CONTEMPORARY PASTORAL COUNSELING

CONTEMPORARY PASTORAL COUNSELING

EUGENE J. WEITZEL, C.S.V., S.T.D.

PARTICIPATING EDITOR

THE BRUCE PUBLISHING COMPANY / NEW YORK

Imprimi potest: V. Rev. John W. Stafford, C.S.V.
　　　　　　　　Provincial
Nihil obstat: John A. Schulien, S.T.D.
　　　　　　　Censor librorum
Imprimatur: ✠ William E. Cousins
　　　　　　　Archbishop of Milwaukee
　　　　　　　Jan. 21, 1969

The *Nihil obstat* and *Imprimatur* are a declaration that a book or pamphlet is considered to be free from doctrinal or moral error. It is not implied that those who have granted the *Nihil obstat* and *Imprimatur* agree with the contents, opinions, or statements expressed.

Library of Congress Catalog Card Number: 75–75032

Copyright © 1969 The Bruce Publishing Company
Made in the United States of America

To
the Holy Family
at Nazareth—
Jesus,
Mary,
and Joseph,
and to
my Brothers
and their Families—
Mr. and Mrs. Frank C. Weitzel
and
Mr. and Mrs. Harold J. Weitzel

INTRODUCTION

Several years ago, the Chairman of the Faculty of the Lutheran Theological Seminary at Gettysburg, Pennsylvania, the Reverend Donald R. Heiges, D.D., wrote that clerics must be "first of all, men of God, men who in a very special sense have been nurtured by Word and Sacrament during their seminary years, men who by daily discipline have learned to live in the Presence of Christ, men who by corporate worship and private devotion have come to know what it means to present themselves as a living sacrifice, men who have welded *ora* and *labora* together to the glory of their Creator and Redeemer." [1]

Though Dr. Heiges, aware that unless a cleric ". . . daily kneels, alone and with his fellows, in the Presence of God, there to receive His forgiveness, guidance, and power, sooner or later the divine call will grow faint, the inner wells of the spirit will go dry, and there will be only a dusty land where the path of commitment has faded away," [2] quite properly stresses the importance of a vital and virile spiritual life, he knows that factual knowledge and the mastery of a methodology are important too. Along with his "knowledge and understanding of what God has already done in history," the contemporary cleric must continually strive to attain "an understanding of contemporary man and his culture as well as proficiency in the use of tools (worship, preaching, teaching, counseling, etc.) with which the Church seeks to minister to this culture." [3] In a word, churchmen of today must become skilled in all phases of pastoral practice.

Other theologians—Protestant and Catholic—without de-emphasizing the need for personal spiritual growth, agree with Dr. Heiges concerning the importance of pastoral theology. Thus, Professor Gibson Winter observes that "training for the ministry is training in apostolate and servanthood." [4] Franklin H. Littell is also convinced of the importance of professional training for the ministry, for he says that:

[1] Donald R. Heiges, "Preface to Theological Study," *Lutheran Theological Seminary Catalogue* 1965–1966, p. 3.

[2] *Ibid.*, p. 3.

[3] *Ibid.*, p. 4.

[4] Cited in C. Williams, *Where in the World?*, 35n.

. . . Sincere believers hope that (America) may yet be Christianized, and to achieve this goal seminaries must become training centers in the church's mission in the world. To this end, they must move beyond the archaic notion fitted to an intact "Christendom" but meaningless in the United States, that the seminary can operate in isolation from the churches and from the social crisis, content merely to equip future clergymen for a known role in a "normal" setting. The seminary for this age must be a theological center for the whole believing people. It must train lay leaders as well as clergy. It must move beyond the mindset of the "normal" parish to equipping the several ministries which implement the Church's total mission.[5]

Under the heading "Bachelor of Divinity Degree," the catalogue of the Lutheran Theological Seminary states that:

In a profound sense, the real goal of the whole theological course is reached in the studies undertaken in the Division of Ministry. The primary purpose of the Seminary is to prepare candidates for effective leadership in the Church's ministry in the world. This ministry is grounded in the biblical, historical, and theological witness of the Church, but is made proficient and effective by careful development of the ministering arts (preaching, teaching, pastoral care, and leadership). Consequently, the major portion of prescribed work in this division appears in the senior year and profits from the concentrated studies in Scripture, history, theology, and socio-cultural experience, the potentially rich and productive internship as well as the increasing maturity of the student.[6]

Today, as always, Catholic leaders insist that ecclesiastics be properly and adequately prepared to meet the ministerial obligations of their particular apostolate. In fact, the *Decree on Priestly Formation* explains quite clearly how this is to be accomplished, for it states that the "pastoral concern which should thoroughly penetrate the entire training of seminarians also requires that they be carefully instructed in those matters which have a special bearing on the sacred ministry. . . . Let them receive careful instruction in the art of guiding souls, so that they can lead all sons of the Church, before everything else, to a Christian life which is fully conscious and apostolic. . . ."[7]

Speaking to a group of newly ordained American priests who were studying at Rome's North American College, Pope Paul VI agreed that:

These are challenging days for your ministry. The world has changed and you will have to bring the message of Christ to a troubled, searching and seemingly confused society. You have studied in Rome during the Second

---

[5] F. Littell, "Protestant Seminary Education in America," *Seminary Education in a Time of Change* (ed. J. Lee and L. Putz, C.S.C.), p. 552.

[6] ————, *Lutheran Theological Seminary Catalogue* 1965–1966, pp. 25–26.

[7] Vatican Council II, *The Decree on Priestly Training* (trans. N.C.W.C.), p. 9.

Vatican Council which has given us the *Decree on the Priestly Ministry*. According to this important document "the purpose which priests pursue in their ministry and by their life is to procure the glory of God the Father in Christ. That glory consists of this—that men working freely and with a grateful spirit receive the work of God made perfect in Christ and then manifest it in their whole lives." Study this document well, and make every effort to make it the touchstone of your ministry to the People of God. Your stay in Rome has produced a special affection for the Church, and we are confident that you will be worthy stewards of the Gospel and ministers of the word. Have courage; have faith; give yourselves wholeheartedly to the task at hand and your fruits will be rich.[8]

The Very Reverend Walter J. Schmitz, S.S., S.T.D., Dean of the School of Sacred Theology at the Catholic University of America, and Professor of Pastoral Theology, wrote in the "Forward" of *Pastoral Ministry in a Time of Change* that "the priest today must not and cannot feel like a stranger, but he must be ready to meet the challenge that the world offers. He must recognize the social changes in the contemporary world and the necessity for the clergy to relate themselves to it intelligently." [9]

In view of what has been said above by both Protestant and Catholic leaders and by many others as well, it is the purpose of this book to come to the assistance of those clergymen who are striving to learn ". . . to use the aids which the disciplines of pedagogy, psychology, and sociology can provide, according to correct methodology and the norms of ecclesiastical authority" [10] by probing rather deeply into one ancillary area of pastoral theology—pastoral psychology.

Traditionally, pastoral theology has embraced the conclusions of the strictly theological sciences—dogma, moral, canon law, ascetics, etc., and included among its ancillary subjects catechetics, homiletics, liturgy, and pedagogy. However, within the past fifty years, in response to the many important social changes that are taking place, pastoral has also embraced the conclusions of pastoral medicine and of the behavioral sciences.

Though it might seem at first that by embracing these new areas pastoral has undergone a change of emphasis, such is far from the truth. For today more than ever the traditional branches of this science, especially liturgy, catechetics, homiletics, and ecumenism, are being strongly emphasized. What has happened, however, is that pastoral theology has, in response to the needs of the times, expanded its horizons without undergoing any

---

[8] Paul VI, *A Talk to a Group of Newly-ordained American Priests Who Are Students at Rome's North American College,* Documentary Service, N.C.W.C. (1965).

[9] Walter J. Schmitz, S.S., "Forward," *Pastoral Ministry in a Time of Change* (ed. Eugene J. Weitzel, C.S.V.), p. vii.

[10] Vatican Council II, *op. cit.,* p. 9.

de-emphasis of its traditional subject matter. In fact, some theologians have indicated that only recently have these newer disciplines been given proper recognition in pastoral theology. But, even at the risk of some de-emphasis of the traditional subject matter of pastoral theology, this science must embrace the newer disciplines if it is to fulfill its function of training general practitioners for the various normal offices of the priesthood.

Father Stafford Poole is aware of the importance of these newer ancillary subjects, for he writes that:

> Greater emphasis could also be laid on the behavioral sciences, for more and more in these days the priest is called on to be a counselor. One psychiatrist has estimated that seventy-five per cent of the people who seek psychiatric help see a clergyman before seeking more specifically professional advice. If this is even partly true, it places on the seminary a heavy obligation to see that the priests of the future are adequately prepared to recognize symptoms of mental disorder, that they understand thoroughly their own limitations in this area, and that they are skilled enough to guide their clients into the proper medical channels. Finally those dioceses which assign their priests to the staffs of high schools should see that they are thoroughly grounded in adolescent psychology and counseling.
>
> In addition to their immediately practical value, the study of such subjects as psychology, counseling techniques, sociology, and anthropology, aids greatly in the formation of intellectual adaptability and of broadness of outlook. Obviously, this is not merely an ability to master the professional jargon, but is a definite point of view which enables the priest better to understand his environment and the forces at work in his parish—whether it be urban or rural, inner city or suburban, wealthy or poor.[11]

A number of other well known authors have also stressed the importance of these disciplines. James Michael Lee, in his chapter "Curriculum and Teaching in Seminary Education," attests to the importance of these subjects when he says that "To be effective in their ministry, priests need to be able to deal with their parishioners' emotional problems, because spirituality cannot be fostered independently of psychological health and adjustment." [12] He therefore strongly urges that seminarians be given courses in pastoral psychology, counseling psychology, mental health and clinical psychology. Because of the already crowded seminary schedule, he suggests that these courses should be taken in the pastoral year.

Writing on this same point, in their book *Fundamental Psychiatry*, John R. Cavanagh, M.D. and James B. McGoldrick, S.J. say that:

[11] Stafford Poole, *Seminary in Crisis*, p. 116.
[12] James Michael Lee, "Curriculum and Teaching in Seminary Education," *Seminary Education in a Time of Change*, op. cit., p. 368.

Theology and philosophy are excellent studies, but an understanding of the nature of God, the mysteries of religion and other theogical metaphysics, the knowledge of being, act and potency, the syllogism, even the study of abstract rational psychology leaves one completely ignorant of the art of helping people with emotional disturbances. . . . Many seminaries, schools of divinity, theologates, and philosophates, have no explicit course in psychiatry, abnormal psychology, or mental hygiene. No one on the staff is competent to teach such subjects, and, unfortunately, priests and ministers are ordained almost entirely ignorant in this respect. They have little knowledge of the problems of neuroticism, and are unconscious or only dimly aware of the millions of neurotic people who are to be found in the society which they are trained to help and save. Sooner or later, most of these (clerical) professionals learn about such matters, but they do it the hard way, by making mistakes, causing pain, and intensifying the problem of people by misdirection. Some never learn, and in this respect become and remain a definite social liability.[13]

Francis J. Braceland and Michael Stock are also convinced of the importance of adequate training in this area, for they write:

. . . a clear and sound judgment on psychiatry as a whole seems particularly important for those who deal with men's souls and spirits and they should be provided for them during the time they are forming their basic outlook on things. This means that psychiatry, at least in its general principles and broad outlines, should be introduced into the major seminaries, not to make professional psychiatrists out of the students there, but to give them a deep and solid orientation toward an area of science which will impinge closely on almost all the other areas they will study.[14]

Therefore, this book treats of the various aspects of pastoral psychology and psychiatry, pastoral counseling, and pastoral marriage counseling. In the course of planning, writing and editing this book, I have continually kept in mind what Joseph F. X. Cevetello, the Editor of *All Things to All Men*, said about the sincere and enthusiastic pastor of souls—"The zealous and true shepherd of souls seeks for, works with and tries to understand souls. It would be a most consoling thing if the priest had to work only with the good, but, as we have seen, Christ said that this is not enough. There are many, e.g., the alcoholic, drug addict, compulsive gambler, the aged, the retarded and mentally troubled, the married or single within the Church, as well as millions outside, who need the priest's special help and

---

[13] J. Cavanagh and J. McGoldrick, S.J., *Fundamental Psychiatry* (2nd ed.), pp. 29–30.

[14] F. Braceland and M. Stock, O.P., *Modern Psychiatry, a Handbook for Believers*, p. 22.

consideration." [15] Consequently, I have asked the many clerical and lay-specialists in their respective fields who have contributed to this book, not only to present the fundamental principles, problems, and possible solutions to these problems within the various areas of pastoral medicine and pastoral psychology, but also to go into some depth in the development of their specific chapter. As a result, we have provided both the seminarian and the ordained cleric striving to become even more competent in these fields with material well suited for obtaining the necessary knowledge and skills for the work they will be called upon to do.

Every contributor to this book is a specialist in the area which he treats, and realizes that he cannot consider every possible aspect of his specialty in one chapter. However, each writer is aware of the contributions that a properly trained clergyman can make in the area of pastoral medicine and the behavioral sciences and has volunteered to contribute to *Contemporary Pastoral Counseling* not only as a means of providing sufficient informational materials and references for future study, but also as a means of encouraging clergymen to become more proficient in these areas. Even if nothing is achieved but the latter, it would have been worth the effort of all of us.

Although this book is primarily intended for seminarians and ordained clerics, it can also be of real value to religious and to laymen. Today, more than ever, knowledgeable and competent religious and laymen are approached by persons who are troubled or confused with the request to talk about their problems. Having mastered the psychological and counseling data contained in books such as this, they are better prepared to deal with the situation, and if necessary, to refer those persons who require professional help.

This book can also be of special use to physicians and surgeons, psychologists and psychiatrists, nurses and technicians, social workers and marriage counselors, and others working in these areas, for not only does this book supply the clergyman with up-to-date psychologico-clinical data, and guide him so that he can make sound judgments and decisions in particular cases that have psychological and counseling implications, but it also forms and guides the psychologist, psychiatrist and counselor so that they can properly form their conscience on those aspects of their practice that have moral implications.

The author-editor sincerely thanks all of those who have in any way contributed toward the publication of this book. Special acknowledgement is due the Reverend John W. Stafford, C.S.V., provincial superior of the Clerics of St. Viator, for his generous approval of this undertaking, and to

[15] Joseph F. X. Cevetello, "Introduction," *All Things to All Men* (ed. Joseph F. X. Cevetello), p. v:

Mr. Aloysius Croft, of the editorial department of the Bruce Publishing Company, whose interest and counsel were invaluable.

Eugene J. Weitzel, C.S.V., S.T.D.

Griffin High School
Springfield, Illinois

CONTENTS

CONTEMPORARY PASTORAL COUNSELING

1

PASTORAL COUNSELING

JOHN W. STAFFORD, C.S.V.

IN THIS CHAPTER there will be an attempt to look at pastoral counseling, as conceived and practiced in our contemporary world, against the backdrop of the history of pastoral care.

A first premise of the chapter is that shepherds of souls have been engaged in face-to-face relationships that can at least broadly speaking be called counseling since the beginnings of Christianity. Such shepherds have assisted souls to grow toward spiritual maturity by means other than the strictly sacramental; they have tried to apply to spiritual problems solutions that have been therapeutic in character.

A second premise is that in our own generation there has developed, within the framework of the general counseling movement, something quite new in pastoral counseling. This development has been possible because of the emergence in our century, and at the end of the preceding century, of powerful new systematic viewpoints and techniques in psychology and psychiatry.

A third premise is that what was new and accepted in pastoral counseling even as recently as five or ten years ago may indeed now be suspect or even obsolete: changes in almost everything today are so frequent, so fast, and so radical, that a truly "contemporary" presentation is scarcely possible.

This chapter then has three themes: a nostalgic melody from the past, a *leitmotif* familiar to anyone older than 25 or 30, and tentative, atonal snatches of sound from tomorrow. Within the limits of the plausible, the three themes will be interrelated, it is to be hoped without a counterpoint of cacophony.

The Antecedents of Pastoral Counseling

It would be easy, but hardly profitable, to document from the history of the Church the statement that those in care of souls have across the centuries performed tasks that could very well be called counseling. Broken marriages are not peculiar to our day, nor are problems of adjustment to authority, drug or alcohol addiction, scrupulosity, sexual conflict, or vocational choice. *Acta* of all sorts as well as the testimony of the literature of all ages show us that these and similar problems have always been the concern of pastors of souls. Indeed, the clergy were about the only group that handled such problems professionally. There were no psychologists or psychiatrists until quite recent times. The orientation of physicians was almost totally somatic. Lawyers, teachers, even court jesters, no doubt occasionally performed functions that today we might call psychologically therapeutic. But all this was incidental, often casual, certainly quite nonprofessional.

Even the clergy in past centuries were by no means professional counselors in a modern sense. But they came closest of all groups to performing counseling functions of any kind professionally.

Perhaps only in the area of spiritual direction do we see even with the clergy any systematic attempt to apply professional skills to personal and psychological problems of human nature. Since even today many clergy find conflict and role confusion between pastoral counseling and spiritual direction, it would be useful to reflect on similarities and differences between the two.

The Development of Spiritual Direction

Although maxims of spiritual direction and what really are systematic viewpoints can be found in Christian writings from apostolic times, spiritual direction as something even remotely resembling a profession seems to have developed with the Fourth Century monks of the desert. Although we have no evidence of appointment secretaries or records of how many interviews were customary per week, there are interesting similarities between the pastoral relationships the fathers of the desert had to the neophyte disciples and the counselor-counselee relationships of the present. At base were often the same problems of tortured human nature a counselor faces today: feelings of inadequacy, anxiety, and insecurity, problems of interpersonal relations, the deep-seated need for adequate and satisfying personal self-fulfillment, the conflict between the "demons" of desire and the ideals of a "higher life." There was a narrative presentation of the problem, a dialogue to explore various solutions, the working out of a program of action to help the "client" to mature. The controlling attitudes were clearly authoritarian, the techniques most certainly not non-directive; but there was the same human anguish, the same compassionate dedication to be helpful, and, we can be sure, oftentimes the same hopeful relief in new vistas for personal development. The "father" was a man of experience who had seen before most problems brought to him by the neophyte. He himself had often been trained in the techniques of an earlier master. The "client" sought him out because of his reputation, saw him repeatedly and often over long periods, and was convinced that a fuller and more satisfying life was a result of the helpful encounters with the master. It would be churlish to see here nothing therapeutic.

It is in the Sixteenth and Seventeenth Centuries that one sees the highest development of the theory and art of spiritual direction, especially in Spain. By this time a technical literature of the "ways" of the spiritual life had grown up. Numerous treatises have come down to us detailing the steps to be followed in "growth in holiness," in "the progress of the soul toward union with God." Many of the classical treatises are filled with studies of highly unusual mystical states and of forms of prayer obviously possible only to the most favored souls. But there was an extensive literature also for the "ordinary" souls, for all aspiring to greater "perfection." And there were practitioners to match the literature. The spiritual director of a house of religious, for example, was a person of considerable prestige, appointed with as much care as we would take today to select a superior or a treasurer. There were itinerant spiritual directors, whose coming to a locality was heralded beforehand and who were consulted by all those who could manage an interview. It was not only the members of the religious orders who had their own spiritual directors; those in positions of power, even kings, had specially appointed masters of the spiritual life to accompany them everywhere.

It is perhaps best to look on the role of such spiritual directors as the outgrowth and expansion of the role of the confessor. Except when used as status symbols, such directors were expected to help their clients grow in love of God. They taught methods of meditation, prescribed practices of penance that would frighten a modern, and advised on the extirpation of habits of sin. Such counsel can be and often is given, even today, through the confessional. No doubt it was also so given then. But it was also given outside the confessional, often at great length in long interviews, and in great detail by correspondence, some of which has come down to us as classics in the literature of the spiritual life.

PASTORAL COUNSELING TODAY AND TOMORROW

In our own generation there has developed, within the framework of the general movement in counseling and clinical psychology, something that can be called new in the area of pastoral counseling. The term itself, "pastoral counseling," is new. There is a new literature that has grown up, in books and in journals. There are training programs, workshops, institutes, and seminars for pastoral counselors. Although for the most part pastoral counseling has become another of the functions of a pastor of souls, along with his functions as proclaimer of the Word of God, his sacramental ministry, and his administrative duties, we do find pastoral counselors whose primary, if not almost exclusive, occupation is that of counseling.

The explicit, professional role of the pastoral counselor, as a subdivision of the more general role of counselor, has developed somewhat later than other counseling roles. The role of the personal counselor, sometimes called a psychological or therapeutic counselor, has developed concurrently with the role of the clinical psychologist; indeed, many find it hard to set up here any really meaningful distinctions. Vocational counseling, with its important correlate, vocational rehabilitation, is likewise an early application of, among a number of other things, some of the insights and techniques of contemporary psychology to the problems of vocational choice. In educational circles there has also been with us for some time what is properly called educational counseling, restricted generally to the academic problems of the school setting itself. Finally, it may be of interest to note that pastoral counseling, especially as anything approaching an explicit and exclusive role, has developed later in Catholic circles than in Protestant or in Jewish.

What the future of pastoral counseling may be, of course, is only speculation. Psychology has undergone radical changes during the present century and it would be foolish to think of its future as static. And as psychology changes, so does counseling, for the principal conceptional basis of counseling is its psychological underpinnings. On the other hand, it can easily be demonstrated that counseling psychology has made notable contributions to the "humanizing" of psychology itself. Thus, the importance of value systems, of truly human goals, of individual responsibility, lost for too long in the quasi-scientific and sometimes pseudoscientific delirium of an ultra-mechanistic psychology, are at the very core of the counseling approach. As psychology, for this and other reasons, becomes more a study of the total human personality and less a fragmented science of selected physiological or sociological aspects of man, it is to be expected that counseling psychology also will benefit. Since pastoral counseling seems to be ever more consciously an application of counseling psychology to pastoral function, it also should change. What the next "new" psychology will be is anyone's guess. Perhaps it will be more existential, with a greater concern for the actual condition of individual man in a world that confronts him almost to the extinction of his personality. Perhaps it will be more communitarian, with a far greater development of social psychology than we have had in the past. Perhaps it will even be more psychosomatic, in some future enlightened age that can really solve the "body-mind" problem; we may then see a historic breakthrough even into physical medicine, built on the slight and tentative insights of today that most of what are called physical ills have a startlingly large component that is psychological. In any of these developments, of course, pastoral counseling will be affected: man *as he exists* will be faced more squarely than today with his personal and often frightening potentialities; man will be seen even more than now as essentially communitarian man, dependent for the flowering of his personality on his interrelationships with others; and who knows but what the pastoral counselor of the future may not, without danger of prosecution for practicing medicine without a license, bring surcease to some of the ills of the body as well as solace to the soul.

COUNSELING AND DIRECTION COMPARED

There are important differences between the counseling that has been dispensed for centuries as a part of the duties of the pastor of souls and the pastoral counseling that is practiced today. The emphasis in the past was not only primarily spiritual, but almost exclusively spiritual. As mentioned above, the role of those engaged in pastoral counseling in centuries past seemed best characterized as an outgrowth of the confessional function of the priest, even though, paradoxically, some notable "pastoral counselors" of the past were not ordained. The outlook was frankly other-worldly. The "world," like the flesh and the devil, was merely an obstacle to personal perfection. The theoretical basis for counseling was doctrinal, dogmatic, spiritual. Although there was use of many insights and techniques that are quite respectable psychology even today, such insights and techniques were used only casually and incidentally. A "pastoral counselor" of days gone by would not have known what you meant if you had said he was psychologically oriented, and if he did understand your meaning he would have been horrified.

Pastoral counseling today is frankly psychologically oriented. It is the explicit application of the attitudes, insights, theories, and techniques of contemporary counseling psychology to pastoral problems. Much of the training of the present-day professional counselor involves work in contemporary psychology that is common to all psychologists-in-training. Whether there need be a specific training program for pastoral counselors is a good question. Perhaps all that is needed is a sound training in counseling psychology; the product of such training should be able to apply his skills to various problem areas, the pastoral, the vocational, the educational, the therapeutic. Even though some may disagree with the above suggestion, the fact that it can reasonably be made indicates that pastoral counseling today is in the mainstream of contemporary counseling psychology and of psychology itself.

The pastoral counselor of yesteryear, whatever he might have been called, had his sights set on the growth in holiness of his client, his personal perfection, his spiritual maturity. These *desiderata* were attacked directly as explicit goals of the relationship between director and directed, counselor and client. The pastoral counselor of today is, of course, not uninterested in the spiritual maturity of his counselee. But it is unlikely that he would attack such a problem directly. He operates instead on the assumption that the solution to the more obviously psychological problems of the individual is often a prerequisite to the solution of spiritual problems and to a growth in holiness. He is just as much in favor of spiritual maturity as his professional ancestor. But he is also dealing with a contemporary concept of psychological maturity, and he is convinced that there can be no true spiritual maturity in the psychologically immature.

The pastoral counselor today faces a problem of conflict of role that could not have been an issue with the spiritual director of the past. The priest-counselor today often has trouble deciding whether he is priest or counselor. It is a quite satisfactory *verbal* solution to say he is primarily a priest, but acting in the capacity of a counselor. But verbal solutions seldom solve. He is often in conflict in the area of moral judgment. Should he condemn a course of action as morally wrong, or even as psychologically undesirable, following the traditional judgmental role of the priest? Or should he refrain from moral judgments, trying instead to help the client achieve an adjustment in which he himself can make appropriate moral judgment? Just as the physician has traditionally spoken of his assumption of "medical responsibility," so also the clergyman has considered himself as responsible for moral judgments affecting the behavior of those under his charge. Indeed, one of the classical, if highly questionable, "treatments" of scrupulosity in the past has been for the confessor to say: "Do as I say;

I assume all responsibility." Anyone who has caught the authentic spirit of the modern approach in counseling psychology will be convinced that we act most responsibly toward a client when we help him assume responsibility himself. Such an approach is not always easy for a clergyman, especially for one who had had an authoritarian type of training superimposed on an authoritarian type of personality. Perhaps one solution to this problem of conflict of role is to counsel this type of pastor of souls to stay out of pastoral counseling.

In our look at pastoral counseling today against the backdrop of the history of pastoral care we have related the contemporary pastoral counselor with the spiritual director of the past. Lest the reader suspect that we have buried all spiritual directors, it might be well to look at pastoral counseling as related to what is indeed today a vital pastoral role, that of spiritual director. Unless the contemporary spiritual director is encapsulated in a cocoon of traditionalism, he has been profoundly moved, perhaps uncomfortably "shook up," by developments in recent decades in psychology. If he is flexible (and if he is not he should never try to be a spiritual director) he has adapted some of the insights and perhaps some of the techniques of contemporary counseling psychology to his own practice. But there are still important differences between him and a pastoral counselor. He is somehow more directly and professionally interested in the spiritual than in the psychological. The role of the pastoral counselor has minimal, if any, sacramental connotations; that of the spiritual director is still very much an extension of function of the confessor, even though never practiced in a sacramental, confessional setting. The spiritual director has a more permanent and continuing relationship with his directee; the pastoral counselor is more the trouble-shooter, to be consulted when a problem arises. Thus, one might report to his spiritual director that he has no problem at present that is bothering him, just as a penitent may tell a confessor he has no sin to confess; but one just does not go to a pastoral counselor unless propelled there by a problem.

If the above attempt at distinguishing between the spiritual director of today and the pastoral counselor should strike one as lacking in rigid logical justification, it may very well be that the distinction between the two is today becoming blurred. Who knows but what in the years that lie ahead the two roles will become merged? Either every spiritual director will be sufficiently skilled in the art of pastoral counseling or every pastoral counselor will accept without qualm the tasks of spiritual direction as part of his pastoral role. Someone may even come up with a new term, perhaps something like "spiritual counselor," to cover the functions of what were two roles in the past.

Man and His Cultural Past

The modern psychological approach to pastoral counseling has developed not merely out of contemporary psychology. It is one of the products of our cultural history. And that history is founded largely on Judaio-Christian concepts of man. Counseling, without the qualification "pastoral," has preserved more of what is good in our cultural history than has the larger body of psychology. This latter, especially in the earlier decades, perhaps the first half century, of its development, was openly hostile to many traditional notions of man. It considered itself scientific, and hence had no place in its theoretical framework for concepts of a religious or a metaphysical nature. Other sciences could pursue their own methodological way with no thought of religion, and with precious little thought of philosophy. But psychology was too close to man for that: it had to face the problem of the whole man, including his metaphysical structure and his religious aspirations. Unable to integrate such thinking into its almost anti-humanistic biases, it simply rejected as mystical and therefore mythical anything resembling the philosophical and religious. That it at the same time rejected much of man was seen only later. And it was the counseling and clinical variety of psychology that began to see what had happened. Hence, when pastoral counseling developed within the framework of psychology, the climate was no longer really antagonistic to man, and could even tolerate the concept of man as a proper subject of pastoral care. Quite lately the American Psychological Association has admitted "Philosophical Psychology" as one of its official divisions.

Freed from its compulsions of protest against traditional man, and open to helpful insights from the long history of man's study of himself, psychology began to take into its own body of theory and practice much that was good from the past. It is useful to see in some detail how the modern psychological approach to pastoral counseling has borrowed from these earlier views of man.

From the beginning, counseling psychology has been characterized by a profound respect for the dignity of the individual. It is hard to see how pastoral counseling could have developed at all unless such respect were there. In the traditional view of man, the basis for his dignity was of course theological: man was created in the image of God, redeemed by God-made-man, and through that redemption elevated by grace to the dignity of a son of God. Counseling psychology saw man through the eyes of an enlightened humanism, based vaguely perhaps on a philosophical analysis of man, and based also on·a sort of self-centered intuition that man must be noble. Man's capacity to think has always led him, even after detours into inhuman philosophical systems, back to a healthy humanism. And man's capacity to admire himself, even if it leads him sometimes into comic absurdity, does enable him to grasp intuitively his nobility and dignity. What the pastor of souls always knew from his theology the counseling psychologist retained from the backgrounds of his culture; hence the pastoral counselor has never been in doubt about the dignity of man. And counseling psychology has come lately to see more clearly what our culture has always implicitly known—the goodness there is in man when he is fully functioning as a human being.

Dignity is not a title to smugness. It is, instead, the basis of responsibility. Here again the insights of the past are preserved in the psychological counseling approach to man. In the past the emphasis on man's personal responsibility had most often a moral character: man has free will, is responsible for the rightness or wrongness of his actions, and will be rewarded or punished accordingly. In Jewish times the sanction would come within one's lifetime, or at least to one's descendants; only in very late Jewish pre-Christian thought was there explicit belief in sanctions in an afterlife. In Christian times from the beginning these sanctions were essentially otherworldly, but also from the beginning and in varying degrees in different periods of Christian history there was the "hundredfold" in this life as reward; and St. Paul's terrifying first chapter to the Romans lets us know that punishment in this world for moral turpitude may also be expected. Whatever the locus and time of the sanction, and whatever, indeed, the philosophical or theological basis, our culture has always in all its institutions accepted as unquestioned man's moral responsibility for his actions. Contemporary pastoral counseling is decidedly in this tradition.

An interesting parallel between pastoral counseling today and spiritual direction and even confessional practice from the past, is the emphasis on the importance of confidentiality, out of respect for the dignity of the individual. Although counseling does not have a confessional "seal," absolute and unbreakable, there is an accepted convention among all counselors of whatever variety that confidences must be respected. Information obtained in connection with counseling, even results of tests a counselor may have given, is normally released only with the authorization of the client.

Another corollary of the insights concerning the dignity of man shared by contemporary counseling and spiritual direction is a hopefulness of attitude about man. Both are based on the assumption that man *can* become more mature through therapeutic encounter with trained and dedicated persons who care. Theologians sometimes say that hope is the forgotten virtue, with faith and charity receiving most of the publicity. Even in those with a facade of confidence and superiority, the basis of personal problems is often a deep-seated feeling of worthlessness. A counseling relationship often does nothing else, and nothing else need be done, than help a person see that his condition is not at all hopeless, that he has strengths and capacities that can be freed for mature development. When a ray of hope illumines a man's perception of himself, then in the light of that hope he can move on to more constructive relationships with others. Unless a counselor himself has an attitude of hopefulness toward people, his encounter with a client without hope will be ineffectual.

This encounter is a highly personal relationship. One even finds at times transference phenomena not unlike those found in psychoanalysis: great attachments of client to therapist, dependencies that must be carefully handled, dramatic extremes of love and of hostility. Some pastoral counseling points of view are based on a theoretical formulation that the interview with the counselor is, as it were, a sort of microcosm of the client's larger context of interpersonal relationships. Since many of the problems of living are simply problems with people, the client is given the opportunity of relating meaningfully and in a non-threatening atmosphere to a particular person; from what is learned here, and the learning is much more an emotional achievement than it is an intellectual acquisition, the client should be able to relate better to the significant persons in his daily living. At the basis of such theory and practice is the conviction, naive as it may sound, that people *are*, indeed, important, and that one's own personal growth and maturity depend absolutely on the goodness of one's interpersonal relationships. Again we have a convergence of contemporary and traditional viewpoints: in even the most theocentric system of spiritual direction the maxim "Love thy neighbor" has always been paramount.

The Thrust of Contemporary Counseling

If contemporary pastoral counseling has roots in the past and debts to the past, we can also say that it is the product of our age. Most of the more or less typically modern aspects of pastoral counseling are important improvements on thinking and practice of the past. The value of some of them is no doubt debatable, but it is difficult to find any that are downright objectionable.

Perhaps the most significant aspect of the new look in pastoral counseling is that it is far, far less authoritarian than has been any type of pastoral care in the past. It is simply a truism that the *world* itself and everything in it are less authoritarian; hence *anything* today would be that way. Pastoral care in ages past, reserved largely to an ordained clergy, shared the authoritarian structures and attitudes of the clergy. I am speaking here not in value judgment, but in fact: it could very well be that a less authoritarian clergy was neither possible nor *desirable* historically. But the fact is beyond doubt: pastoral care for centuries has been paternalistic, hierarchical, authoritarian, and, in its worst manifestations, downright arrogant.

Pastoral counseling today is less authoritarian not only because the world is that way: it has not only followed the way of contemporary thinking but has itself helped significantly to fashion that thinking. As counseling, it is the direct beneficiary of what many consider one of the great theoretical breakthroughs in contemporary thought—the emergence of the nondirective point of view. Technical treatises on the development of this point of view, and of the therapeutic methodologies derived from it, are readily available. As this approach has passed over even into the non-technical thinking of our contemporary age, it has become distilled into a point of view not inaccurately characterized as follows: one does not solve problems for a client, but provides an opportunity for him to solve his own problems. This seemingly simple statement is charged with content. In the past the approach was very definitely solution-oriented. In this there was a startling resemblance to the point of view of medicine throughout the ages, including our own: something is wrong, a skilled practitioner is consulted whose job it is to find an answer. If an arm or leg is broken, the physician sets it; if diagnosis reveals pathology, then the appropriate therapy is applied. In matters of the soul, the approach through the prescribing of remedies was likewise accepted practice. But in the non-directive approach there is a radical difference: the client himself must find *his own* solution. No solution that he cannot accept as his own and live with can be of any value. The contribution of the counselor is not to prescribe, not to direct, not to lead. This does not mean, as was said cynically in the early criticisms of the non-directive approach, that the counselor does nothing. It means, instead, that he does something that is very definitely therapeutic, but that is quite different from what his predecessors would have done when faced with similar problems.

Thus, in times past a spiritual director would "direct"; indeed, his clients came to him explicitly for professional "direction." If the client were having difficulties with others—with a wife or husband, with superiors, with peers —there would be a lecture, a homily, a giving of directions on what to do to achieve more harmonious living with other people. The approach, incidentally, was almost exclusively intellectualist. There is a problem; it has a cause; find that cause and apply the reasonable, logical solution. Today the approach is as much through the feelings as through the intellect. Some in fact would say it is exclusively an affective approach, and that one of the greatest hindrances to improvement is "over-intellectualization" of one's difficulties.

The modern approach is far less symptom-oriented, far less casuist, far more positive. Pastoral care always stressed positive development of the individual—his "growth in holiness," for example. But there was also a fearful lot of emphasis on the negative aspects of life: faults and imperfections, sin—venial and mortal and original, the dangers of occasions of sin, how to combat temptations, those familiar pitfalls to perfection—the world, the flesh, and the devil. Even spiritual directors today who would not call themselves counselors have a basic approach that is much more positive than negative, much more supportive and developmental and even joyous than casuist or legalistic. And the contemporary pastoral counselor may not even bother at all about a diagnostic study of what is wrong; his emphasis is on how the client can be helped to live a richer, fuller, more satisfying life.

In ages past there was a sharp focus on the individual himself and his direct, personal relationships with God. The Christian view of man as a member of the society of his fellow man was certainly there. But "other people" were too often seen as obstacles to perfection or as sources of problems. There was less insight than we possess today of man's essential dependence for his own personal development on his interpersonal relationships with others.

Pastoral counseling today is based on a body of theory, some of it debatable, much of it still in the process of development, but most of it hardly questioned. In the past there was no formulated theory even of personal development except what was implicit in the body of Christian thought. And it remained just that, largely implicit. As psychology has begun to come of age theoretically and to develop a well-rounded body of theoretical constructs to guide its experimentation as well as its techniques, so has the counseling psychologist been able to use a systematic body of concepts to aid his thinking and his practice. The importance of the experiences of early childhood is now recognized by almost everyone as being overwhelming in the development of the personality. The counselor knows that *he* cannot himself change a client. And he also knows that, given even the most ideal therapeutic environment, the client can change himself only within certain definitely circumscribed limits—circumscribed by all his past experiences with others, but especially those of the first year or two of life. Hence there has been systematic development of the notion of "acceptance": facing reality as it is, including the reality of one's own deficiencies and the limitations of one's capabilities, all of which was laid down in a distant past. The personality as molded in early childhood may be modified within limits, but to try to modify it beyond those limits may end in disaster. In the attempt to assess oneself as he really is, not only will limitations emerge, but also unsuspected potentialities. Thus, instead of the pursuit of unrealistic ideals that will lead only to frustration, there is the exploration of hitherto unknown avenues of development that now appear as possible and desirable.

Another powerful set of theoretical concepts today focuses on the importance of the unconscious in human life, especially unconscious motivations. If the pastoral counselor is sufficiently trained and sufficiently skilled, he will be able to assist his client to see that much of his behavior, though apparently guided by conscious motives, is really caused by deeper drives of which he may be only vaguely conscious, if conscious at all.

Over the centuries the focus in the care of souls has undergone change. For centuries the focus was on evil, a strictly moralist approach. Then, without a denial of the obvious presence of evil in the world, with little attempt to explain the *Mysterium iniquitatis*, but still with no urge to explain it away, the emphasis became what we might call medical. Souls are sick rather than evil: they are given no exorcism, but only treatment from an expert. Today the approach is best called existential. The soul is not viewed as a lost soul in the moral sense of meriting the fires of hell; nor is it a sick soul in need of treatment. It *is* a lost soul, but in a far different sense. It is a soul—let us now say a person—that is depersonalized and alienated, wandering about in a hostile world without meaning, a confused individual unable to find meaning even in himself.

Another contribution of the modern point of view is the importance of training. Counseling psychology as a movement originated as much in the development of training programs as it did in the emergence of theoretical guidelines and the uncovering of new information through research. Perhaps the case could be made out that, along with clinical psychology, it has avoided extremes of ridiculous theorizing and of wild, irresponsible practice, largely because from its origins there has been a very close interplay of theory, research, and practice. Theory as soon as formulated has been applied to practice, and the results of the practice evaluated by research. The experience of practice has led to modifications of theory. Research has not only been used to evaluate both theory and practice but also been germinative of further advances in both. And training has never been just the "how to do it" sort of thing. In the best training institutions, at least, it has been a fine balance of sound theoretical foundation, carefully supervised practice, and highly sophisticated research. Some of the research, even, has contributed techniques of investigation that have become widely diffused into the whole of psychological science and have been influential even beyond. This almost unique blend of theory, practice, and research is characteristic of long-term programs leading to the doctorate, of post-doctorate institutes and internships, as well as of short-term institutes and workshops for almost all levels of training. Counseling psychology has indeed come of age in our contemporary world.

CONTEMPORARY CONTRIBUTIONS TO PASTORAL WORK

What can the priest learn from these modern developments that might help him in his pastoral work? If he decides to take specialized training as a pastoral counselor, he will become equipped to function within the contemporary framework of counseling as outlined above. If he does not obtain such training, he can still use insights, and perhaps certain techniques, developed in the counseling movement to assist him in his thinking and in his practice.

Foremost of these contributions might well be the impact of the non-directive viewpoint on his own approach to souls: he will consider himself less as the director of souls and more as an agent assisting a person who comes to him for help in finding that help himself. The positive development of the person's resources will be encouraged by the total acceptance given by the priest; and that very acceptance will help the client to accept himself, with his limitations but also with his potentialities. Through the experience of a healthy interpersonal relationship developed with the priest, the client will come to see how important, rewarding, and possible are harmonious relationships with others. It is not implied here that the values of positive development, of acceptance, and of good relationships with others have been neglected in the past. But the heavy emphasis on these values today should help the priest who is open to influences for improving his ministry to avoid authoritarianism, over-intellectualism, and any more or less lofty "take my advice" attitude or approach.

The focus today on the crucial place of the emotions in the healthy functioning of the personality should help any priest realize that what is often presented as a problem for rational decision is really a deeply-charged emotional problem. Alert to the impact of unconscious emotional drives on behavior, the priest will not readily assume in every case that the present problem is really the basic problem at all. He will be aware that sound emotional health is most important in spiritual development. To assist a client in overcoming crippling emotional blocks to effective performance of any kind may often be all that is needed to free him to advance through grace to dazzling heights of spiritual development.

Although not qualified to engage in treatment that is properly psychological or psychiatric, the priest would be better able to recognize cases requiring such specialized theory. Thus he would avoid the danger of trying such therapy himself and would be aware of the need for proper referral. Even without elaborate formal training, the priest today can easily pick up through reading, lectures, and special institutes sufficient information to help him recognize many of the more characteristic forms of emotional disturbance.

Even though our theologians and psychologists have not yet worked out all the answers, much is known today about the impact of psychological disturbances, serious and slight, on moral responsibility. Since pastoral care still quite properly has a focus that is primarily moral and spiritual, the priest will be better able to assist his client in solving his moral problems and in his spiritual development by insights into the psychological components of the moral life.

A New Climate in the Church

It can be predicted that along with professional counseling psychology, pastoral counseling will continue to develop in the directions indicated in this chapter. For the future there will be, no doubt, more existential influence and less medical. Techniques will be further refined through the experiences of the counselor and through the empirical controls of research. Since man will probably progressively be seen as more and more communitarian, the focus of both theory and practice in counseling will be more and more on his relationships with his fellow men. As psychology comes more and more to see our transactions with others as "constitutive" of personality and not merely as influences in its development, so too will counseling aim to reduce the self-other tensions in everyone. As psychology matures even more, so shall psychological counseling.

It is not only psychological counseling that is undergoing change. Far greater changes are taking place in the Church, indicating that the task of the pastoral counselor in the "New Church" may be vastly different from what it has been in the past. This change began most perceptibly when Good Pope John in 1958 became the leader of The People of God and of all men of good will. He let it be known that he would be a "pastoral pope," and that precisely was what he was, the faithful follower of the Good Shepherd, in love with all mankind. His personal warmth and availability, his obvious concern for people and his joy in being with them, his selflessness and dedication, surely made the traditional role of a Minister of Christ seem less hierarchical and far more pastoral. Against the historical background of a priesthood not entirely free from authoritarianism, triumphalism, and even arrogance, his emergence in history "at the top of the heap," as he refreshingly put it, swept away centuries of diffidence and somehow made it possible for all pastors, and, let us say, pastoral counseling, to be more respectable. Without losing a bit of the divine, all ministers of things divine suddenly became also more human, more loving, more helpful.

The Ecumenical Council begun by Pope John in 1962 was to be, as everyone knows, a "pastoral" council. And it was that, with all the richness of its pastoral implications not yet totally perceived and certainly by no means completely realized. Pastoral counseling in the Church of the future may very well be predicted on the basis of our insights as to what the Church itself will become. The Council has seen man as more mature, more responsible, and possessed of greater human dignity than ever before in history. This is no doubt partly because man, indeed, *is* this way. But the emphasis of the Council on all this will certainly assist man in achieving faster the greater maturity his cultural advancement across the centuries has been nurturing. The possibilities of man's true coming of age seem greater now than ever before in history. The task of the pastoral counselor is thus made more crucial, and at the same time the climate for his contributions to man's development made more appropriate.

The Council has re-emphasized in a striking way the responsibility of the individual, something dear to the heart of every counselor. Decisions are to be made, it is now clearer than ever before, on the basis of one's own conscience, and not imposed by an outside authority. The teaching role of the Church is still intact, and every priest, whether functioning as pastoral counselor or not, must continue to interpret the Good News of Christ as a faithful minister of that Gospel. But there is a difference in emphasis. The traditional role of individual conscience as the arbiter of action is now seen more sharply than in the past; the role of the pastoral counselor will be far less directive, as in the "giving" of spiritual direction, and far more focused on helping the individual properly form his own conscience. The need stressed by the psychoanalysts for norms of morality to become completely "interiorized," a need seen by moralists of all ages, is now re-emphasized by the insistence of the Council that man indeed can achieve such personal interiorization of the moral law. In doing so man becomes still more mature, still more himself, capable of entering still more into rich and rewarding relationships of cooperation with others rather than settling for less noble relationships of dependence.

Thus man's *communitarian* existence will be seen as more important than ever. The pastoral counselor of the future, satisfied that the current counseling emphasis on the importance of relationships with others is in the right direction, will even more than today see his task as helping a client live more harmoniously and more rewardingly with others. If selfishness is at the root of all the ills of the world and, as some insist, the major cause of all personality problems from temper tantrums to paranoia, the other-ness that is inevitably implied in living a greater life of community will bring greater happiness and fulfillment to all. With the counseling relation-ship a microcosm between counselor and client of the world of inter-rela-tionships "outside," the pastoral counselor of the future, with new insights of the brotherhood of all under the Fatherhood of God, will no doubt even develop new techniques to help transfer from the counseling office to the larger world of people the therapeutic results of the counseling experience.

Persons are only a mass of people unless they are loved. Pope John, in invoking the Spirit of Love in a New Pentecost, and in living himself a mag-nificent life of love, has let all pastors of souls see again the truth of Christ that "God is Love" and that men can be helped to God and to their own highest development only through a ministry of love. The theoretical im-portance of love in interpersonal relationships has been explored fruitfully by contemporary counseling psychology. This exploration should continue. And a far greater implementation in practice of the doctrine of love should be the task of every pastoral counselor of the future.

The dominant theme, then, will be a theme of love, with a haunting melody still there from ages past but rescored and reorchestrated into a mighty Canticle, so that all of every land and color and condition may be helped to sing to the Lord a new song of joy.

BIBLIOGRAPHY

Bingham, W. V., and Moore, B. B., *How to Interview*, New York: Harper and Brothers, 1941.

Blum, Milton L., and Balinsky, Benjamin, *Counseling and Psychology*, New York: Prentice-Hall, Inc., 1951.

Brewer, J. M., *History of Vocational Guidance*, New York: Harper and Brothers, 1942.

Cox, R. D., *Counselors and Their Work*, Philadelphia: Archives Publishing Co. of Pennsylvania, 1954.

Curran, Charles A., *Counseling in Catholic Life and Education*, New York: The Macmillan Co., 1952.

Faber, H., and Van Der Schoot, E., *Art of Pastoral Conversation*, New York, Nashville: Abingdon Press, 1965.

Godin, Andre, S. J., *The Pastor as Counselor*, New York: Holt, Rinehart and Winston, 1965.

Hahn, Milton E., and MacLean, Malcolm S., *General Clinical Counseling*, New York: McGraw-Hill Book Co., Inc., 1950.

Hiltner, S. *The Counselor in Counseling*, New York, Nashville: Abington Press, 1950.

Hiltner, S., *Context of Pastoral Counseling*, New York, Nashville: Abington Press, 1961.
——, *Pastoral Counseling*, New York, Nashville: Abington Press, 1952.
——, *Preface to Pastoral Theology*, New York, Nashville: Abington Press, 1958.
——, *Journal of Pastoral Care*, Council for Clinical Training, 475 Riverside Drive, New York, New York.
Kraines, S. H., *Live and Help Live*, New York: The Macmillan Co., 1950.
Rogers, Carl R., *Client Centered Therapy*, Boston: Houghton Mifflin Co., 1951.
——, *Counseling and Psychotherapy*, Boston: Houghton Mifflin Co., 1942.
Shostrom, E. L., and Brammer, L. M., *The Dynamics of the Counseling Process*, New York: McGraw-Hill Book Co., Inc., 1952.

2

MENTAL HEALTH AND MENTAL ILLNESS

MAGDA B. ARNOLD

THE CONCEPT of mental illness is one that has aroused violent controversy. There are psychologists and psychiatrists who claim that mental illness is an illness like any other except that it attacks the brain. There are
others who think that mental illness is the result of psychological conflict,
that is, that it is *psychogenic*. Still others insist that there is no such thing
as mental illness and that abnormal behavior is merely a reaction to various
difficult situations.

Actually, the term "mental illness" was never intended to include all the
difficulties that bring people to a psychotherapist. Only the most severe
disturbances have been termed "mental illness": *psychosis*, which always
implies some confusion and irrationality, whether it is schizophrenia (characterized by bizarre behavior, peculiar talk, and inappropriate emotions)
or manic-depressive states (characterized by flight of ideas in the manic
phase, apathy in the depressive phase). Milder emotional disturbances,
chronic anxiety or irritability have usually not been labeled mental illness.
They are called *neuroses* and are characterized by severe anxiety.

There are other difficulties such as family or marital problems which cannot be resolved, or difficulties in school or on the job for which no solution
can be found that bring people to a psychotherapist. In these cases there
is usually no question of mental illness. These are situations that have become hopelessly tangled because the people involved do not have the
necessary knowledge or needed resources to find a solution. The longer the

problem remains unsolved, the more intense the emotional suffering until weeks and months may be required to reestablish frictionless relations.

Most psychotherapists see mainly patients in the last two categories because severe psychotics have to be referred to a psychiatric hospital for their own and their family's protection. The task of the therapist is always to help the patient control his behavior. Success in this task may easily lead to the conclusion that all unacceptable behavior is produced by the occurrences that first brought it about. From there it is only a step to the conviction that all abnormal behavior is the result of traumatic experiences or that abnormal behavior is the normal reaction to abnormally difficult situations.

What is abnormal behavior? The first answer that comes to mind is that it is odd, bizarre, peculiar behavior. But not all odd behavior is abnormal. Flagpole sitting or crowding six people into a telephone booth is odd enough, but at one time or another it has been the favorite pastime of scores of young hopefuls. Because peculiar behavior is not always a sign of abnormality, it is sometimes said that odd behavior must be unacceptable to the social group before it can be considered abnormal. But then the question arises how large this group must be before its norms can serve as a standard of normality. Obviously, it cannot be a subgroup within a given culture. Homosexuals, no matter how large their number, cannot provide the norm for sexual behavior and so cannot judge what is unacceptable in this area for the rest of mankind. Even a national group is not large enough. In Hitler Germany, for instance, brutal treatment of prisoners in concentration camps was not only permitted but commended—thus accepted as "normal" in that particular situation. That such behavior was considered neither normal nor acceptable by the rest of the world was proved by the universal outcry when conditions in concentration camps became known.

This seems to show that at least humanity at large has some notion of what can be reasonably expected of normal people. If we judge someone's actions as queer or peculiar or hateful because they do not conform to what is generally done, we assume that he could or should act as we do but is either unwilling or unable to do so. If he wears feathers instead of hats, we might merely call him queer. If he marries two women at once or shoots people in peace time, we call him a criminal. But if he acts in such a way that we cannot conceive of any reason at all for his behavior, for instance if we see him fighting someone who isn't there, we call him abnormal. In every case, we assume that there are rational principles of conduct that are binding on all members of our society and ought to be obeyed by anyone who is not ill or incapacitated. The nonconformist meets with disapproval because he apparently can but will not act rationally. Punishment is inflicted on him when he acts against the interests of the community (as the criminal does) because it is hoped that the pain or restraint he is made to suffer will make him willing to conform. Incapacity for rational behavior is assumed only when neither punishment nor disapproval has the slightest effect, as in the case of the mentally ill or mentally retarded. To conclude, as some anthropologists do, that the notion of rationality has no meaning because different cultural groups have different notions of what is rational conduct is no more reasonable than to suppose that there is no electricity just because some cultural groups may believe that thunder and lightning are signs of divine displeasure.

Indeed, the notion that normal is what is socially acceptable has a core of truth in it because by and large what is socially acceptable is also rational conduct. Unfortunately, such a norm depends on casual untrained judgment embodied in custom which holds that everything judged right in a given culture is also according to right reason.

Sometimes normality is thought simply to consist in freedom from symptoms of ill-health. But this would mean that we must be able to recognize a symptom—and how can we do that unless we know what normal functioning is like? Unfortunately, normal mental functioning is not as easily described or defined as normal physical functioning. There are some functions that may be defective without affecting the normality of actions. Shortsightedness, deafness, partial or even total paralysis may handicap the sufferer but they do not make a man abnormal in his thought, speech, or action. It is different with other mental processes: when memory is severely disturbed so that a man does not remember his wife or children or is no longer able to read or write though his eyesight and muscular coordination are unimpaired, his actions are bound to appear peculiar. The same is true when his judgment is disturbed so that he believes himself to be immensely wealthy or makes grandiose plans for sinking a tunnel to the Antipodes; or when his imagination plays tricks on him so that he thinks he is being persecuted, that spies are following him, or that people are always talking about him. Usually, more than one of these mental functions (they used to be called "internal senses") are disturbed in mental illness.

The first requirement for normal behavior, then, is normal functioning of the internal senses: memory, imagination, judgment. A man who can remember things and recognize them, who is able to speak, to understand what he hears and reads, who can find his way around, is normal even if his memory is not as accurate as he would like it to be. A man who can distinguish between imagination and reality, who can judge correctly what is good and bad for him, who can draw on his fantasy when useful and on his memory when necessary will be firmly anchored in reality.

Over and above the normal functioning of the internal senses, a deliberate organization of human activities is required also. A man may be able to think and judge rationally, to imagine the consequences of his actions, yet decide on doing something that will bring great pleasure today and bitter sorrow tomorrow. His internal senses are functioning normally but he has never learned to resist the emotional pull of immediate pleasure. He may regret his decision later but follow his impulses again next time. Not until his unwise decisions land him in serious trouble may he be willing to seek help in controlling his desires.

Fear and anger also interfere in man's rational conduct. When such interference leads to undesirable consequences and makes reasonable decision and action difficult, expert help is necessary. This does not mean that people who are emotionally disturbed are abnormal or ill. It does mean that they have problems they may be unable to solve without help; or that they have never developed emotional control, so that the least extra pressure will be too much for them.

Emotional control and the ability to act reasonably even under trying circumstances is usually called "emotional maturity." In adults, normal behavior means not simply the absence of symptoms of mental ill health but emotional maturity. This is not something that comes inevitably, like physical maturity. Emotional maturity means that we relinquish childish ways. The child wants what he wants immediately and brooks no waiting. The adult must learn to weigh immediate pleasure against later consequences and must be able to assess what is important from a long-range view. He must have a goal in life that he is willing to work for—whether that is a job or a family or the good of his country and his fellowmen. He must be willing to subordinate his own pleasure to what is truly important.

Every human being tries to better himself in some way: through study, through working and earning money, through fulfilment in human relationships. Even the man who is gambling away his inheritance hangs on to the notion that his luck may turn and make him rich over night. But in the unlikely case he does draw a winner, he still has no psychological gain. Man grows only by what he works at, for only those things he tries and finds he can do are at his disposal later on. Work is no curse; it is idleness that is the real enemy. In idleness, a man stagnates and never has the chance of finding out what he can do if he tries. Unfortunately, so much of the work that has to be done is routine and allows little ingenuity and less innovation and so deprives the worker of the emotional satisfaction and the psychological gain he is entitled to. This may change abruptly in the years to come, as soon as automation relieves the worker of most of the routine jobs. It is to be hoped that the hours of leisure so created will be used to develop some interest rather than allowing more time for television. Sheer passive enjoyment may enrich the imagination but if these riches are never drawn on, they are like a miser's hoard, of no use to anybody.

Love and friendship also enrich our life, but only if we take an active part. The maxim: "It is better to give than to receive," holds doubly in love. We must love before we can enjoy being loved. Unwanted love is a burden. To love means wanting the well-being of the beloved, means being concerned about his best interests. It does not mean making love the touchstone of right conduct nor does it mean flitting from one love to another. Human relationships have their own logic. Unless the lover is committed to the beloved, he misses the best part of love, and unless he recognizes a higher law than that of mutual love, his fickleness will prevent him from reaping the fruits of love. Human relationships take time to ripen and it is part of maturity to build for the future.

The mature man or woman has his life so organized that his time is appropriately divided between his work, his family life, and other interests. He is open to others, enjoys his work as well as his leisure, is interested in the larger issues that concern him, and finally, is committed to a living faith. In all the upheavals of recent years it is impossible not to see that man needs some mainstay and some guiding line that will make it possible for him to order his life. If he has no faith in God, he puts his faith in something else, be it science or sex, money or power. Whatever it is, it forces every other interest in life into submission. To subordinate himself and what he loves to science or sex, money or power, is to court humiliation. To subordinate self, love, and work to God is to gain dignity and peace.

The mature person is happy because he uses what powers are necessary and uses them harmoniously. He may face difficulties, sorrow, and pain in his life but his inner serenity will win out. He may live through emotional upheavals but will win back to tranquillity. This is true self-realization, the use of man's powers for a worthwhile purpose. Maslow has studied such self-actualizing people and has remarked how extraordinarily confident, yet humble; how charming, yet dependable; how altogether remarkable they are. These are the truly *normal* personalities, for they are the norm of what human beings can become. These are the people who do more than their share yet are fun to be with, who are the hope of the human race.

TRANSITORY DISTURBANCES

Adverse circumstances will affect even a man whose life is well ordered, and whose mind is serene. He cannot help suffering in mind and body when he is bombed out, starving, fatigued, exhausted, or seriously ill. But such suffering need not disturb the rational ordering of his life though he may need help to overcome these difficulties.

It is also possible that at some time or another he may have to face a particularly difficult situation which may lead him to doubt his life goals: an unhappy marriage may finally become insupportable; his job may be threatened because of personal differences with a demanding superior; a child's waywardness may bring dissension to the home; a neurotic husband or wife may make life a burden. In all these cases it is advisable to seek help because personal involvement makes it impossible to deal with such problems objectively. What is needed here is counseling and not therapy. Indeed, the counselor can be of help only insofar as he helps the troubled persons to decide on the important values and can suggest ways in which they can overcome their emotional disturbance and settle the problem objectively.

Traditionally, counseling has not been the domain of the doctor but that of pastor or spiritual guide. In the past, when anyone became confused about his goals and values, he used to discuss his problems with parents, older friends, teachers, or clergymen. The physician in the guise of the psychiatrist has been added to the list comparatively recently because of a growing conviction that man is an organism and not a person. If something goes wrong with the human organism, we call the physician—just as we call a technician when something goes wrong with a machine. But a difficult situation cannot be smoothed over with a pill, and an ethical conflict is not solved by a tranquilizer.

In these personal problems, the clerical counselor has the advantage over the psychotherapist, for he knows about the values to which his parishioner is committed and can help him decide the kind of solution he wants to achieve. But it will undermine the counselor's effort and harm the person he wants to help if the counselor sees a neurotic disturbance in the emotional upset of a person who finds himself in an unbearable situation. Particularly when confronted with a weeping woman, the clergyman may be tempted to make an end of an uncomfortable situation by referring his parishioner to a psychiatrist. He should remember, however, that an emotional upset (with or without tears) is the normal reaction to a difficulty which cannot be resolved easily. The counselor's task is to help find a solution, not to deal with the emotional upset. Neurosis, on the other hand, is a chronic anxiety state without apparent cause. The neurotic does not weep, usually, but is excited and anxious. He may blame various people or circumstances for his state, but the effect seems out of all proportion to the alleged cause.

PERSONALITY DISORDERS

When it seems clear that the difficulty is not a temporary disturbance but a lifelong behavior pattern, the priest counselor may come to grief unless he asks for expert help. Among the various types of personality disorders perhaps the most puzzling is a type of character development that has been called by many names, from "moral insanity" to "psychopathic inferiority" and "sociopathic personality." Despite the use of medical terms, the psychopath certainly is not ill. He is usually charming, even suave, makes friends easily and can talk well and persuasively. He forms no strong attachments and feels not the slightest reluctance to use his friends for his own purposes, and even to sacrifice them for some passing pleasure. He manipulates people and usually manages to extract money and other favors from them. He may lie, steal, cheat, profess remorse when he is caught but go on as before as soon as he is free again. The psychopath usually charms the therapist as much as he does casual acquaintances. He may start out as a juvenile delinquent and be in and out of psychiatric hospitals, always showing insight, always promising to do better, until he is finally diagnosed as a psychopath. Since neither punishment nor psychotherapy seems to be of the slightest use, incorrigibility has become the hallmark of the psychopath. Since he sets no standards for himself and so never feels he falls short, the psychopath has no conflicts and no anxiety. No wonder he is cheerful and confident, altogether charming on first acquaintance—and absolutely devastating as a friend, husband, or father.

We know that without purpose in life a man will develop into a drifter. But we have no idea whether the psychopath cannot or will not organize his life by commitment to a long-range goal. It would seem that a strong attachment should make it possible for him to reform, and that it should be possible for any man to form a strong conviction; but this is precisely what the psychopath does not seem able to do. Nothing is worth enough to him to make an effort, to discipline himself, to concentrate on some work, to be loyal to a friend. It is almost as if the psychopath had no memory for affection or punishment so that he encounters each situation anew, without the ready reminder of past benefits or past dangers.

For the counselor, the psychopath is an occasion of distress and brings a feeling of helplessness and incompetence. Because he knows that not every plausible juvenile delinquent is a psychopath, he dare not refuse to try. But as soon as it becomes clear that his efforts bring no improvement, he will be well advised to concentrate on protecting the psychopath's family as best he can rather than expect a change of heart in a youngster who has no heart.

The psychopath is almost a textbook example of immaturity, the opposite of the mature human being described earlier. It is tempting to think that this built-in immaturity is not altogether his own fault, that he has an innate deficiency that predisposes him to impulsive actions. Such a deficiency could be the lack or weakness of "affective memory," what Thomas Aquinas has called "memoria." When a man has no special welcome for a friend, feels no restraint in speaking to someone he dislikes, when he remembers past danger merely as an occurrence, not as something that deeply affected him, he may appear even-tempered, friendly, courageous, when in reality he can form no clear judgment of the situation because he feels neither remembered affection nor remembered fear or dislike. If this is the psychopath's defect, it is not surprising that he cannot learn from experience, for the affective ingredient of experience is missing.

For the clergyman, the problem is how to recognize a psychopath and to whom to refer him. To recognize a man as a psychopath, dependable reports on his dealings with business associates, family, and friends are necessary. Personal interviews with several family members or business associates may be required to round out the picture. When faced with the evidence, the psychopath may admit that he has occasionally done the wrong thing, but he will usually insist that here and now his point of view is the right one. For this reason, there is very little hope of persuading him to change his mind and act in a responsible way. Sheer force and absolute necessity are the only factors that may prove stronger than the psychopath's desire. Not a clergyman or psychotherapist but a lawyer may be needed to convince a psychopath that his intended course of action may not only hurt his family and associates but himself as well.

Another type of personality disorder is homosexuality. The classification of homosexuality as a personality disorder (see AMA Standard Nomenclature) is based on the notion that homosexuality is not an illness nor a temporary disturbance but a lifelong pattern in which sexual desire is directed toward the same rather than the opposite sex. At the same time, it is well recognized that both men and women may have isolated homosexual experiences (e.g., in boarding schools, camps, reformatories or prisons, during a time of enforced abstinence) but later continue to be heterosexually oriented.

It has been said that everyone is "bisexual," that is, he has unconscious inclinations toward the same as well as the opposite sex, just as he has both male and female sex hormones though in different proportions. According to this interpretation, homosexuality would occur when the proportion of male and female sex hormones in a given person differs from that of normal members of his sex. Unfortunately for this theory, the vast majority of homosexuals do not differ from their normal fellows in their hormonal balance, and injections of male sex hormones in male homosexuals and of female sex hormones in female homosexuals do not change the direction of their sex drive.

According to psychoanalytic theory, a boy develops into a homosexual because he is unconsciously afraid of women and defends himself by identifying with the aggressor (the mother). Similarly, homosexuality in women is said to be based on an unconscious fear of men and identification with the aggressor-father. But the only evidence for this view is found in the "dynamics" of homosexual patients as interpreted on the basis of the same theory.

In human beings, sexual desire is not isolated from love. Whenever admiration or love is aroused, sexual desire may be aroused as well. Because of this, a very young girl may develop a crush on an older one which easily leads to intimacy; in this way she may be seduced before she has experienced any heterosexual attraction. And once she has experienced emotional as well as sexual satisfaction in this relationship, her desire may be permanently directed toward women. Early seduction by older boys or men is a factor also among boys. No doubt there are other factors as well; fear of women may play a role in some though not in all male homosexuals.

Usually, the homosexual does not consider himself abnormal in any way. He may deplore the social stigma but usually refuses help unless his behavior has caused him serious trouble. When a clergyman is approached by one of his parishioners with a problem of this kind, he must first decide whether this is a case of true homosexuality or of occasional homosexual inclinations. If it is the latter, the pastor may be able to deal with the problem of conscience and in addition give the assurance that occasional physical excitement in the presence of a member of the same sex does not make a person a homosexual. However, if he has satisfied himself that he is dealing with a person whose whole pattern of thought and of action is directed toward his own sex, he should not try to undertake any counseling. It takes expert help by a psychiatrist or psychologist who has considerable experience in this field to make any progress, and even then the outcome is not at all certain.

PSYCHOSOMATIC REACTIONS

Of these, *anxiety states* (neuroses) are the most frequent. Anxiety may be diffuse and all-pervading or it may be sharply focused into a phobia or compulsion neurosis.[1] None of these states indicate mental illness but they do imply that there is a serious emotional disturbance. Anxiety states are

[1] Cf. Fr. Harvey's statement on compulsion, p. 112 below.

accompanied by definite physical complaints: palpitation, breathlessness, diarrhea, dry mouth, tremors, sweating. All these are physiological symptoms of fear.

There is considerable controversy as to the origin of the chronic fear state we call neurosis. Normally, any fear experience is soon forgotten, though its shadow remains. This is "affective memory" which is re-lived as soon as any similar situation is experienced. When the original fear was very intense, the resulting affective memory is correspondingly strong.

Usually, the man who experiences such affective memory does not realize that he is reexperiencing past emotions. He feels fear, sometimes extremely strong fear, yet cannot discover the cause of it. He either comes to believe that there must be some danger because he feels such fear, or he begins to wonder whether he is not "losing his mind," particularly when he is afraid more and more often without discoverable cause. Freud thought that the original experience was "repressed," that is, automatically prevented from being remembered; and that the drive attached to it now connects with similar situations and so brings about the old anxiety. But the traumatic experience may never have been forgotten and yet the anxiety connected with it is re-lived over and over. To give an example:

A young man of twenty-five consulted me because of his excessive anxiety whenever he had to speak to the director of his department. He felt that he not only made a poor impression but also that his fear made progress in his profession almost impossible. He could not bring himself to ask for a raise in salary, could not voice the most reasonable suggestions or complaints, in short, was reduced to a quivering bundle of nerves as long as his employer was in the room with him. After every such occasion, he felt completely exhausted . . . and was almost convinced that he was suffering from a severe and progressive disability.

I asked him when he had first experienced a like feeling. . . . He thought for a while and then recounted an experience he had had as a boy of seventeen. He had worked for a friend of the family during every vacation all through high school, had been treated almost like a partner, and had felt a great sense of achievement and responsibility. He had intended to make this occupation his life work as soon as he should graduate. During his last summer before graduation, however, he noticed some serious irregularities in his employer's business. At first he tried to draw his friend's attention to what he believed to be an oversight, but with little result. Later during the same summer a business friend of the firm, apparently with his employer's tacit consent, asked the boy to take his daughter to a dance. The boy did not want to take the evening off from work but finally decided to oblige his employer's friend. Next day he was called into the office and dismissed on the spot for his neglect of duty—in spite of his explanations and in spite of the unclouded and cordial relationship that had existed before. This was a severe blow to the boy, who saw not only the summer's job disappear but also the opportunity to be accepted into the firm and establish himself. In addition he lost a

personal friend whom he had admired and idolized. His world was in pieces—
no wonder that he had all the signs of a severe fear reaction. This reaction
with its full complement of physiological symptoms was repeated afterward
every time he had to talk to an employer again.[2]

In this case, the traumatic experience was not repressed but was a vivid
and bitter memory. But the young man remembered the disappointment,
not his physiological reaction. His later fear together with its distressing
symptoms was not recognized as an *affective* memory and so not connected
with the experience he had had only eight years before.

In this case, it was not too difficult to make the young man aware of
the connection between the old disappointment and his present symptoms.
With other patients it may take considerable time, particularly when it is
a series of emotional reactions rather than one traumatic experience that
has built up their anxious attitude. What has to be done is to make the
patient see that his anxiety is an emotional hangover, as it were, that has no
connection with his present life. He has to learn to face whatever he is
afraid of, supported by the therapist, until he knows by experience that he
can overcome it. Different schools of therapy achieve this in different ways.
Freudian psychoanalysis dredges up the traumatic memories and motivates
the patient to face his problems through his confidence in the therapist.
Jungian psychology isolates the patient's emotional attitudes by dream
analysis and free fantasy and helps him change by working through his
difficulties in imagination before he solves them in fact. Rogerian client-
centered counseling reflects the client's feelings and so helps him to recognize them.

Often, physical complaints have to be tackled before any psychological
change can be brought about. This is often done by prescribing tranquilizers, or using relaxation techniques together with psychotherapy. The physical symptoms merely indicate that the patient is afraid. But they are so
insistent that he may take them for symptoms of a dangerous illness (e.g.
heart trouble) and becomes afraid on this count as well. The new fear adds
new symptoms and the vicious circle is complete.

When anxiety becomes focused on some physical organ, it develops into
a so-called *organ neurosis:* the anxiety either increases the symptoms directly
(palpitations in heart neurosis) or it produces a feeling of malaise and
sometimes pain which eventually contributes to the difficulty (e.g. abdominal pains, upper chest pains, itching skin that may contribute to inflammation). But anxiety may also be focused on a particular object: subways,

---

[2] Arnold, 1960 I page 187. In this chapter sources cited in footnotes will be found in
the bibliography, page 43 below.

open spaces, closed rooms, dogs, mice, etc. This is called a *phobia*. It may be so severe that the patient is unable to face the thing he fears and avoids it at any cost. This severely restricts his freedom of movement and often makes it necessary to change his way of life radically.

In *compulsion neurosis*, the patient feels constrained to repeat certain actions: to make the bed or wash his hands over and over, to try the key again and again to be certain he has locked the door. He goes over these actions repeatedly because he is panic-stricken at the thought of what would happen if he did not make the bed perfectly, did not wash his hands, did not lock the door or turn off the gas.

Though phobia seems to be an emotional hangover like the anxiety state, compulsion is more in the nature of a defense against it, albeit an ineffective one. In phobia, the trouble seems to stem from a singular concentration on what is feared, with never an attempt to overcome the fear. Fear, like every other emotion, does force such a concentration; but most people manage to face the danger again in a happier hour and learn to overcome it; this provides a corrective experience and reduces the affective memory. Hence the counsel to drive or fly again as soon as possible after a minor accident, to make friends with horses or dogs or whatever animals have inspired fear. If that is done successfully, there is no chance of developing a phobia.

In compulsion there is just as exclusive a concentration on the possible dangers that threaten if the compulsive actions should be omitted. The patient seems to be inordinately afraid of being blamed or of falling short of the ideal of perfection he has set for himself. Such an ingrained attitude requires a thorough reeducation which is best accompanied by techniques designed to reduce the physical symptoms of anxiety.

Neurasthenia or *psychasthenia* is the name given to the exhaustion that follows in the wake of long, drawn-out anxiety. It has been called "effort syndrome," when anxiety was accompanied by exhausting effort, as, for example, in combat personnel during the last war. The physiological changes that come with fear are very similar to those brought on by exhausting effort. However, they do not bring the increase in muscular strength that comes with exercise. Rest will help only if the anxiety is eliminated as well. Combat personnel improve quickly with rest and relaxation, particularly if their tour of duty is over. But when neurasthenia is the result of a persisting personal problem, the problem must be tackled before rest will restore the patient.

Reactive depression which is a reaction to some misfortune—loss of love, job, or fortune—is also considered a neurosis although the anxiety is not obvious. The patient becomes despondent, feels that his loss has ended his chances for success or happiness, loses his appetite, becomes apathetic, often suffers from sleeplessness and various physical complaints. He is not only afraid of the future but has given up hope altogether. This is a state beyond anxiety and beyond sorrow for the loss is felt to be so great that nothing else is worthwhile. Reactive depression usually requires psychotherapy to shorten the time of recovery.

Hysteria or conversion reaction is also considered a type of neurosis even though the patient shows no anxiety. According to psychoanalytic theory, anxiety is "converted" into a physical disability that helps to cope with the original danger. One example of this is the patient of Freud who suffered a hysterical contracture of the arm with which she had warded off a blow. Another is the case of the soldier who develops a paralysis of his right arm because he is afraid that he might strike a hated officer. But the notion that anxiety is "converted" into a symptom does not really explain the mechanism by which it is brought about. The phenomenon could be explained by the patient's single-minded concentration on the feared event. Thus, regarding the examples given above, the girl was so intent on defending herself in a highly emotional situation that this posture became fixed, while the soldier was so intent on not using his arm in the wrong way that he completely eliminated it from his thinking and "forgot" it so completely that he was finally unable to use it.

It is a fact that concentration on a movement (or on muscular relaxation) will bring it about. Motor imagination can innervate muscles or prevent innervation. When imagination turns into firm belief through emotional concentration, muscle paralysis or contracture can be brought about in the same way as in hypnosis. But it takes suggestible people who have little inclination for self-criticism to develop hysterical symptoms. This is the reason why suggestion and hypnosis, or a sudden emergency can often abruptly restore the use of such spastic or paralyzed limbs. Increased psychological sophistication has materially reduced hysterical reactions; but when they do occur, they need psychotherapy.

Amnesia is a fugue state related to hysteria. When a man finds himself in a situation that exerts a great deal of pressure and he cannot see any way out, he sometimes manages to "forget" his past life, his very identity. He may come to in entirely unfamiliar surroundings without any notion how he got there. He may not remember his name, his job, his family, and have to start life afresh. But however bewildered he may be at the time, he usually recovers his memory over a period that may range from a few months to a few years. After head injuries such fugue states are particularly likely to happen because there is usually a memory loss for the period immediately before the accident. If there is a driving reason for forgetting, the memory loss may stretch over a person's whole past instead of the few hours usual after concussion.

Multiple personality is another phenomenon related to hysteria. It is curious that the classic fictional case of multiple personality, that of Stevenson's Dr. Jekyll and Mr. Hyde, speaks of two different egos in a man whereas practically all the reported cases seem to have been women. Moreover, Dr. Jekyll had to take drugs to bring about the transformation, but the women reported in real life managed it all by themselves.

There are several well authenticated cases on record in which two or three entirely different personalities may appear one after another in the same person. What seems to have happened in such cases is that the dominant personality has led a severely restricted life so that a whole area of experience has been closed to it. Given a woman who is largely unaware of her inner wants because she severely suppresses them, it is possible that a whole new personality will emerge who does all the things her straitlaced *alter ego* denies herself. Most of the reported cases were cured; that is, the diverging personalities were, in the course of lengthy psychotherapy, integrated again into a new personality at once more flexible and more attractive.

Neither neurosis nor hysterical (conversion) reactions should be treated by the clerical counselor, with two possible exceptions: scrupulosity and reactive depression. Only the mildest forms of scrupulosity (which is a type of obsessive-compulsive reaction) should be attempted. If the penitent is willing to let the confessor decide whether a sin has been committed and how serious it is, and if he manages to do his work without great disturbance, well and good. But when such counsel cannot be followed and the penitent is in a continuous state of anxiety which impairs his efficiency, it is far wiser to refer him to a psychotherapist. In reactive depression, companionship can often help a man find new interests and help him over the preoccupation with his loss. For this reason, it is often a great boon when he can talk to a sympathetic counselor because his family and friends have long exhausted their ingenuity and patience.

PSYCHOSIS

Psychosis is the only deviation from the normal that deserves the name "mental illness," but is usually described euphemistically as "mental breakdown." Whether it has a known organic cause or is termed "functional" (because, as yet, no organic cause has been discovered), psychosis implies a definite abnormality in thinking and judgment that makes it impossible for the patient to act responsibly.

Paranoid states are perhaps the least abnormal of the various psychotic deviations. The paranoid patient believes that he is suffering malicious persecution, that spies are after him, and that he is the victim of a Communist or rightist plot (depending on circumstances). However, in every other way he seems entirely rational. These are the patients who complain that the malice of their relatives or enemies has put them into the mental hospital—and often they manage to convince a jury of the injustice of their commitment. Just as often, such patients are never committed because they are comparatively harmless and are able to look after themselves.

The paranoid is so normal (except for his delusion) that it is often difficult to recognize his mental abnormality. The first paranoid I talked to as an intern was a man who had been pointed out to me by the superintendent of the mental hospital as a textbook case. He was a personable young man, a bookkeeper, unmarried, who talked easily and well. We talked about his job, his family, the hospital, about current events and anything I could think of. After almost an hour, I still could not detect any signs of mental illness. When I asked him why he was in the hospital, he said he had been overworking and the doctor thought he had better take a rest. I was completely nonplussed. Finally, I asked him how he liked the hospital. "Why," he said, "I like it all right, except for the nurses." When I tried to find out what the nurses had done to him, it all came pouring out. He complained that all the nurses were after him, they dropped down from the ceiling, came out of cracks in the wall and out of the faucets as soon as he turned on the water; they got in his bed and made love to him. In short, they were bothering him all the time and he did not have a moment's rest. When I inquired whether he had made a complaint to the doctors, he assured me that he had and that the chief psychiatrist had been very sympathetic and had encouraged him to defend himself against them. Since then it had been much better. When asked how he defended himself, he explained: "You see, first I break off their arms and legs and then I break off their head—and then they disappear." Fortunately, he was in excellent shape physically, so the real nurses never had any call to come too close to him.

It is perhaps easier to explain paranoid states as being the result of psychological difficulties rather than any other psychosis. We have all met people who had some pet notion that seemed impossible to dislodge: that all businessmen take advantage of their customers, that all doctors are charlatans or all lawyers are crooked, and there is no way of convincing them that they are generalizing one unfortunate experience for, indeed, sometimes they cannot even point to one incident to support their conviction. These are the people who engage in lawsuits at the slightest provocation or write letters to Governor or President complaining of abuses for which they can give no evidence. It seems credible enough that a lifetime of such suspiciousness may eventually lead to paranoia, and, in fact, in many cases, it does. Sometimes a period of stress, an illness or operation seems to unleash a man's suspicions and bring about violence, and so lead to his commitment to a mental hospital. Just as often, particularly with educated and well-to-do people, those who are rather cantankerous often retain a shadow of reasonableness so that their sanity is not suspected no matter what trouble they cause to neighbors, friends, and family.

Why do some people develop such suspicions in the first place? Affective memory accounts for a man's disposition to be suspicious once he has experienced someone's malice. But it does not explain why he never seems to correct this attitude. Unfortunately, once a person is willing to believe the worst about his fellowmen and treats them accordingly, they will often retaliate and may sometimes attack. But even if their temper remains even, he will put the worst interpretation on everything they do or say, and keep wondering what is the ulterior motive for their friendliness.

For whatever reason, the paranoid's judgment seems definitely warped. It is almost impossible to change his attitudes, even in long-term psychotherapy, because he suspects even the people who try to help him. Neither family nor friends can disarm his suspicions. If they try reasonable persuasion, they convince him only that they too, are against him. The full-blown paranoid may become dangerous because at some time his delusions may compel him to attack. Nevertheless, as long as his delusions are comparatively harmless, the community perforce has to put up with him. But at least it should be recognized that his judgment is so warped that he is no longer capable of a just and objective evaluation where his delusion is concerned.

Schizophrenia (often called "split personality") is not, as the layman often thinks, the same as "multiple personality." The latter is akin to hysteria, as has already been pointed out. There is a split in schizophrenia, but it is a split between emotion and reason and not a split between different personalities in the same person. The patient may say over and over: "Everybody is sick because of me. I am to blame for everything," but show no emotion at all. The schizophrenic is confused, disturbed in his thinking and irrational in his behavior. He is out of touch with his environment, sees things no one else sees, hears voices, misinterprets other people's words and actions, and ascribes malicious intention and baneful influences to all sorts of things. He may say that the radio is shouting abuse at him, that he is being influenced by thought rays or cosmic forces, or that people are using a laughing or tickling machine on him. He may insist that he is Napoleon, Christ, a king or a pope, and has power over other people. He cannot be convinced by logic or evidence that his hallucinations are not real or that his delusions are not true. Apparently, he *feels* that he is powerful or called on to do great things, and tries to account for this feeling by insisting that he is Napoleon or Christ, or some other important personage. Most of his peculiar convictions seem to be rooted in a similar abnormal experience. They cannot be dislodged because he believes his experience, his feelings, rather than other people's reason.

Schizophrenic delusions change with changing times. In centuries past, a patient might talk of being bewitched, of consorting with the devil, of participating in the Witches' Sabbath. Today, patients talk of radio, TV, machines or rays that influence them, but also of men from Mars. They have changed their interpretation of the weird feelings they experience, but the experiences themselves seem to have remained remarkably similar over the centuries.

Since the turn of the century, when Kraepelin and Bleuler first described schizophrenic states as a definite disease, our understanding of this disturbance has not improved much. Kraepelin called it "dementia praecox" because the mental deterioration that goes with schizophrenia sets in so early in life. But Bleuler did not consider this early loss of mental faculties the essential feature of the disease. Rather, it seemed to him to consist essentially in a split between reason and emotion or between different kinds of thinking. His term "schizophrenia" has been generally accepted. But today schizophrenia is no longer considered a single disease but a variety of abnormal mental states.

Usually, four types are distinguished: simple, hebephrenic, catatonic, and paranoid. In simple schizophrenia, the patient shows loss of energy, apathy, and indifference, in contrast to his earlier behavior. He is deteriorating rapidly, occasionally seems confused but usually shows no marked psychotic symptoms. The following case is a good illustration:

Miss S. aged twenty-seven, has had three periods of residence in mental hospitals since the age of nineteen. She was a slow but not unusual student in (grade) school and in the first two years of high school. Until she was seventeen she showed no evidence of mental abnormality and had many friends. During the second and third years in high school she became apathetic and complained of loss of energy, vague pains, and occasionally said that things seemed unreal to her. Her parents noticed a slow but pronounced change in her character and she seemed to lose all interest in things which she had formerly enjoyed. There was no evidence of delusions or hallucinations.

Because of her apathy and slovenliness, she was finally brought to a mental hospital, where she became even more disinterested and apathetic. She appeared to be mentally deteriorated, so that after six months her behavior and conversation were similar to that of a feeble-minded person. Her family took her home from the hospital on two different occasions, hoping that home surroundings would stimulate her and make her more normal in behavior. At home she continued in the same deteriorated fashion. Her lack of attention to her person and her untidiness interfered with the family life to such an extent that she had to be returned to the hospital on each occasion. At age twenty-seven she behaved like a stupid girl of six or seven, giving no evidence of any of the intellectual ability which had enabled her to reach high school.[3]

The *hebephrenic* type is the most frequent. The patient has hallucinations and delusions, uses labored round-about ways of talking, often high-flown language and odd word combinations. He is out of touch with his environment and shows all the other schizophrenic symptoms. He may have periods of acute excitement during which he may try to harm himself or others. He usually neglects habits of cleanliness and personal hygiene and shows gradually deepening deterioration.

The *paranoid type* is a schizophrenic whose delusions take the form of a persecution complex. He differs from patients suffering from paranoia in that his delusions are only one of many psychotic symptoms and are not nearly as well systematized. He usually has hallucinations and tends to be confused. There are many psychiatrists today who refuse to recognize paranoia as in any way different from paranoid schizophrenia, at least when it is full-blown. The patient mentioned above in the discussion of paranoid states was diagnosed simply as paranoid despite his hallucinations of nurses disturbing him, because he was so entirely rational in every other respect. However, because he is convinced that people are after him, the schizophrenic paranoid frequently has periodic acute outbursts which take a violent and often very dangerous form. Such a person may commit crimes of senseless violence which are often the first indication of his disturbed mental state.

Catatonic schizophrenia is diagnosed when the patient shows a peculiar stiffness, ungainliness, and mannerism in his movements, or remains motionless, standing or sitting in bizarre postures for hours. He is practically inaccessible at these periods, does not answer questions, and apparently does not know what is going on around him. From the accounts of recovered catatonics, we know, however, that they are usually aware of everything, but for their own reasons neither move nor answer. This catatonic period does not last. Sooner or later, the patient begins to speak again, moves more normally, and is in contact with others at least to the extent that he will answer questions. When the catatonic episode is over, his symptoms are no different from those of other schizophrenic patients.

[3] Landis and Bolles, pages 146–147.

In recent years, another variety of schizophrenia has been described. It has been called "preclinical," "early," or "pseudoneurotic" schizophrenia. The disturbance is milder, comes in repeated episodes, and may not develop into true schizophrenia throughout life. The patient has many complaints and seems to suffer from anxiety just as the neurotic does. But, while the neurotic is adept in dissecting his mental state, is engrossed in his emotions, and can analyze his and other people's motives perfectly, the pseudoneurotic complains of emotional flatness and an inability to give or return affection. This patient gives a vague, rather stilted description of his difficulties and shows little evidence of emotion. An acute episode usually starts with excitement and general apprehension; it is at this time that the psychotic episode can easily be mistaken for neurotic anxiety. But, whereas the true neurotic is afraid of various external dangers with which he feels himself unable to cope, the pseudoneurotic is fearful because of his changed thought life and the inrush of alien impulses and ideas. However, as the psychotic episode develops and the patient begins to have hallucinations and delusions, he can no longer be mistaken for a neurotic.

Childhood schizophrenia is another variety that has been described only comparatively recently. It may be noticed in early childhood or even in infancy. The schizophrenic child seems to have difficulty in relating to other people. He is extremely dependent on his mother without showing much affection, seems to be preoccupied all the time, and is difficult to interest in anything. It has been noted that the maturational spurt at puberty often brings the child into closer contact with reality so that adolescence is the best period in his life. But it may also happen that such children eventually reach an adjustment that is not far from normalcy. It was reported in one study that only about 12 per cent of children diagnosed as "infantile psychosis" were regarded as schizophrenic years later.[4]

From this discussion it is clear that schizophrenia has many faces. The core seems to be the same but the symptoms may differ widely, and the disturbance, acute episodes alternating with a more placid period, may be present in infancy or develop later in childhood or early adulthood. Schizophrenia may be so severe that commitment in an institution is necessary even during the quiet periods; or it may be milder, allowing the patient to stay at home except for the acute episodes. Most theorists agree that there is a constitutional (genetic) predisposition that is activated either during stress or at a particular time in the life of the patient (e.g., during pregnancy or after childbirth). Just what the schizophrenic fault could be is not easy to say. Various physiological factors (biochemical, hormonal) seem to play a role. For instance, the blood of schizophrenics contains

[4] Reiser and Brown.

elements not found in the blood of normal persons.[5] Also, electrical activity in certain brain structures differs decisively during a psychotic episode.[6]

There is dispute even about the basic psychological defect in schizophrenia. To speak of "thought disorders" is simply to describe the effect, and not to pinpoint the cause. Often it is said that the schizophrenic withdraws from reality to live in his fantasy world. But studies with projective techniques have shown that the schizophrenic complains of things being weird, and frightening. He is painfully aware of his difficulty in thinking and of his inability to communicate his experience to others. Such a patient complains that he is exhausted and unable to do what others do so that he cannot manage without their support; yet they do not understand him and he does not understand them.[7] These reports seem to indicate that the schizophrenic has suffered a serious interference with his mental powers so that he cannot function as others do. However, it is not he who has withdrawn from reality, but rather his disability has cut him off from it, much against his will. Consequently, we might infer that several of his internal senses are affected, but in particular his intuitive appraisal of people and things. In simple schizophrenia, this function seems to be sluggish, and the patient is apathetic because he does not—and cannot—appraise anything as worthwhile. Consequently, he has no impulse to do anything, not even to keep himself clean. In hebephrenia and other forms of schizophrenia, this appraisal seems to be biassed toward dislike and strangeness, and so produces fear. Since the estimative sense is used also to distinguish between past, present, and possible experiences, he is often unable to distinguish between reality, memories of the past, and imagination. In addition, his imagination seems overstimulated so that images appear, voices are heard, and influences are felt that rival real experiences in intensity. And finally, the victim of hebephrenia seems to be unable to draw on memory when needed, with the result that his answers to searching questions are approximate, he uses round-about ways of talking, and often makes up words. In catatonia, motor imagination seems to be affected as well, so that the patient imagines and acts out postures that have a magical significance for him.

It is unlikely that such defective functioning of the internal senses could be produced by unresolved conflicts or traumatic experiences. Emotional disturbance can interfere with recall (as in stage fright and fugue states), or it can give rise to chronic emotional attitudes (e.g. anxiety, or suspicion) but it cannot produce the deterioration seen in schizophrenia. Only ab-

[5] Heath, 1964 and Frohman *et al.* 1960.
[6] Heath, 1964.
[7] Vassiliou.

normal functioning of the brain structures that mediate appraisal, memory, emotion, and imagination could be responsible for such bizarre changes in psychological experience. A beginning has been made in identifying these structures; [8] and there is considerable evidence that they show abnormal electrical discharges during psychotic episodes.[9] What it is that interferes with their normal functioning remains for future research to discover.

Not only is the cause of schizophrenic disorders in doubt, but their cure is an even bigger problem. Usually, even when the patient is discharged from the mental hospital he is not cured though the psychosis has been arrested. Psychotherapy, when successful, has enabled the patient to disregard remaining symptoms, to control his behavior and get along with others. In recent years, tranquilizing drugs have been used frequently by both clinics and mental hospitals. As a result, the acute violent episodes so destructive to life in the family or in the hospital ward have been reduced or shortened. Furthermore, the patients are more able to cope with their fears and their peculiar feelings, and to take part in group therapy, which in turn gives them a feeling of fellowship they badly need. "Behavior modification" is a still more recent technique which consists in giving small rewards (candy or certain privileges) for conforming with hospital routine, refraining from "sick talk," or helping in the ward. This technique seems more effective than supportive therapy for seriously ill patients because these are not able to see the desirability of abstract goals like orderliness or getting well, but are able to appreciate an immediate reward.

Manic-depressive psychosis is called an affective disorder to distinguish it from thought disorders. It was first described by Kraepelin, who pointed out that mania, depression, and the so-called circular insanity, in which mania alternates with depression, are all forms of the same disease process and can occur singly or in combination. One patient may show a period of severe depression, then return to normal and after some years have another attack of depression without ever going through a manic phase. Another patient may experience only the manic phase, alternating with normal periods. Finally, a third class of patients may go from the manic phase through a normal period to depression, or experience a depression immediately after the manic phase. Kraepelin, and others after him, thought that this disorder has a constitutional basis.

The depressive phase is not too different from the reactive depression in neurosis, except that it is usually more intense. It may consist in an extraordinary slowing of mental functions so that the patient is unable to think or to talk. When he attempts to answer a question, he has such

[8] Arnold, 1960, Vol. 2.
[9] Heath, 1964.

difficulty expressing his thoughts that he has forgotten the question as well as the intended answer before he has finished his sentence. Or he may experience agitation instead of the usual slowing of mental functions so that he weeps, wrings his hands, literally tears out his hair, and storms up and down, wailing and accusing himself of the greatest sins and crimes. There is no mental deterioration and it is just a matter of time before he recovers. Even so, the individual's suffering is extreme, for as one recovered patient says:

> Suffer? And what is the verdict of people who have undergone the most excruciating physical pain, and then been mentally ill? These people say: "Rather all the physical illnesses—everyone of them—over again, than mental breakdown." Or, more simply, "That's the real hell." Torture. There is never any getting away from it. Your body seems shaken by it. It gives you no rest. It is like a mental flagellation—always, day and night. The minute you wake up it is there. All day long it is there. Whatever you try to do, it stands in your way. And sometimes it is like a big, threatening obstacle. But you have to put up with it. You think: "Isn't there something the doctor can cut away?" It is like a monster, it is like a growth. It presses down on you. It mocks you. It exhausts you. It makes your thought go spinning around like a squirrel in a cage, and it wears you out just as going around in a circle physically would wear you out. "If I could only press a lever to stop this whirring," you say to yourself. Yet you *cannot stop*. You cannot "snap out of it." If only you might. For just a minute, for just a second. No wonder so many depressives long for death.[10]

This is an account of agitated depression. Retarded depression, as the apathetic form of depression is called, is a veritable paralysis of suffering, the closest approach to living death.

In the manic phase, the patient initially has an extraordinary feeling of well-being because his mental functions are speeded up. He has an uprush of plans and ideas, and feels capable of doing almost anything. One patient, an engineer, conceived grandiose plans of building a bridge over the Gulf of Mexico, and neglected all his work because of this fantasy. After recovery, he realized how far out his calculations had been. Later attacks brought back the same wild notion, his grand bridge, and so he finally signed in to a mental hospital as a voluntary patient.

As the excitement progresses, the patient has more and more difficulty ordering his thoughts; he talks rapidly and excitedly, and resorts to puns, rhymes, and plays on words. He jumps from one topic to the other until no one can follow his flight of ideas, and gradually, the connection loosens and he begins to be incoherent and irritable and abusive when others attempt to control or restrain him.

[10] E. Krauch, 1937, page 95–96.

Manic-depressive psychosis, like schizophrenia, has not yet yielded its secrets. Whether it is toxic in nature as Kraepelin believed, or the exaggeration of the cycloid personality with short and rounded body build (as schizophrenia would be the exaggeration of a schizoid personality with tall and thin build) as Kretschmer suggested, there is as yet no evidence for either view. However, following Kraepelin's theory, if a general slowing of function could be caused by some agent inhibiting central nervous functioning (but what that agent could be is anyone's guess), then it would seem that a manic flight of ideas could be caused by some agent accelerating brain function. It is known that electroshock, which throws every muscle into violent convulsions, is almost a specific remedy for retarded depression. On the other hand, neither agitated depression nor the manic phase are materially shortened by electroshock, but tranquilizers seem to be quite effective. In the period between attacks, psychotherapy can help the patient to guard against attitudes that might bring about a depressive or manic phase. Clifford Beers, one of the pioneers of the Mental Health Movement tells us in his autobiography how he finally learned to prevent or reduce his manic attacks. The book is an extremely interesting account of his illness and his attempts to prevent recurrences.

Senile psychosis or *senile dementia* is the result of brain damage. The changes in old age are primarily organic, and include such changes as the gradual loss of energy and muscular power, the hardening of arteries, and the poorer nutritional state of tissues. As a result of the reduced nutritional conditions of the brain cells, memory becomes uncertain and learning is more and more difficult. Thus it is easier for the aged to repeat routine tasks than to establish new habits or make new plans. Most old people are reluctant to start something new, to leave home, or to travel. They carry an additional burden in knowing that every day brings them closer to physical helplessness that will end only with death. Fortunately, emotions also are more sedate so that they are to some extent insulated from distress.

Though normal old age brings with it much discomfort, it need not bring senility. But when there is serious "softening" of the brain, mental deterioration follows rapidly. The first symptom is usually an inability to think of common words, which makes conversation painful for all concerned. The oldster may either become irritable and blame others when they do not manage to understand what he wants, or he may become confused, emotionally unstable, weeping and laughing in the same breath. As memory deteriorates more and more, he no longer recognizes family or friends and may wander away from home, unable to find his way back. Frequently too, his conversation rambles and he gives an impression of confusion and general disorientation. This general disorientation cannot be arrested, though tranquilizing drugs may reduce emotional excitement.

Other psychoses. Other nervous system diseases and brain damage can also produce mental abnormalities. Their seriousness and kind will depend on the extent of the damage and the location of the lesion. The usual symptoms are severe memory defects, personality changes, or a deterioration of judgment. Drugs also can reproduce one or the other symptom of psychosis: delirium tremens, an acute psychotic episode with luxuriant hallucinations, result from excessive use of alcohol. The mental state produced by LSD seems to consist in changed perception in which the world seems recreated in weird, fanciful, or frightening shape, one that hints at a reality more impressive by far than the individual's humdrum everyday life. High fever also produces hallucinations and often delusions. With such proof that mental disturbances with psychotic symptoms can be produced by physical means it is difficult to exclude an organic origin even of the so-called "functional" psychoses.

The clerical counselor will rarely be tempted to substitute counseling for the expert help that is needed in mental illness. But to recognize a psychosis in the early stages is not always easy; and an acute schizophrenic episode is sometimes mistaken for an acute anxiety attack even by experts. Usually, the psychotic is recognized by his thought disturbance (in schizophrenia), his flight of ideas (in a manic episode) or his extreme apathy (in psychotic depression). Long before he can be committed to a mental hospital, he will have become a problem to his family who may be superstitiously afraid of his "insanity." But it is important to remember for all who come in contact with a psychotic that this is a human being fighting against an enemy which has taken possession of what is almost the last stronghold of the person—his mind. With the sole exception of gross brain damage, there is always hope that with expert help this enemy can be contained, if not defeated.

RELIGION AND PSYCHOSIS

It is difficult to assess the role of religion in psychosis, for while on the one hand, religious images are woven into the system of delusions and hallucinations, on the other, the psychosis may produce thoughts and convictions about the meaning of life that would never have occurred to the patient before. Boisen and Mowrer both believe that psychosis (by which Boisen primarily means schizophrenia and Mowrer psychotic depression) is often the means of conversion.[11] Be that as it may, the core of the person,

[11] Boisen, A., and Mowrer, O.

the remnant of normality that still exists in every psychosis (the "observer," as some have called it) can only be strengthened by firm faith in a God who loves all men, even those who no longer love themselves.

BIBLIOGRAPHY

Arnold, M., *Emotion and Personality*, 2 vols. New York, 1960.

Arnold M.,—Gasson, J., S.J. eds., *The Human Person*, New York, 1954.

Boisen, A., *Exploration of the Inner World*, Chicago, 1936.

Deutsch, A.,—Fishman, H. eds., *The Encyclopedia of Mental Health*, 6 vols. New York, 1963.

Freud, S., *The Basic Writings of Sigmund Freud*, Tr. A. Brill, New York, 1938.

Frohman, G., *et al.*, "Evidence of a Plasma Factor in Schizophrenia," *Arch. Gen. Psychiat.*, 1960, 2, 255.

Heath, R. *et al.*, "Developments toward New Physiological Treatments in Psychiatry," *J. Neuropsychiat.*, Aug. 1964.

Jung, C., *Modern Man in Search of a Soul*, New York, 1936.

Krauch, E., *A Mind Restored*, New York, 1937.

Landis, C.,—Bolles, M., *Textbook of Abnormal Psychology*, rev. ed. New York, 1950.

Maslow, A., *Religious Values and Peak-Experience*, Columbus, Ohio, 1964.

Mowrer, O., *The Crisis in Psychiatry and Religion*, Princeton, N.J., 1961.

Prince, M., *The Dissociation of a Personality*, 2d ed. New York, 1913.

Reiser, D. E.,—Brown, J. L., "Patterns of Later Development in Children with Infantile Psychosis," *J. Amer. Acad. Child Psychiat.*, Aug. 1964.

Rogers, C., *Client-Centered Therapy*, Boston, Mass., 1951.

Vassiliou, V., *Motivational Patterns of Two Clinical Groups as Revealed by TAT Sequence Analysis*. Unpubl. Doctoral Dissertation, Loyola University, Chicago, 1962.

3

PSYCHOLOGICAL ALIENATION AND THE PROCESS OF COUNSELING

Alexander A. Schneiders, Ph.D.

Introduction

PSYCHOLOGISTS and psychiatrists have long been aware of what we are referring to here as the psychology of alienation—that peculiar and sometimes tragic process of estrangement of person from person, or of person from reality. But it was not until Harry Stack Sullivan's theories of interpersonal relationships forced their way into psychological theorizing and therapeutic practice that professional counselors and psychotherapists became more keenly aware of the impact and the significance of alienation.[20]* It would be difficult to think of an area of human behavior or of human relationships more important than this one, especially from the standpoint of a meaningful and useful diagnosis of aberrant and distorted human responses. Countless persons today live in an almost complete psychological isolation even when surrounded by loved ones, friends, relatives, classmates, colleagues, or co-workers. Because of dynamic factors that have become an integral part of their personalities and whatever relationships they are able to maintain (factors that we shall study later on) these victims of the process of alienation find themselves unable to reach out to others in any effective manner, to accept and to love other persons, to be

---

* Numbers refer to items in the list of References and Bibliography following this chapter.

accepted by others, or to generate those feelings and relationships that would make their island of life become a part of the mainland, where other persons are busily engaged in events and activities that constitute the mainstream of life. They are in a sense like mummies, so wrapped up in their feelings of anxiety, or guilt, or self-hate that reaching out to others in a psychological sense has become impossible.[17]

This psychological block to behavior and interpersonal relationships suggests quite clearly why the phenomenon of alienation is closely relevant to the processes of counseling and of psychotherapy. It has been stated over and over again by persons from many different orientations and even different disciplines that one of the primary tasks of counseling is the reduction or removal of psychological hindrances to effective response and self-realization. Clearly, alienation is such a hindrance, and it is the business of the counselor to help reduce and eventually to eliminate feelings of anxiety, hostility, or guilt, when these feelings are of a depth or magnitude as to preclude the growth of healthy relationships with other persons. As we shall see, this is not an easy task for the counselor, because feelings—especially those that are negative and self-destructive—have a way of embedding themselves within the very marrow of the personality, and strongly resist every effort to dislodge them. This is true not only of feelings such as guilt and hostility, but others as well, including insecurity, jealousy, envy, inferiority, and obsessive phobias.

In counseling and in psychotherapy, therefore, it is of primary importance to understand the logic as well as the psychological development of self-destructive feelings, and especially those that generate alienation.[17] As we shall see more fully later, the logic of this aspect of psychic development can be more important to therapeutic attack than its psychological development. This point we shall study more closely when we examine the relationship between the psychology of alienation and the process of counseling.

THE PSYCHOLOGY OF ALIENATION

As we have already suggested, alienation is a characteristic of contemporary society that is so common as to be almost universal. Paradoxically, the more efficiently that man builds intricate systems of communication that circle the earth and reach far into outer space, the more isolated he becomes within his own existential being. In a way, systems of communication tend to foster isolation. Many persons are content to limit interpersonal relationships to some form of written communication. Others find it more comfortable and less threatening to maintain lines of communication via the telephone, especially now that long distance telephoning is so facile and inexpensive.

But the psychology of alienation is deeper and more complex than this simple interpretation would suggest. Man becomes alienated from himself and from others when value systems begin to disintegrate and supportive units like the family begin to fall apart. It should be noted at this point that the gradual emancipation of the adolescent from the family system, in his striving for independence, identity, and adult status, creates a typical form of alienation. It is obvious that the conflict between the adolescent and his family in matters of dating, friendships, use of the family car, money, late hours, etc., often causes the adolescent to become estranged from the family and particularly from the parents, this estrangement resulting in considerable anxiety, conflict, guilt, and hostility. Thus a great many of the problems encountered by the adolescent in his movement toward maturity fit into the framework of the alienation syndrome.

In addition to the erosion of value systems and the breakdown of social institutions there are also the isolation and the alienation that are almost inevitable by-products of the brittle and unreal urban life which has replaced friendly and accepting neighborhoods with towering and ugly apartment buildings, in which families are stacked on top of families, and among whom there is little or no communication. It is difficult to trade experiences, confidences, and gossip over a back fence when there is no back fence to begin with. Many urbanites live in an encapsulated arena of three or four rooms that are heavily barricaded against neighborly intrusion by fear, suspicion, or mistrust of people in general, and of "neighbors" in particular. Much of this is traceable to the lack of cohesiveness in contemporary family living, in which the idea is supported if not fostered that as soon as the wedding bells start ringing it is time for the children to desert the family nest and to begin living an isolated life of their own. These conditions are of course sociological, but they provide a strong background for the emergence and development of those personal feelings that underlie the psychology of alienation.

In this connection it is interesting to note that distance or separation often removes psychic barriers to the extent that the person functions more effectively. This is particularly noteworthy in the case of stutterers who often divest themselves of their handicap when talking with someone on the telephone. We may note also that in contemporary society, as compared with an earlier era, travel and mobility are much more common phenomena, and the more that persons engage in these activities the more they reduce the possibilities of effective communication. Mobility especially tends to destroy those deep roots that foster pervasive interpersonal relationships. We see the same thing in the habit of spending hours staring at the television screen, because here again communication is reduced to a minimum, and one person is isolated from another within the confines of the same room.

It should also be observed that at times the closer people are *to* one another the more difficult it is for them to relate *with* one another. Many persons have little or no contact with their next door neighbor, whereas persons living on farms, separated by great distances, manage to establish much closer relationships than city dwellers by using the Saturday shopping trip to town as a means of reaffirming close bonds and enjoying one another's company to the utmost at the hoedown or the Saturday evening barn dance. For all its proximity, city dwelling seems somehow to isolate people from one another and to set up barriers to communication. This isolation provides the groundwork for alienation.

The process of alienation, as already noted, can assume many forms, but in this essay we wish to study only four principal types: guilt, shame, hostility, and anxiety. These forms of alienation are perhaps the most commonly encountered in counseling and in psychotherapy, and are certainly in the front ranks of those processes that interfere with personality development, or that cause serious damage to the personality once they are set in motion. For these reasons they offer the most serious challenge to the counselor intent upon helping his client overcome the obstacles that stand in the way of self-fulfillment. Significantly, no one of these dynamic feelings can be tolerated for any serious length of time without erosion of the personality.

An important characteristic of these four reactions is the common quality of alienation. Guilt, for example, is an alienation from significant existence, or to personalize the characterization, *an alienation from God*. Shame, which often has the same origins as guilt, is nevertheless a different kind of process—*an alienation from self*. Guilt, therefore, stems from the realization, conscious or unconscious, that one has become estranged from a truly *worthwhile existence*, or from some significant person, whether a parent or God, whose acceptance and love are necessary to personal worth. Shame, on the other hand, is a process which involves estrangement from an *ideal* that is loved and needed because it is a reflection of what one ought to be. Guilt is a constant, nagging reminder of what parents or God wants one to be; shame is a nagging reminder of what a person wants himself to be. The dynamics of these two processes will be examined more closely later on; but it is clear at this point that the two processes are most closely allied in their development and in their effects on the personality.[16, 24]

In much the same way that guilt and shame involve alienation, so do the processes of anxiety and hostility. Anxiety is widely recognized as one of the most important determiners of psychological problems, and is regarded by many as the core of mental disorganization. The experience of anxiety can be interpreted in several different ways—first, as a relatively mild, normal fear reaction to a stressful situation that suggests difficulty or failure. For example, a student manifests anxiety when confronted with a final examination. In the more acute state, anxiety takes the form of a strong and pervasive fear reaction that tends to interfere with or to paralyze effective functioning. This is typical of the anxiety neurosis. It may be object-bound or free-floating, but in either case it has a severely limiting effect on personality.[5, 7, 9, 21]

In the present connection, as a form of alienation, the experience of anxiety may best be thought of in relation to reality—the everyday reality of experiences, events, problems, demands, and relationships to which every human being must respond and work out whatever compromises are necessary. The feeling of anxiety—as a pervasive, dominating force embedded within the psychic apparatus—can thus be interpreted as an *alienation from reality*. This concept means that pathogenic anxiety sets up a barrier between the personal psyche and objective reality that cannot be explained in terms of experience or development. This peculiar circumstance is best exemplified in free-floating anxiety because in this instance there is an alienation from reality that cannot be explained in the usual manner by threat, danger, or other suitable cause. In anxiety of this type the person is literally *estranged from reality*—a reality that he does not understand, cannot cope with, and from which he feels almost completely alienated.

The fourth principal form of alienation is expressed in the process of hostility, which may be defined quite simply as *alienation from other persons*. Where anxiety is a derivative of fear, hostility has its source in anger, and anger is a first step in the process of undermining human relationships. Whereas anxiety, like fear, is more passive in character and fulfills its purpose by a pulling away from reality, hostility, like anger, is a thrust *against* reality situations. Yet it is this very thrust that creates the condition of alienation from others, because hostility is an excellent means for setting up barriers between the hostile person and those other persons who are motivated by acceptance, love, or charity.[17] We see, then, that all four of these critical processes—guilt, shame, anxiety, and hostility—lead inevitably to some kind of alienation from self or from reality that makes it impossible for their victims to function effectively in the work-a-day world. It is this fact that must be taken into careful account in any counseling or therapeutic approach to the problem of alienation.[12, 14, 15]

INTERRELATIONS OF ALIENATION SYSTEMS

We have already noted certain similarities and identities among these different processes of alienation, but for purposes of adequate diagnosis and treatment it is necessary to draw out still further other relationships that bind one or more of these processes to the other. Let us examine first of all the interpenetration of guilt and shame, two reactions so closely similar that they are often confused with one another. However, as we saw, guilt involves a different kind of alienation than does shame, because the latter process has a distinct reference to the personal self. In addition, we may now note that the etiology of guilt and shame is different in some respects; nor are they expressed in the same symptoms or behavior.[11, 16, 17, 18]

First of all, it must be observed that we are not referring here to *objective* guilt, since this type, derived from ethical values rather than psychic developments, is little more than the intellectual conviction of code violation. This form of guilt may cause some psychic anguish until it is expiated by contrition or confession, but ordinarily it causes little psychic difficulty unless it evokes and becomes bound up with neurotic guilt. Within this framework it then functions in the same way as neurotic guilt. The following case will illustrate these several points.

Mary Jo was a senior in a Catholic high school when she was referred for counseling. She was one of several children from a devout Irish, Catholic family, and was deeply committed to her religious convictions. She attended the sacraments regularly, but complained of considerable difficulty with confession. This was especially the case with so-called "sins of impurity." At the time of the initial interview, she was obviously upset, extremely nervous, and frequently burst into tears in trying to explain her problem. For some months prior to the interview she had been dating a boy from the same high school and had become involved in minor behavior infractions that bordered on intimacy. This involved nothing more than holding hands, occasional kissing, and close embraces. Mary Jo felt very guilty about this behavior to the point where she was on the verge of breaking off the relationship. The guilt which she experienced spread to other forms of behavior, and she found it increasingly difficult to distinguish one form of behavior from another. It soon became obvious that this client had been troubled all through her adolescence by a deep and pervasive scrupulosity, and that it assumed even greater pathological proportions with the development of a personal and quasi-intimate relationship. After six months of weekly interviews the scrupulosity was largely dissipated, and Mary Jo was better able to evaluate her own moral problems.

This case study illustrates several important facts about guilt. First of all, objective or normal guilt is very different from abnormal or pathological guilt, both in its dynamics and in its effect on personality and behavior. Pathological guilt, which is always determined by unconscious factors, expresses itself much more clearly in the syndrome of alienation, and tends strongly toward the development of the obsessive-compulsive neurosis. This is not true of objective guilt. It is equally clear from this analysis that subjective or abnormal guilt must be distinguished from shame. The feeling of shame results when a person *fails himself* rather than some objective norm or being (like God), or significant authority figure. That is why we defined shame as alienation from self. It is the sign of a person's failure to live up to his own self-imposed standards of behavior, and thus expresses itself in the typically self referent responses of blushing, downcast eyes, or bitter self-renunciation. Yet the two processes of guilt and shame have much in common, and the counselor cannot afford to lose sight of this important fact. Both involve a type of alienation, and both are objectively based upon personal failure. Both, too, are psychologically very painful. For these reasons the two experiences are invariably linked together.

The second important relationship within the syndrome of alienation is the interpenetration of guilt and anxiety. This is not true of shame, since shame is basically self-referent and does not involve alienation from reality. But there is some of this estrangement in the experience of guilt. When the feeling of guilt reaches fairly large proportions, especially if determined by unconscious factors, it will at the same time evoke anxiety, because guilt always stimulates fear of abandonment. The dynamics of this aspect of guilt will become clearer when we study the psychological origins of guilt later on. But even at a purely conscious level, where only objective guilt is involved, there is at least a nascent fear of abandonment, and it is this fear that generates real anxiety.

Thus the guilty person, whether objectively or subjectively guilty, will manifest signs of real fear; fear that his misguided or improper action will somehow overtake him, fear that he will be found out, fear that because of his wrongdoing he will be severely punished or ostracized, fear that he will be abandoned by those on whom he relies for understanding and support. This interpretation does not preclude the possibility that guilt also reflects the need for punishment as several writers have pointed out.[16, 17, 23, 24] This concept actually supports the preceding interpretation since punishment leads to expiation, and in this way both the guilt and the fear are gotten rid of.

The following statement of one patient will exemplify these ideas clearly.

"I don't know what's wrong with me, Doctor, but I feel so terribly afraid all the time. It is as though some awful fate is hanging over my head ready to destroy me at any moment. I can't figure it out. I have a good job, plenty of money, a devoted family, just about all the things that any person wants. And yet I have this awful feeling that fate or whatever you want to call it is going to strike a decisive blow at any moment."

"Have you any idea how this started?" the counselor asked. "Do you remember at all when it started?"

The patient hesitated for a moment, seemingly lost in his own memories. Then he replied, "It all seems to go back to a period six months ago when I made a trip out to the west coast. I was attending a convention and met this lady who was a buyer for a large eastern firm. We had a lot of fun together—all of us did, in fact—and when the evening was over I took her back to her hotel. She invited me to her room, and I felt that I should not go because I knew that it would displease my wife very much, but I went anyhow. We listened to music, danced a little, and had several drinks, and then I left. But almost immediately when I got back to my room I began to feel terribly guilty. I knew my wife would disapprove bitterly if she knew what I had done, and I could not shake the feeling of guilt. I tried to tell myself that I had done nothing wrong, but the guilt stuck like a burr inside my mind. And the more guilty I felt, the more afraid I became, and the anxiety seemed to increase the guilt. I am half out of my mind with this endless go-around of guilt and fear. I keep telling myself that I have nothing to be guilty about or to be afraid of, but no amount of reasoning seems to do any good."

This case is of particular interest to the study of guilt and anxiety because it exemplifies so clearly the development of guilt even when there is nothing to be objectively guilty about. Subsequent analysis revealed an unconscious desire in the patient to have an affair, but the idea was so revolting and frightful to him that he had completely repressed it. Nevertheless, it was real enough to generate considerable guilt, and it was this unconscious guilt concerning desire that caused his rather innocent foray to assume a guilty cast. Once the guilt process was set in motion at both the unconscious and the conscious levels, anxiety was inevitable. When the patient was able to confront his desire for an illicit affair, and to realize at the same time that he had the strength to resist the temptation, the guilt and the anxiety disappeared.

The reader can see from these analyses that anxiety is one of the leading determinants of alienation. Some element of it is always found in any situation involving alienation. Hence there is also a marked relationship between anxiety and hostility. Earlier we characterized hostility as an alienation from other persons, which serves the purpose of protecting the victim of hostility from contacts and experiences which he fears would be harmful or damaging in some way. This is not the whole story of hostility because there are several forms which it may assume; but when we study both the etiology and the logic of hostility, as revealed in case histories, we soon find that in the majority of cases hostility is used as a defensive measure to ward off relationships that could lead to disappointment, heartache, or rejection. By this defensive use of hostility the patient thus alienates himself from other persons and avoids the risk of unhappy or damaging personal relationships.[14, 15, 17]

An example comes to mind of a young man, sixteen years of age and a sophomore in a parochial high school, who literally seethed with hostility toward his parents, his teachers, his counselor, and any other person in authority who in any way endangered or threatened his freedom to act in whatever way he pleased. This boy had been severely rejected and somewhat brutally chastized by his father who was deeply disappointed by his son's academic interests and his lack of activities in sports. By this rejection, the father effectively alienated the boy who in turn generated a strong feeling of hostility for any authority figure or other person who might treat him in the same way as had his father. This boy trusted no one because of his alienation from the father, and he was able to resist all intrusions into the inner sanctum of his mistrust by the simple expedient of using hostility to limit personal relationships. Thus he very effectively matched the alienation imposed by his father with an alienation of his own from all other persons, and this is the essential meaning of the hostility pattern.

This kind of total alienation quickly tends toward the development of anxiety, because of the natural fear of isolation that all persons experience. Hostility, as we have just seen, is an effective isolator, and isolation generates anxiety because of the fearful condition of being alone and having no one with whom to share one's anguish. Thus, as we saw in the case of guilt and anxiety, hostility also becomes associated with anxiety and for much the same basic reason. Both of them are grounded in alienation, and thus one is quite likely to lead to the other.

Let us now consider the relation between anxiety and shame in terms of the theory of alienation. We had said that shame is essentially alienated from self, and that anxiety is alienation from reality. In terms of these definitions, it is not too difficult to see why the one process should be related to the other. The self is also a part of reality, and therefore when there is estrangement from self because of some personal failure there is bound to be some measure of anxiety. Failure itself is always to some extent anxiety-producing, because it signifies personal inability to cope effectively with reality demands. There is, for example, the simple case of the sophomore in college who failed to complete a necessary assignment. Her reaction to this failure illustrates clearly the congruence of anxiety and shame.[7, 9, 11]

"I don't know what's the matter with me, Professor, but I just can't seem to get going this semester. I've never had this experience before. I feel so awful. I'm so ashamed of my failure to hand in the assignment I could just die. I wish I knew what was wrong. I'm just not myself, and it frightens me. Maybe I ought to see a psychiatrist or something."

In this little story, so typical of numerous college students, the process of alienation from self and from reality is strikingly exemplified. To fail one's self is disturbing to many persons, and is at the same time a serious reflection on their ability and perhaps their integrity. Thus do shame and anxiety fuse together into an over-riding process of alienation.

Here we have four of the clearest instances of the interrelationships that exist among different processes of alienation. Other relationships, perhaps of lesser significance, could also be described. Certainly there is a close connection between hostility and guilt as well as between hostility and shame. These different relationships point up the important fact that the process of alienation is itself an *organized syndrome* which expresses itself in different forms of emotional experience, to which we attach terms like guilt and anxiety. The emotional processes in turn are revealed in various symptoms and symptomatic behavior, and eventually in distinctive personality characteristics if and when alienation becomes a chronic, pathological process.

Sources of Alienation

The various forms of alienation discussed earlier in this chapter, as well as their interrelationships, cannot be fully understood until we probe deeply into their various sources within the personality, and within the environmental-cultural complex in which the personality develops.[5, 6, 9, 17] At the very onset we can be certain that there is little in the innate physical or emotional dispositions of the human personality that would initiate the process of alienation, which is not true of other pathogenic processes like inferiority or inadequacy, which often have their genetic beginnings in physical weakness, structural deformity, or inadequate emotional disposition. However, we often find in the personal history of patients with the alienation syndrome a group or a series of traumatic experiences that serve to estrange the young child from other persons, from reality, or from significant figures. Even where physical factors are concerned, it is conceivable that gross physical deformity or ugliness could cause self-alienation, especially if physical characteristics evoke disgust or repulsion in other persons in the child's environment. In any event, it would not be wise from a counseling or therapeutic viewpoint to ignore the possibility that there are significant factors in the personal history of the patient that could set the stage for alienation.[17, 18]

More to the point in ferreting out the etiology of the alienation syndrome is a study of the network of *interpersonal relations* that characterized the early history of the patient who shows signs of alienation. This is particularly true where parent-child relationships are concerned. For example, it is often observed in clinical practice that the history of the patient suffering from pathological guilt or scrupulosity is surfeited with instances of parental neglect, rejection, or discriminative favoritism. Children with this type of background are quite likely to develop excessive and self-destructive guilt on the premise that rejection by the parents must signify that they are evil or worthless. Once this logic is established, they soon develop deep, unconscious, and pathological guilt which rises into consciousness in the form of compulsivity, ritualism, and scrupulosity. In such cases it is easy to see how the groundwork for alienation is securely laid.

A similar development often occurs in the relationship between the child and siblings, members of his peer group, or fellow students. Just recently a case of this kind was brought to the writer's attention with the referral of a fourteen-year-old girl, then a freshman in a private girls' high school. This young lady was already suffering from self-alienation because of differential treatment by her parents, a condition that was severely aggravated by the rejecting attitude of her classmates. Because of the rejection by her parents, and the nagging criticism of her three sisters, Kathy had developed an extremely sullen manner which she quickly projected to other persons in her environment. This sullenness was intolerable to her classmates who soon excluded her from their company. This exclusion served to nurture Kathy's hostility, and the alienation from other persons became complete. As a result, Kathy learned to despise the school, began to do poorly in her subjects, and was making every unconscious effort to get herself transferred to another school. This is a typical instance of the process of isolation which has its beginning in hostility and alienation from others.

The process of alienation can also be traced to the social matrix within which the child develops. This concept, of course, includes the family, but it extends beyond the family to the wider social order. We can see this process exemplified in the aggressive and rejecting behavior of delinquent youth. In its deepest roots delinquency is of course an estrangement from society. It is the boy's or girl's way of expressing resentment against the existing order of things and the world created by adults, and at the same time it is the means by which youth can alienate itself from a society which it has learned thoroughly to mistrust.

The most striking aspect of delinquent behavior is its quality of rebellion

—rebellion against rules and regulations, mores and morals, laws, restrictions, and authority as well as authority figures. Rebellion is, naturally, a form of hostility; and as we have noted several times, hostility is an effective means of achieving or maintaining alienation, especially alienation from other persons. This rebellion against the social order is as much a defense reaction as it is a means of rejection and alienation; and this defensiveness indicates again the relationship between hostility and anxiety. By developing hostility and rebellion, the delinquent protects himself from the attachments, dependencies, acceptance, and other social relationships which he despises and fears at the same time. However, this reaction also isolates him from his fellowman, from his family, and from society, and hence leaves him without the support that everyone else derives from the social order. It is this state of affairs that creates basic anxiety.[19]

Alienation has its source also in *outmoded patterns of thinking,* as we see clearly today in the reactionary responses of many persons to ecumenism, ritualistic changes, and alterations in moral, racial, or religious attitudes. The so-called "sexual revolution" is a case in point. The old standards of sexual morality, derived from the anxieties of Puritanical and Jansenistic phobias more than from canons of morality and ethics, have been eroding at a rapid rate in many parts of the world during the past quarter century. And this erosion has alienated a large group of stand-patters who insist on believing that sexual morality is immutable and cannot tolerate change of any kind. The same situation obtains with respect to birth control, premarital sexual freedom, and abortion. For many persons the *status quo* and the familiar are much more tolerable than change, disruption of existing patterns, or innovative thinking. This group is alienated from the mainstream of contemporary events by their crippling unrealism, and thus their characteristic reaction of anxiety can be typified as an estrangement from reality.

A similar development can be observed in the current trends that are swirling around traditional religious concepts, dogmas, and practices. On the one hand we witness extensive changes in the liturgy, and on the other broad inroads into the domain of ecumenism. On the one side we see the somewhat startling example of priests getting married in large numbers, and on the other the secularizing of a Catholic institution of higher learning. The religious atmosphere is permeated with concepts of religious freedom, freedom of conscience, situation ethics, meat on Friday, folk Masses, and numerous other innovations that strike fear if not terror in the hearts of many believers for whom tradition rather than modernism is the sacred cow of religion. All such persons experience the process of alienation from reality which expresses itself, as always, in general anxiety.

When innovative thinking and ritualistic change touch them personally, they also experience the alienation of hostility—hostility toward a Church and a hierarchy that do not have the common sense or the thoughtfulness to "leave well enough alone."

On the other side of the picture are those religionists who are more than ready to jump the gun and abandon the age-old concepts of licit birth control, the sanctity of the family, or the evils of abortion and divorce. They are the freedom riders in the various religious camps, who want to create history rather than learn from it. In this process they too experience the alienation of anxiety because of their sudden and harsh desertion of beliefs and practices that they had accepted for a good part of their lives. Here again we see the molding of anxiety and hostility, because in their searing break-away from ancient mores and traditions they can most effectively rationalize their behavior by becoming angry at, and therefore hostile toward, those persons and institutions that support the older view of things. There is a strong likelihood, too, that shame enters into their experience, so that the process of alienation becomes even more complete.

A similar situation exists with respect to outmoded thinking on various social and political issues, as we see exemplified in both the New England and the Southern states. Steeped in its own rigid conservatism, the politics of New England and its staunch adherents are almost completely alienated from the political realism of other sections of the country. And in the Southern states there is an almost pathological estrangement from the realities of both history and politics, particularly in their attitude toward racial equality and toward the sanctity of Southern life. In both instances lack of realism has generated a great deal of anxiety as well as a corresponding hostility that is used as a defense against the encroachment of new ideas that threaten their outmoded and often distorted way of life. It is the Southerner's anxiety about the equality of the Negro which generates his massive and sometimes pathological hostility; and here again we see how the processes of alienation function to reinforce one another.

One other example of current thinking that has supported the processes of alienation in our society involves such time-honored concepts as the home, parental discipline, and parent-child relationships. No one would seriously question the fact that a great deal of alienation has grown out of the changing concepts of the home and the family in America during the past fifty years. With 400,000 divorces hammering away each year at the bastions of the American home, and with untold numbers of separations and destructive family conflicts, anxiety and hostility must certainly characterize the personal lives of many Americans, thus causing considerable alienation between parents on the one hand, and between parents and children on the other. These estrangements will in turn generate guilt and shame, so that all forms of alienation can be involved in the breakdown of the family.

In addition, changing concepts of authority, of discipline, of the respective roles of the parents, of independence and freedom, and of various other aspects of family life tend to encourage the development of alienation. Quite often the parents are estranged from each other, and the children from the parents. In some families anxiety, guilt, and hostility are constant companions that set one member of the family against another and that provide an unusually rich breeding ground for maladjustment and neurotic disorder. These relationships and outcomes the counselor must keep in mind if he wishes to understand the origins and the dynamics of the alienation syndrome.

Alienation and the Process of Counseling

From everything that has been said so far it is obvious that the alienation syndrome has many implications for the counseling process. Without a knowledge of how this syndrome develops, and how its different aspects are related to each other, the counselor is at a loss in trying to understand the problem with which he is confronted. From the outset we must understand that alienation is a social-cultural phenomenon as well as an individual reaction to self, other persons, and reality. To counsel a person with this type of syndrome it is essential that we understand thoroughly his background, developmental history, interpersonal relationships, and significant experiences. This approach is of course the beginning of a precise and careful diagnosis which must take into account every significant aspect of psychological development. Particularly important is a sensitive probing of unconscious content, including repressed traumatic experiences, attitudes toward self, pathological feelings and frustrated impulses.

It is at this point that projective devices, such as the Rorschach and the TAT, and classical dream analysis are important tools for diagnosis. It is only when these unconscious factors are brought into the spotlight of self-awareness and direct confrontation by the patient himself that progress is likely to be made. In addition, of course, there is the classical method of dream analysis so brilliantly developed by Freud.[4] When Freud said that the dream is the royal road to the unconscious he gave us a principle of diagnosis that is of great practical import for counseling and psychotherapy. Thirdly, depth diagnosis can be accomplished by a careful, precise interview approach whereby unconscious material can be brought into the arena of consciousness. This is a difficult skill to develop, but once it is mastered, it can be very helpful. It involves several steps: (1) a clear definition of the patient's problem; (2) an evaluation and interpretation of symptom complexes related to the problem; (3) the formulation of several hypotheses as to the background, etiology, and dynamics of both symptoms and problems; (4) the careful testing of each hypothesis against material produced by psychodiagnostic evaluation and interviewing; and (5) validation of the hypothesis through continuing diagnostic interviewing.[19]

Perhaps it would be helpful to clarify this process by means of an example. A young woman, 30 years of age and unmarried, complained of extreme unhappiness, compulsive hand-washing, strong dislike of her parents, religious conflicts, social isolation, and intensive scrupulosity revolving around sexual matters. She was an attractive young woman who lived alone in a small apartment in New York City, and whose social life was almost entirely limited to occasional office parties, which she found uninteresting and unenjoyable. With this symptom complex, it was not at all difficult to formulate several useful hypotheses. The hand-washing, the scrupulous sex attitudes, and the religious conflicts certainly suggest massive, unconscious guilt and self-rejection. The attitude toward the parents indicates further that the guilt was in some way related to parent-child relationships, particularly in early life, and this is exactly what a continuing diagnosis revealed. The mother's attitude toward child rearing was extremely rigid, rejecting, punitive, and surfeited with threats of sinfulness and damnation. This attitude, and the child's reaction to it, clearly explained the religious conflict and the development of pathological scrupulosity, at the core of which is extreme guilt. This unconscious guilt, as we noted previously, is always reflective of excessive moral demands and of parental rejection, the two combining to produce a deep, unconscious sense of wrongdoing or evil, and therefore of guiltiness. The testing of these hypotheses was a relatively simple matter, and when the young lady was able to confront this damaging background and discover the reason for her hatred of her parents, her personality began to improve noticeably.[17,18,24]

Therapeutic counseling, of the kind that we are describing here, involves other psychological processes that are necessary to recovery or to problemsolving. First of all are the twin processes of *abreaction* and *desensitization*, which involves bringing into the focal point of consciousness what is historically unconscious. This process is part of the classical analytic technique. This insight can in turn be utilized to accomplish another aim of treatment, namely, the *dethroning of feeling*, which is one of the most essential steps in recovery from psychological damage.[17] Until a person is able to rid himself of destructive guilt and shame, anxiety and hostility, he cannot free himself from the alienation and the social isolation which these feelings inevitably breed. This is perhaps the most critical and difficult task of therapeutic counseling, because feelings become developmentally embedded in the psychic structure to an extent that only the most intensive psychological surgery is effective in dislodging them. This statement is especially true of feelings that have their start in early childhood and manage to secure a stranglehold on the patient's psychic makeup. When, in addition, they serve a defensive purpose, they are even more resistant to treatment.[17]

Another important therapeutic step is in helping the patient gradually to achieve *a personal-historical perspective* relative to his own psychological development. He must learn to see himself as he is at the present moment (*confrontation*), but he must also learn to view himself in historical perspective so that he can understand the origins of his own personality. This is a broader view of the older concept of insight which is generally regarded as an important tool for the therapist. As abreaction and desensitization increase, and confrontation becomes increasingly less painful, and as feeling is more effectively dethroned and the patient develops an insightful perspective on himself, then another important step becomes possible—the *growth of self-control*. Every neurotic and maladjusted person is characterized by poor control; and it is not until he regains possession of himself—his feelings, ideas, attitudes, behavior, and interpersonal relationships—that he starts back on the road to mental health.

Finally, and this is the most important step of all for the treatment of alienation, the therapeutic process should be directed ceaselessly toward the conversion of alienation into self-acceptance, the acceptance of other persons, the capacity to love, acceptance of reality, an awareness of being and of becoming, and an acceptance of God or other transcendent being. This is the whole purpose of psychological counseling in relationship to the process of alienation. Alienation must be therapeutically undermined, and until it is, it will remain as the patient's only defense against a dangerous and threatening reality.

References and Bibliography

1. Alexander, F. *Fundamentals of Psychoanalysis.* New York: Norton, 1948.
2. Burton, A. and Harris, R. *Case Histories in Clinical and Abnormal Psychology.* New York: Harper, 1947.
3. Buss, A. *The Psychology of Aggression.* New York: Wiley, 1961.
4. Freud, S. *A General Introduction to Psychoanalysis* (Trans. by Joan Riviere). New York: Liveright, 1935.
5. Garre, W. *Basic Anxiety.* New York: Philosophical Library, 1962.
6. Goldstein, M. and Palmer, J. *The Experience of Anxiety: A Case Book.* New York: Oxford, 1963.

7. Hoch, P. H. and Zubin, J. (eds.) *Anxiety*. New York: Grune & Stratton, 1950.
8. Houselander, C. *Guilt*. New York: Sheed & Ward, 1951.
9. May, R. *The Meaning of Anxiety*. New York: Ronald, 1950.
10. Nuttin, J. *Psychoanalysis and Personality* (Trans. by George Lamb). New York: Sheed & Ward, 1953.
11. Piers, G. and Singer, M. *Shame and Guilt: A Psychoanalytic and a Cultural Study*. Springfield, Illinois: Thomas, 1953.
12. Redl, F. & Wineman, D. *The Aggressive Child*. New York: Free Press, 1957.
13. Reik, T. *Myth and Guilt: The Crime and Punishment of Mankind*. New York: Braziller, 1957.
14. Saul, L. "Inferiority Feelings and Hostility." *Amer. J. Psychiat.*, 1951, *108*, 120–122.
15. Saul, L. *The Hostile Mind*. New York: Random House, 1956.
16. Schneiders, A. Clinical Manifestations of Guilt. In Bier, W. C. & McCall, R. J. (Eds.) *Three joint symposia from the ACPA-APA meetings of 1957, 1958, 1959*. New York: Fordham University, 1960, 7–18.
17. Schneiders, A. *The Anarchy of Feeling*. New York: Sheed & Ward, 1963.
18. Schneiders, A. *Personality Dynamics and Mental Health*. New York: Holt, Rinehart & Winston, 1965.
19. Schneiders, A. *Counseling the Adolescent*. San Francisco: Chandler, 1967.
20. Sullivan, H. *The Interpersonal Theory of Psychiatry*. New York: Norton, 1953.
21. Winter, J. *The Origins of Illness and Anxiety*. New York: Julian, 1962.
22. Worchel, T. Hostility: Theory and Experimental Investigation. In D. Willner, (ed.), *Decisions, Values, and Groups*. New York: Pergamon, 1960, I, pp. 254–266.
23. Zilboorg, G. *The Psychology of the Criminal Act and Punishment*. New York: Harcourt Brace, 1954.
24. Zilboorg, G. A Sense of Guilt. In A. Schneiders (Ed.) *Proceedings of the Institute for the Clergy on Problems in Pastoral Psychology*. New York: Fordham University, 1956.

4

THE MORAL AND PSYCHOLOGICAL
ASPECTS OF SCRUPULOSITY

REV. GEORGE KANOTI, C.R.

THE IMPACT of psychology upon counseling procedures and theory has left much of the traditional pre-psychology pastoral counseling a vast wasteland strewn with outdated opinions and archaic techniques. Nonetheless, despite the great aid and insight given to the pastoral counselor by psychology, he has found one concrete problem very resistant to the therapeutic techniques offered by psychology: scrupulosity. It is almost as if scrupulosity has a built-in immunity to therapeutic tools. This frustration is understandable when one considers that cases of obsessive-compulsive personalities (the clinical term for scrupulous persons [1]) are usually so resistant to ordinary therapy that they are referred to "experts" in the treatment of obsessions. The pastoral counselor can at least find some solace in the fact that even professionally trained therapists find this problem very difficult.[2]

This paper makes no pretense at solving the problem of therapy, but hopes to update the reader on some of the relevant therapeutic thinking on the question of the scrupulous personality. The paper will follow this plan: the problem will be defined, the current etiological insights indicated, the broad diagnostic norms will be presented, and pastorally relevant thera-

[1] A. Lauras, *The Treatment of Scruples*, tr. M. Carrol, 8–9.
[2] D. MacCalman, *Modern Practice in Psychiatric Medicine*, ed. J. Rees, 210.

peutic procedures will be reviewed. Finally, some traditional approaches to the problem will be reinforced, others rejected.

THE PROBLEM

Every pastoral counselor with even a modicum of experience knows the problem. The penitent who devours a quarter of an hour of the confessor's time on Christmas eve with a recitation of sins, supposed sins, doubts, circumstances, etc. and the distraught anxious person who cannot be solaced in any way are examples of the scrupulous person. The trying experiences that scrupulous persons give their counselors have earned them the sobriquet "the confessor's bane." [3]

Probably the most apt description of the obsessive personality was offered by Wilhelm Reich when he called them "living machines." [4] The description is apt because it captures both the subjective experience of the obsessive person [5] and the counselor's reaction to the person. The scrupulant recites sins, doubts, circumstances, minutiae of every type *because he must.* His admission of faults, sins, doubts, etc. reminds the counselor of a computer spewing out data on neatly punched cards which are printed "do not fold, spindle, or mutilate in any way." But the scrupulant lacks the cold precision of the computer. Paradoxically, he exhibits an agitated precision. Furthermore, the counselor's words, exhortations, admonitions, admonishments, etc., seem to be sloughed off and rendered as ineffectual as if the counselor were attempting to merely vocally program a computer. The counselor's judgments concerning the scrupulant's activity are turned aside by him almost as if his "data" of life should not be "folded, spindled, or mutilated in any way" by the counselor.

The religious modality of the scrupulous person is characterized by a "persistent and unreasonable fear that he has sinned or is about to sin at every turn." [6] His approach to religion and morality is colored by anxious, obsessive, neurotic sensitiveness to problems of conscience which tends to falsify guilt and, at times, reflects a deeper fear of accepting culpability for his actions.[7] But there is no need to describe the problem any further. The definitions or descriptions of scrupulosity remain basically the same today

[3] P. Larere, "Conduite pastorale en face des scrupuleux," *Cahiers Laennec* 20 (1960) 67.

[4] W. Reich, *Character Analysis,* 199.

[5] The terms "obsessive" and "scrupulous" will be used synonymously throughout this paper. "Scrupulosity" merely describes the religious tone of obsessive behavior. Furthermore, since there is little distinction between an obsessive and a compulsive behavior pattern, the term "obsessive" alone will be employed. c.f. D. MacCalman, *op. cit.,* 211; D. Hendersen and R. Gillespie, *A Textbook for Psychiatry,* 471.

[6] G. Hagmaier and R. Gleason, *Counseling The Catholic,* 146.

[7] H. Gratton, "The Cause of Scrupulosity," *TD* 10 (1962) 52.

as they were in the time of Alphonse Liguori.[8] The phenomenon has been faithfully reported. The unanswered questions concern the causes, the nature, and the therapeutic approaches to scrupulosity.

SOURCES

A review of the theoretical explanations for obsessive behavior is necessary because of an unwritten assumption found in all therapy: the practical techniques used bear some relationship to the causes of the abnormal behavior.[9] The dissatisfaction generally experienced by the counselor indicates that the techniques employed in obsessive cases are ineffectual and thus there is suspicion that the theoretical explanations for the sources of obsessive behavior (from which the techniques have evolved) are inadequate. This inadequacy is readily admitted today.[10] Nonetheless, the dissatisfaction has produced *more research* and will continue to challenge more and more research into the problem.[11]

The theoretical explanations for the sources of obsessive behavior range far and wide. On one side of the spectrum are the rather naive and oversimplified "diabolical intervention" theories.[12] On the other side are the rather complex, sophisticated and often obtuse psychoanalytical theories which place the origin of obsessive states in the ambivalent feelings of love and hate produced by repressed hostile feelings.[13] None of these theories have provided the total answer to the question. In fact, both extremes have wielded a suffocating influence on advancement in this area by the weight of their authority (both that of spiritual authors and the psychoanalytic founder).[14]

Fortunately, psychologists have been able to resist arguments from authority in their study of abnormalities. More recent thinking on the question of abnormal behavior tends to emphasize the existential person—the concrete person here and now and his particular "style" of behavior.[15]

[8] See: Alphonse Liguori, *Tractatus de Conscientia*, 1. 10 ed., 1793, n. 10–19; Brocard de Saint-Nicolas, *De Conscientia*, ques. II, art. 5 1730; J. Rossell, *Tractatus sive praxis deponendi conscientiam in dubiis et scrupulis circa casus morales occurentibus*, 2 ed., 1661; A. Tanquerey, *The Spiritual Life*, 2 ed., tr. H. Branderis, S. S., Tournai, 1930.

[9] L. Salzman, "Therapy of Obsessional States," A. J. of Psychi., 122 (1966) 1139.

[10] N. Mailloux, "The Problem of Scrupulosity in Pastoral Work," *Proc. of the Institute for the Clergy on Problems of Pastoral Psychology*, 1956, 61–62.

[11] *Ibid.*

[12] A. Tanquerey, *The Spiritual Life*, 444.

[13] S. Freud, "Notes Upon a Case of Obsessional Neurosis," in *Collected Papers* 3, 293–383.

[14] cf. A. Tanquerey, *op. cit.*, 443; L. Salzman, *op. cit.*, 1139.

[15] "By 'style' I mean a form or mode of functioning—the way or manner of a given area of behavior—that is identifiable in an individual through a range of his specific acts." D. Shapiro, *Neurotic Styles*, 1.

Today there is less delving into the person's history, less seeking of the cause of his poor "superego integration." [16] More emphasis is placed on the current relationship between the person and the counselor.[17] This shift in theory indicates a radical change in therapeutic techniques which will be delineated later in this chapter.

Contemporary analysis of the obsessive personality has followed this new trend. The behavior of the obsessive is analysed to discover what particular function it serves the person in the therapeutic relationship. Some interesting facts have begun to emerge from this analysis of the obsessive.

The obsessive person utilizes a particular "style of life" (to a greater or lesser degree depending on the severity of his obsession) which reflects his particular way of thinking or his way of perceiving reality: he is rigid. Rigidity is the most universal characteristic of obsessive persons. The obsessive manifests this characteristic in any number of ways—by a ram-rod posture, by a frozen social manner, by constant concern for order (these people are inveterate "list makers"), by meticulous cleanliness (these are the "nit pickers"), etc.[18] But more important, rigidity is a *style of thought* for the obsessive person. His thought patterns are fixed. In fact, he believes everyone should think in his way—precise, intense, sharply focused. The counselor invariably confronts this "stylized thinking" when the scrupulant approaches him for advice. After patiently listening to the litany of detail, the counselor launches into an exhortation and even some trenchant insights into the problem only to have the scrupulant reply: "Father, I think I forgot to tell you that I think I neglected to recite grace before meals eight times instead of six times and three of the eight times I could have possibly given scandal to two of my three children." The counselor's frustration can be mollified only by his realization of the intensity of the problem.

The obsessive person exhibits an intense, sharply focused concentration on detail. His attention is very limited in scope and mobility. He seems to be concentrating all the time. He has no "hunches," no flashes of insight. He is usually insensitive to the "tone" of a social situation. When he finds a patient confessor or a kind friend, he often becomes a bore because he cannot respond to the other person's discomfort, his pressing appointment, his lack of time, etc. In a sense, the obsessive seems to be actively inattentive to any external influence, any new idea which would threaten his

---

[16] L. Salzman, *op. cit.*, 1141.

[17] *Ibid.*

[18] For a statistically isolated and defined list of obsessive characteristics see: J. Delay, P. Pichot, and J. Perse, "Personnalite obsessionnelle et charactere dit obsessionel: Etude clinique et psychometrique," *Rev. Psychol. Appl.* 12 (1962) 232–62.

rigid, dogmatic concern for detail. He has presented his "data" to the counselor and it must not be "folded, spindled, or multilated in any way."

This rigidity is increasingly evident in the obsessive's external activity in proportion to the seriousness of his obsession. There is evidence to substantiate the hypothesis that catatonic schizophrenia (an acute psychotic state characterized by withdrawal from reality and extreme postural rigidity) [19] is the extreme limit of the obsessive-compulsive's solution to conflict: rigidity.[20] Even in the milder stages of obsessive behavior the function of rigidity (as seen in the rituals, the constant state of doubt, the unwillingness to commit himself to a definite decision, etc.) seems to be a constant attempt to control himself and his universe so that he can guarantee his security, safety, and survival.[21]

The constant attempt of the obsessive to control himself and reality points to another general characteristic of his style of life. His life is intense, colorless, joyless, and in a special way, *directed*. The obsessive is rarely a jolly person. He rarely shows any emotionality other than gloom, anxiety, and grim determination. His life pivots around intense work; there is a sense of tense deliberateness around everything he does. His work, his play, his life in general is not "hard" but "labored." There is a definite sense of trying, of effort in everything he does. He is "driven" to do better, to do the best. There is a singular lack of enthusiasm in all his activity. Much like the uninspired, unenthusiastic piano practicing of a young athletically minded boy on a warm Spring afternoon, the obsessive does things "because he has to." His lack of enthusiasm reflects a state of self-imposed pressure. "I should" is the constant theme of his life. The *oughtness* serves as a directive, a reminder, a warning, an admonition to the obsessive person. In sharp contrast to the emotionally mature person the obsessive person acts as an over-seer to himself. He attempts to constantly and willfully direct himself, even to the extent of directing his own desires and emotions. Impulse is an enemy to the obsessive person.[22]

This "sense of oughtness" which drives the obsessive seems to be motivated by the obsessive's great need to be absolutely safe and certain about everything. In order to remain safe and certain he must know everything. Only by knowing everything can he predict the future and be prepared for any and every eventuality. The point is not so much that he must know everything, but that with this knowledge he will rarely risk being wrong;

[19] J. Coleman, *Abnormal Psychology*, 2 ed., 266.
[20] K. Blacker, "Obsessive-Compulsive Phenomena and Catatonic States," *Psychiatry* 29 (1966), 185–94.
[21] L. Salzman, *op. cit.*, 1140.
[22] D. Shapiro, *op. cit.*, 37.

he will rarely not know what he ought to do; he will not be forced to decide to take a certain course of action or commit himself where there is risk of error.[23] This area is precisely the point where the religious manifestation of obsession makes its most dramatic entrance. When rules are presented, when the obsessive "knows" what he must do, he can operate. The overseer in his religious life is God; the rules are His commandments and the laws of His Church. These provide a framework within which he can operate. His choices are then just so many technical decisions. He merely applies the rules to the case and acts accordingly. Fulfilling the rule does not give the satisfaction which comes with the challenge of freedom and decision; but, to the obsessive, the satisfaction is the satisfaction of temporarily pleasing the overseer, God.

Unfortunately, reality and life are not spelled out in every detail even by the most classical of the moral casuists. There are many areas, many circumstances where no rule is available, no definite word has been spoken. A mature person faces such a situation aware of the risks; but responsive to the exigencies of the situation. He makes a decision based on his experience, the relevant facts available, and his capacity for anticipation and elementary planning. Not so the obsessive! His need for security and certainty leads him to a "doubt," to indecision which will guarantee his remaining right by not acting. He remains safe and secure by not acting. And so, the obsessive comes to the moral guide—the counselor—so involved in the problem, so threatened by the possibility of error that he cannot be touched by any verbal, intellectual or spiritual help. If he is forced to decide by circumstances, his action will be a "leap" not a choice or indication of preference.[24]

In summary, the current psychological analysis of the characteristics of the obsessive person emphasizes two main points: 1. the obsessive is rigid, quite often in his external behavior, but invariably in his thinking; 2. he is driven by an "oughtness"; he seeks to control his behavior by a self-imposed (or at times an authoritarianly imposed) overseer so that his entire behavior can be safe, secure, protected from any mistakes. These two characteristics—rigidity and fear of error—are the obsessive's "style of life." All his contact with human beings and with God are tinged with these factors.

This psychological analysis of the obsessive is strikingly reinforced by the following comment from a priest-counselor who has extended his warm humanity as well as his professional skills to scrupulous persons over a period of more than twenty years:

"A characteristic of scrupulants which does not seem to be usually men-

---

[23] L. Salzman, *op. cit.*, 1140.
[24] D. Shapiro, *op. cit.*, 48

tioned by writers . . . is their unconscious, unformulated desire to be pure and sinless in the eyes of God. *In reality, they would like to be sinless (and even temptation-less) in their own eyes.* Some of them come to recognize this in the course of counseling. Although they may have heard about man's . . . limitations, his imperfections . . . etc., they do not apply these things to themselves. There is a defect . . . in their ability to accept themselves as they are. They live and act as if perfection were expected of them. For them to achieve the insight that perfection is a goal of striving is a kind of revelation to them and affords them a measure of relief." [25]

DIAGNOSTIC NORMS

Although the theoretical analysis given above will help the counselor gain insight into the scrupulous person's style of life, it does not aid the counselor in a more basic question. How does one identify and distinguish the various degrees of severity in cases of obsession? Identification is no easy task since there are many types and variations of the obsessive pattern which range from what may be called mere personality traits (such as, the dedication to detail that a professional airline pilot manifests prior to takeoff) to incapacitating obsessions (e.g., the person who compiles a continuous list of sins).[26]

Although any attempt at classifying types of scrupulous personalities is open to all the limitations and defects of classification, it does have the practical value of giving the counselor a framework or background against which he can compare the person who seeks his advice. The danger of classification is that a given counselor will apply the norms too mechanically. A sensitive counselor is much like an excellent chef. He uses the cook book recipe as a general guide. But he responds to the inspiration of the moment by altering the precise cook book proportions with a pinch more of this, a bit less of that, and some of this. The counselor will also use the norms as a guide but will utilize all his personal resources and his sensitivity to respond to the uniqueness of the personality and the problem before him.

It may help, first of all, to distinguish the "false positive" behavior patterns (those which have the characteristics of obsessive behavior but which are not truly obsessive) from true scrupulous behavior. Mis-judgment about some particular moral or religious obligation may indicate ignorance or lack of maturity in a person, but not scrupulosity. This type of behavior has been traditionally called "erroneous conscience." [27] A classical example of

---

[25] E. Janusz, *Personal Correspondence to Author,* October, 1966.
[26] A. Noyes, *Modern Clinical Psychiatry,* 447.
[27] J. McCall, "Scrupulosity," *Guild of Cath. Psychi. Bull.* 5 (1957) 6.

this is the elderly woman who confesses missing Mass on Sunday even though illness or infirmity prevented her from participating with the community in worship. Another "false positive" is the genuine state of doubt or indecision. Genuine indecision is not an example of scrupulous behavior. When the choices have reasonable grounds supporting each horn of a dilemma, the state of genuine doubt occurs.[28] A contemporary example of this condition can be discovered in the state of indecision many honest Catholics find themselves in over the birth control question. Their state of doubt, all things being equal, is not scrupulous. Finally, the sensitivity of a maturing Christian, shown by his awareness of subtle forms of selfishness in his behavior and his insensitivity to the demands of the moment upon his generosity is not scrupulosity. Ascetical authors describe this type of person as one who has a "delicate conscience." [29] Any attempt to describe this person and to distinguish him from the scrupulant is difficult because of the many intangibles which are the crucial distinguishing factors. The total personality is the crucial factor here. A truly "delicate conscience" belongs to a maturing Christian. The maturation shows itself in the lack of anxiety over the faults confessed and in the general stability of the person. This type of person is not depressed, anxious, or agitated over the confession of faults.[30] This person listens to the confessor and integrates the applicable advice to himself. There is an honest openness about the person. Where the scrupulant is actively inattentive to the confessor, closed to suggestion, and anxious, agitated, or depressed, the maturing Christian is attentive, open to advice, and calm.

Briefly then, the scrupulant is *not* a person who is ignorant, in sincere doubt, or equipped with a developing sensitivity to the demands of his Christian life. The scrupulant is quite different.

In instances of actual scrupulous behavior the first diagnostic judgment the counselor must make is: is this a case of a transitory or "permanent" scrupulosity? The judgment is important since normal personalities can experience transient crises which induce obsessive behavior. But the obsessive behavior is only temporary. It exists as long as the person is under the pressure of the crisis. As the person works through the crisis with the help of a counselor the obsessive behavior tends to slacken and usually vanishes altogether. The crisis can be any number of experiences: a change of life (adolescence, menopause, debility of old age), a religious experience (such as conversion to a religious group with a strong set of morals), a sudden jarring emotional experience (death of a close friend, illness, etc).[31]

---

[28] *Ibid.*
[29] A. Tanquerey, *op. cit.*, 444–5.
[30] A. Lauras, *op. cit.*, 65–67.
[31] *Ibid.*, 59.

The diagnostic indications of a case of transitory obsession are: 1. the lack of obsessiveness in the history of the person; 2. the existence of some crisis which precipitated the obsessiveness; and 3. the presence of a basically well adjusted personality.[32] The last point needs some elucidation. The obsessive patterns these persons exhibit—the doubts, hesitations, guilt feelings, etc.—do not constitute a style of life for them. For the most part these people have good insight into the problem and they have considerable control over their thoughts. They do not experience the acute pain of indecision or doubt. These persons can offer constructive information to the counselor. They can point out relevant facts, such as the crisis they find linked to the onset of the obsessive behavior. And generally speaking, the obsessive symptoms occupy their attention fleetingly and only partially.[33] The symptoms usually capture their attention when they are in a reflective mood, e.g., while preparing for confession, not in their everyday activity.[34]

However, in the case of a permanent obsessive, the pattern of doubts, hesitations, fears, etc. has become the style of life for the person. The severity of the problem will indicate to what degree the obsessiveness rules the person's life and the particular form the obsessive behavior will take. In severe cases the obsessive behavior is accompanied by other symptoms which are obvious indicators of severe mental disturbance. These persons become overly emotional; their moods swing dramatically without warning or reason; they can become hysterical; they can be emotionally "flat"; they do incongruous things. The obsessive behavior they reveal is usually bizarre, persistent, and disruptive to their everyday behavior.[35]

The severely obsessive person may say that he has a fear of giving in to an almost uncontrollable impulse. He may be agonized while attending Mass because of persistent obscene thoughts. The obsessive urging to begin singing an obscene song during the consecration, the obsessive thought that the priest slurred the words of consecration so that the host is merely a wafer disturbs the person to such an extent that he begins to react physiologically by perspiring heavily, tensing his muscles, shaking his head to rid himself of the thoughts, etc. These symptoms make the severely disturbed obsessive rather easy to recognize. Generally speaking, these persons are beyond the competency of the usual pastoral counselor. But the severe cases are rather rare and easy to recognize because of their uniqueness. About all the usual counselor can offer these persons is support and gentle direction to a professional therapist.

[32] P. Sifneos, "Psychotherapy for Mild Obsessional Neuroses," Psychi. Quart., 40 (1966) 273.

[33] D. MacCalman, op. cit., 212.

[34] For a treatment of childhood obsessions see: L. Judd, "Obsessive Compulsive Neurosis in Children," Arch. of Gen. Psychi. 12 (1965) 136–43.

[35] J. Coleman, op. cit., 209.

The more frequently met "permanent" obsessive is the mildly severe case. In addition to their frequency of occurrence these mildly severe obsessional persons present a great variety of obsessional problems. Their obsessions usually center on the observation of laws, civil, ecclesiastical, and divine. These persons can conjure up more problems about observing laws than even the most imaginative casuist. Their problems are so varied that they defy classification. However, the presence of doubt and fear is universal to these mildly severe cases.

There are distinguishing factors present to their fears and doubts which indicate the mild severity of their problem. First of all, the problem is absurd. It would not even occupy the attention of a mature person. For example, a mother with obsessive problems experiences great fears and guilt feelings when she attempts to decide whether or not she should spend a Saturday evening with her husband. She fears that her baby sitter may become so exhausted caring for her children that she will not be able to attend Church on Sunday. The absurdity of the fear is obvious to the out-side observer and even to the mother herself. In fact, the knowledge of the absurdity of her fear is a contributing factor to the anxiety of her state. She knows the fear is absurd but nonetheless it is all too real. She struggles against the fear and feels the anguish and anxiety of the struggle. But like some parasite, the absurd fear cannot be shaken. As is the usual case, her struggle results in a failure to act, a hopelessness which subtly pervades her entire life pattern.

Besides the struggle, the recognized absurdity of the fear, and the failure experienced by the mildly severe obsessive, his general approach toward a specific obsession indicates the severity of the problem. Once again, let us use the example of the scrupulous mother to illustrate this factor. The mother recognizes the absurdity of the fear. She tells herself: "Let's be reasonable about this." Then with a herculean effort she begins to recon-struct all the similar decisions she faced in the past, her counselor's advice, the seeming relevant facts of the present situation, etc., etc. Finally, she becomes so involved in the details of reconstruction that confusion floods upon her. Note that she dwells in the past. Under the guise of a logical reasonable approach to the decision, she becomes so involved in the past that she effectively avoids confrontation with the existential before her. While she recalls what happened before in similar situations, the subtle drive to be absolutely safe about the present situation flows into her think-ing. The gnawing fear that she may make a mistake, the fear that somehow this case is different from those of the past, the infinite variety of possible circumstances make her more and more insecure. Finally, she either goes out with her husband on impulse (and has a miserable evening worrying about the baby sitter) and then accuses herself of wrongfully placing the baby sitter in danger of missing Sunday Mass, or she refuses to decide by staying home. In the latter case, she probably will accuse herself of a lack of charity toward her husband.[36]

Quite apart from the characteristics of the obsessive's approach to concrete problems certain pertinent personality characteristics usually reveal themselves to the counselor through his interaction with the obsessive. These persons have a tendency to present their problems and their approach to life in general in opposing terms of good and evil, in blacks and whites without any greys. Much like a child's view of life their view of life and problems is very concrete and magical. Things are good or bad. There is only one way to act. If only they could find it! Furthermore, these obsessives show a marked lack of spontaneity. No attempt to lighten the heaviness of the conversation will meet with favorable response from the scrupulant. The obsessive's attitude toward the counselor is mechanical and basically dehumanizing. To the obsessive, there is a "right" way to act toward an authority, a "right" way to act toward the counselor, a "right" way to act toward the salesman, another "right" way toward the neighbor, etc. These persons attempt to live in a world of absolutes.[37] Their platonic approach to life really means that they refuse to become involved in life. Thus they act in the "right" way toward the counselor. They approach the counselor as an information vender who will tell them the "right" way to act in the circumstances they find so trying. They treat the counselor impersonally.

Another personality characteristic is egocentricity. The deep drive for absolute certainty and absolute perfection makes their lives center constantly on themselves. Unconsciously they place themselves at the center of the universe. This is the root cause of the deep sense of frustration the counselor experiences in his attempt to communicate with the obsessive. The scrupulant is isolated; he is further and further removed from reality. He has an idealized image of himself which can rarely be successfully challenged. If the counselor attempts to challenge this image, the obsessive renders him ineffectual by turning him into an object and not a person. The counselor also senses that unconsciously the obsessive thinks of himself as being a fascinatingly unusual case who requires special care. He also gives the impression that deep in himself he believes that he is a victim of this spiritual plague. Actually, he is pure, "angelic," innocent, totally incapable of evil even when he accuses himself of the worst crimes.[38]

The mildly severe scrupulant can be described as a person who has a

---

[36] A. Lauras, *op. cit.*, 209.
[37] G. Mora, "Psychotherapy for Scrupulous Patients," in *Cross Currents of Psychiatry and Catholic Morality*, ed. W. Birmingham & J. Cunneen, 250.
[38] *Ibid.*

history of scrupulous behavior; who presents a black and white picture of life; who spends much of his life ruminating; who presents absurd problems and questions to the counselor; who is distant in the interpersonal contact with the counselor; and who uses his obsessiveness as a guard against any possibility of error or mistake in his life.

In summary, the pastoral counselor will meet various types of obsessive personalities. He will find some "false-positive," some transitory, and some permanent obsessives among those who seek his aid. In each of these categories he will find an amazing assortment of variations. The most frequently met and the most troublesome of all these types is the mildly severe permanent obsessive.

Counseling Techniques

Although the weight of contemporary evidence points to a psychological rather than a spiritual source for scrupulous behavior, the pastoral counselor will discover that scrupulous persons present their problems only as religious problems. Any attempt on the part of the counselor to discuss the problem as a psychological one will usually meet with great resistance. This reality underscores the necessity of every pastoral counselor possessing the fundamentals of good counseling technique. Especially important are the initial contacts with the obsessive which must provide the basis of rapport between the counselor and the scrupulant. The counselor must do his utmost to provide a climate of confidence for the scrupulous person. He does this by being non-judgmental, by expressing concern for the person not so much in word as in behavior. The concerned counselor does not yawn or drum his fingers or show signs of boredom. He does not intrude into the obsessive's stream of detail and slough off the obsessive's words with a curt: "Don't worry about that!" (Although the establishment of the climate of confidence will differ from a sacramental confessional situation to a more professional face-to-face counseling session, the importance of trust is primary for any hope of success.)

Once sufficient trust is established, the counselor can proceed to the diagnostic and therapeutic aspects of the relationship. If the counselor discovers the person is a severely disturbed obsessive, his attitude toward the person and his decision is clear and simple: this person must be referred to a professional therapist—a psychiatrist, or psychotherapist.[39] His familiarity with the professional sources available in his community will enable him to suggest or even arrange such professional care for the person.

If the person is a transitory obsessive, the counselor is in a position to

[39] *Ibid.*, 251

offer help. Since these persons do not find the obsessive patterns dominating their entire life pattern, they are usually receptive to suggestion. Brief questions can quickly determine the status of the problem. "Is the obsessive problem linked with an illness, a change of life, etc.?" "Did this problem ever cause you any difficulty before this time?" "Do these thoughts and doubts disturb you throughout the day? everyday?" Once the counselor has determined this is a transitory problem he can structure his counsel to the age and intelligence of the person. Basically, he wants to reassure the person that the problem is a transitory one. He should reinforce the good judgments of the person and give continual support to the person during the time of the crisis.

The greatest aid the counselor can give the transitory obsessive is supportive. Since the obsessive behavior is atypical, his typical, more mature, behavior patterns will regain their prominence (provided there is no physiological source for the scruples), if the person receives the necessary support and encouragement during the time of crisis.

The most difficult counseling problem is the mildly severe obsessive. When the obsessive's problem is full blown, it is more refractory to treatment than a mild psychosis.[40] Despite the poor prognosis of this type of problem, the pastoral counselor should not despair of being able to help the mild obsessive at all. The pastoral counselor brings more to the counseling situation than mere expertise. He also brings the sacramental dimension of his pastoral office. In fact, it is precisely this dimension which usually stimulates the obsessive to approach the pastoral counselor in the first place. Thus by utilizing this sacramental dimension the confessor can develop the human-sacred relationship between himself and the obsessive into a therapeutic tool. In his role of director and forgiver the confessor can trace with the obsessive the route of the doubts and fears of the penitent to their source, to the deep need the obsessive has to be pure, sinless, and mistakeless, and to the deep rooted pride in the person.[41]

The counselor will avoid the traditional "blind obedience" technique which proved to be so ineffectual. The great sense of "oughtness" which drives the obsessive is actually fed by the blind obedience approach. The obsessive uses the confessor as a surrogate "overseer." He uses him as an escape from facing the "here and now" decisions which demand personal choice and risk. If the counselor uses the blind obedience technique he only provides the obsessive with another "overseer" behind whose words the obsessive can hide from life.

Since the obsessive uses the past to hide from the present realities, the

[40] A. Noyes, *op. cit.*, 447.
[41] G. Mora, *op. cit.*, 252.

counseling approach should be quite different from the traditional procedures. Instead of dwelling on the past or projecting to the future, the counselor should emphasize the *present* behavior of the obsessive in the counseling relationship. This will help the obsessive see and understand exactly how he behaves. When the "here and now" is used as the subject matter the behavior is clear, the facts are pinned down, the person's reaction to the occasion and the steps he takes to handle the anxiety he feels are obvious. He cannot ignore or run away from these facts.[42]

In a confessional this procedure of "existential therapy" is inappropriate for the most part because it is a psychological, therapeutic instrument. The "existential therapy" should be employed by a trained pastoral counselor outside the confessional. But a knowledge of this dynamic as well as the dynamics of the obsessive can be of great help to the confessor. If he meets a person (usually a young adult or an adolescent) who is in the initial stages of the mildly severe obsessive style of life, he can delineate the dynamics behind the obsessive behavior. He can indicate that engrossment in the minutiae of decision and the paralysis of fear and anxiety serve as effective means of removing the person from the realities of decision which face him. The counselor can show that the obsessiveness leads the person to a deeper and deeper egocentricity which thwarts any real psychological and spiritual maturation.

This "existential therapy" might be described as "now" therapy. The "now" indicates the attitude which both the counselor and the obsessive must take toward the problem. The stress must be on what is occuring here and *now*. The obsessive must be brought to see how he utilizes both the past, and fear and doubt to avoid the "now" decision. The counselor must slowly lead the person to see the importance of the everchanging opportunities for grace present in the person's existence. He must aid the obsessive in restructuring his hierarchy of values on the firm base of Christ and not on the vapid, self-feeding ego.

In the case of the fully developed mildly severe obsessive there is little that the confessor can do besides offering him the sacramental presence of himself and the consolation of the sacrament of forgiveness. He should remove the case from the confessional and divert the person to a competent therapist.

PRACTICAL PROCEDURES

In summary, when the confessor meets an obsessive person for the first time, he should be accepting, nonjudgmental, and actively building a "cli-

[42] L. Salzman, *op. cit.*, 1142.

mate of confidence." If there is no possibility of follow up with this particular person, the confessor must offer his humanity to the person by his
concern and his patient acceptance of the obsessive's problems. Little or no
advice other than urging a permanent confessor or professional therapist
seems to be the best advice in this case. If the penitent can and will return,
the confessor can plan to ask some questions which will help him decide
the severity of the problem.

If the problem is severe, the counselor should slowly guide the person to
a professional therapist. This is a delicate procedure which requires time
and patience. But if the problem is a transitory one, the procedures outlined above will be a good starting point for the counselor. If the problem
is a mildly severe one, the confessor will do well to transfer the counseling
out of the confessional into a more structured counseling situation. His aim
may be to guide the person to a professional therapist, or, if he himself is
competent, to employ some of the existential therapy techniques suggested
above.[43]

Undoubtedly the scrupulous person will continue to remain the "bane
of the confessor." But with the influx of more positive and less purely intellectual catechetical approaches to the Christian life and liturgy we hope
the incidence of the scrupulous person will slowly recede until scrupulosity
will become a rare illness mentioned in pastoral literature but rarely seen in
a severe state.

BIBLIOGRAPHY

BOOKS:

Coleman, J., *Abnormal Psychology and Modern Life*, 2 ed., New York, 1956.
Freud, S., *Collected Papers*, New York, 1959.
Hagmaier, G., C.S.P., Gleason, R., S.J., *Counselling the Catholic*, New York,
1959.
Henderson, D., Gillespie, R., *A Textbook of Psychiatry for Students and Prac-
titioners*, New York, 1948.
Lauras, A., *The Treatment of Scruples*, tr. M. Carrol, Techny, 1964.
MacCalman, D., *Modern Practice in Psychological Medicine*, ed. J. Rees, New
York, 1949.
Mailloux, N., O. P., "The Problem of Scrupulosity in Pastoral Work," in
*Proceedings of the Institute for the Clergy on Problems in Pastorial Psychol-
ogy*, ed. A. Schneiders, New York, 1956.
Mora, G., "Psychotherapy for Scrupulous Patients," in *Cross Currents of Psy-
chiatry and Catholic Morality*, eds. W. Brimingham, J. Cunneen, New York,
1964.
Noyes, A., *Modern Clinical Psychiatry*, 6 ed., Philadelphia, 1963.
Reich, W., *Character Analysis*, New York, 1949.

[43] For a fuller treatment of the existential therapy see L. Salzman, *op. cit.*

Shapiro, D., *Neurotic Styles*, New York, 1965.

Tanquerey, A., *The Spiritual Life*, 2 ed., tr. H. Branderis, S.S., Tournai, 1930.

Allers, Rudolph, *The Psychology of Character*. New York: Sheed and Ward, 1940.

Bier, William C., S.J., ed. *The Adolescent: His Search for Understanding*. New York: Fordham Univ. Press, 1963.

————, *Personality and Sexual Problems in Pastoral Psychology*. New York: Fordham Univ. Press, 1964.

Kelly, Gerald, S.J., *Guidance for Religious*. Westminster, Md.: Newman, 1956.

Mora, G. "The Psychotherapeutic Treatment of Scrupulous Patients," *Cross Currents*, 7 (1957), 2940.

O'Flaherty, Vincent, S.J., *How to Cure Scruples*. Milwaukee: Bruce, 1966.

Oraison, Marc, *Illusion and Anxiety*. New York: Macmillan Co., 1963.

Terruew, A. A. A., M.D., *The Neurosis in the Light of Rational Psychology*. New York: P. J. Kenedy and Sons, 1960.

Weisner, Wayne M., and Riffel, Pius, S.J., "Scrupulosity: Religion and Obsessive Compulsive Behavior in Children," *American Journal of Psychiatry*, 117 (1960), 314–318.

ARTICLES:

Blacker, K., "Obsessive-compulsive Phenomena and Catatonic States," *Psychiatry* 29 (1966), 185–94.

Gratton, H., "The Cause of Scrupulosity," *TD* 10 (1962), 51–56.

Larere, P., "Conduite pastoral en face des scrupuleux," *Cashiers Laennec*, 20 (1960), 67–78.

McCall, J., "Scrupulosity," *Guild of Cath. Psychi. Bull.* 5 (1957), 5–9.

Salzman, L., "Therapy of Obsessional States," *A. J. of Psychi.* 122 (1966), 1139–46.

Sifneos, P., "Psychoanalytically oriented short term dynamic or anxiety-producing psychotherapy for mild obsessional neuroses," *Psychiatric Quart.* 40 (1966), 271–82.

5

MASTURBATION: SOME PRACTICAL CONSIDERATIONS

Eugene J. Weitzel, C.S.V., J.T.D.

MASTURBATION is a rather common practice among adolescents and even among certain classes of adults. Indeed so widespread is the practice, that many authorities agree that under present cultural conditions it can be considered psychologically normal and/or common,[1] not only during adolescence, but even in adulthood when sexual relations with a person of the opposite sex are impossible, or when the individual persists in a severe habit acquired during adolescence. This position is strongly supported by statistical research conducted in both the United States and in Europe in recent years. Furthermore, these statistics have been accepted by most Catholic writers.[2]

Using the statistical data acquired from these various studies in conjunc-

[1] The expression "psychologically normal" as used in this article "is meant to refer to that which is usual, typical, and/or common as inferred from whatever empirical observations are available and without reference to whether or not what is so termed complies or conflicts with the natural or moral law. The term "normal," then, is used somewhat in a statistical sense to refer to what is found in a majority of cases, and specifically to indicate behavior which in itself is not considered pathognomonic of severe psychiatric or emotional disorder." Robert J. Campbell, "Masturbation and Homosexuality," *The Adolescent: His Search for Understanding*, edited by William C. Bier, S.J., (New York: Fordham University Press, 1964) pp. 53–54.

[2] *Ibid.*, p. 54; J. G. Prick and J. A. Calon, "Masturbation Among Boys. (a) Medical Aspects," *New Problems in Medical Ethics*, edited by Dom Peter Flood, O.S.B., (Cork: The Mercier Press Limited, 1955), pp. 19–20.

tion with the most recent census figures, one arrives at some rather startling facts regarding the possible frequency of this practice. In the United States today, there are approximately 19.0 million boys and 18.5 million girls between the ages of ten and twenty-one. If at least some of these studies are valid, and if it is true, as many authors writing in this area assert, that between 85 and 92 percent of all boys and 50 percent of all girls practice masturbation, the figures shows that between 16.2 and 17.5 million boys and 9.3 million girls may masturbate once or more than once in the course of their pre-teen and teen-age years. Fortunately, however, the vast majority, or 65 percent, spontaneously and permanently abandon the practice within four years' time. Another 15 percent, according to accepted statistics, abandon it before reaching the age of twenty-one. The remaining 20 percent (3.8 million of the total population of boys) may continue the practice in adult life.

Although the age of onset varies, available studies also accepted by most Catholic writers, clearly show that it peaks in the years from ten to twelve. That the age of onset peaks during these pre-adolescent years may well be accounted for by the fact that most of the boys had acquired considerable sex information during their pre-adolescent years, in fact, before they reached age 10. These statistics strongly support the view that it might be wise to instruct sub-teens regarding the moral and social dangers inherent in this practice rather than to wait until they are freshmen or sophomores in high school and, perhaps, already involved in habitual masturbation. Even with ten and twelve year olds, the emphasis must be on education and they should be provided, prudently, of course, with more knowledge about sex and reality, on the theory that forewarned is forearmed. Priests and teachers should use various methods of developing the consciences of these young people and of impressing upon them the importance of self-control and the value of mortification.

The frequency of masturbation in terms of times per week also varies. While the average teen-age boy may masturbate from two to three times per week, nearly 17 percent, according to Dr. Campbell, masturbate as often as six to seven times per week. The group with the highest frequency practices acts of masturbation on an average of twenty-three times per week in early adolescence. However, even in this group there is a gradual decrease in the frequency so that by the age of twenty the frequency drops to 15 times per week, by the age of fifty to 6 times per week, and by the age of sixty to once every fortnight.

While the statistics tell us many things about the problem, they are most valuable in a discussion of the causes of masturbation. For, if it is true that most adolescents engage in this practice at some time, and that the average fifteen-year-old boy might masturbate two to three times a week, then, it would seem unwarranted to conclude that masturbation is the result of a psychopathological problem, and that the act of ipsation is actually a symbol of defeat and helplessness of a person who cannot love and a regression of personality back to the stage of infancy. Rather, they would seem to indicate that the first cause of masturbation is to be found in the physiological and sociological factors, and only secondly in the psychological. However, before considering the causes of ipsation, it is important that we first provide the reader with other pertinent information.

Authors use various terms to identify this practice—onanism, *molities*, *pollutio voluntaria*, ipsation, self-abuse, and masturbation. The latter two are the most common designations. Perhaps the most complete definition of this act is found in the *Dictionary of Moral Theology* which defines self-abuse as the production of orgasm by excitation of the genital organs, as by manipulation or friction, without heterosexual intercourse. In a moral sense it stimulates complete satisfaction outside of copulation; thus, it comprises not only the emission of the semen (in the adolescent and adult male) but a complete sexual satisfaction, whether it be in man or woman, adolescent or child, eunuchs, etc., if they are capable of it.[3] Another definition provided by Doctor Robert J. Campbell is also worthy of note, since it calls our attention to the fact that even impure thoughts, desires, looks, and touches (of another person's body) can bring about a discharge of semen without any direct physical manipulation. He defines self-abuse as "direct self-manipulation of the genitals, most commonly by the hand, accompanied by phantasies that are usually of a recognizably sexual nature, and having as its aim the discharge of sexual excitation."[4] He then points out that it is also possible to recognize "psychic" masturbation where sexual discharge is effected by phantasy alone and not by any direct physical manipulation.

Although most of the other definitions of ipsation are acceptable, there is one definition formulated by Doctor Frederick von Gagern, M.D., which could be rather misleading. According to this definition, masturbation is "sexual excitement and satisfaction sought either alone or with others as a means to procure pleasure or relief, usually as a reaction brought about by motives in the unconscious."[5] Regarding the large majority of cases of both adolescents and adults, it is difficult to accept Baron von Gagern's contention that masturbation is a reaction brought on by motives in the uncon-

---

[3] Francesco Cardinal Roberti, *Dictionary of Moral Theology*, edited by Pietro Palazzini, and translated by Henry J. Yannone, (Westminster, Maryland: The Newman Press, 1962) p. 852.

[4] Robert J. Campbell, *op. cit.*, pp. 52–53.

[5] George Hagmaier, C.S.P. and Robert Gleason, S.J., *Counselling the Catholic*, (New York: Sheed and Ward, 1959), p. 74.

scious. From my own experience as a confessor and counselor of boys, and from all of the empirical data available it would seem that for the vast number of people who indulge in this practice, masturbation is a consciously wanted and freely accepted exercise of the reproductive function for no other reason than that they are unable to have the desired normal sexual relations. They do it for lack of anything better—*faute de mieux*. Dr. Henri Gibert seems to sense this point when he writes,

> Now, it must be made very clear that this nearly universal stage of masturbational conduct is not at all essential to the acquiring of adult maturity in sexuality. It is nonetheless true that the state of change in an adolescent's sexual instinct, his ignorance concerning women, and his misconceptions about the realities of human sex all tend to make pubertal masturbation practically so unavoidable, except for pathological cases of sexual disinterest, that it must appear to be biologically normal and the object of neither amazement or fear, despite its frequency.[6]

The Effects of Masturbation

To anyone experienced in counseling or treating persons who practice self-abuse, it is clearly evident that this practice produces certain physical, mental, emotional, moral, and sexual effects. However, most of these effects are of minor importance. In the physical order, "we find at most unspecific symptoms of bodily exhaustion, or nervous eroticism," such as 1) loss of muscle tone, 2) pains in the region of the loins (back-pains in the areas extending from the lower ribs to the hip-bones), 3) Loss of appetite, 4) sometimes, loss of sleep. In almost every case, these effects are of minimal importance. Contrary to popular belief (a belief shared at times by pastors and confessors), masturbation is not the cause of pimples, acne, insanity, weakness, impotence, or feeblemindedness.

While masturbation does not cause insanity or feeblemindedness, its practice does often result in a lessening of attentiveness and of memory. Since attention and memory are essential for success in school, the practice of self-abuse may affect a student's performance to the extent that his academic work suffers. However, since the mental consequences of masturbation are also of minimal importance, teachers, especially, should be most reluctant to judge that every student who does poorly in school, or who shows signs of slipping academically is practicing masturbation. In almost every case, the causes of poor scholastic achievement lie elsewhere.

Many authors also agree that for the great majority of adolescents the

[6] Henri Gibert, M.D., *Love in Marriage*, (New York: Hawthorn Books Inc., 1964), p. 168.

emotional and moral effects are not too serious either, since the practice usually disappears of itself with the maturing of the personality. Perhaps the most serious of these are the feelings of guilt and depression that follow upon the act itself. However, in most instances, the feelings of dejection, guilt, and distress are relatively fleeting and the personality is not permanently scarred. Only in the case of a very small minority—perhaps, among the group with the highest frequency—will masturbation become a possible cause of neurosis. Several authors take this position regarding the seriousness of the emotional and moral effects of self-abuse, because they are convinced that when it is nothing more than a form of sexual behavior, it is closely associated with what from a psychological point of view appears to be usual development, and will usually be limited to a certain period or periods of life. [7]

Furthermore, while it is true that the practice of self-abuse is a more serious matter when it persists even in adult years, we could argue that it is also wrong to conclude, for the large majority of cases, that "adult masturbation" is a sign of an immature personality which has remained too firmly fixed in self-interest. Is it fair to those in need of help to speak of it as "confinement within the ever shrinking bounds of a fear-struck, impoverishing and selfish gratification?" Certainly not. Furthermore, in reference to the large majority of un-married adult cases, it cannot be maintained, as some few authors do, that " 'The act of masturbation is really a symbol of defeat and helplessness of one who cannot love' . . . a regression of personality back to the stage of infancy." [8] In fact, again there is good reason to contend that the vast number of un-married adults who masturbate do so primarily because they are presently deprived of sexual intercourse with persons of the opposite sex.

Even in the case of the married man who continues or resumes the practice of self-abuse, it is wrong immediately to assume that a psychopathological problem exists. Because of certain circumstances (advanced pregnancy, serious illness on the part of the wife, the use of the rhythm method, military service or employment that takes the husband away from the home for extended periods of time, etc.), it may be difficult or impossible for the couple to have normal marital relations. Consequently, the husband finds himself in the same situation as the un-married adult. Even the married

[7] Robert J. Campbell, "Autosexuality: Habitual Masturbation," *Personality and Sexual Problems*, edited by William C. Bier, S.J. (New York: Fordham Press, 1964), p. 209.

[8] Henri Gibert, *op. cit.*, p. 175. Ludovico Bender, O.P. writing in the *Dictionary of Moral Theology*, observes that, "Sometimes masturbation is practiced by adults unable to have normal marriage relations (e.g., in jail or prison); in such cases, its psychopathological significance is non-existent." p. 902.

man who is able to have normal and regular sexual relations with his wife may not be suffering from a psychopathological condition. A considerable number of men (between 15 and 20 percent) enter marriage with a long-established and sometimes persisting habit of masturbation. Again, there is good reason to believe that in the majority of cases this situation is merely the result of psychological and physiological conditioning (conditioned reflexes), and not the result of "an uncompleted stage of instinctive sexual behavior which has remained self-centered, with all the more or less obsessional elements involved." [9]

From what has been said, it would be wrong to conclude that there are no cases of habitual masturbation that are indicative of pathology. Certainly, when habitual masturbation continues in later life it may subsume the function of preference by an adult for autoerotic activity to normal heterosexual intercourse, or it may be an attempt to relieve sexual tension denied any other outlet because of neurotic inhibition. However, while there are instances of compulsive masturbation, which is usually the expression of neurotic conflict, as such, it is the symptom rather than the cause of neurosis.

In describing the other consequences of masturbation, this writer has already touched upon the sexual effect, which involves the creation of conditioned reflexes due to repeated masturbation. This conditioning takes place at both the physiological and the psychological levels and leads to habitual masturbation which is actually a form of addiction. Consequently, we can properly speak of the autosexual addict, and classify him as an individual who has become physically and emotionally dependent upon the act so that he is strongly inclined to maintain a certain frequency of performance. Since a person can become addicted to masturbation, this practice is difficult to break and may persist in adult life. Even a penitent who is making serious efforts to lead a life pleasing to God may find that his progress in overcoming this practice is impeded because of his addiction.

STAGES OF MASTURBATION

Many authorities in this area of sexual behavior identify three stages of life during which masturbation occurs, or is likely to occur. The first of these is called the prepubescent or phallic stage. Though masturbation is

[9] Henri Gibert, *Ibid.*, p. 172. However, I do agree with Doctor Gibert when he says that masturbation, "of course, has more or less deep repercussions on the harmony of the married couple, not only in the matter of sex relations, but also from the psychological and spiritual point of view. It will also contribute, in more than just a slight degree, to making more difficult the already delicate task which two human beings face when they want to become adapted to each other." p. 172.

often in evidence in earliest infancy, the age of onset varies, with a peak in the years 4 to 6. Since the phenomenon of infant masturbation is quite common, and, in fact, to be expected, it should be understood that it in no way involves responsible guilt or sin. In fact, the discovery of pleasurable sensations in the genital area must be considered as part of the natural process of growth. This period usually ends in the sixth year, and is followed by a four to six year period of latency during which sexual activity does not occur. The child who is sexually active during this period is usually neurotic.

The second stage begins with the onset of puberty. It is referred to as the pubescent or adolescent stage. From the statistics that were quoted at the beginning of this chapter, it is evident that most youngsters masturbate during this period. Within this second stage, three types or forms of masturbation can be identified. These include 1) non-habitual masturbation, 2) habitual masturbation, and 3) compulsive masturbation.

Between fifteen and twenty percent of all boys pass through their adolescent years and never or seldom masturbate. Those who masturbate only a few times during these years are classified as non-habitual masturbators, and, incidentally, present little difficulty for the confessor in this area. Contrary to what some psychologists would have us believe, those boys who never or seldom masturbate do attain to a healthy maturity.

The second type or form of masturbation includes the very large majority who acquire a habit of masturbation that, even though it may continue anywhere from a few months to four or five years, is of little or no psychopathological significance. The individuals in this grouping resort to masturbation only as a makeshift, "while dwelling in (their minds) upon the ideal of normal intercourse of which self-abuse is an inkling." [10] Though in the case of these individuals self-abuse can be linked to depression, insecurity, a lack of confidence in self, difficulties at school, a lack of affection in the home, inadequate boy-girl relationships, an undue preoccupation with guilt and sin, and even a difficulty in giving sex and love their proper and proportionate place in healthy emotional living, it should not be regarded as indicative of pathology. In fact, these cases fall well within the domain of the confessor and spiritual director.[11]

The third type or form includes only a very small percentage of those who

[10] Henri Gibert, *op. cit.*, p. 177.

[11] On this point, Robert J. Campbell says, "In the treatment of habitual masturbation, you might first consider if it might be only a relatively temporary problem best handled on a counseling level. I think it would be most helpful in the treatment of habitual masturbation to find out what it is the masturbator is expressing. We have discussed masturbation as a form of sexual behavior which appears with great frequency. Such masturbation from the psychological point of view is part and parcel of what seems to be usual development, ..." "Autosexuality: Habitual Masturbation," *op. cit.*, p. 209.

have the problem of masturbation. These are classified as compulsive masturbators, because their actions are the expression of neurotic conflict. However, it should be noted that in these cases, masturbation is the symptom rather than the cause of neurosis. In other words, masturbation may be the presenting symptom or complaint in a variety of mental states—from a very benign to the most malignant forms of mental disorder. Furthermore, as Dr. Gibert points out, there is the possibility that persons in this third group will be "led to intensify the excitation, with the risk of perversions like sadism and masochism, unless he becomes openly narcissistic and derives sexual pleasure from the contemplation of his own body in the state of sexual excitation." [12] Most persons in this group require psychiatric treatment, and great care should be exercised in handling these cases.

The third stage is called post-pubescent or adult masturbation. It includes the twenty percent of the adolescents who carry the practice into adult life. As in the adolescent stage, three types or forms of masturbation can also be isolated. These types are identical to those described in the previous paragraphs, with approximately the same distribution in each of the groupings. Though post-pubescent masturbation is a more serious problem than is pubescent self-abuse, and while there are certainly some psychopathological cases, most instances of adult ipsation should not be regarded as indicative of pathology. In fact, as has already been indicated, most adults continue this practice either because they are using masturbation as a makeshift while dwelling upon the ideal of normal intercourse owing to the fact that they are temporarily or permanently deprived of normal sex relations, or because they have developed a psycho-neurological need pattern (severe habit) which creates an ebb and flow of demand and release quite apart from the voluntary choice and external stimulation.

SOME CAUSES OF PUBESCENT MASTURBATION

Though there is valid evidence for contending that the chief reasons for adolescent masturbation are the two I have already mentioned—the substitution of self-abuse for the ideal of normal intercourse during the time when they are temporarily or permanently deprived of it, and/or the development of a habit of masturbation—there are other causes which can bring on non-habitual or habitual masturbation, which deserve some consideration here. However, before listing them, it seems advisable to say a word or two about the "makeshift" cause stated above, and point out that it has a strong cultural basis as well as a psycho-biological one. For, while the hormonal changes that occur cause the sex urge to become extremely

[12] Henri Gibert, *op. cit.*, p. 177.

powerful during the adolescent years to the extent that the male reaches the peak of sexual potency at about the age of sixteen, our culture does not permit him at this age to consider the possibility of marriage with its normal sexual release, though it bombards him with sex in movies, magazines, TV, dress, and even in various forms of active and passive recreation.

Of the other causes of pubescent masturbation, perhaps the most frequent is just plain curiosity—"What does it feel like?" Furthermore, almost every teen-ager is tremendously influenced by others of the same age and group, and the resulting pressure to be "one of the boys" can be a strong inducement toward masturbation. High on the list also must be "The common helplessness, insecurity, and anxiety felt keenly by many a teen-ager, who must live in the halfway house between childhood and adulthood, which propels him to seek brief comfort and reassurance from masturbation. Other causes stem from the failure of many parents to impart adequate sex education; the partial or complete absence of affectionate interchange and understanding between so many of today's family members; and, clashes of authority between parents and young adults which may lead the individual to substitute masturbation for confident, independent kinds of activity that young people dream of, but are not permitted to try. All of these causes must be considered jointly by the confessor or spiritual director and the adolescent when they are attempting to arrive at a solution to the problem of masturbation." [13]

Pastoral Notes

A few years ago it would not have been necessary to consider the objective morality of ipsation, because at that time no theologian questioned the traditional teaching of the Church that masturbation is objectively a mortal sin since it had traditionally been regarded as a grave violation of the natural law. Traditionally, theologians have taught that for procreation nature requires intercourse, and hence masturbation is unnatural, because it causes semination without copulation, either alone (self-abuse, solitary vice, masturbation), or with another (softness). The late Francis J. Connell, C.SS.R., after explaining that any act of impurity is a grave sin, includes masturbation among the different classes of sins against purity, goes on to explain that, self-abuse, is the inordinate use of the sexual faculty by oneself. Even as contemporary an author as Bernard Häring, C.SS.R., insists that masturbation is an unnatural deviation of the sexual craving to one's own sexual instinct and its complete satisfaction or gratification, and that, every free and deliberate act of masturbation is a grave sin.

[13] Cf. George Hagmaier, C.S.P. and Robert Gleason, S.J., *op. cit.*, pp. 76–80.

However, within the past few years, several authors, including this writer, have begun to question this traditional position. One interesting example of this new line of thinking is the position held by the Most Reverend Francis Simons, Bishop of Indore, India, who contends that while, on the one hand, the traditional position of the Church on ipsation seems to be the right one, and that most would hold that it is gravely illicit freely to obtain venereal pleasure through self-abuse, or to cause it without good reason, since harmful causes would follow, on the other hand, other viewpoints cannot be ignored. Thus, in his opinion, consideration must be given to the views of those outside the Church who seem to hold that masturbation is licit when it is used for the voluntary release of a strong sexual tension that has arisen voluntarily or as the result of some justified activity and which is seen to persist for a longer time and probably will lead to self-release, whether voluntary or involuntary. The Bishop also points out that people who work with youth, among them, psychologists, priests, and educators, believe that more than 90 percent of boys and a large percentage of girls do go through a protracted period of recurring sexual tensions which lead to self release. He is also aware that many youth, even those who hold that masturbation is objectively a grave sin and struggle against it, are often unable to avoid becoming habitual masturbators.

The Bishop of Indore offers three arguments for modifying the Church's traditional teaching on masturbation. However, before considering these arguments, it seems most useful at this point to present Bishop Simons' views on all aspects of sex and sexual morality. In this area, the Bishop writes:

> One field of activity in which traditional views have come under strong and prolonged attacks, and are now rejected by many, is that of sex. Among many Catholics, it must be admitted, in this matter of sex there is a strong psychological block which makes it more than ordinarily difficult to approach questions concerning the use of the genital organs with detachment and objectivity.
>
> If their free and unrestricted use had no consequences for the good of man, the question of morality, I think, would not arise. The pleasure as such, attached to their use, cannot make the morality of the use suspect, rather the contrary. Nature has attached its greatest rewards, also in pleasure and joy, to the acts which are most necessary and valuable, and the joy associated with human love, in the meeting of bodies and minds, is but a faint foretaste of the delights found in the loving meeting of man with God in the beatific vision. The strong pleasure attached to their use does, however, make the danger of their excessive use very great, but in order to be qualified as immoral the excess has to be measured in terms of harm to the individual and to mankind. It is the same as with eating. Pleasure is attached to eating, and according to each person's taste, to the eating of particular dishes; yet eating

for pleasure, eating beyond what the health of the body requires, is not usually considered illicit, unless it goes to the excess of causing harm to the body or of evidently degrading the person who eats to excess. We would all qualify as degrading and illicit the disgusting habit of some wealthy Romans, who ate to excess and induced vomiting to begin again, but I do not think that any serious moral theologians would qualify even this as gravely or "mortally" sinful.

The pleasure attached to the use of the sexual organs is for most people much greater than that connected with eating, and thus the danger of excessive use, of immoderate occupation with sex to the harm of bodily and mental health and of other duties and tasks, is very great. Moreover, the inner structure of the sexual organs is certainly directed towards procreation. And since a child needs, for its protection and healthy upbringing, the love and care of a father and mother, the use of the organs is, in the case of man, by its inner structure directed towards a family life. In this man differs from the animals, even from those who for some time look after their young. There is another difference between man and most animals: in them the sexual organs are liable to activation only at very restricted periods; man is able to activate them almost at will, and thus to use them as a means of expressing and fostering tenderness and love, but also to indulge in them to excess for mere pleasure.

It is the opinion of most human societies, primitive as well as civilized, and it is the traditional view of Christianity, that the danger of the excessive use of sex and its harmful, potentially disruptive consequences for the individual and for society are so grave that all use of sex outside the circle of the family, between husband and wife, is gravely illicit. Most societies have, therefore, erected strong safeguards against sexual relations outside marriage, though more especially to shield women against extra-marital relations. There are good reasons to believe that these societies are right. The latest thorough experiment in favor of the opposite view was tried in Russia after the Communist revolution and was soon abandoned because of the disastrous consequences.

As has already been pointed out, by admitting that the good of humanity is the final criterion of morality, we are not given any easy solution for all our moral problems. Least of all, we do not find it in a basis for a moral minimalism or an encouragement for selfishness. Although man has in the course of history imposed on himself a multitude of laws and taboos to which he was not bound by any moral obligation and which he might rid himself of with a great sense of liberation and frequently with profit—as witnessed by the freedom Christ brought from the many restrictions of the Jewish law, the obligation to seek the common good—or what is the same, to love one's neighbor—is no stimulant or free pass to egoism. The sharpening of our moral sense has already led us to condemn many ancient forms of cruelty, injustice, abuses of power and sex, and to seek out new and better forms of social service. This progress towards a keener awareness of the rights and needs of others and of the demands of the common good, goes on uninterrupted. It is unavoidable, however, that in their legitimate desire to emancipate themselves from ancient taboos and to remain bound only by the real demands of the common good, many should be misled into seeking liberty also from some genuine moral obligations. In choosing, for example, extra-marital sexual relations man seems to set aside a genuine moral law which protects an important common good. Though in many cases such relations may cause some benefit, the permission of promiscuity would, it seems, produce far more harm than good, even to the cause of deeply satisfying human relations.[14]

Turning our attention now to Bishop Simons' arguments favoring a modification of the traditional teaching on masturbation, it is interesting to note that all three of the prelate's arguments seem to be more or less based on the generally admitted psychological normalcy of self-abuse. Concerning the fact, previously mentioned, that more than 90 percent of boys and approximately 50 percent of girls are unable to avoid the problem of masturbation, the Ordinary of Indore insists that, "For one who believes in God it is intolerable to have to think that God made the observance of His law so difficult that a large proportion of young people find it impossible not to fall into grave immoral acts." He then follows up this brief argument by saying that those who are convinced of the cogency of this argument, believe that there must be a flaw in the traditional Catholic view. Though the validity of the Bishop's argument and his conclusion may not be immediately apparent, it is worthy of further consideration, especially in terms of the more recent considerations of theologians concerning the nature of sin—a point that shall be considered later in this chapter.

Still keeping in mind the large number of young people who have difficulty with masturbation, Bishop Simons states that if the criterion of morality is the welfare of mankind, the real question facing the Church and her theologians is: ". . . which is the better, less harmful or more beneficial way of acting—considering the totality of cases in question—voluntarily to release such strong tension, or to continue to fight it and thus prolong it?" [15] The Bishop then answers his own question by stating that there is good reason to believe that the more psychologically healthy solution is voluntarily to release these strong tensions. This reply is based on the bishop's belief that voluntary masturbation under these circumstances enables the individual not only to avoid prolonging the tension for long periods of time, but also to exclude from their minds a morbid preoccupation with sex. The Bishop compares this solution—an early release in those instances when the individual foresees that he faces a lengthy struggle, and that the outcome is doubtful—to marriage, which traditionally, Catholic

[14] Francis Simons, "The Catholic Church and the New Morality," *Cross Currents* (Fall, 1966), pp. 439–441.
[15] *Ibid.*, p. 442.

moralists have regarded as healthy, because, like marriage, it enables the individual to form an excessive preoccupation with sexual matters. In a word, voluntary early release is truly a *remedium concupiscentiae*, "It makes sexual matters less prominent in the mind of the young and so is conducive to a healthy development and a healthy marriage." [16] From what has been said above, it is evident that this argument applies only to those instances where voluntary masturbation is sought for the release of tension, and not for other reasons.

The third argument presented by the Bishop, though not unrelated to the one given above, seems to be based on the importance of the spiritual well-being of the individual. In this argument, the author contends that

> . . . The psychological harm done by a regular prolonged fight and occupation with sexual tensions is immensely heightened for those who believe that a voluntary release is a grave sin. The misery and moral harm inflicted on such youth, the warping of their notion of God, the breaking of their spiritual ardor, are incalculable.[17]

Bishop Francis Simons also parenthetically and briefly debunks an old "argument," when he writes: "(For those who in this matter like to contrast the 'chastity' of animals with the 'beastiality' of man, it may be useful to mention that recent studies, as well as earlier observations, show that some animals practice self release regularly.)" [18]

It is interesting to note that the Bishop's position, as indicated by his first two arguments, is based on the principle: the good of man is the criterion and basis of morality, rather than on the traditional principle which makes any act of impurity a violation of the common good of mankind, a sin against social justice (at least).

Contrary to the teaching of the Church, most protestant theologians do not regard masturbation as sinful, at least under certain circumstances. Thus, the theologian Helmut Thielicke, when considering homologous insemination, teaches that:

> . . . In homologous insemination, however, this objection (that the masturbation which the operation necessitates is contrary to Christian moral law), is hardly valid, since it is based upon a theologically untenable doctrine of works. For Reformation thinking, at any rate, the worth or unworth of a "work" depends not upon its isolated form as such, but rather upon the state in which the person is with respect to God, and also the intention or purpose he is pursuing in this work or act.[19]

[16] *Ibid.*, p. 442.
[17] *Ibid.*, p. 442.
[18] *Ibid.*, p. 442.
[19] Helmut Thielicke, *The Ethics of Sex* (New York: Harper and Row, 1964), p. 255.

Though Dr. Thielicke certainly allows masturbation to obtain semen from the husband for the purpose of artificial insemination, it is evident that he does not allow this practice for any other reason. On this point he writes:

> . . . Masturbation is as a rule regarded as offensive for the following reasons. First and above all because in masturbation sex is separated from the I-Thou relationship and thus loses its meaning as being the expression and consummation of this fellowship. Second, because the sexual phantasy is no longer bound to a real partnership and therefore roves about vagrantly. Third, because as a rule the absence of this bond leads to physical and psychic extravagance. The ethically decisive thing is therefore not the offensiveness of the physical function as such—in this area the criteria of taste, hygiene, etc. are involved rather than theological criteria—but rather the personal situation that underlies the masturbation, the being turned in upon himself (*incurvitas in se*). All acts which are centered not upon God and my neighbor but upon my own self are actualizations of sin.[20]

The Reverend J. Kenneth Morris, a Director and Counselor at the Marriage Counseling Service of the Diocese of Upper South Carolina of the Protestant Episcopal Church, when discussing the morality of masturbation, argues in a manner similar to that of Bishop Simons, for he writes that:

> This is a sexual outlet on which Christian ethics is divided. However, we have learned through our research in sex knowledge, both on the infrahuman and human levels, that masturbation is too universally practiced to be considered a moral problem per se; rather, it is an attempt to satisfy sexual needs, just as eating or exercise are expressions of other physical needs. We know that masturbation, which is a deliberate external manipulation or frictional stimulation of the sex organs, is enjoyed by infants and small children before they are able to appreciate the right or wrong of it as experienced emotionally by adults. May not masturbation be one way by which nature calls attention to and emphasizes the importance of sex? Medical studies show no physical ill effects from masturbation. However, it does sometimes accompany feelings of self-pity and association with unwholesome fantasies that are mentally unsatisfactory. Also, since masturbation in marriage deprives oneself and one's spouse of the expression of sex through the mutual experience of coitus, it therefore becomes a selfish act.[21]

Without doubt, the argument that the very universality of the practice of masturbation makes it difficult to consider it as a moral problem *per se*, especially for those who practice it merely as a means of satisfying sexual needs and when it is not accompanied by feelings of self-pity and/or by

---

[20] *Ibid.*, p. 256.
[21] J. Kenneth Morris, *Marriage Counseling*, (Englewood Cliffs, N.J.: Prentice Hall, 1965), p. 178.

mentally unsatisfactory fantasies has some persuasive power. However, it would seem that any theologian inclined to show that masturbation is not a moral problem when used merely as a *remedium concupiscentiae* with moderation and when there are no psychological implications, should look for more basic and compelling principles on which to base such a conclusion. Such a theologian might well argue from the Church's traditional teaching regarding the definition of sin and its distinctions.

Sin is defined as AN OFFENSE AGAINST THE LAW OF GOD BY A PERSON'S OWN DELIBERATE ACT. The key words in this definition are, of course, the "law of God," and this brings up two questions: what is the law of God? and, is masturbation really opposed to the law of God? The law of God includes both the natural law and divine positive law (the ten commandments, except the third, are not positive-divine legislation in the strict sense, because they are merely expressions of the natural law). Therefore, the law of God as concerns matters of impurity is the natural law. However, the natural law, which is defined as that portion of the eternal law which governs human beings, has as its proximate foundation human nature considered in its entirety. In other words, the fundamental norm of morality is human nature itself. Thus, a human act is morally right and good if it is in conformity with man's nature considered in itself and in all of its relations.

Since masturbation does not cause serious or permanent physical, psychological or moral harm to a very large majority of those who practice it even habitually, and since, especially in the case of the unmarried, it does not seriously (or even slightly, for that matter), harm the common good— most persons, even those who practice self-abuse habitually for a considerable period of time, eventually marry and become parents—it is most difficult to see how this practice can *per se* be included among the list of grave sins.

What we are saying here, in effect, is that even habitual masturbation, when practiced with full advertance by the unmarried to achieve the only kind of sexual fulfillment available to him, is not a violation of the law of God because it is not injurious to or in disagreement with human nature with its inherent characteristics and propensities, that is to the individual or to society.

Ignace Lepp seems to support this point of view, for he writes that:

> The adolescent who must gather together all of his energies to become fully himself, is generally turned in on himself and little open to others. His sexual instincts take a narcissistic form: he himself is the object of his libido. Masturbation, the sign par excellence of autoeroticism, might be considered, at least statistically, as normal for the adolescent. Moralists of former times

were too ready to link it with moral turpitude, with sin. But this attitude can transform autoeroticism, in itself a simple biopsychic phenomenon, into a vice. Today we have happily become much more enlightened on this point for few priests or educators are as set against the "solitary vice" as they at one time were. We are quite sure that this development will have happy effects on the moral plane.

Normally, at about fifteen or sixteen years of age, the sex impulse begins to direct itself toward others, toward a person of the opposite sex, and to become integrated with love. By virtue of this the young man and the young woman gradually emerge from their narcissistic "shell," become open by the intermediary of the object of their love to people in general, to the world and to the concrete life as it is lived about them (while as adolescents they lived in a largely imaginary world), and become capable of disinterest and true generosity. The love of one person is like an apprenticeship to universal love. St. John already warned us about pretending to love the whole universe without loving our neighbor. Such love of humanity is abstract, without warmth, and frequently goes hand in hand with real cruelty toward others as we observe in the life of a Robespierre and other seekers after an ideal "purity." [22]

A similar argument can be constructed from the position held by St. Thomas that sin is either an offense against God, oneself, or one's neighbor —"For it is evident from what has been said that by the theological virtues man is directed to God; by temperance and fortitude, to himself; and by justice to his neighbor." Thus, only those acts are sinful which are either against God—heresy, despair, blasphemy, or against oneself—intemperance, suicide, or against one's neighbor—theft, calumny. Now, it is quite evident that self-abuse is not directly against God, since it does not involve matters of faith or things due to God alone. Furthermore, it's not against oneself in the large majority of cases not only because the physical and mental consequences are of minor importance, but also because it rarely leads to a moral and/or psychological crisis. (Henri Gibert, M.D., observes that: "It is nonetheless true that the state of change in an adolescent's sexual instinct, his ignorance concerning woman, and his misconceptions about the realities of human sex all tend to make pubertal masturbation practically so unavoidable, except for pathological cases of sexual disinterest, that it must appear to be biologically normal and the object of neither amazement nor fear, despite its frequency.")[23] Finally, masturbation for the large majority of persons, and when it is clearly a "solitary act," is not against one's neighbor except in those rare instances when a person enters "the marriage state handicapped with a long-established and sometimes persisting habit of masturbation . . . (which has) deep repercussions on the

[22] Ignace Lepp, *The Authentic Morality*, (New York: The Macmillan Company, 1965), pp. 180–181.
[23] Henri Gibert, M.D., *op. cit.*, p. 165.

harmony of the married couple, not only in the matter of sex relations, but also from the psychological and spiritual point of view . . . (or when it also contributes) in more than just a slight degree, to making more difficult the already difficult task which two human beings face when they want to become adapted to each other." [24]

> Autoeroticism, whether or not it manifests itself in masturbation, begins to be a moral problem when it goes beyond adolescence. It then stops up the release of emotional energies, inhibits the natural generosity of man, and renders the subject inept for love of an individual person, for humanity, and the common good. Every time I meet a markedly egocentric person I suspect him of being autoerotic; in those cases I have been able to verify I have never yet been wrong.
> Thus the "new morality" also considers autoeroticism an evil, but not because it turns the seed, supposedly so precious, away from its "normal end" but because it prevents the blossoming of that generosity and love without which man cannot be authentically moral. Moreover, the narcissistic fixation is often the cause of serious psychic troubles.[25]

Theologians argue that ipsation is an intemperate act because it is an inordinate use of the sexual functions (by oneself) in as much as this act seriously interferes with the principal purpose of the sexual function, which, according to the law of God, is the procreation of children so that the human race will be preserved and propagated. However, if it is true on the one hand that as many as 85 to 92 percent of all boys and nearly 50 percent of all girls practice masturbation, and, on the other hand, that most of these marry and raise families, it is extremely difficult to see how, for the very large majority of cases, even those who continue to masturbate throughout the course of their married life actually interfere with the primary function of the sexual faculty.

Pleasure is the general term for an agreeable feeling of satisfaction, ranging from a quiet sense of gratification to a positive sense of happiness. Enjoyment—getting pleasure from—is a synonym. Theologians, who divide pleasure or enjoyment not only into that which is absolutely necessary, but also pleasure without which man cannot live conveniently, teach that pleasure of itself is not opposed to the law of God, and therefore, a person is entitled to a reasonable amount of enjoyment or pleasure in his life. Furthermore, these same theologians explain that pleasure in some activity can be regarded as a morally good act when the activity is not forbidden by any law. This is true, they say, even when the pleasure is not necessary under either of the aspects mentioned above, that is, neither for the *esse*

[24] *Ibid.*, p. 168.
[25] *Ibid.*, p. 169.

nor for the *bene esse* when done with moderation as regards time, place, occasion, and suitability to environment. In other words, if the pleasure is used in moderation, and if the object and circumstances of the pleasure are rational, the pleasure itself is rational.

When theologians speak of "moderation" in regard to pleasurable activity, they are referring to the rule which temperance imposes on the carnal appetites: "Indulge only as necessity requires and duty allows." However, since pleasure is a means whose end is some reasonable need of life, the term "necessity" can be understood quite broadly, so as to include not only the essentials but even the conveniences of life.

While the pleasure of masturbation cannot be included among the higher sensible pleasures such as the enjoyment derived from beautiful scenery or classical music, or even among the joys of physical well-being such as the refreshment of sleep or the relaxation of exercise—though it frequently produces similar psychological and physical effects—because it is a much stronger pleasure than these and can lead to excess, nevertheless, the pleasure as such that is attached to ipsation does not determine its morality. Rather, the morality of even a carnal act such as ipsation is determined by the harm that is done to the individual and to mankind. On this point, Bishop Simons observes that "pleasure is attached to eating, and according to each person's taste, to the eating of particular dishes; yet eating for pleasure, eating beyond what the health of the body requires, is not usually considered illicit, unless it goes to the excess of causing harm to the body or of evidently degrading the person who eats to excess. Why can't the same be said of the moderate use of masturbation which for the large majority of cases does no more harm to the individual or to society than does the moderate use of gourmet foods or intoxicating beverages?" [26]

Since more and more confessors, counselors, and theologians are having second thoughts about the traditional Christian teaching regarding non-compulsive masturbation, especially on the part of adolescents, but, under certain conditions, even for both unmarried and married adults, because they see the cogency of the arguments presented above, and find it difficult to prove that masturbation is objectively a mortal sin by arguments from reason alone, it seems advisable at this time to suggest that the Church and her theologians restudy the question in much the same way that she and her moralists, as well as others competent to study the question, are now doing with regard to birth control.

Father Charles E. Curran, a member of the Faculty of the School of Sacred Theology at The Catholic University of America argues that the act of masturbation does not always involve grave matter, that is that mastur-

[26] Francis Simons, *op. cit.*, p. 439.

bation is not an action which is *ex toto genere suo* grave. In presenting his arguments, he considers sin in the Theory of the Fundamental Option, and asks the question: "Does the act of masturbation so involve the core of the person, that man generally makes a fundamental option with regard to it?" Father Curran then answers his question by stating that empirical evidence clearly shows that "masturbation, especially among adolescents, does not involve a fundamental option. Since masturbatory activity is symptomatic, it can have many different meanings. The ambiguous nature of masturbation argues against the theory that masturbation always involves grave matter. It would seem impossible to conclude, even as a presumption, that every masturbatory act as such involves a fundamental option." [27]

In response to a most precise question, namely, "Does the single act of masturbation constitute a substantial inversion of a very important order of nature?" Father Curran offers five reasons that seem to indicate that a single masturbatory action does not constitute an inversion of a very important order.

(1) Older theologians have had too narrow and unilateral an understanding of masturbatory activity. From a purely biological and physiological viewpoint, masturbation may constitute a substantial inversion of sexual actuation. However, a total human consideration embraces much more than the mere biological emission of semen. The psychological understanding of masturbation does not seem to warrant the severity with which moral theologians speak about masturbation. Masturbation as a total human action does not seem that important or serious.

(2) Consideration of the gravity of masturbation has again been too narrow and unilateral in concentrating almost exclusively on the relationship of sexuality with procreation. Sexuality must also be considered in relationship to other persons and to the individual himself. Masturbation might indicate a narcissistic behavior pattern, a period of temporary stress, or a developing stage of adolescent sexuality. Since masturbation is a complex human reality involving a multiplicity of relationships, the moralist distorts reality by considering masturbation solely in terms of procreation.

(3) Inadequate physiological knowledge merely heightened the unilateral emphasis on the procreational and biological aspects. Since science thought that semen was the primary and only active agent in procreation, the arguments against masturbation stressed the teleology of the semen. Only in the last century did theologians begin to realize a consideration based on the teleology of the semen was too unilateral because it did not explain the reality of female masturbation. However, a disordinate stress on the teleology of semen has contributed to a misjudgment about the seriousness of masturbation.

(4) It does not seem that a single masturbatory action can constitute a substantial inversion of an order of very great importance. Perhaps in the

[27] Charles E. Curran, "Masturbation and Objectively Grave Matter: An Exploratory Discussion, "*Proceedings of the Twenty-First Annual Convention*, (June, 1966), p. 101.

past theologians have illegitimately transferred to the individual act the importance that belongs to the sexual faculty. I am not saying that individual actions are never important; but in the total consideration of masturbation, individual actions do not always constitute a substantial inversion of human sexuality.

(5) Most contemporary theologians and educators recognize that in the past there was an overemphasis on sexual sins. The overly spiritual heresies from Gnosticism to Jansenism have warped our understanding of human sexuality. The inadequate and distorted notions of the past have contributed to the importance and gravity attached to individual masturbatory actions. A word of caution, however, is in order. Today, when many are espousing the "Playboy philosophy," Catholic teaching must uphold the dignity and importance of human sexuality. However, Catholic teaching must avoid the temptation of overreacting to laxist, and ultimately inhuman, notions of sexuality.[28]

It seems quite certain that the doctrine that masturbation is objectively a mortal sin has never been authentically proclaimed explicitly and with the greatest solemnity by the Sovereign Pontiff. Nevertheless, most theologians hold that the Church is so completely committed to the moral teaching that masturbation is intrinsically and gravely immoral that she cannot make a substantial change in her teaching on this point. Those theologians who are convinced that the traditional doctrine regarding masturbation is taught infallibly *ex iugi magisterio,* point out that not only does Holy Scripture condemn ipsation as a sin which excludes a person from the Kingdom of Heaven, but that the Church regards it as the execution of a generative act implying the frustration of its primary purpose, the procreation of children, and therefore opposed to a very great social good; an act of lust against nature. Furthermore, this position, according to most theologians, is expressed by several decrees issued by ecclesiastical authorities. The first of these was issued by Alexander VII on September 24, 1665, and along with various other moral errors condemned the proposition: "Voluptuousness, sodomy, and beastiality are sins of the same species, and so it is enough to say in confession that one has procured a pollution" (D.B., 1124). A second decree issued on March 4, 1697, by the Holy Office, during the reign of Innocent XI, condemned the proposition that: "Voluptuousness is not prohibited by the law of nature. Therefore, if God had not forbidden it, it would be good, and sometimes obligatory under pain of mortal sin" (D.B., 1199). Two other decrees issued in more recent times by the Holy Office on March 24, 1890, and August 2, 1929, state that pollution artificially provoked either for artificial insemination or for laboratory testing is unlawful; "Whether masturbation procured directly is permitted to

[28] *Ibid.,* pp. 105–106.

obtain sperm by which a contagious disease blenorragia (gonorrhea) may be detected and in so far as it can be done, cured. Reply: In the negative" (D.B., 2201).

However, turning to more practical matters now, it seems appropriate to say a few words about the subjective morality of masturbation. Certainly there are often circumstances which diminish imputability to the point where an individual is not guilty of serious sin, or which destroy it altogether so that the individual is not guilty of any sin at all. On the other hand, it is impossible to justify that extreme position which urges the confessor or spiritual director to make sweeping presumptions of non-responsibility in almost every case of teen-age or adult masturbation. So, to guard against just such an extreme position, it seems important to point up the following three considerations: 1) Catholic teaching and practice take it for granted that normal individuals are capable of committing mortal sin; 2) Catholic tradition takes it for granted that mortal sins frequently take place in the world; and, 3) the Catholic doctrine of grace.[29] In other words, on the question of imputability, I choose to follow a middle course; one that avoids both extremes.

Though there is no procedure for determining imputability in an individual case that will give the confessor or spiritual director absolute certitude in the matter, there are some guide lines that can be helpful in this matter. However, before developing these points, it should be noted that considerable harm is done by those pastors and confessors who "take personal offense" when masturbation is discussed or confessed, or who berate a youngster and give him to understand that he or she is a "bad boy," or a "bad girl," or perhaps, even a juvenile delinquent, or sex deviate. Furthermore, considerable harm is also done by those who refuse to admit that masturbation is psychologically normal during adolescence, and consequently are inclined to regard every case of masturbation as pathognomonic of severe psychiatric or emotional disorder.

There is also good reason to be extremely impatient with those who continually turn first to psychology and psychiatry rather than to biology and sociology to find the basic causes of pubescent masturbation. They seem to forget that at the age of puberty a youngster undergoes a rather extensive biological upheaval induced by massive hormonal changes with the result that the sex urge becomes extremely powerful during the adolescent years. In view of these biological facts, is it any wonder that an adolescent seeks sexual release through masturbation? Consequently, it is difficult to understand how society can, on the one hand bombard young people with sex

[29] John C. Ford, S.J. "Auto Sexuality: Moral Aspects," *Personality and Sexual Problems, op. cit.,* p. 217.

symbols and sex stimuli in almost every media of communication and in so many forms of recreation, and then on the other hand ignore the obvious reasons for masturbation in favor of some more exotic ones.

Returning to the problem of determining imputability in an individual case, it should first be pointed out that a confessor, spiritual director, or pastoral counselor cannot possibly form a prudent judgment concerning the state of a penitent's soul unless he takes the time and makes an effort to do so. Since a priest frequently does not have sufficient time in the confessional, many of these cases of self-abuse can be dealt with much more effectively by the spiritual counselor outside the confessional. However, when the confessor, spiritual director, or counselor does endeavor to determine imputability, he must rely principally on the conscious data supplied by the penitent himself. But, even here there is need for caution, for many penitents are ignorant or confused and thus are poor witnesses of their own inner experiences. Nevertheless, the conscious data supplied by a penitent with "an enlightened conscience" are extremely valuable.

Besides the information supplied by the penitent, two questions, "Did you realize fully it was a grave sin?" and "Could you have resisted?" can be very useful to the confessor. It should be noted, however, that affirmative answers do not indicate conclusively that mortal sin has taken place. On the other hand, intelligent negative answers can indicate clearly that mortal sin has not taken place.

Furthermore, the following criteria can be very helpful in enabling the confessor or spiritual guide to arrive at a prudent judgment, and when one of them is certainly present it should lead the confessor to judge leniently the question of guilt in individual cases. This is even more true when several of these criteria are present together, for there is even more reason for assuming that there is no grave culpability. These points are:

1. Is there a history of mental or emotional illness, nervous breakdown, etc.; is the penitent presently under psychiatric or neurological care?
2. Does the penitent have a severe habit, i.e., one of long duration and inveterate frequency, but which he is seriously trying to overcome?
3. Did the penitent resist and refuse consent up to the point where passion is very intense, or orgasm is almost at hand? Sexual passion can be overpowering when thoroughly aroused.
4. Was psychological liberty reduced by the fact that there occurred on the part of the penitent a "fascinated narrowing of consciousness to one all-absorbing object of desire, to the extent that it excluded any realistic appraisal of the alternatives to that desire?" In other words, was the penitent capable of sufficient reflection and full consent of the will?
5. Was there a sudden onslaught of passion that caught the penitent

unawares and thus eliminated the opportunity for sufficient deliberation?

6. "The indulgence of fantastic ideas during the struggle with temptation . . . and similar confabulations or irrational defenses show that a person is not himself and are arguments against grave culpability."

7. "Senseless, unsatisfying, frequent repetitions of the act of self-abuse within a short time are a sign of pathological impulse and an indication of greatly reduced responsibility."

8. "If a penitent is making serious efforts to lead a life pleasing to God; if he is sincerely trying to overcome this habit and avoid the individual acts; if he avoids the occasions that are avoidable, frequents the sacraments and is consistent in prayer; and especially if on the individual occasions when temptation comes he does not yield except after a long struggle or a hard one—the confessor should be lenient in judging the case." [30]

Once the confessor or spiritual director has made a prudent judgment concerning the imputability of an individual penitent he should then help the penitent to know the true state of his soul. In a spirit of kindness— there is never an excuse for unkindness, impatience or lack of understanding either in the confessional or the counseling situation—the confessor should then tell the penitent the truth as he sees it with appropriate advice and encouragement. If the priest is convinced that the penitent has committed mortal sin, he should tell him so, kindly, and in accordance with the usual pastoral way for dealing with sinners. If, on the other hand, the confessor judges that mortal sin has not been committed, he should also tell the penitent. However, he must be careful not to lull the penitent to think that because the acts already performed were not gravely guilty, this automatically absolves him from all responsibility for them. It would be worse to allow him to think that he has no responsibility for the future, or leave him with the idea that he is the helpless victim of his own passions, with neither the obligation nor the ability to do anything about his habit. On this very point, Rupert Angemair says,

> Above all the priest must not forget that, even if the subjective character of particular cases can be judged mildly, the attitude of the onanist (masturbator) in general must be looked upon as highly regrettable. For this reason the priest must never regard his task as finished when he has passed judgment upon the sins of the past; he is the shepherd of souls and his function as judge must be supplemented by giving responsible aid for the future.[31]

[30] John C. Ford, S.J. and Gerald Kelly, S.J., *Contemporary Moral Theology*, (Westminster, Maryland: The Newman Press, 1958) pp. 240–242.

[31] Rupert Angemair, "Moral and Theological Notes on the Problems of Self-Abuse," (Appendix) Gagern, Frederick von, *The Problem of Onanism*, Translated by Meyrick Booth. (Westminster, Maryland: The Newman Press, 1955) pp. 116–117.

Even if the priest is doubtful about grave guilt, he should tell the penitent, for this will be very helpful and encouraging to a penitent who has been sincerely trying to avoid this practice. And, as Father John C. Ford, S.J. observes,

> . . . Furthermore, it will keep him trying, when a lapse occurs in the future. Too often these penitents, after failing once, conclude that they have already sinned mortally when this point is actually doubtful. They then give up, say: "What's the use?," and make no effort to avoid further falls before the next confession. Telling them the truth as far as it can be discovered will be the best spur to continued resistance against temptation, besides being the best basis for collaboration in eradicating the habit.[32]

A Plan for Eradicating The Habit of Masturbation

Since there is a great similarity between the psychological and physiological need for self-stimulation in the person who has a habit of masturbation and the psychological and physiological need in the alcoholic, many of the principles and techniques that are used by Alcoholics Anonymous can, with some modification, be employed by the person with the problem of self-abuse. The following suggested twelve steps to overcome the habit of masturbation have been taken in principle from the suggested twelve steps to recovery used by A.A. These steps are:

1. Admit that you are weak willed in matters of impurity—especially masturbation—that your life has been complicated by this sin.
2. Believe that God can give you the grace to overcome this habit of sin.
3. Make a decision to turn your will and your life over to the care of God.
4. Make a fearless and searching examination of conscience.
5. Admit to yourself and to God in the confessional (Go to confession weekly.) the exact nature of your wrong-doing.
6. Be entirely ready to cooperate with the grace of God to remove not only this problem, but all of your defects of character.
7. Humbly pray and ask Him to remove your faults and short comings.
8. Make a list of all the persons, places, and things that tempt you to commit this sin, and be willing to avoid them from now on.
9. Do avoid all persons, places, and things that tempt you to commit this sin, except when to do so would be a violation of the virtues of justice or charity.
10. Continue to examine your conscience daily, and when you see that

[32] John C. Ford, S.J., and Gerald Kelly, S.J., *op. cit.*, p. 244. Also, Cf. pp. 243–245.

you are not making progress or are slipping backward, admit it and do something about it.

11. Strive through prayer and meditation to draw closer to God, praying only for knowledge of His Will for yourself, and for the power to carry it out.

12. Having become more aware of the presence of God as a result of these steps, go to Mass and receive the sacraments frequently, and try to help other teenagers observe the virtues of modesty and purity by being cautious in the things that you say and do, and in the way you dress.

The person who has a serious problem with self-abuse, like the person who has a serious problem with alcohol, must often live "just for today."

Just for today he must try to live through this day only, and not tackle his whole life problem at once. "I can do something for 24 hours that would appal me if I felt that I had to keep it up for a lifetime."

Just for today he must be happy. (Never become discouraged or give up.) This assumes to be true what Abraham Lincoln said: "Most folks are as happy as they make up their minds to be."

Just for today he must try to strengthen his mind and will. When at school he must study hard and not be a mental loafer and day dreamer. Before retiring every night he should read something of interest that requires effort, thought, and concentration.

Just for today he should exercise his will in two ways: he should do two things he doesn't want to do—just for the exercise of his will.

Just for today he should have a definite program. He may not be able to follow it exactly, but he should have it, and it should not leave time for him to be alone where he can easily fall into temptation.

Just for today he should be unafraid. Especially, he should not be afraid to enjoy what is beautiful, and to believe that as he gives to God and to his fellow men, so God and his fellow men will give to him.

Just for today he should set some time aside to pray and to meditate, so that he can try to get a better perspective of his own life. He should say three Hail Mary's for the virtue of purity.[33]

CONCLUSION

This chapter attempts to point out that while unfortunately masturbation during puberty and even in adulthood is a very frequent phenomenon, it should not be the object of amazement and fear, either for the confessor

---

[33] These suggestions for eradicating the habit of masturbation have been adopted from literature published by Alcoholics Anonymous

or the penitent, nor should it ordinarily be regarded as indicative of pathology. Furthermore, while it cannot be denied that there exists, even in the normal, healthy, adolescent, unstable psychological, as well as physiological conditions, the physiological (and even the sociological) conditions should be stressed rather than the psychological ones. Again, while it is understood that the whole personality is involved, it is difficult to conclude, as some few authors do, that masturbation is a symbol of defeat and helplessness in either the adolescent or the adult in most instances, nor is it a regression of personality back to the stage of infancy.

Again, while it is true that there exists a variety of causes, including that of helplessness, insecurity, and anxiety felt keenly by many young people, it would seem that most adolescents take up this practice and continue in it either because they simply enjoy the pleasure of sex in much the same way that most people enjoy the pleasures of eating, and are seeking a substitute for normal sexual intercourse, the highest form of that pleasure, or they have developed a severe habit, the result of physiological and psychological conditioning.

Though it is impossible to reject the proposition that each and every act of masturbation is objectively a grave sin, it is reasonable to maintain, as do many other authors, that there are often instances when the penitent is not fully responsible for his actions and consequently imputability can diminish to the point where an individual is not guilty of serious sin. On the question of determining imputability, every confessor and spiritual director should be cautioned to follow the guidelines established by the Church and her reputable theologians.

Finally, with the exception of the compulsive masturbator who usually needs psychiatric help, there is good reason to believe that most sincere penitents will respond to the kindly guidance of an informed, interested, and above all prudent confessor or spiritual director.

BIBLIOGRAPHY

Angemair, R., "Moral and Theological Notes on the Problem of Self-abuse," Appendix to Von Gagern, F., *The Problem of Onanism*. Westminster, Md., 1955.

Bier, William C., S.J., *Personality and Sexual Problems*. New York: Fordham Univ. Press, 1964.

Curran, Charles E., "Masturbation and Objectively Grave Matter: An Exploratory Discussion," *Proceedings of the Twenty-First Annual Convention of the Catholic Theological Society of America*. June, 1966.

Fleckenstein, H., "The Moral and Religious Guilt of the Act of Self-abuse." Appendix to Von Gagern, F. *Op. cit.*

Ford, John C., S.J. and Kelly, Gerald, S.J., *Contemporary Moral Problems*, Vol. I. Westminster, Md.: Newman, 1958.

Gibert, Henri, M.D., *Love in Marriage*. New York: Hawthorn Books Inc., 1964.

Lepp, Ignace, *The Authentic Morality*. New York: The Macmillan Company, 1965.

Morris, J. Kenneth, *Marriage Counseling*. Englewood Cliffs, N.J.: Prentice Hall, 1965.

Simons, Francis, "The Catholic Church and the New Morality," *Cross Currents*. (Fall, 1966) pp. 439–441.

Snoeck, A., S.J., "Masturbation and Grave Sin," In Flood, P., O.S.B. ed. *New Problems in Medical Ethics*, Vol. I. Westminster, Md., Newman, 1953.

Von Gagern, F., *The Problem of Onanism*. Westminster, Md., Newman, 1955.

6

SOME PASTORAL REFLECTIONS
ON HOMOSEXUALITY

Rev. John Harvey, O.S.F.S.

THE PURPOSE of this article is to develop various insights concerning the problem of homosexuality gained through study and counseling, and to investigate more thoroughly certain aspects of this problem in the light of recent developments.[1] I shall approach the subject from a practical and pastoral point of view, keeping in mind not only priests, but also all those professional men and women who struggle with the problem on many different levels. Time spent conducting workshops in this area has encouraged me to present the viewpoints contained in this article. I shall assume that my readers already know the general nature of homosexuality, but, like myself, are searching for deeper understanding as a necessary preliminary to effective pastoral practice.

CAUSES OF HOMOSEXUALITY

While the causes of homosexuality need scientific study, recent thought tends to focus attention more on the father than the mother in the development of the male homosexual, and on the mother rather than the

---

[1] (Editor's note) Father John Harvey, O.S.F.S., has written extensively on this topic. Some years ago he wrote an article for *Theological Studies* treating the pastoral aspects of homosexuality. This article, which appeared in the March, 1955 issue, is entitled: "The Pastoral Problem of Homosexuality." Other contributions by the author are included in the bibliography.

father in the growth of the female homosexual.[2] Homosexual boys usually have mothers who are too possessive and fathers who are detached and unconcerned. Homosexual girls usually have critical mothers who belittle their daughters' femininity, and fathers who tend to allow their wives to domineer. In the development of both male and female homosexuals it is significant that one finds a weak father figure, indeed in many cases a neglectful and alcoholic character.

It seems, moreover, that in the analysis of the multiple contributing factors to homosexuality sufficient attention has not been given to what may be called the "learning experience," that is to say, some form of seduction coming in childhood or early adolescence, which precipitates the person into seeking the same pleasure again. The initiating factor may be fear of the opposite sex or lack of opportunity to contact them. Of course, in the broader sense of the word, the future homosexual has "learned" from his early childhood attitudes toward the opposite sex which become the seed ground of adolescent seduction. This is not to say that very early attitudes formed toward both parents make adolescent seduction inevitable, but they certainly predispose the youngster to gravitate toward his own sex and away from the opposite. In this movement toward deviation personal frustrations of a non-sexual character play a large role. Deprivation of normal family life remains a key factor in the development of homosexuality.

In a recent study of female homosexuality Dr. Wilbur stresses fear of the opposite sex, heightened by frequent parental warnings concerning heterosexual contact, as a significant predispositive cause.[3] A similar fear is found in many male homosexuals. In the male, however, the fear may assume the disguise of idolization of woman as something clean, immaculate, and unreachable, whereas in the female fear assumes the images of castration, of pregnancy, of venereal disease, of penetration and injury. Sometimes in females early heterosexual trauma (rape) are found. Finally, in both sexes present evidence suggests that homosexuality is the result of psychodynamic factors rather than physiological ones.[4]

FEMALE HOMOSEXUALITY

The incidence of female homosexuality remains unknown for a number

[2] Landis, Paul H., *Social Problems in Nation and World* (Chicago: J. B. Lippincott Co., 1959), 236–237; Wilbur, Cornelia B., *Sexual Inversion: The Multiple Roots of Homosexuality*, "Clinical *Aspects of Female Homosexuality*," Judd Marmor, ed., (New York: Basic Books Inc., 1965), 269–272; Bieber, Irving, "What You Should Know About Homosexuality," *Parents' Magazine*, 41: May, 1966, 62, ff.

[3] *Op. cit.*, 278–280.

[4] *Op. cit.*, 273–280; also Bieber, Irving, et alii, *Homosexuality*, Basic Books, 1962, N.Y., N.Y. (study of causality).

of obvious reasons, particularly the attitude of society which allows two women to live together without suspicion but immediately suspects two men in similar circumstances. As already indicated, the causes of female homosexuality are similar to those of male homosexuality. In some instances, however, one notes among Lesbians a kind of contempt for men, as if men were incapable of any deep tenderness or affection, as if the only purpose of women as far as men are concerned was to give them sexual satisfaction. Heterosexual women, it is true, express the same sentiments, but either they do not marry or they remain in marriage for the sake of the children although all attraction for the husbands has disappeared. It is not unknown in pastoral practice that married women lapse temporarily into a homosexual relationship because of such contempt for their husbands.

There are many different kinds of female homosexuals, ranging from the feminine type to the very aggressive type, called dykes. The tomboy adolescent girl is not to be confused with the mature, masculine woman. The dyke assumes the role of the man in relationships, while the feminine homosexual assumes the role of the female. But in many Lesbian relationships the roles are interchangeable, and usually expressed in mutual masturbation. Many feminine homosexuals are prostitutes, a fact interpreted by some psychiatrists as evidence of their contempt for men, to whom they give no personal response. The fact that a feminine homosexual can submit to intercourse makes it possible for her to continue her marriage more easily than a married male homosexual. But were a woman to realize before marriage that she is homosexual, she should not marry because she will not be able to respond to her husband.

Besides providing sexual release the homosexual relationship seems to serve a variety of irrational defenses. Between the two females there is often extreme jealousy, and the discovery of infidelity on the part of the other may disrupt the relationship. Besides jealousy, there is hostility, verbal arguments, and sometimes physical fighting. Both partners often lack insight into the reason for their relationship, and their ambivalence is a sign of the relative instability of their relationships. No doubt, there are exceptional cases, but much in homosexual relationships is destructive.

As in the male homosexual, so also in the female, there is guilt over masturbation, indeed, it seems more guilt over masturbation than over homosexual acts. A female homosexual who is struggling to free herself from overt practices will often suffer the torment of phantasy and will take refuge in drink. In this seemingly hopeless situation she will be tempted to suicide and will succumb to the temptation unless someone can reach her and give her some kind of support.

One of the ironies in the development of the female homosexual is the attitude of her parents. Lack of sexual education and frequent warnings about heterosexual dangers during the adolescent period are meant to keep the teenager from sexual harm, but often lead to the opposite. But parents must also communicate something else to the future homosexual, because many girls who received the same warnings and suffered from the same lack of sex education turn out very normal. We can only guess concerning the ways in which parents can contribute to the formation of a homosexual attitude in their daughters; but one thing seems clear to the writer, namely, that homes in which there is good order, in which the child finds a positive paternal image, and warm but not possessive love from the mother, usually do not produce homosexuals, *male or female*.

In general, female homosexuals do not persevere in psychiatric treatment, mainly because the same pressures are not upon them to change as are exerted upon the male homosexual. A woman can maintain a homosexual relationship in relative anonymity.[5] On the other hand, she can manage a life of complete chastity more easily than the male homosexual once she makes up her mind to dedicate herself to some work of service to God and to society. She can avoid the occasions of sin more easily; and she will not have to answer questions concerning her non-married status, to which inquiry the virtuous male homosexual is constantly subjected.

THE MORALITY OF HOMOSEXUAL ACTS

It used to be taken for granted that sexual activity among humans always possessed a procreative orientation, but in recent years even in Catholic writings attempts have been made to separate the procreative purpose of sexual intercourse from its meaning as an expression of love between man and wife. Others have gone further and asserted that intercourse between lovers who could not yet get married could be both contraceptive and licit. It was not long before the next logical step was taken, granting the premise that sexual intercourse can have a meaning totally divorced from both marriage and procreation. If man and woman can express love by contraceptive intercourse, why may not man and man or woman and woman express love by the homosexual equivalent of heterosexual intercourse? The plausibility of such a line of argumentation is strengthened by the approach of the homosexual in Morris West's *Devil's Advocate*. He tells the Monsignor that such is the way that God has made him and he intends to act according to his nature. To gainsay this kind of reasoning one must turn to an analysis of the meaning of sex within human life, as that meaning is uncovered by reason, revelation, and the authoritative directives of the

[5] Wilbur, Cornelia B., *op. cit.*, 269–279.

Church. Preliminary, however, to development of the objective morality of homosexuality one may ask whether the homosexual is responsible for his condition.

A. *Subjective Responsibility for Condition*

It is as unrealistic to presuppose that a man wants to be homosexual as it is to believe that he desires to be alcoholic. As a result of medical science, psychiatry, and the experience of Alcoholics Anonymous, the general public has taken a more tolerant and sympathetic viewpoint toward the alcoholic, but it has not yet reached a similar level of understanding of the condition of homosexuality. While the homosexual may feel that God has made him "that way," the ordinary person feels that the homosexual himself is responsible for his condition. Usually, however, by the time an individual discovers his homosexual tendencies it is too late to do more than to learn how to control them. In case histories or in novels like *Finistère* one of the crucial moments is the person's discovery that he is drawn erotically toward his own sex, and not the opposite.

Obviously, the tendency had been developing for years without the person's being aware of it. Frightened by his own insight, he is at a loss what to do about it. He may try to prove that he is heterosexual by indulging in promiscuity for a while, but this proves fruitless and he is left with the decision of seeking self-control or of yielding to the already matured tendency. Sometimes, luckily, the tendency is not yet formed when an adolescent feels there is something wrong with him, and by both psychological and spiritual guidance he can be rescued from it.

In the practical order, then, it may be assumed that the individual is not responsible for the condition of homosexuality. It is reasonable to suppose that a person is not going to choose a psychological state which will bring him much suffering. *De facto*, very few people who become alcoholics realized that they were heading in that direction; even more so in 'the case of the homosexual, he does not realize that his desire to be constantly with another member of his own sex is the result of an already ripened condition. Sometimes without a single external act of inversion the individual realizes that he is a homosexual, because the desire for physical acts has remained in consciousness for a long time.

His responsibility for indulging the tendency is another and very complex matter, because it involves the degree of freedom which an individual possesses when he is obsessed with desires for homosexual acts. Since in such a person a modicum of freedom remains he must learn how to use it. The point to be made is that a homosexual has the obligation to control his tendency by every means within his power, especially by various forms of psychological and spiritual counsel.

B. *Objective Morality*

By its essence, however, the homosexual act excludes all possibility of transmission of life. This assertion needs no demonstration, inasmuch as physical acts of sexual union between members of the same sex cannot be procreative. Such an act is an inordinate use of the sexual faculty. Since the only ordinate union of the sexual faculty involves a member of the opposite sex in an act that always remains primarily procreative in nature, while not excluding the secondary purpose of expression of mutual love, it follows that any other use is out of order, inordinate. Sexual acts between members of the same sex are contrary not only to the primary purpose of the sexual faculty, namely, procreation, but also to the secondary purpose, which is to express mutual love between man and wife.

Since it runs contrary to a very important goal of human nature, it is a grave transgression of the divine will. The procreation and education of children within the framework of the family is the primary purpose of the divine institution of marriage and a very important goal. Since homosexual acts make this goal impossible, perverting the purpose of the sexual act outside the divine institution of marriage, they constitute a grave violation of the divine will. The more important the goal, the more objectively grave is the frustration of that goal. It is also a deviation from the normal attraction of man for woman, which leads to the foundation of the basic unit of society, the family. So natural is the attraction between man and woman that whenever one mentions romance he leads others to believe that a man and a woman are involved. Recently a psychiatrist read to a class of student nurses several "love letters," and asked the students what they thought about them. The students referred to the "girl" who was receiving these letters, and were shocked to be corrected by the psychiatrist-teacher: The "girl" was another man. Said one of the nurses: "I never dreamed such a condition existed." Her reaction is typical of the young when they are first made aware of the existence of homosexuality. (Incidentally, teen-agers should be made aware of it).

To that *corpus* of homosexual literature which holds that it is "natural" for homosexuals to express mutual love by physical acts a rebuttal should be made that as soon as one separates completely the procreative function of the genital faculties and of the marital act from their personal and individual values, there remains no reason why "any mutual act of two people, married or unmarried, of opposite sexes, or of the same sex, can be condemned as immoral, if they simply state that this is the way they choose to express their mutual love." [6]

[6] Joseph Duhamel, "The Catholic Church and Birth Control," Paulist Press pamphlet, 1962, p. 17.

While there are several passages in Holy Scripture whose homosexual connotations are doubtful, there are six references definitely referring to homosexual acts: five to males, and one to females. In all cases the practice is condemned. Derrick Bailey in *Homosexuality and the Western Christian Tradition*,[7] gives an exhaustive treatment of both the doubtful references and the clear passages. Among the doubtful references are *Apocalypse*, 21:8 and 22:15. According to some authorities, the *ebdelugmenoi* (THE ABOMINABLE), 21:8, and the *kunes* (DOGS), 22:15, refer to those who engage in unnatural sex practices. Bailey, however, doubts that these passages refer to homosexual practices. At most, it is *possible* that 21:8 has this meaning, but extremely improbable that such is meant in 22:15.[8]

The first two definite references are in Lev. 18:2 and 20:13. Lev. 18:2: "Thou shalt not lie with mankind, as with womankind: it is an abomination." Lev. 20:13: ". . . If a man lie with mankind, as with womankind, both of them have committed abominations: they shall surely be put to death; their blood shall be upon them" (King James Version).

In the New Testament three passages refer to male homosexuality: Rom: 1:27; I Cor. 6:9–10; and I Tim. 1:9–10. Rom. 1:26 should be taken in conjunction with 1:27: "For this cause God has given them up to shameful lusts; for their women have exchanged natural intercourse for what is against nature, and in the same way men too, having given up natural intercourse with women, have burned in their lusts towards one another, men with men practicing that well-known shamelessness and receiving in their own persons the fitting punishment of their perversity." Notice the context in which the practice of homosexuality occurs. The pagans had refused to worship the true God, and God "has given them up" to the practice of unnatural vices, i.e., He has withdrawn His grace from them in punishment for their idolatry. I Cor. and I Tim. regard the sin of homosexuality as very grave; I. Cor. 6:9–10, V. 10: "Make no mistake; no fornicator; no idolater, no adulterer, no pervert, no homosexualist, no thief. . . . will inherit the kingdom of God." I Tim. 1:9–10 refers to the Mosaic Law punishing various forms of crimes, including "homosexualists." (All Pauline passages are from the Kleist-Lilly translation).

Rom. 1:26 can be understood with references to acts between women. The above quotation makes it clear that homosexuality was also found among women in St. Paul's time, and that it was equally heinous.

The Sodom and Gomorrah Account (Gen. 19:4–11) is controverted, although in past ages it was assumed to be the *Locus Classicus* of the divine condemnation of homosexual acts as most heinous. After a careful

---

[7] London: Longmans, 1955.
[8] *Op. cit.*, p. 41.

study of the so-called traditional interpretation of the Sodom story, Derrick Bailey [9] concludes that the biblical account has "no direct bearing whatever upon the problem of homosexuality or the commission of homosexual acts. Hence, it is no longer possible to maintain the belief that homosexual practices were once punished by a Divine judgment upon their perpetrators so terrible and conclusive as to preclude any subsequent discussion of the question. Still less can it be held that an act of God has determined once for all what attitude Church and State ought to adopt toward the problem of sexual inversion. This is not to say that homosexual acts may not, in a greater or lesser degree, be sinful; but only that their morality fails to be decided (like that of other human acts) by reference to the natural law, and in accordance with the principles of Christian ethics and moral theology, and cannot be considered settled by a natural catastrophe which occurred in the remote past."

RESPONSIBILITY AND FREEDOM

The present responsibility of the homosexual may be understood only by full consideration of his freedom or lack of it. This can be determined only by one who knows him very well over a long period of time, and even such a one will find it almost impossible at times to judge whether a given person was fully free in the act of homosexuality. There are so many environmental and constitutional factors involved.

It is important to distinguish between a tendency toward homosexuality, expressed by dreams and daydreaming, and deliberate consent to such movements. One may experience erotic dreams, or daydreams about one's own sex, and not commit any sin of homosexuality. The same holds true with regard to similar dreams and daydreams about the opposite sex. Only when deliberate consent is given to daydreams of this sort is any violation of the moral law involved. This distinction should be made clear to any person suffering phantasies, so that knowing he has committed no sin, he will be encouraged to the practice of further virtue. Incidentally, from the fact that one regularly has carnal daydreams about his own sex we can infer that he is homosexual.

Many homosexuals act under compulsion, at least on the interior levels of erotic phantasy. One of the most characteristic signs of the homosexual is obsession with erotic phantasy. No matter where he goes, he runs into more phantasy. His very fear of this obsession causes even greater tension. On the external side all seems well with him, but within his soul there is a daily fixed battle. In a given instance of a young homosexual it is difficult

[9] *Op. cit.*, p. 28.

to know whether from the moment he made plans to seek out another homosexual he was *free*. It could be that he was not free from the very beginning, acting under impulse *before* he sought out his accomplice.

Compulsion is a narrowing of consciousness concerned either with a fascination for some object or with obedience to an impulse regarded as intolerable unless accepted. In a broader sense, the term also includes the conviction, born of bitter failure to control it, that the urge is irresistible. The individual comes to regard his struggle to overcome his tendency as hopeless. Sometimes, as a result of indoctrination, for example, by homosexual literature or by harsh and vengeful religious writings, the individual despairs of his ability to overcome his tendency. Since homosexual behavior is found in the tangled background of neurosis of which it is one symptom, it is not surprising to find compulsive elements in the invert. The compulsive nature of his acts may be surmised from the sordid circumstances, coupled with risk, in which the typical liaison takes place. Reciprocal masturbation in a public washroom, for instance, is not the sort of thing which would appeal to a normally free agent. Some inverts, moreover, tend to appraise sexually and to contemplate solicitation of every man encountered, whereas the normally sexed individual does not try to seduce every woman or man.

Under certain circumstances some inverts may be unable to resist temptation, and their weakness will be exploited by others, who, for example, will stand in a public rest room in a state of arousal or will make their genitalia prominent in the hope that some other invert will be attracted by this sight, and then will be unable to resist the temptation. Despite the fact that previously he had been able to avoid any external act of homosexuality, he is *now* unable to stop the chain of events precipitated. He does not think, as a general rule, of the serious consequences which he may suffer from the civil law if he is caught in the act.

It is to be noted that only under specific circumstances does the behavior of the homosexual become compulsive. There is no categorizing the kinds and degrees of compulsive homosexual behavior. Each person reveals a different degree of compulsion within a different pattern of personality traits. It is practically impossible to say in a given case that the action was the result of a compulsive urge. A man who one day acts freely may act compulsively the next, and his neighbor would be none the wiser. "We cannot know anything about the nature of alleged irresistible impulses," says Dr. Rudolf Allers, "unless we know all we can find out about the total personality." [10]

[10] "Irresistible Impulses: A Question of Moral Psychology" *American Ecclesiastical Review*, vol. 100 (1939), p. 219. J. C. Ford and G. Kelly, *Contemporary Moral The-*

In the same article, Dr. Allers points out that a compulsion may seem perfectly free to others, because it is a result of preparatory steps. What is not observable is that the subject is absorbed with one dominant purpose, shutting out all other thoughts from his mind, thereby eliminating at this time the chance of any counteracting motives' having efficacy. The mind is filled with one big idea. Again, as the result of intense concentration on an object of desire comes great tension, tension so overpowering that the person feels that he has to give in or suffer an intolerable situation. He has to seek physical satisfaction from an unknown man. Now, it happens that an individual may *not* be subject to the above described narrowing of consciousness, yet in a short period of time may suffer what he regards as intolerable tension. It *seems* that he retains more freedom despite the tension than the individual who prepares for the action over a long period of time through "monoideistic narrowing of consciousness." [11]

Usually compulsive phantasy leads to compulsive masturbation. This is not difficult to understand. The individual generally has more control over temptations to sin with others than over the ingrained habit of self-abuse. What can be done about it I shall discuss now and later.

In these circumstances the homosexual is bound to seek help either to live with the compulsion without giving voluntary consent to its movements or to rid himself of it by therapy, if that is possible. It may seem contradictory to assert, on the one hand, that the sexual drive of the homosexual is no stronger than that of the heterosexual, and on the other to speak of compulsive drives in the homosexual. But it should be noted that heterosexuals also have compulsive tendencies of various sorts, including self-abuse, and that the source of the compulsion in both heterosexual and homosexual is not in the strength of the sexual instinct as such but in deeper disorders within the whole person which find readiest expression in sexual phantasies or acts. In most instances the homosexual is capable, albeit with the help of grace, of refusing at the onset to give in to the compulsive forces. With the help of therapy he usually acquires greater self-control over a period of time. He may not be able to rid himself of his homosexual compulsions, but he can learn to live with them as a result of the insight which usually comes with therapy.

If the homosexual temporizes with this interior disorder by fostering habits of indiscreet reading or by cultivating dangerous friendships, he is guilty of placing himself unnecessarily in the proximate occasion of sin. As long as the homosexual seeks counsel and resists spontaneous carnal desires,

---

ology, Westminster: The Newman Press, 1959, vol. 1, develop the same problem: pp. 201–247.

[11] Allers, *op. cit.*, pp. 214–215.

he is not accountable for possession of homosexual tendencies. Obviously frequenting homosexual haunts, reading their literature (of which there is plenty), and cultivating friendships which one perceives may lead to sins of the flesh should be assiduously avoided.

Since individuals vary in their ability to control apparently compulsive tendencies, only therapists and spiritual counselors familiar with the invert's background can form reliable judgments concerning his ability to avoid consent to these drives. Compulsions are insidious. Concerning this Dr. Allers has this curious insight, which applies to impulses of a heterosexual nature as well: "There is one very curious and very important feature worthy of mention in these irresistible impulses. They become irresistible, so to say, before they have fully developed. People have a presentiment of the impulse arising; they know that within a short time they will become entangled in a situation from which there is no escape, much as they desire one. They know that they are still capable, this very moment, of turning away and that by doing so they will avoid the danger—but they do not. There is a peculiar fascination, a lurid attraction in this kind of danger, and there is evidently some anticipation of the satisfaction that the *partes inferiores animae* will derive from indulging in the 'irresistible' attraction. The action itself may, therefore, not carry any responsibility and nevertheless not be excusable, because in fact, the person has assented to its development." [12]

Generally the counselor's judgment should incline toward compassionate leniency. Nevertheless, the spiritual counselor should make the homosexual realize that in the development of the so-called "irresistible impulse" described above there are elements *of latent insincerity in his claim that he did not want the temptation,* and that the way the impulse develops is often "a disguised expression of a desire for sexual satisfaction." [13]

It is necessary for the homosexual to be rigorously honest with himself in evaluating the occasions of sin. As Allers has pointed out, in many instances of the *almost* irresistible urge the individual could have stopped the whole process of mounting passion at an early stage, but he did not do so.

GENERAL PASTORAL CONSIDERATIONS

Before one can counsel the homosexual he must possess some understanding of the attitude of society toward the homosexual and of the homosexual toward society. Most people regard the homosexual as super-sexed and so dangerous that he must be kept under surveillance lest he seduce

[12] *Ibid.,* 216–217.
[13] Ford, J., and Kelly, G., *op. cit.,* p. 233.

the innocent. The known or suspected homosexual's difficulty in getting acceptable employment or in making ordinary social contacts and non-sexual friendships indicates the distrust and dislike with which most people regard the homosexual. Homosexual behavior is such a stigma that black-mail is used effectively against inverts by the unscrupulous.

Now, many homosexuals assimilate the horror which society manifests toward homosexuality and unconsciously hate themselves. A woman in her thirties discovered that she possessed homosexual tendencies and sank into a mood of self-reviling, bordering on suicide. A seminarian who thought he had such a tendency was ready to leave without really examining closely the nature of his own disorder. And so on. The mood of self-condemnation is followed by bitterness toward God and society. Bitterness leads to isola-tion and loneliness; loneliness, to seeking the exclusive company of other homosexuals. This sexual ghetto spirit creates the illusion of a superior breed who view with contempt heterosexual behavior. All unconsciously, many homosexuals transfer hatred of their own condition unto society.

It is not surprising that the confirmed homosexual possesses a kind of hopeless air about him. Since he feels there is no remedy for his condition, he is tempted to give in to his tendencies or to commit suicide, an alterna-tive worse than the homosexual condition itself. What William F. Lynch has written about the mentally ill applies also to the homosexual:

> In hope there is a future. That there be a future is part of the nature of hope. If there is a future to which we can look forward, we can endure all things in hope. . . . In mental illness, however, the image of the future is restricted. The future dies as the disease grows. But what then is there? There is only the past, and it is endless. The sick are trapped in the past. [14]

A counsellor can communicate hope by accepting the homosexual as a person, and by not suggesting ways of controlling the tendency until he understands the complete situation. Proposing a plan of life with stress upon some meaningful service to others can come later. At first, he will be frightened by the very idea of abstinence from overt homosexual activity, but, as he discerns another way of living for the invert, he will gain courage gradually, interspersed perhaps with relapses, often of a solitary and phan-tasy character. Some years ago, I made specific proposals for a plan of life for the invert who is aware of the fruitless frustration of purely emotional attachments and who is in search of some means of serving God. These proposals were based on the conviction that the invert can find his place in the divine plan and can discover his purpose in life if he learns to see

[14] *Images of Hope* (Baltimore: Helicon, 1965), p. 58. (Mentor-Omega pb. 1966). An excellent book for both invert and counsellor.

the totality of his life within the deeper viewpoint of faith; "His life must have purpose, and discover it he must in some form of apostolic labor." [15] As I explained it at that time,

> . . . A plan of life is a radical rethinking of an inadequate viewpoint of life, a deep determination to redirect the will in the pursuit of God, and of values leading to Him, and a gradual formation of systematic practices which are designed to help the invert to fulfill these thought-out objectives. Ascetical practices selected to achieve the goal of supernatural rehabilitation are not all of the same value. Some contribute more than others, as meditation, for example, is more important than the rosary. The stress, however, is not upon the practice, but rather upon the spirit which infuses it. The good act must flow from a new view of life and it must express new striving for eternal values, now viewed as alone worth possessing. Pervading all must be a sense of overwhelming purpose.[16]

In discussing this plan, I pointed out that it must possess two qualities. First of all, it must be specific enough to include certain spiritual exercises for every day, and secondly, it must be pliable enough to allow for the normal variations in a person's daily schedule. The following is an example of a plan of life which might be used as a basis:

1. Morning prayers, including some form of meditation for at least fifteen minutes.
2. Mass as often as possible during the week.
3. Examination of conscience at least once a day.
4. Short spiritual reading every day (about ten minutes).
5. Carefully chosen regular confessor.
6. Some form of devotion to the Virgin Mary and to the saints.
7. Some service to the Lord.

Though I do not intend to go into further detail concerning these proposals at this point, I would add the following advice concerning modesty, and the homosexual's social life.

A. Modesty

Homosexuals cannot be too modest in the use of their senses or in dress. What would be prudery in the heterosexual is necessary precaution in the homosexual. Virtuous homosexuals do not linger near homosexual haunts, visit homosexual bookstores, do not wear tight clothing, or frequent public toilets. The ordinary heterosexual can be rather free in the use of his eyes without serious moral danger, but not so the homosexual. One might be inclined to believe such modesty unnecessary were it not for the cumu-

---

[15] *Homiletic and Pastoral Review,* Jan. 1962, p. 328. Cf. also, *Bulletin of Guild of Catholic Psychiatrists,* Oct., 1963, pp. 204–214.
[16] *Homiletic and Pastoral Review, ibid.,* p. 329.

lative evidence of homosexuals themselves. The homosexual, for example, who indulges in the practice of "cruising" (walking or driving slowly through a homosexual district looking for other inverts) usually slips into overt acts sooner or later. This "cruising" is one expression of the compulsive tendency of the homosexual to get sexual satisfaction. Oftentimes he will go through a prolonged agony of indecision as he flirts with temptation. In this respect he is as immature as a teenage boy reading a salacious novel with ambivalent feelings of guilt and excitement; but the difference is that the teenager will probably grow up. Thus when the homosexual tells his counselor that he does not want to go to places like movie houses or swimming pools, he must not be advised that he is too timid or prudish. Curiously, the female homosexual has similar difficulty with women who dress immodestly.

B. Social Life

Usually pastoral practice goes on the assumption that the homosexual who wants to practice virtue must not associate with other homosexuals for fear of mutual seduction. For this reason the idea of an organization analogous to A.A. has been dismissed as too dangerous to be practical. But one may wonder whether an association of virtuous homosexuals could not be of mutual help to all the members. Already the principles of A.A. have been applied to divorcees and drug addicts. Recently Neurotics Anonymous came into existence.[17] Of course, the principles of organization would have to take into account the specific dangers of the homosexual condition, but the project is worthy of thought. Whatever dangers such an organization might entail would be justified when one considers the current condition of many homosexuals living in haunted isolation, and subject to all the phantasies of the lonely. The least that can be done is to try new approaches to an old problem. The writer knows one virtuous homosexual who has befriended a younger invert with the express purpose of keeping him from slipping into the underground and has succeeded up until now. The younger man does know the inversion of the older man. For many inverts, moreover, the alternative to association with virtuous homosexuals is a life of overt homosexuality. Such an association could include heterosexual members of both sexes as well, just as A.A. has many non-alcoholic members.

An encouraging sign that homosexuals can give some positive help to one another is the work of Dr. Samuel Hadden. First, he had noted that homosexuals did not do very well in group therapy whenever they revealed their homosexual problem too early in a group which was not sufficiently mature

[17] Neurotics Anonymous International Liaison, Inc., P.O. Box 21134, Kalorama Station, Wash., D.C. (20009).

to accept them; later, he discovered that "the homosexually oriented patient can be treated successfully in mixed groups when the group is quite mature and when they achieve a certain measure of acceptance before they expose their socially unacceptable symptom. However, it is my firm belief that the homosexually involved are more successfully treated in groups made up exclusively of those who have homosexuality as their most significant symptom." [18]

Dr. Hadden calls homosexuality a symptom, "because it is but one manifestation of an overall pattern of maladaptation." [19] He considers homosexuals not as homosexuals, but as neurotics "whose preference for sexual experience with the same sex is one of their symptoms." [20]

Through group therapy an attempt is made to uncover the experiences which may have caused the homosexual syndrome. At first the individual may claim that he prefers his homosexual condition but in the dynamics of group therapy this rationalization is broken down. The previous members of the group give support and encouragement to the new member, while some of them report changes for the first time. No pressure is put on anyone to change his outlook. But as group therapy progresses, each benefits by the recounted experiences of the others; "This emotional reliving of traumatic experiences with others lends an impact to the reliving that seldom occurs in the one-to-one relationship." [21] Gradually members of the group come to realize that their condition is a privation of what they wanted to be. Certainly the investigations of Dr. Hadden demand further research inasmuch as they open up a vista of hope for many homosexuals.

Despite the widely held theory which places the origin of male homosexuality in fear of women, some homosexuals find real support in the friendship of women of both their own age group and that of their parents. Very probably this fear must be understood in terms of sexual intimacy. Again, many homosexuals find adequate satisfaction in the social life of heterosexuals, both relatives and non-relatives.

SPECIFIC PASTORAL CONSIDERATIONS

A. Marriage

What can be done to demonstrate the invalidity of a marriage in which one party semed to be homosexual before marriage? To treat this question

[18] Newer Treatment Techniques for Homosexuality, American Academy of Occupational Medicine, Arc. Environ. Health, vol. 13, Sept. 1966, 284–288 at 286.
[19] Loc. cit.
[20] Loc. cit.
[21] Op. cit., p. 287.

adequately, it seems necessary to study not only the question of the homosexual's capacity for marital consent, but also the problem of psychological impotency. First of all, because of his inability to make a complete dedication of himself to a person of the opposite sex, there is reason to believe that the homosexual lacks the capacity for marital consent.[22] Secondly, since the homosexual neither understands nor experiences heterosexual attraction he is psychologicaly impotent; a fact that he is sometimes unaware of until later in marriage. The fact that he has consummated his marriage and has a family does not alter the psychological problem, for he is still incapable of true marital love and consent. Unfortunately, however, a consummated marriage involving a homosexual remains practically unbreakable in the present state of canonical legislation. Yet the revision of canon law may provide some release for many persons involved in a homosexual difficulty on the part of the opposite spouse. Admittedly, the practical difficulties of proving *prior* homosexual condition are familiar to both canonists and psychiatrists, but these can be overcome. What is needed at the moment is a consortium of moralists, canonists, psychiatrists, and other concerned professionals to work out discernible criteria of true homosexuality, which would make a revision of the pertinent canon law of practical value.

Once these canonical criteria have been determined, it would be necessary to demonstrate that the homosexual condition renders the person incapable of marital consent, because, in effect, it is equivalent to impotency. Studies like those of Gerald Oesterle and Charles Ritty, quoted extensively by Cavanagh, in *Counseling the Invert* (Bruce, 1966) seem to prove this point. It is known that Declarations of Nullity in cases of sexual pathologies have been granted.[23] While it is true that the case noted is one of nymphomania, still the compulsions found in homosexuals are similar. Perhaps while the Church is waiting for an updating of canonical legislation on homosexuality, petitions for declaration of nullity might be initiated and diligently pursued. In this way a "praxis Rotae" would facilitate further research into the problem, and the results of research would encourage a more informed "praxis Rotae." At any rate, more discussion at higher levels, both canonical and moral, is urgently needed.

The other side of this problem is immediately pastoral. What do you do with a married man (woman) who seems to be homosexual? This writer feels that one should encourage the person to make the best of a bad situation, particularly if children are involved. Of course, when the apparent

[22] For fuller treatment see the author's article in *Homiletic and Pastoral Review*, Nov. 1966, pp. 170–174.

[23] *Monitor Ecclesiasticus*, T. 90, 1965, pp. 409–415, Summarized in *Ephemerides Theological Lovanienses*, XIII, June, 1966, p. 160.

homosexual condition is discovered after marriage, it seems wise to keep knowledge of it from the other spouse. I take this position for a number of reasons, including the fact that I know of one instance where the unknowing spouse had a nervous collapse because of the apparent homosexual's neurotic desire to confess. Everything must be encouraged which will help the marriage to continue, and in the contingency that psychiatric help is beyond financial reach the counselor must provide as much supportive guidance as possible.[24]

B. Prevention of Homosexuality.

Consideration of the homosexual marriage leads us to wonder what can be done to prevent children from becoming homosexual. Concern for children in institutions was voiced during the Catholic Charities workshop in New Orleans (1966). One suggestion was to develop meaningful personal relationships with various surrogates. Another was not to give such children so much privacy that they can begin these practices with little probability of detection. It remains a baffling problem. While living in dormitories rather than rooms would seem to make the practice less likely, it does not eliminate it. The advantages in privacy gained by the majority when they share relatively smaller units seem to outweigh the increased dangers in such new quarters. Part of the solution seems to be in placing at least five or six in units. The much larger problem is the youngsters themselves. There is a period in the development of a child in which he has latent tendencies toward homosexual practices. If these are arrested in various ways, he may develop normally; but if he is a victim of seduction, he will develop in a homosexual way. It is a question of adequate sex instruction over the years of child development. Youngsters should be warned about this practice. With the mere facts about sex so available even to children, there is no value in the argument that one should wait until the teenage period before discussing the danger.

Admittedly, one does not wish to disturb the relative peace of the child with such instruction, but effective steps toward prevention are better than any efforts to remedy an already existing situation. Traditional adherence to modesty in dress has been recommended by psychiatrists who have discovered that homes where immodesty was the rule are seedbeds of various sexual deviations. Parents who go about immodestly in the presence of their children, or who fondle them far beyond infancy in a passionate way, or who touch the genital organs of the growing child while bathing him, can stimulate sexual desires prematurely, and this has been known to lead to homosexual practices: "Examples of all degrees of parental seduction of

[24] Harvey, J. F., "Homosexuality and Marriage," *HPR*, Dec., 1961, pp. 227–234.

the child occur more commonly than it is comfortable to contemplate, regardless of the socioeconomic status of the family. The seduction may be as subtle as a caress or as blatant as actual incest. . . . The conventional restraints of common modesty respected outside the home are ignored where the children are concerned. The parents parade about the house in all degrees of nudity, sleep with the child, bathe with the child, and fail to respect bathroom privacy. . . . The behavior may extend to such more frankly seductive practices as playing with the child's genitals. . . . and the parent and the child stimulate each other." [25]

In the writer's opinion, however, the most powerful preventive of homosexual development in children is a positive father figure with whom the boy may identify and to whom the girl looks for support. Of course, the girl also needs a woman with whom she can identify. Social workers and relatives can provide for children of broken homes the kind of positive relationships the children need. Institutions, however, should be cautious in the choice of counselors, because immature individuals may seduce the young instead of helping them.

A positive influence during the formative years which may compensate for deficiencies in the parental relationships are effective peer relationships from the early years of life. A child who is able to romp and play from 18 months to five years will experience warm human relations with his companions. This will help him relate to others in later life. But the boy who is deprived of this experience may never develop normal peer relationships and may tend to seek physical fulfillment with peers whom he regards as more masculine. "Inability to make normal peer contacts with the resultant aloofness is a factor in the development of homosexuality in many males who offer themselves as sexual objects to be accepted and embraced by peers or males with whom they want to make contact." [26]

More recent research has indicated that one is able to predict which children will develop effeminate homosexuality.[27] The external mannerisms of the effeminate child are more discernible than the external behavior of the future non-effeminate homosexual. The effeminate homosexual learns of homosexuality at an earlier age, and is more likely to repeat the homosexual act sooner and with the same person. In homosexual relations he is likely to be passive. In these patients effeminacy seems to be the primary

[25] Johnson, Adelaide and Robinson, David, "The Sexual Deviant (Sexual Psychopath), Causes, Treatment, and Prevention," *Journal of American Medical Association*, Aug. 3, 1957, vol. 164, no. 14, 1559–65. (It is significant that this quotation is not from a moralist, but from two psychiatrists.)

[26] Hadden, *op. cit.*, 288.

[27] Holeman, Eugene and Winakur, George, *American Journal of Ortho-Psychiatry*, "Effeminate Homosexuality," 41: 78–83 (November, 1965).

problem. All these characteristics in addition to his greater homosexual activity than the non-effeminate homosexual make prognosis more certain, and suggest that the sooner such a child or youngster is sent to a psychiatrist the better are the chances that he will be able to achieve heterosexuality, or at least control of his sexual impulses.[28]

HOMOSEXUALITY AND THE CIVIL LAW

The present civil laws concerning homosexuality need drastic revision for a variety of reasons: lack of proportion between the homosexual act and the kind of penalty inflicted; the fact that the law is applied only to men; occasions of blackmail; forced homosexual practices in prison; the unsavory tactics of police entrapment, and the like. "The laws are ineffective, serving neither a deterrent, preventive, nor rehabilitative function. No argument in favor of these statutes, based on social utility, has substance enough to condone the harsh penalties. In fact, these statutes represent the enforcement of a code of morals for their own sake, a grave misuse of American criminal law. Learned and powerful voices, clerical and lay, both here and in England, have been and are being heard for the adoption of laws which recognize that morals and their inculcation are not the province of the state, and that, accordingly, consensual acts of adults in private are beyond the proper scope of the criminal law." [29]

As a result of the Wolfenden Report of over ten years ago the ferment for change in the civil law continues to gather strength in Great Britain and in the United States. Only in Illinois at the present writing are private, consensual acts between homosexuals not a civil offense, unless force is used. Steps should be taken by all concerned groups to make the civil laws just. In supporting a revision of the law clergymen are not affirming that homosexual acts are moral, but simply that it is not the province of civil law to cover such private acts. A change in the law could be justified as the lesser of two evils. The greater evil remains in our present body of legislation, which cannot be effectively applied, and which has given rise to so many abuses. While some will identify a change in law as a kind of moral ratification of homosexuality, education can correct this misunderstanding.

Much has been accomplished in research into homosexuality, but much remains unfinished. More than anything else America needs a more just and merciful judgment of all those who suffer from the disorders of homo-

[28] Bieber, *op. cit.*, 62.
[29] Cantor, Donald, "Deviation and the Criminal Law," *The Journal of Criminal Law, Criminology and Police Science*, vol. 55, no. 4, 441–453, at 453 (December, 1964).

sexuality. It is not a disease in the sense of something beyond human control, but, in the minds of many psychiatrists and pastoral guides, it is a neurosis and should be treated as such. By the grace of God homosexuals can be guided into a fruitful life of service to God and man. But they must bring to the counselling session an abundant faith in God's care, a vigorous trust in His sustaining power, and a persevering love of the Redeemer who loves them just like all other persons.

SELECTED REFERENCES

Anomaly, The Invert, 2nd edition, Baltimore: Williams & Wilkins Co., 1948.

Bailey, Derrick S., Homosexuality and the Western Christian Tradition, Longmans, Green, 1955 (Excellent on Scripture).

Berg, Charles, and Allen, Clifford, The Problem of Homosexuality, New York: Citadel Press, 1958.

Bieber, Irving, et alii, Homosexuality, Basic Book Publishers, 1962.

Cantor, Donald, "Deviation and the Criminal Law," The Journal of Criminal Law, Criminology and Police Science, vol. 55, no. 4, 441–453, December, 1964.

Cavanagh, John R., Counseling the Invert, Milwaukee, Bruce, 1966.

Cory, Donald Webster, "Homosexuality," Encyclopedia of Sexual Behavior, ed. Albert Ellis & Albert Abarbanel, I (1961), pp. 485–493.

Hadden, Samuel, "Newer Treatment Techniques for Homosexuality," American Academy of Occupational Medicine, Arc. Environ. Health, vol. 13, Sept. 1966, 284–288 at 286.

Harvey, John F., O.S.F.S., "Homosexuality as a Pastoral Problem," Theological Studies, XVI, March, 1955, pp. 86–108.

Harvey, John F., O.S.F.S., "Homosexuality and Marriage," Homiletic and Pastoral Review, December, 1961, pp. 227–234.

Harvey, John F., O.S.F.S., "Counseling the Homosexual," Homiletic and Pastoral Review, January, 1962, pp. 328–335.

Harvey, John F., O.S.F.S., "Working with the Homosexual," All Things to All Men, (ed. J. Cevetello), Wagner, N.Y., 1965, pp. 183–207.

Harvey, John F., O.S.F.S., "The Pastoral Treatment of Compulsion in the Homosexual," (ed. J. Cevetello), Wagner, N.Y., 1967.

Harvey, John F., O.S.F.S., Bulletin of the Guild of Catholic Psychiatrists. October, 1962. "Counseling the Invert in Religious Life," vol. 9, no. 4, 210–222. October, 1963. "Counseling the Apparent Adolescent Homosexual," vol. 10, no. 4, 204–214. Article on Homosexuality in New Catholic Encyclopedia.

Harvey, John F., O.S.F.S., Book Reviews on Homosexuality in Theological Studies, March 1956 (pp. 128–132), Sept., 1960 (pp. 491–495) and Dec. 1966 (pp. 720–721); in Homiletic and Pastoral Review, Nov., 1966, 170–174.

Henry, George W., All the Sexes, New York: Rinehart and Co., 1955.

Holeman, Eugene and Winakur, George, "Effeminate Homosexuality," American J. of Ortho-Psychiatry, 41: 78–83, November, 1965.

Johnson, Adelaide and Robinson, David, "The Sexual Deviant (Sexual Psychopath), Causes, Treatment, and Prevention," Journal of American Medical Association, vol. 164, no. 14, Aug. 3, 1957, pp. 1559–65.

Landis, Paul H., *Social Problems in Nation and World*, Chicago: J. B. Lippincott Co., 1959, 236–237.

Lorand, Sandor (ed.) *Perversions, Psychodynamics and Therapy*, New York:
Random House, Inc., 1956.

Rees, J. Tudor and Usell, Harley V. (ed.), *They Stand Apart*, London: Heine-
mann, 1955.

Tobin, William J., *Homosexuality and Marriage*, Rome: Catholic Book Agency,
1964.

7

VENEREAL DISEASE

Norman J. Rose, M.D.

Introduction

THE VENEREAL DISEASES may be defined as those diseases peculiar to man which are acquired and transmitted, with few exceptions, through sexual intercourse, or venery. There are five diseases classified as the venereal diseases. In order of incidence, they are gonorrhea, syphilis, chancroid, lymphogranuloma venereum, and granuloma inguinale. The first two are considered the major diseases while the latter three are the minor ones and are of low incidence in this country.

Because syphilis and gonorrhea comprise better than 95 per cent of the venereal disease in the United States, this chapter will deal with them exclusively. Syphilis and gonorrhea are considered a part of the communicable diseases. However, because of the nature of these illnesses and the manner in which they are acquired, health agencies give special attention to reporting and investigational procedures.

The American Social Health Association, in its "Joint Statement" released in January, 1967, reports the following: "In 1966, for the first time since 1957, there was a slight decline rather than an increase in the number of cases of primary and secondary syphilis reported in the United States. The number of persons reported as newly infected with syphilis in 1966 was 22,473, a decrease of 3.3 per cent from the 23,250 reported in 1965. The rate per 100,000 population dropped from 12.3 to 11.6. Despite this slight decrease, the 1966 incidence of reported primary and secondary syphilis still represents an increase of 259.5 per cent over the low of 6,251 cases reported in 1957." [1]

In reviewing the incidence trends over the six-year period from 1960–1965, a decrease in the rate of infectious syphilis in larger population centers with a corresponding increase in the smaller cities and rural areas is noted. The latter rate has increased from 3.9 to 7.1 per 100,000 population while rates in the larger cities (200,000 population and over) were slightly less in 1965 than in 1960.

The report, based on information from questionnaires sent to every state health officer, also includes statistics regarding the incidence of gonorrhea: "In contrast to the reduction in new cases of infectious syphilis reported in 1966, the reported incidence of gonorrhea increased in 1966 by a larger percentage than during any of the past eight years. The 334,949 cases of gonorrhea reported in 1966 are 8 per cent more than the 310,155 reported in 1965. The rate per 100,000 population increased from 163.8 to 173.6. Since 1957, reported gonorrhea has increased by 54.7 per cent."

The true incidence of gonorrhea is unknown, but it is conservatively estimated that about 100,000 cases occur each month or roughly 1,200,000 per year. Gonorrhea represents the most frequently reported of the nationally notifiable communicable diseases among teen-agers and young adults under 25 years of age. Except in fiscal year 1962 when there was a slight reduction in the number of reported cases of gonorrhea, there has been a steady increase each year since 1957. The increase has been about 7 per cent per year—a greater increase, percentage-wise, than the population. It is of interest to note that proportionately more males are reported as gonorrhea cases than females. The difference in reporting by sex may be more apparent than real because of the difficulty of diagnosing gonorrhea in the female.

In reviewing gonorrhea case reporting by specific age groups, it is clear that teen-agers and young adults (i.e., 15–24 years of age) are responsible for more than 50 per cent of the reported cases of gonorrhea. The age specific rate for the true teen-age group—15 to 19—has increased steadily over the four years from 358.0/100,000 population in 1962 to 400.8/100,000 in 1965.

For a while after penicillin was rediscovered in 1943 (Sir Alexander

[1] "Joint Statement on Today's Veneral Disease Control Problem," a comprehensive report written and published annually by the American Social Health Association and sponsored by the American Social Health Association, the American Venereal Disease Association, and the American Association of State and Territorial Health Officers, with the cooperation of the American Medical Association. It is prepared from detailed questionnaires completed each year by state and local health officers.

Fleming first discovered it in 1929,[2] but for the next fourteen years, no importance as a therapeutic agent was attributed to it), many who hailed it as a wonder drug felt that these alarming statistics would soon be reversed and that syphilis and gonorrhea would be banished from the face of the earth.[3] So much faith was placed in this drug that both federal and state budgets were reduced for venereal disease control purposes.

The resurgence of the venereal diseases is not limited to the United States. The World Health Organization, which receives reports from 105 countries, estimates that over 60 million new cases of gonorrhea occur each year.[4] Of 12 of the nations reporting to the World Health Organization and studied by them, 7 showed that over 50 per cent of the cases of syphilis and gonorrhea were among the teen-agers.

Many official and non-official organizations, including every religious faith in the United States, are concerned with the appalling incidence of the venereal diseases in the 15–21 age group. Father Trafford P. Maher of St. Louis University states,

> The daily record indicates unmistakably the rising incidence of venereal disease. This illness is reaching down to younger age levels; it is cutting across all socioeconomic, ethnic, religious and racial groups.[5] Obviously, keeping people ignorant about any subject, especially sex, does not induce more moral behavior. We need more forthright, objective, sound sex education taught in proper focus and context. We need to start earlier and according to a developmental point of view.

A Protestant minister, Rev. Virgil A. Kraft, Administrative Pastor of the Peoples Church of Chicago, Illinois, comments,

> Since venereal disease is not a private malady, it becomes a moral issue involving a sense of social responsibility. This means that in addition to the need for physiological education in this area, we must improve the effectiveness of our character-building agencies. It is the current rebel-emphasis on individuality and personal rights which has accelerated disregard for law, disrespect for custom and ignoring completely the values of community living. Venereal disease is a social disease, and along with imparting practical information about it, requires a deepened sense of social responsibility, not only among the victims but also among those responsible for their welfare.

[2] Fleming, Alexander, Sir, *Penicillin, Its Practical Application* (Philadelphia: Blakiston Company, 1946).

[3] Mahoney, J. F., Arnold, R. C., and Harris, A., "Penicillin Treatment of Early Syphilis," *Journal of Venereal Disease Information*, 24 (1943), 355–357.

[4] *Bulletin of the New York Academy of Medicine*, 40 (October 1964)

[5] Trafford P. Maher, S.J., Ph.D., Chairman, Department of Education, Human Relations Center for Training and Research, St. Louis University, St. Louis, Missouri.

Rabbi Herman E. Schaalman of Emanuel Congregation, Chicago, has said,

The very cornerstone of our civilization as it grows out of its Biblical roots is the fundamental recognition of the sanctity of each person and of the prime importance of the family. Both individual and family are, of course, to be understood not only in terms of theology or economy, etc., but equally decisively in terms of biology, of sex. One of the most persuasive trends in Jewish religious practice has been the attempt to hallow the sexual life and to make it appear as a precious part of the divine gift of life to man. Some of the most consistent and strenuous efforts of the Jewish historic community were spent in developing and maintaining a level of inter-personal relationship within the family and between the sexes that at times genuinely approached such levels of sensitivity as to touch the realm of the holy. It is, therefore, all the more appalling to realize how the devaluation of the individual, brought about in large part by the technological industrial society and its dislocations and disturbances in value structure which are threatening the nature of the family, have led to a degree of sexual freedom and experimentation particularly among the young which exposes them to serious dangers of soul and body. Every measure, therefore, that can be devised by public authorities or the private sector of our society concerned with education and communication designed to the concept and function of family life must be encouraged and supported to the fullest. This includes sex education, dealing both with the physiological and psychological aspects of the matter. In fact, the need for this and many other similar steps is so imperative that it is to be hoped that all religious forces would endorse such steps and measures jointly, in order to launch the most effective attack possible upon the danger that so very clearly threatens the central nerve of the entire conception of man as derived from scriptures and tradition.

The National Congress of Parents and Teachers, also concerned about the rising incidence of venereal disease, at its national meeting in May, 1966, approved a resolution calling for a "sound and adequate program of venereal disease education in every school system in the United States, beginning at least by the eighth grade . . ."

Sociologists, psychologists, and psychiatrists, in an effort to account for the rise of venereal disease, have conducted numerous studies, and consequently, are in general agreement that a multiplicity of factors are responsible for the high infection rate in this particular age bracket.

Social and environmental factors are perhaps the major causes of this increase. The relaxing of moral and cultural values in present-day society has brought about greater promiscuity in young people. Emphasis, false though it may be, has elevated sex to a status symbol of glamor, happiness, and success. There is continuing emphasis on sex in advertisements, movies, television and every other communication media, including books and magazines. It is paradoxical that society condones promiscuity but condemns the acquisition of a venereal disease. Perhaps, what is needed is an intensive, mass education program, for as Dr. Freeman of the District of Columbia Health Department, states,

> Every adult should know the facts of venereal disease—facts of symptoms, of prevention, of availability of treatment facilities. . . . The entire community should be organized systematically so that there will be no adult who has not heard the story and learned the facts. Syphilis and gonorrhea must be discussed as infectious diseases calmly and impersonally. . . . Misconceptions, prudery and guilt complexes must be replaced by frank discussions of symptoms, prevention and cure.[6]

Another possible cause of the spread of this disease may be the contraceptive pill. However, there is a paucity of information in the United States regarding the effect the contraceptive pill may have on the incidence of the venereal diseases in this country, but professional workers in England have expressed their thoughts concerning the effect of the pill as evidenced by the following statement made by the British Federation Against Venereal Disease. "Wider use of the pill will increase the incidence of venereal disease . . . Teen-age girls in the clinics inform us that they are obtaining the pill from all sorts of unofficial sources. They make it clear that it is fear of pregnancy and not venereal disease that holds them back from promiscuous relations and the pill removes that fear." [7]

SYPHILIS

Syphilis is a word of curious origin. It comes from two Greek words, *sys*, a swine and *philos*, loving. The hero of a 16th century poem by Fracastoro of Verona was called Syphilus, because he tended animals, presumably including swine. He was said to be the first sufferer from the disease and he contracted it, not in the orthodox way, but as a punishment for blaspheming against the Sun and raising altars to his earthly master—

> And first th' offending Syphilus was griev'd
> He first wore Buboes, dreadful to the sight,
> First felt strange Pains and sleepless past the Night
> From him the Malady receiv'd its Name.

The question has been asked many times, "Where did syphilis come from and when?" The most common and widely accepted answer has been that the crews sailing with Christopher Columbus in 1492 brought it back from the new world on their return to Spain. This answer seems no longer tenable in view of the extensive review of anthropological, sociological

[6] Freeman, C. Wendell, "The Chain of Venereal Disease Control," *Medical Annals of the District of Columbia*, 35 (July 1966), 355–356.
[7] *The American Medical Association News*, January 23, 1967.

and ethnological material by Hudson.[8] He theorizes—and quite lucidly—
that the disease syphilis is only one manifestation of four diseases caused by
the same organism—syphilis, yaws, pinta and endemic (non-venereal)
syphilis. According to Hudson, these diseases should be called Treponematosis. On this point he wrote:

> The thesis here advanced suggests that treponemal infection of man orig-
> inated in Equatorial Africa as yaws in Paleolithic times, that it accompanied
> the hunter-gatherers in their migrations and that it changed to endemic syph-
> ilis in cooler and dryer areas. Endemic syphilis found an exceptionally favor-
> able environment in the village, a social invention of Mesolithic/Neolithic
> time which spread over the world, the New as well as the Old. When urban
> civilization evolved in the Middle East, conditions were favorable for the
> parallel evolution of venereal syphilis. It is suggested that this transition from
> endemic to venereal syphilis has occurred in many places where village life
> has been exchanged for city life. Treponematosis is a flexible disease which
> has changed to conform with man's social history. In this view environmental
> factors, including climate and man's social habits, have produced the four
> syndromes.

Further evidence substantiating Hudson's theory may be found in Stitt,
Clough and Branham's *Practicale Bacteriology, Hematology and Parasitology*, in which the authors mention that Brickell in 1737 noted in the
colony of North Carolina, yaws was very common among the slaves and
also prevalent in the West Indian slaves from Africa. They also mention
that when a white man acquired yaws in the tropics, he had syphilis when
he returned home. However, more will be said about the agent of syphilis
later.

Syphilis is known as the great imitator because of its capability of imitat-
ing many other diseases or conditions from athlete's foot to cancer (a fact
that will become more apparent as the stages of syphilis are discussed),
it is a disease of the whole body caused by the *Treponema pallidum* identified by Schaudium and Hoffman in 1905. The *Treponema pallidum* is a
small corkscrew-shaped organism about the diameter of a red corpuscle in
length. The treponeme or spirochete of syphilis, as it is also called, is a
very delicate organism. It cannot withstand drying and will die within
seconds in an environment that is not moist and warm. Soap, water, and
the mildest of antiseptics will readily kill the spirochete on contact. The
organism does not occur naturally in other animals. Man is its only host.

Because man is the only host for this disease, he then is the only reservoir
for syphilis. Unlike some other communicable diseases, syphilis does not

---

[8] Hudson, Ellis H., "Treponematoses or Treponematosis?", *British Journal of Venereal Diseases*, 34 (1958) 22; "Historical Approach to Terminology of Syphilis," *Archives
of Dermatology*, 84 (1961) 545; "Treponematosis and Anthropology," *Annals of
Internal Medicine*, 58 (1963) 1037.

develop into a chronic infection carrier state as do typhoid fever, diphtheria, infectious hepatitis and many other communicable diseases. When the infectious period of the disease which sometimes lasts as long as 2 to 4 years, has passed, the individual will not transmit the disease through sexual or body contact with another. For as with any communicable disease, as long as the organism causing the disease stays within the host there will be no further cases. An exception to this is the untreated or inadequately treated pregnant female. However, this does not mean that the individual who has passed through the infective transmissive stage of the disease will not suffer any consequences, for the effects of their disease, which will be discussed later, are numerous.

The treponema, in order to cause an infection, must penetrate some covering of the body—skin or mucous membrane—where it finds the proper environment to multiply. After it has entered the body, it is disseminated throughout the body by way of the blood stream and lymphatic system. (Congenital syphilis is an exception.)

Once having entered the body, the organisms multiply and spread rapidly. The parasite may be recovered from the small papule (a slight reddened elevation of the skin) which may precede the primary lesion, or chancre, of syphilis. The pustule may scab over or even disappear, only to return, but nevertheless, the infection is progressing at the site of inoculation. The lymphatics draining the area of the chancre are invaded and blood stream dissemination follows with the localization of the spirochetes at multiple foci in the body.

The first visible clinical evidence of the disease is the appearance of the chancre. This will usually occur anywhere from 10 to 60 days after exposure. The most common period of incubation is between 14 and 21 days. Approximately 90 per cent of the chancres are "typical"; that is, the chancre may be the progression of the papule at the site of inoculation or develop at the same site without any apparent forerunner. The fully developed chancre is observed as a circular elevated sore with a depressed, eroded or ulcerated center within a "rolled" rim. The lesion at this stage of development is "hard" to the touch and is likened to a button in the skin. (The "hard" quality differentiates the syphilitic chancre from the "soft" chancre of the minor venereal disease, chancroid.) The chancre is usually a solitary lesion, excepting a "kissing" chancre may appear on a site directly opposite the original lesion where the skin surfaces touch each other. Chancres are *painless* unless secondarily infected! As the primary lesion is developing, the lymph glands draining the area begin to increase in size, and if the chancre is genital, a solitary gland, bubo, in one groin will become palpable but soon enlarged glands may ultimately occur in both groins.

Extragenital chancres (those not associated with the genitalia) are not usually typical. As a rule, they are painful when they occur on the fingers and lips. The lymphadenitis associated with the extragenital chancre is unilateral—at the elbow or under the armpit when the primary lesion is on the finger, and at the base of the jawbone when on the lip.

The chancre uncomplicated by secondary infection heals spontaneously within 2–4 weeks, depending upon its size, but may be observed for as long as 6 weeks or more. The chancre disappears without noticeable scarring; however, on very close inspection, a "cigarette-paper" thin scar may be seen at the site of the healed chancre.

In addition to the preceding findings, the appearance of the secondary rash is often found. The patient may also have generalized symptoms similar to those that occur before the onset of any of the common communicable diseases, namely, headache, sore throat, fatigue and a rise in temperature.

The secondary stage of syphilis actually does not occur suddenly as the term may imply. However, it usually begins in six to eight weeks after the appearance of the chancre.

The secondary skin rash of syphilis, as previously stated, may mimic any of the dermatological diseases or conditions, from the rash of measles to the pustules of smallpox. The most common type of rash—about 33 per cent of all types—is the macular. The macular rash looks much like measles except that it is not blotchy and confluent. The lesions vary from ¼ to ½ inch in diameter but may be larger. There may be grouping of the lesions; they do not itch.

In addition to the secondary skin lesions, the mucous membrane of the mouth shows skin changes also. They are comparable to those of the skin and differ only in that the moisture—saliva—of the mouth gives them a different appearance. The covering, as it were, of these lesions is affected by the saliva and washed off, leaving thin eroded areas called mucous patches. Secondary syphilis lesions are infectious—the mucous patches more so than the skin type.

The term latency or latent syphilis is applied to that stage of the disease that follows the infectious stages, i.e., primary and secondary syphilis. Because of the possibility of relapse to an infectious stage, latency has been arbitrarily divided into early and late latency. Early latent syphilis is the period of time from the acute infection to two years post-acute infection. Late latent syphilis is the period of time subsequent to the early latent period, and it is usually during this period that the complications of syphilis occur. The most common complications involve the cardiovascular system and the central nervous system. The involvement of these systems occurs late in untreated or inadequately treated cases. Cardiovascular syphilis develops in about 12.5 per cent of untreated patients, some 10 to 30 years post-primary infection. Central nervous system syphilis develops in about 9.5 per cent of untreated patients, usually 5 to 10 years post-primary infection.

The most common form of cardiovascular syphilis is aortitis—inflammation of the aorta and its valve, followed by aortic aneurysm (sacculation). Damage to the aortic valve produces severe disability and ultimately death. The aneurysm is also a serious complication, as with the passage of time the sac increases in size with associated thinning of the sac wall. Terminal hemorrhage occurs when the sac ruptures.

In central nervous system syphilis, the most common type is tabes dorsalis (locomotor ataxia), with general paresis in second place. Tabes dorsalis occurs when certain nerve pathways within the spinal cord are destroyed. The onset of this complication begins with numbness, a prickling sensation and shooting pains in the legs. Progression of the disease produces severe attacks of abdominal pain. As destruction of the cord proceeds, the patient finds he cannot walk in the dark as he does not "know where his feet are." Finally the patient is wasted and bedridden.

General paresis, unlike tabes, affects the brain. The early manifestations are insomnia, headache, forgetfulness and instability. Progression of the disease results in psychotic personality changes. There is lack of judgment and delusions of grandeur. Speech is indistinct and unintelligible because of slurring, hesitancy and the dropping of syllables. Paralysis with confinement to bed precede death.

First admissions of patients with neurosyphilis to state and county mental hospitals dropped from 312 in 1963 to 260 in 1964, the latest year for which data are available. However, the number of patients resident during 1964 in tax-supported institutions because of neurosyphilis was 17,130 representing an annual cost to taxpayers of more than $46,000,000.[9]

Because the spirochete has invaded the body and produced localized foci of infections, any of these foci may arise from their dormant stage and produce disease in any organ or system of the body—bone and muscle tissue not excepted.

CONGENITAL SYPHILIS

This term applies to the infant born of a syphilitic mother. The time of infection of the mother—or to state it differently, the duration of the mother's infection—is important, both as to the chances of the infant's acquiring the infection in utero and, if acquired, the ultimate outcome.

If the mother is infected at the time of conception, the chances of the

[9] U. S. Department of Health, Education and Welfare, *Venereal Disease Status Report*, Atlanta, Ga., Fiscal, 1966.

infant escaping the infection are minimal. The mother would, if untreated, show a primary lesion, if a thorough physical examination was not made at the right time, or if the chancre were not observed, she would show signs of secondary syphilis at a later date. Conversely, if the mother is infected late in pregnancy the baby may escape the infection. The baby may also escape infection if the mother has untreated syphilis of over four years' duration.

Congenital syphilis is wholly preventable or at least can be satisfactorily treated in utero. (Proof of this is the low incidence of congenital syphilis in states having both the premarital and prenatal blood-testing laws.) When the mother is treated during the first 16 weeks of gestation, the infection is prevented in the baby.[10] This is due to the fact that the *Treponema pallidum* does not cross the placental barrier until after the 16th week of gestation. When the mother is treated after the 16th week, this actually is treatment also of the baby in utero.

Regardless of when the mother acquired her infection, treatment will, almost without exception, prevent the birth of a congenital syphilitic baby. It is of interest that a baby may be born with a positive cord blood test, by usual testing methods, but not be infected. This results from the cross-placental transfer of the material substance (reagin) which causes the serology of the infant to react positively but is not evidence of an actual infection. This type of reaction in the infant's blood will disappear by the time the baby is three months old.

However, it is possible for the infant to have a negative blood at birth and develop syphilis within three months. This occurs when the baby is infected shortly before birth and is still incubating the disease after it is born.

The product of conception of a syphilitic mother may result in spontaneous abortion (gestation under 20 weeks), miscarriage (gestation under 36 weeks), the birth of a premature baby or a full-term infant. The premature or full-term baby may show signs and symptoms of congenital syphilis at birth. These, briefly, are fissures at the corners of the mouth, bulging fontanels, lesions of secondary syphilis. He usually has a high-pitched whining cry.

Later complications of congenital syphilis are blindness due to optic nerve involvement or to scarring of the cornea, the area of the eye directly in front of the pupil. The nervous system may become affected and this results in various types of mental retardation and muscular incoordination. Bone changes—malformation of the leg bones—is not uncommon and destruction

---

[10] U. S. Department of Health, Education and Welfare, *Syphilis, Modern Diagnosis and Management*, Public Health Service Publication No. 743, U. S. Government Printing Office, Washington, D.C., 1960.

of the nasal cartilage occurs, resulting in "saddle nose." The front teeth and the molars will have characteristic shapes and notches. The pitiful result of a congenital syphilis infection is that treatment will only arrest the disease but not correct or remedy any of the already developed defects.

DIAGNOSIS OF SYPHILIS

The diagnosis of syphilis may be relatively easy or most difficult, depending upon the stage of the disease in the patient. Also, the greater the physician's "index of suspicion," the greater will be the number of cases diagnosed most readily and most early.

The earliest and most reliable diagnosis is based on finding the spirochete in secretions from the primary lesion. This particular microscopic test is known as the darkfield examination. The darkfield examination is performed by having the specimen slide illuminated in such a manner that the organisms or cell debris appear brightly lighted on a dark to black background. When the spirochetes are seen, by magnification of about 1,000 times, the laboratory will report "Darkfield positive."

A blood test (frequently referred to as an S.T.S.—standard test for syphilis) will be negative as a rule if the chancre has been present for only seven days or less. The chance of a positive serology increases proportionately with the passage of time. Approximately 25 per cent of the blood tests will be positive by the end of the first week after the appearance of the chancre, with the rate increasing progressively up to 100 per cent by the end of the fourth week. If a darkfield is not or cannot be performed (it must be done on a fresh moist specimen), the diagnosis can be established by periodic serologic tests for syphilis at weekly intervals. Not only will the test become positive but as time passes, it will become more strongly (quantitatively) positive—commonly expressed as a rising titer.

It is possible to obtain darkfield positive specimens from mucous patches and secondary skin lesions. However, because of other spirochetal organisms in the mouth it is rather difficult to identify the T. *pallidum* in such specimens. The secretions or scrapings from early secondary skin lesions may show spirochetes present. One can also aspirate the lymph glands involved and examine for spirochetes. The darkfield examination is seldom done on lesions other than the primary lesion. A history of exposure can usually be elicited by patient, kindly and diligent questioning (very important for control purposes).

The old-time Wassermann [11] test has been modified as the result of increased knowledge in the field of immunology. Today the test is for the

[11] Kahn, Reuben L., *Serology in Syphilis Control* (Baltimore: Williams and Wilkins, 1942).

presence of specific syphilitic antibodies instead of the almost non-specific reagin.

All positive serologic tests for syphilis (excluding the specific antibody tests) do not necessarily mean the person has or had syphilis. A positive serologic test may result from any of the viral diseases, smallpox immunization and about 100 other conditions including cancer, malaria and diseases affecting the blood and blood-forming organs.

When the physician has a patient whose S.T.S. is positive—usually in low titer—and the history is negative with no apparent signs and symptoms of syphilis, he can request one of the special treponemal (antibody) tests be done and the diagnosis problem can thus be solved in better than 95 per cent of these equivocal cases.

Most hospitals include a blood test in their routine admission tests, there are two main benefits to be derived from this procedure. First, a person who has syphilis that has not been recognized will benefit from the discovery that he has syphilis. Treatment will follow and thus prevent the possibility of late complications of the disease. Secondly, should the patient have early syphilis, his contacts can be traced and other cases of syphilis discovered and subsequently treated. Prophylactic treatment may be indicated in certain of his contacts.

TREATMENT OF SYPHILIS

The treatment of syphilis is relatively simple and is almost 100 per cent effective in preventing progression of the disease. Penicillin is the drug of choice for the early stages of the disease as well as the later stages. The only contraindication to its use is patient sensitivity to the drug. When the allergy is present, the so-called broad-spectrum drugs are used.

As little as one injection of 2,400,000 units of a long-acting penicillin will "cure" the disease in 90–95 per cent of the cases. Most physicians and clinics prefer to administer at least 6,000,000 units of penicillin to bring the treatment failure rate to almost zero. Several visits will also present an opportunity for repeated interviews for additional contacts. Complications such as cardiovascular syphilis and central nervous system syphilis are treated with from 12,000,000 to 18,000,000 units of penicillin.

Some 39 per cent of the people with untreated syphilis can be expected to develop some destructive lesions of syphilis, and 23 per cent of the entire group of untreated syphilitics can be expected to die primarily as a result of syphilis.[12]

[12] U. S. Department of Health, Education and Welfare, *Venereal Disease Status Report, Fiscal Year 1966*, Atlanta, Georgia.

The blood test is not a consistent indicator of the effectiveness of treatment. Cases of primary syphilis treated when the blood test is negative will not, as a rule, develop a positive serology. When the disease is treated for the first time in the late latent stage, the serology usually remains positive and no amount of treatment will change it. In essence, the earlier a case of syphilis is treated after acquisition of the disease, the better the chance of having a negative serology and also, and more important, a decreasing risk of complications.

GONORRHEA

Gonorrhea—(Greek: a flow of semen)—is an acute local contagious disease caused by the gonococcus of Neisser,[13] affecting the genito-urinary tract in both sexes but capable of systemic disease by widespread dissemination of the organism throughout the body.

Gonorrhea is believed to be a disease of antiquity, though there is no conclusive proof to support this belief. The old Chinese and Japanese writings as well as Biblical and Egyptian prescriptions allude to such a disease, but all are considered to be vague generalities.[14] In fact, so little was known about gonorrhea that in the 15th century, gonorrhea was considered to be the first symptom of syphilis. This misconception was further strengthened by Hunter when he inoculated himself with pus from a supposed case of gonorrhea and contracted syphilis. Hill in 1790 and Bell in 1792 proved conclusively that syphilis and gonorrhea were separate and distinct diseases. The organism causing gonorrhea was identified in 1879 by Neisser.

The organism responsible for the disease belongs to the "cocci" group of the bacteria—"cocci" meaning round. The individual organism is actually kidney-shaped but occurs in pairs with the concave surfaces facing each other. The gonococcus is really an organism of low viability. It will die in a dry environment. Soap and water and the mildest of septics will kill the organism.

The reservoir of this organism is the human body. No other animal harbors it. This reservoir is composed of acute cases, missed cases (undiagnosed) and chronic cases without symptoms. The male segment of the reservoir is pretty well known because of the clear signs and symptoms the disease produces in this sex and his subsequent seeking of medical care. The escape of the organisms from the reservoir to the new host, with two excep-

[13] Stitt, E. R., Clough, Paul W., and Branham, Sarah B., Practical Bacteriology, Hematology and Parasitology, 10th Edition, (New York: Blakiston Co., 1948).
[14] Garson, Warfield and Thayer, J. D., Bacterial and Mycotic Infections of Man, 3rd Edition, (Philadelphia: Lippincott, 1958).

tions (ophthalmia neonatorum and vulvo-vaginitis) is through sexual intercourse.

If the organisms are present in the mother's vaginal tract at delivery, they can and do produce an eye infection in the baby known as ophthalmia neonatorum. Many states require the immediate post-delivery application of a prophylactic medication—usually 1% silver nitrate in the infant's eyes to prevent this disease which may result in blindness.

True vulvovaginitis of gonorrhea etiology is not too common. When seen it is usually in the middle years of childhood. Before puberty the lining of the vulva and vagina is made up of a different type of cellular layer than post-puberty. This makes those parts of the female anatomy more liable to infection. With the change in cell character of the lining and its subsequent increase in acidity, a more protective environment ensues.

In the summary of Dr. Nazarian's article on gonococcal infections in children,[15] it is stated ". . . Gonorrhea in children is increasing and takes the form of conjunctivitis, arthritis, or genitourinary infection. The infection seems to be transmitted most often by contamination in the infant, involuntary sexual contact in the young child, and voluntary sexual contact in the older but not necessarily pubescent child. The physician treating children must be aware of the prevalence and characteristics of this type of infection and should use his influence in a preventive manner as well."

Because the symptomatology is not as clear-cut in the female, i.e., there are fewer and less severe signs and symptoms as a rule, and because she has a tendency to think of a vaginal discharge as "one of those things," she seldom seeks medical care. The promiscuous female is capable of having a greater number of contacts over a given period of time than the male and because of this fact, combined with the few-to-none signs and symptoms, the undiagnosed, untreated female makes up the larger segment of the reservoir. The female's chances of acquiring the disease through intercourse with an infected partner are greater than those of the male because of anatomical differences.

The incubation period may be as short as 36 hours or as long as 28 days. The most usual period is between three and five days. The first symptom in both male and female may be a slight burning sensation on voiding—dysuria, frequence of voiding and finally the appearance of a thick whitish-yellow pus. The disease may be localized in the urethra in the male and in the urethra and cervix in the female. The organism may also spread by contiguity to cause infection of the gonads in the male (epididymitis),

[15] Nazarian, Lawrence F., "The Current Prevalence of Gonococcal Infections in Children," *Pediatrics*, 39 (March 1967) 372.

prostatis, proctitis (rectal infection) and in the female, salpingitis (infection of the tubes), cystitis, kidney infection, and peritonitis.

Because the complications of gonorrhea in both male and female produce serious and irreparable damage, a brief discussion of them is indicated.

Complications in the Male: Infection of the prostate gland is the most common complication of gonorrhea and is the precursor and associate of other complications. Generalized infection of the gland will produce temperatures of 103°F to 104°F. The patient is ill. He will have frequent and painful urination. Pain at the base of the scrotum (perineum) may be intense. Occasionally the acute stage may develop into abscess formation. The patient is sicker and the temperature higher. There may be retention of the urine. However, the most unfortunate complication of gonorrhea is epididymitis—an infection of the epididymis, the sperm-collecting tubules of the testes. Scarring frequently occurs which blocks the tubes and if both testes are affected, sterility results.

Complications in the Female: Salpingitis (infection of the Fallopian tube(s) is the most serious and important local complication in the female. It may accompany the acute stage or follow shortly thereafter. This complication may occur without any preceding signs and symptoms of gonorrheal infection. The acute stage of salpingitis may resolve into a chronic stage. This stage of the disease and its subsequent course results in backache, abdominal pain, frequent vaginal discharge and general ill health. The seriousness of this complication parallels that of epididymitis in the male, because if both tubes are involved, sterility results. The scar tissue that occurs in the tubes predisposes to the lodging of the fertilized ovum in the tube resulting in a tubal pregnancy. When the tube ruptures, hemorrhage is usually severe and death may result.

Occasionally the glands secreting the lubricating substance in the vagina may develop abscess formation. When this occurs, surgery is usually indicated.

DIAGNOSIS OF GONORRHEA

The diagnosis of gonorrhea can at times present a greater problem than that of diagnosing syphilis. In the male presenting the classical signs and symptoms of gonorrhea—burning and the frequency of urination, and a discharge—the diagnosis can be made clinically and can be easily confirmed by the microscopic examination of a stained smear of the discharge. When such a preparation is made from an acute case, the organisms appear as pairs within pus cells. As the disease progresses, fewer gonococci are observed and they may also occur outside the confines of the pus cells.

The stained smear under a microscope is the simplest method of laboratory diagnosis of gonorrhea but it is also the least reliable. This is particularly true for the female for two reasons. First, it is more difficult to obtain a good specimen for examination because of the anatomy of the female genitalia and secondly, because the organisms seem to lodge in the many glands of the urethra and cervix. It is estimated that only one-third of the actual cases of gonorrhea in females can be confirmed by the laboratory when only the stained smear is examined.

A better and more accurate diagnostic laboratory method is the culturing of the organism, for this method will bring about a two-fold increase in identifying cases over the "smear" technique. However, the difficulty of delivering viable organisms to the laboratory for culture is a major problem. As previously pointed out, the gonococci will not survive drying or temperatures below normal body temperature. Even the growing of the organisms in the laboratory is not a simple procedure and the majority of small hospital and private laboratories do not perform this test.

Perhaps the best test is one called the fluorescent antibody test. The principle of this test is to attach a specific fluorescent dyed antibody to the gonococcus; if this organism is present, it will fluoresce when viewed under the microscope when ultra violet light is used for illumination. The equipment for this test is very expensive and the technique most delicate.

Over the years, attempts have been made to develop a blood test for gonorrhea. The latest version of this test has proven quite successful in sure hands even though one of the components of the test is difficult to standardize. A negative test does not rule out a diagnosis of gonorrhea but a positive test will appear in four to six weeks post-infection.[16] The perfection of this test would be most helpful in the diagnosis of gonorrhea in the male homosexual and the symptomless female.

TREATMENT OF GONORRHEA

Even though gonorrhea is a less serious disease than syphilis, its treatment is becoming more and more difficult. The reason for this is the decreasing sensitivity of the gonococcus to penicillin. Since 1955 the gonococcus has become so insensitive to penicillin that the dosage of penicillin for treatment of the uncomplicated case of gonorrhea has increased four-fold. Should complications occur—prostatitis, epididymitis, etc., in the male, and abscessed glands, tubal abscesses, etc., in the female—hospitalization is mandatory. The problem in the treatment of gonorrhea is further com-

---

[16] Questions and Answers—"Complement Fixation Test for Gonorrhea," *Journal of the American Medical Association*, 172 (1960) 639.

pounded by patients who have developed a sensitivity to penicillin. In these cases other, though less effective, antibiotics are used.

Causes of failure in the treatment of gonorrhea with penicillin, in addition to the organism's increased resistance to this drug, are reinfection, improper diagnosis, insufficiently high blood or tissue levels of antibiotics, and poor natural defensive mechanism of the host.[17]

IMMUNITY

The body reacts to an invasion by the spirochetes of syphilis very similarly to that provoked by other bacteria. Two factors influence the development of immunity and they are related. Time is the first factor. The longer the person has his untreated infection, the more solid his immunity becomes to re-infection. The second factor influencing the development of immunity is the stage of the disease in which treatment is given. A rather solid immunity is developed in about three months after the appearance of the chancre. One may wonder why a patient should be treated as soon as possible after the diagnosis is established if this will prevent the development of immunity. Two principles dictate the need for immediate treatment. First, the patient's risk of complications is greatly lessened by killing the spirochetes before they are too well established in the various organs of the body and second, immediate treatment results in "chemical" sterilization of the case because the spirochetes will disappear from the lesion within 48–72 hours post-treatment and therefore the case will expose fewer individuals to possible risk of infection.

Gonorrhea, unlike syphilis, does not produce a reaction of immunity in the host. This is obvious when one becomes aware of the large number of repeat infections. The re-infection rate for male patients as reported by the venereal disease clinic in the city of Boston is 15 per cent; one patient was re-infected with gonorrhea 14 times in one year.[18]

THE CONTROL OF THE VENEREAL DISEASES

Actually the control of the venereal diseases begins with the individual who has or suspects that he has a venereal disease. It is obvious that we cannot solve a problem unless we know that it exists.

The control of the venereal diseases is relatively simple in principle; discover the infectious cases and treat, prophylactically, if necessary, all their

[17] Simpson, W. G., and Brown, W. J., "Current Status of the Diagnosis and Management of Gonorrhea," *Journal of the American Medical Association*, 182 (1962) 63.
[18] Fiumara, Nicholas J., Personal communication to author.

sexual contacts. To achieve this control, (1) every case or suspected case should be identified and reported to the public health agency responsible for the prevention and control of the venereal diseases; (2) when the case or suspected case is reported, the public health officials or their agents should interview every individual so reported in order to learn about their contacts, and (3) bring them to examination and treatment, if indicated. These three steps are the factors in the administrative control of the venereal diseases. In the absence of any single one of these factors, control will fail.

Even though there is a chapter on homosexuality, in this book, mention of it should be made at this time because of its contribution to the incidence of the venereal diseases. The actual incidence of the venereal diseases attributable to homosexual practices is most difficult to ascertain due to the refusal of the homosexual to admit he is a deviate and to name his contacts.

There is a misconception among male homosexuals that a venereal disease can be acquired only from a female partner! Nothing could be farther from the truth. The organisms causing syphilis and gonorrhea, as previously pointed out, can and do live in and on those areas covered with mucous membranes. The spirochete of syphilis may produce the primary lesion in the mouth, the so-called extra-genital chancre, as well as in the mucous membrane lining the rectum. Likewise, the gonococcus can grow and multiply in both of these sites.

Fiumara,[19] in a personal communication to the author, mentioned three cases of culturally proven pharyngeal gonorrhea—one of these cases also had the urethral type of the disease. Male contacts to these cases were proven to have gonorrheal disease.

One may estimate—and it is only an estimate—the incidence of infectious syphilis among male clinic patients. Estimates vary from 5 per cent to 50 per cent. The variation in the estimates results from the marked differences in the clientele of the clinics providing the information. For example, venereal disease clinics in certain areas of the large cities cater almost exclusively to male homosexuals.

Dr. Randolph Whitfield,[20] venereal disease clinician at Los Angeles, California, states, "For the year 1966 almost 36 per cent of male cases of infectious syphilis treated in this clinic named an average of three male contacts. Our figures show that over the past few years, homosexual prac-

[19] Fiumara, Nicholas J., "Gonorrheal Pharyngitis," *New England Journal of Medicine* (in press).
[20] Randolph Whitfield, Jr., M.D., Surgeon (R), United States Public Health Service, Division of Venereal Disease Control, County of Los Angeles Health Department, Los Angeles, California.

tices are from two to three times more common in the white race than in the Negro."

Dr. Vernal Cave,[21] of New York City, comments that 35 per cent of the male patients interviewed in that city during 1965 and 4 per cent of the female patients named contacts of the same sex during the critical period of infection. In addition, he states that it appears that the younger the patient, the greater the possibility he or she will admit to a homosexual exposure.

Dr. Seymour Weinstein, Acting Director, Municipal Social Hygiene Clinic, Chicago Board of Health (perhaps the largest venereal disease clinic under one roof), whose patients comprise both sexes and all races, estimates that between 5 per cent and 15 per cent of all infectious syphilis cases result from homosexual practices.

Prostitution as a factor contributing to the spread of the venereal diseases played a more prominent role a decade or two ago. This is not to say that prostitution has been abolished in the United States; it has not, but its modus operandi has been changed. Instead of the "houses" of the past with their madams, pimps, etc., prostitutes work alone as "call girls" with their own apartments to transact their business or "on call" to travel to their clients. Needless to say, their services are expensive. The majority of the girls are under constant medical supervision which provides them with prophylaxis and immediate treatment when indicated. These persons do not contribute much to the incidence of reported venereal disease. Some girls who work in or frequent taverns are prostitutes and are a constant source of venereal disease infections.

The American Social Health Association has been instrumental in reducing prostitution in the United States. They employ investigators who make on-the-spot personal investigations in every state in the nation on the extent of prostitution in any community. The reports from the American Social Health Association on these investigations are confidential and are supplied only to official health and law-enforcement agencies.

The importance of the premarital and prenatal laws in practically eliminating congenital syphilis has been previously noted.

The control of gonorrhea is much more difficult; first, because of the short incubation period of the disease; secondly, because of the difficulty of diagnosing the disease in the female, and thirdly, the higher treatment failure rate for the female than the male.

If the female partner is not adequately treated at the same time as her male partner, or vice versa, the disease will be transmitted back and forth

[21] Vernal G. Cave, M.D., Chief, Division of Social Hygiene, New York City Department of Health, New York, N.Y.

between the two individuals, a condition termed "ping-pong" gonorrhea.

If it is possible to bring the incidence of the venereal diseases to an irreducible minimum by the means referred to above, it will be, as previously stated, the first time a disease will be conquered by treatment alone.

The American Medical Association's position on the physician's responsibility in venereal disease control is stated as follows, "He (the physician) is the one who is seeing the venereal disease patient and the primary responsibility for the ultimate control of the disease lies in his hands."

Earlier, the importance of the reservoir was discussed. In order to control or hopefully eradicate the venereal diseases, the reservoir and suspected reservoir must be found and rendered non-infectious. James F. Donohue, U. S. Public Health Service statistician,[22] has theorized that if every 1,000 cases of infectious syphilis were treated during the primary stage of the disease, there would be only 5 new cases resulting from these 1,000 cases at the end of the year. However, if these patients were treated in the third week of their secondary stage, there would always be 1,000 cases of syphilis for the 1,000 treated cases. In other words, the level of infectious syphilis would remain constant. By treating every one of the primary syphilis cases during the first week of infectiousness and finding and prophylactically treating all contacts to the case, syphilis would be eradicated.

At present, researchers are developing a vaccine against syphilis. One may expect this to be a reality in the not-too-distant future. The moral issue associated with the use of such a vaccine is left to the reader.

[22] James F. Donohue, Chief, Research and Control Statistics Unit, Program Services Section, Venereal Disease Branch, National Communicable Disease Center, Public Health Service, U.S. Department of Health, Education and Welfare, Atlanta, Georgia.

8

DRUG DEPENDENCY AND ABUSE

ROBERT JEAN CAMPBELL, M.D.

"DRUG ADDICTION appears to be a more widespread problem in the United States than in other countries, and perhaps because of this we are more concerned about its control; addiction is a social and health peril of great magnitude, yet there is continuous controversy, sparked by bias, prejudice, and confusion, about how to manage the problem." Valid as the foregoing statements might be, they were made in 1928 by Terry and Pellens, in their book *The Opium Problem*. It would be unfair to say that we know no more about addiction than we did 38 years ago, for we do know a great deal about the extent, origin, and nature of drug dependency, especially in teenagers; but we still know pitifully little about how to rehabilitate the teenage or adult drug user.

No doubt the prejudices and misconceptions that many of us have about addiction have obstructed progress in this field, and it might be relevant to examine some of these. One is that drugs create sex maniacs. This is certainly not true of narcotic drugs; they are so depressing to sexual impulses and sexual metabolism that erotic desire disappears almost entirely during addiction, and in women the menses cease.

Another misconception is that drugs make killers; the fact is, narcotics are as depressant to aggressive impulses as they are to sexual impulses. Certainly the killer type, the aggressive psychopath, can and does use opiates, but he is atypical. Still more often one hears how much more dangerous addiction is than alcoholism. But such statements ignore the direct deteriorative effects of alcohol on brain tissue, on the liver, and on other organ systems of the body; they also ignore the larger social problems represented by alcohol, such as the constellation of people with whom the alcoholic comes into disruptive relationship, the costs to the public from loss of productive work, the lives lost through drunken driving, family distress, and all the rest. It is hard to explain society's attitude toward addiction, when that same society condones cigarette smoking and alcohol intake; when many of that society take various tranquilizing, stimulating, and depressant drugs habitually, for essentially the same reasons for which heroin is taken, namely, to function better; and when some of that same society must be equally at the mercy of their suppliers of insulin for their diabetes as are addicts for their supply of narcotic.

This is hardly to say that drug addiction should be espoused as a national way of life. Indeed, since we know that many more people could become addicts than actually do, we must do all in our power to maintain strict control over the procurement and dispensing of narcotics, and keep them as unavailable as possible to those who might fall prey to their enticements. At the same time, we cannot ignore the fact that any battle we try to wage against addiction will be a losing one if we continue to delude ourselves about the enemy's nature. The problem of addiction is much more than one of drug abuse and restriction of supplies; it hinges upon our ability as a society to develop healthy members, and to rehabilitate unhealthy people so they need not have recourse to addicting substances. If we permit ourselves to take credit for spawning the successes in our society, we must also accept some of the responsibility for producing its failures. We must try to define how they have come to fail, and under what conditions; we must search for ways to by-pass their limitations and make maximal use of their assets. And we must try to keep our efforts focused upon the problem as it really exists—not on a monster woven from phantasy and conjecture, nor on an homunculus whose significance has been shrouded by our myopic unconcern. We need to know who uses drugs, what drugs they use, under what conditions, and to what extent. What is the rationale for their use? What is the end result, not only for the user, but for his family and society in general? And finally, we might do well to examine the current attitudes of society toward drug use, if for no other reason than to determine what might be the best way for society to approach the user.

DEFINING TERMS

The first order of business might well be to try to define what we mean by addiction, drug-dependency, drug-abuse, and some of the other terms that one frequently encounters in the literature in the field. Technically, addiction refers to strong dependence, both physiologic and emotional, upon alcohol or some other drug. True addiction is characterized by the appearance of a typical abstinence syndrome of organic origin when the drug is withdrawn. It appears that in the addicted person the presence in the body of the addicting drug becomes necessary to maintain normal cellular functions, and when the drug is withdrawn, distortion of physiological processes ensues and abstinence symptoms are provoked. An addict, in other words, is a person who, whatever the apparent reason, has become physically and emotionally dependent upon a drug, substance, or compound, so that he must maintain a certain level of intake of that substance. Often, in addition, the craving for the substance has a compulsive, overpowering quality, and may be complicated by the tendency to use the substance in ever-increasing amounts. One very simple definition of an addict is any person who feels normal on drugs. Addiction is considered to be a state of periodic or chronic intoxication, detrimental to the user and to society, produced by the repeated consumption of a natural or synthetic drug. The user has lost the power of self-control, at least in relation to the drug, and his behavior comes to be determined to a considerable extent by the use of chemical agents.

Those who have had clinical experience with addicts, drug-abusers, or drug-dependent persons will see at once that such definitions can only approximate the broad range of conditions that are in fact presented. Largely, this seems to be because addiction to opiates remains the exemplar against which dependency on other drugs is measured. Except for alcohol, addiction to which was recognized even in ancient medicine, the opiate group was the first to be identified as potentially addictive. Like alcohol, the opiates were known from ancient times and used to reduce or abolish pain, to reduce emotional tension, and to prevent the damage produced by either an excess of pain or an excess of anxiety, or both. Opium was the earliest member of the group and remained an essential element of the pharmacopea until quite recently. Despite the extensive knowledge that physicians through the centuries had of opium, and despite their widespread use of it in medical practice, it was not until the early years of the 18th century that opiate addiction was clearly recognized and adequately described.

In similar fashion morphine, one of the first chemicals to replace opium in the therapeutic armamentarium, had been in extensive use for decades before it was recognized as a drug of addiction in the 1870's. Heroin was not identified as an addicting drug until 1898. But having been made, the point that any opiate derivative was potentially addicting was almost too well taken, for opiate addiction has become a standard to which every other drug is compared.

The need for pain relieving drugs—whether their primary effect is on physical pain or on mental pain—will always be with us, and the search for more and more effective pain-relievers will remain a commendable goal of clinical investigations. But we can predict that any drug that will, in fact, relieve physical or mental pain will also be subject to abuse. For every such substance with which we have had experience to date has been misused, and in some patients drug dependency has become a major complication of therapy. Certainly this was true of the bromides, of chloral hydrate, paraldehyde, and of the barbiturates. The most recent arrivals on the scene—tranquilizers—have also been subject to abuse, and while this has not been of any importance with the so-called major tranquilizers (such as chlorpromazine), severe dependency on the minor tranquilizers such as meprobamate and chlordiazepoxide appears to be on the increase. Furthermore, recent years have seen the development of psychotomimetic agents —drugs whose effects simulate symptoms of the affect disorders or the schizophrenias—and their effects on consciousness, thinking, mood, and relationship to reality have been ineluctable enough to some that now they, too, constitute a drug-dependence hazard.

Of course, it is impossible to say how many more such threats will be added to an already large pile, but we must be careful to evaluate each of them independently and to distinguish between the different patterns of use that characterize each group. With the opiates, for example, we have tended to describe the addiction and dependency patterns in terms of tolerance, habituation, physical dependence, and abstinence. We might now review some of those characteristics, so that we can later see how other drugs differ and to what extent.

Tolerance denotes increasing resistance to the effects of a drug. It is an outstanding characteristic of the opiates and the amphetamines, and only somewhat less marked with the barbiturates. Although tolerance is not an essential for the development of drug dependence—the cocaine addict, for example, does not develop tolerance for his drug—it is an important consideration in any instance of drug dependence. For linked to tolerance is the need for increasing dosage to maintain or recapture the desired effect; and in general the more saturated the body cells become with any substance, the longer will be the period required to rid them of all traces of the drug. Tolerance of any marked degree, in other words, usually means that the addict has serious reality problems in keeping himself supplied with drug, and that withdrawal will tend to be a prolonged and often arduous process.

Closely allied to tolerance is physical dependence, the need to have some quantum of drug present within the body—or at least within some of its cellular elements or organ systems. Like tolerance, physical dependence is not essential to the development of drug dependence, but when present it presages difficulty when and if the drug is withdrawn. The abstinence syndrome is the symptomatic expression of physical dependence—cells that have become accustomed to functioning under a mantle of drugs tend to fire or discharge or otherwise function in chaotic disorder when that mantle is suddenly removed. Withdrawal symptoms can be very severe and on occasion even life-threatening, as in the case of barbiturate or glutethimide withdrawal, and even more dramatically but not so dangerous in heroin withdrawal, but they are not the basic issue in drug dependence.

Habituation is the psychic craving for, or emotional dependence upon, any substance. One can make a habit of anything, from absinthe to zwiebach, yet this factor more than any other is the quintessence of addiction. For the craving of the drug dependent person is a pathologic need for a specific effect of that drug on his mood or state of consciousness. When such effect(s) becomes life's primary goal for the user and displaces all other essential aims, true drug dependence has been established.

Whatever the reasons that lead a person into drug abuse in the first place, the specific drug that is used influences the characteristics of his dependency state.

At the present time, the following types of drug dependency are especially differentiated in the proposed (1968) revision of the American Psychiatric Association's "Diagnostic and Statistical Manual for Mental Disorders."

(1) opium, opium alkaloids and their derivatives, such as morphine, heroin, codein, dilaudid, laudanum, paregoric;

(2) synthetic analgesics with morphine-like effects, such as Demerol and Methadone;

(3) barbiturates (other classifications have included alcoholism and alcoholic addiction within this general category);

(4) other hypnotics and sedatives or "tranquilizers";

(5) cocaine;

(6) Cannabis sative (hashish, marijuana);

(7) other psychostimulants, such as the amphetamines;

(8) hallucinogens, such as lysergic acid (LSD);

(9) a miscellaneous group, not of great importance in the United States although elsewhere in the world other drugs, such as khat, are separately specified because of the prevalence of their use.

Opiate Dependency

Opium is a narcotic and analgesic that is obtained from the juice of the unripe seeds of the poppy plant. The milky juice is dried in the air, where it first turns into a brown, gummy mass and, with further drying and roasting, into a powdery substance. In the flowering season the juice emits a characteristic odor that on warm and humid nights can be so strong and cloying as to give the passerby a dizzy headache. It is the characteristic odor, incidentally, that gave rise to the dark, heavy hangings of the old opium dens; the curtains were there not as part of an erotic mystique but rather to prevent the odor from seeping into the street and alerting the police. Ingestion of opium produces flushing of the skin within a few minutes; the pupils constrict, the mouth becomes dry, but soon thereafter the imbiber feels a warm glow and becomes progressively less sensitive to pain. He feels dreamy and lightheaded, relaxed, and free of tension and anxiety. Thoughts come rapidly but somewhat disconnectedly, and the subject finds it difficult to concentrate. With larger doses, he passes into a deep, dreamless sleep.

Usually, opium was smoked. A pill of the syrup was picked by the needle (or yen hock) and cooked over a lamp whose heat was directed by a cone. When the syrup began to smoke, the yen hock was held over a pipe. The smoker inhaled slowly and deeply, and gradually eased into a light coma, often with vivid sexual dreams, but with no push or drive or interest in translating phantasy into activity. Over a hundred years ago, Thomas De Quincey described his own experiences after imbibing laudanum—tincture of opium—in *Confessions of an Opium Eater.* "For it seemed to me as if then, first I stood at a distance and aloof from the uproar of life: as if the tumult, the fever and the strife were suspended; a respite granted from the secret burdens of the heart; a Sabbath of repose: a resting from human labors. Here were the hopes which blossom in the paths of life, reconciled with the peace which is in the grave, motions of the intellect as unwearied as the heavens, yet for all anxieties a halcyon calm, a tranquility which seemed no produce of inertia, but as if resulting from mighty and equal antagonisms, infinite activity, infinite repose." "Kubla Khan," Samuel Taylor Coleridge's famous poem, was said by him to have been composed during an opium reverie.

To be sure, opium itself has never accounted for much drug dependency in the United States, and since the passage of the Harrison Act in 1914 morphine use has also been fairly restricted in this country to physicians, and to some women in the upper socioeconomic groups. Since 1914, heroin (or H) has been the most common opiate of drug abuse and accounts for as much as 75% to 90% of the total problem. Probably the major reason for heroin's popularity is its potency (three times that of morphine), which makes it relatively easy to smuggle it across borders in powdered, undiluted form; overall, its effects on the habitual user are little different from those caused by the other members of the opium family.

Until shortly before the outbreak of World War II, heroin (and morphine too, for that matter) was typically taken by subcutaneous injection, or by inhalation of the dry form. In recent years, however, heroin has generally been taken by intravenous injection of a solution made by dissolving the powdered drug and one or more diluents in water. Lactose used to be the diluent, but in the 1930's it was replaced by mannitol and quinine. The latter was added as a way of preventing the epidemic spread of malaria among addicts, and that the maneuver has been successful is attested to by the fact that since 1943 no cases of artificially transmitted malaria have been reported in "mainliners" (addicts who inject the heroin solution intravenously). The "junkie" (addict) buys his drugs in bags ("nickel bags" cost five dollars each, "treys" cost three) from a "pusher" (the middle-man, who is usually a junkie himself). Once he has "scored" or "copped" (made a "connection" with the pusher and bought as many bags as he needs or can afford), he races home with his "fix" and starts to put it through the "works." He dissolves the powder content of the bag in a small amount of water, and heats it to a boil by a match flame in a teaspoon or bottle cap ("cooker"). He draws the solution into an eyedropper through a small wad of cotton (to filter out solid particles of undissolved material), affixes a "spike" (needle) to the dropper, binds his arm with a tourniquet made of a cord or a wire or a stocking, and injects the mixture (variously termed "getting off," "taking off," "shooting up"). Sometimes, instead of shooting he "boots" his fix—he squeezes a few drops into the vein, then lets some blood flux back. The booting technique is believed to prolong the drug's initial effect; its chief disadvantage is that the needle is more likely to clog. In that case, the addict returns the blood and drug mixture to the cooker and starts all over again; the second try is "shooting gravy" (because gravy is cooked blood).

It is obvious that the mainliner gives little if any attention to sterile injection technique, and it is surprising that fatal septicemia does not end addiction early in the game in every case. Some do develop complications—septic abscesses at the point of injection, tetanus, serum hepatitis (jaundice)—but fewer than one would predict. Fatality from overdose is also seen, and such deaths have increased steadily over the past 15 years, and particularly since 1961 (at least in New York City). A particularly dangerous form of opiate addiction that has become increasingly popular in recent years is shooting "blue velvet"—a combination of paregoric with pyribenzamine. Paregoric, which can be purchased without prescription in many states, is boiled in a pan until it forms a thick sludge that contains not only opium but any number of impurities. This is made into a suspension with water, and pyribenzamine is added for an extra feeling of euphoria; the pyribenzamine imparts a bluish tint to the mixture, and thus its name.

In any event, once the opiate is in his blood stream, the addict's cares and anxieties vanish, and the problems of the world recede into nothingness; he is totally at peace, and his mind begins to wander pleasantly. His pupils become constricted ("pinned"), and everything starts to move slowly, easily, painlessly. If he has injected just the right amount, he stays "high" (euphoric), but if he has taken too much he may "go on a nod"—his eyelids become heavier and heavier, and although he speaks coherently he speaks slowly, too deliberately, and may stop in the middle of a sentence as though he had fallen asleep on himself. He denies that he is sleepy, and his main feeling is a *not* feeling—the worst thing in the world could happen to him and it would seem as nothing. But when he recovers from the nodding, he berates himself for having slipped so far.

As the effects of his fix wear off—whether sooner or later depends on the quality of the powder he bought, whether it was "garbage" or "dynamite"—his eyes begin to water, his nose starts to run, his constricted pupils begin to dilate, he feels cold and shaky, he loses his appetite, and his skin seems to crawl with gooseflesh. By the third day of withdrawal he is feverish, restless, inundated with anxiety that threatens to mount to panic proportions, his blood pressure rises, he starts to retch and vomit, has diarrhea, and his whole body aches. Sometimes, though rarely, the addict dies during withdrawal.

A single fix will stop all his symptoms, so it is little wonder that no matter how good his intentions, the addict is rarely able to "kick" his habit and go clean on his own. Nor is it hard to understand why he will do almost anything to get the drug—he will lie and steal for it, he will beg for it and sell himself for it, he will devote his every waking moment and, indeed, his entire life to it, he will even risk death for it.

Some people—but very few—become addicts innocently; and some children are born addicted to a drug used by the mother during her pregnancy. Most of these children, incidentally, used to succumb because their condition was not recognized as such. Their irritability, constant crying, vomiting, diarrhea, twitchings and convulsions were typically misdiagnosed as tetany or central nervous system injury; hence they were not treated appropriately. The danger of iatrogenic addiction, i.e., unknowingly being made dependent on narcotics because of their over-long use as therapy for some other illness, is very small. It is interesting that the ordinary person gets no particular lift from morphine or codeine when these are prescribed for him. Most addicts, on the other hand, have an immediate "This is for me" feeling and are introduced to the drugs knowingly, with the idea of getting high, and hitting a peak of euphoria that has been described to them by other addicts.

About half of addicts begin by taking drugs for the relief of some un- pleasant physical or emotional condition; the others begin to use them through simple curiosity. Addicts themselves often trace the beginning of the habit to use of the drug as a hangover remedy. Recent estimates by the Federal Narcotics Bureau and others place the number of heroin addicts at somewhere between sixty and eighty thousand, although less official esti- mates indicate there may be two or three times that number. Most of them, perhaps as many as 80%, are men, typically under 35 years of age, and almost half of them live in New York City. The others are concentrated in the slum areas of Detroit, Los Angeles, Washington, and Chicago. In New York City since 1947, about 500 new cases of juvenile heroin use have come to public attention each year. A decade ago, most of those youths came from the most deprived slum areas, were typically Negro or Puerto Rican males, were usually unemployed or in the unskilled labor group, and con- fined their habit to heroin alone. Just as this represented a change from the pattern of narcotic abuse in 1914—when there were about 175,000 addicts, 75% of whom were women—so has the picture changed markedly within the past decade.

More and more users come from upper-middle-class suburbs and from university campuses, and more and more are multiple drug users—barbitu- rates, amphetamines, marijuana, and hallucinogens such as LSD are used along with heroin. Furthermore, the degree and range of psychopathology to be found among users is much broader than was characteristic of addicts as recently as 1950. About one in every five narcotic addicts admitted to the U.S. Public Health Service Hospital in Lexington, for example, is physically dependent on barbiturates, and still others have a similar dependence on non-barbiturate sedatives such as glutethimide (Doriden), ethchlorvynol (Placidyl), and meprobamate (Equanil, Miltown). Those with such com- bined dependency tend to have passive-dependent or inadequate personali- ties, are more likely to be white than Negro, and seek oblivion from current conflict and anxieties rather than euphoria. As another example of change in addict populations is the finding that, while Negroes are still over- represented in Manhattan's addicts, in the middle of the "black ghetto" in a nearby suburb it is not the Negro who is the prime abuser but the lower middle class Italian. Males continue to outnumber females among addicts by approximately four to one.

About 45% of known addicts began the habit in their teens, and another

45% started in their twenties. The recent increase in adolescent addiction is partially offset by the "maturing out" phenomenon, the tendency for many to discontinue the habit as they become older and less rebelliously antagonistic to conventional society. Further, the teenage heroin user is not likely to be severely addicted. Perhaps largely because of the low concentration of heroin available in the street market, many are weekend or irregular users, or have what they call a "small habit."

The classical picture of drug addiction, and one favored by many textbooks, is a person who undergoes progressive mental deterioration characterized by intellectual inefficiency, loss of interest in the environment, and loss of self-respect. Physically the addict is enfeebled, debilitated, and emaciated, with a sallow, grey complexion, dry skin and hair, small sluggish pupils, a coated tongue, and foul breath; his cold extremities are scarred by puncture marks and old injection abscesses. He becomes morally and socially bankrupt, and develops more and more criminal features as he grows older.

But that is far from the true picture, at least so long as the addict can maintain a source of supply. Physicians, for instance, have an incidence of drug addiction that is forty times greater than that of any other professional group, and as addicts they can often carry on successful, even brilliant, careers. For it is not moral degeneracy per se that leads to addiction; rather, addiction, with its dangerous bedfellow tolerance, forces the victim to sacrifice money, social position, and ethical and moral standards in order to pay for his needed dose. A pound of heroin may cost between $1,500 and $2,000 when purchased abroad; but by the time it goes through increasing dilutions in a long chain of pushers it may cost the addict in this country as much as $400,000. Looked at in another way, even a moderate habit may cost $20 a day, or $7,300 a year—or considerably more than the median annual income for Manhattan residents (where, in 1959, white families had a median income of $5,870; non-white families, $4,050; and Puerto Rican families $3,460). The average powder sold as heroin in New York City actually contains only about 5% of heroin; thus, in order to get the necessary supply, the addict must often resort to stealing, pimping, prostitution, and pushing. Whenever a premium, monetary or otherwise, is placed on a pleasurable substance, crime enters the picture, either in the buying and selling of the commodity or, if the cost is too high, in stealing and other means of making large sums of money dishonestly in order to buy the article. This is not, then, specific for drugs, but it does mean that the user is likely to be in trouble with the law because of the cost of his habit. In New York City, heroin addicts commit one of every 6 burglaries (but only one in every 50 felonious assaults). As his need for more and more bags of heroin mount, the addict may arrive at a point where he cannot realistically steal enough to support his habit, for the fence pays him only 20¢ on the dollar for whatever he has stolen. So he may admit himself to a hospital voluntarily for detoxification, not because he intends to give up the habit, but in order to decrease his daily requirement to one or two fixes.

Generally, the addict gives a slovenly, dirty, unhealthy appearance. His habit depresses his appetite, except for sweets, so he is thin and he slouches limply as he stands even though his expression is one of intense anxiety and hopeless desperation. He is usually bundled in a sweater, and the long sleeves he wears even in the heat of summer are used as much to cover the needle marks and scars on his arms as to keep him from shivering with the cold he always feels. But no matter how long the sleeves, they fail to hide the bruises and the swellings that come from shooting the veins on the back of his hands. His gaze is shifty, and his eyes have a hunted look, for indeed he is a prey—a prey to the detectives who he fears are on to him, a prey to his habit. He walks a thin line between the terrors of withdrawal and the dangers of an overdose which could push him into a fatal coma. He is out of drug now and wonders if he will connect with a pusher and get his next fix. And can he pay for it? If not, what will he steal, from whom, and will he be able to dispose of it in time to score? And if he does manage to steal the right thing, can he stay out of reach of the law?

Whatever his degree of involvement with the law, he is also likely to be in trouble in other ways. His habit is an entire way of life, one that isolates him from his contemporaries and traps him in a quagmire of self-doubt, uncertainty, and unrelatedness. The present is so uncertain there is no thought of planning for the future. Goals, aspirations, hopes, all these have had to give way before the insistent press of his habit. He cannot tolerate change, he cannot adapt himself to others, he has no more confidence in his family or society than he has in himself. He becomes increasingly self-absorbed and lets all of life pass him by. He has no interest in the opposite sex, for he is unsure of his sexual identity and acutely uncomfortable when he mixes with girls. He feels lost and apart even within his own family, if there is any of that left intact.

His closest tie is to his mother, with whom he may have a mutually parasitic relationship, while the father—if he has not already been separated from the family by illness, death, desertion, or divorce—seems distant, forbidding, elusive, or otherwise unsatisfactory to the young user. Toward the environment, he may be manipulative, demanding, exploitative, and undependable; he can accept no responsibility for the dissatisfactions he complains of, and he resents the reality that fails to gratify his every whim.

Without any real feeling for others, he avoids the "squares" of his neighborhood and finally drifts to the delinquent fringe. There he maintains contact, not because of any wish to embroil himself in violent attacks against the society he distrusts, but as insurance against closing of his avenue of drug supply. While he is "straight"—feeling in top form when he has had just the right amount of heroin, not so much that he is on a nod, and not so little that he is still edgy and dismayed—he is soft-spoken, well mannered, incredibly non-aggressive, gentle, and likable. And even at his lowest he is not violent or vicious, but only restless and whining, or morose.

Whether the personality that has been sketched is the same for all who are drug dependent or are drug abusers, or whether it holds true only for the heroin addict is difficult to say at the present time. Heroin addicts have been better studied than other groups, and it is only recently that fairly stringent controls over the use of all potentially hazardous drugs have been imposed. But even within the heroin group it is clear that not all users are poured from the same mold. For some, heroin seems to be a tranquilizer that eases anxiety in social situations, particularly when these involve establishment of some kind of sexual identity or the expression of competitive, aggressive strivings, and permits an easier and smoother adaptation to life. For others, the drug is used as a way to escape from reality, to withdraw into a phantasy world. Many of these latter are latent psychotics, and even though their adjustment with the help of heroin is still inadequate and borderline, it seems probable that it is a more satisfactory one than they could achieve without it. And for an increasing number, particularly in the upper socio-educational group, heroin is used episodically as a way of rebelling against the establishment, much as alcohol is used by many more of their classmates. No doubt other types could be identified; the point to be noted, however, is that different types do exist within a single drug group, and the hypothesis that is forwarded is that each of those types might require a different approach and different management. It seems likely that those different types will also be represented in the abusers of other drugs, and a consideration of some of them follows.

Barbiturate Dependency

Like the opiates, the barbiturate-alcohol groups of drugs are associated with high tolerance and physical dependence, and thus withdrawal symptoms can be severe. Further, despite the fact that he becomes tolerant to incredibly large amounts of barbiturates, the addict may on occasion react to his usual maintenance dose as though he had never before used barbiturates. As a result, the amount he has been accustomed to will suddenly produce acute intoxication, and the patient will be plunged into dangerous, and often fatal, coma.

Chronic intoxication with barbiturates, or addiction, was first reported in 1949, but even today we have few reliable estimates of how many barbiturate addicts there are. We do know, however, that their use is on the increase, much as in heroin addiction, but unlike heroin, their use is not confined or especially concentrated in metropolitan areas. Rather, barbiturate abuse is spread through all of society, from hamlet to megalopolis, through all parts of the world; at present barbiturates are high on the teenage user's list of favorites. Barbiturates can be of inestimable value when used properly, and under medical supervision. But until 1966, there were few controls imposed on their distribution and sale, so at least half of the supply manufactured found its way into illegal channels. Each year, some 3,000 people in the United States die because of barbiturate ingestion, and barbiturates head the list of drugs most often used to abuse. Because of their direct action on the central nervous system, they are potentially much more dangerous than the opiates; they are directly depressant to the cerebral cortex and the cerebellum. They interfere with intellectual functioning, with judgment, with speech, with gait, with muscular control and coordination. Their action on vital centers within the brain can cause fatal respiratory depression. Their interference with judgment, with the user's thought processes, and sense of time, leads to many accidental overdoses.

Barbiturates are synthetic derivatives of barbital and are manufactured in liquid, tablet, and capsule form. They are subdivided into three groups on the basis of speed of onset and duration of their action: the short-acting group, such as secobarbital; the intermediate group, such as amobarbital; and the slow-starting, long-acting group such as phenobarbital. Their usual dose ranges from 50 milligrams (¾ grain) to 200 milligrams (3 grains) as a hypnotic, or from 15 to 30 milligrams (¼ to ½ grain) three to four times a day as a sedative. It is of some significance that under ordinary clinical conditions, patients (epileptics, for instance) can be treated with daily doses of barbiturates for a lifetime without developing addiction, and without developing tolerance. Abusers of barbiturates, on the other hand, often require 30 to 40 capsules a day to maintain their feeling of well-being, and the author has treated one patient (a physician) whose daily intake amounted to 120 100-milligram capsules of secobarbital.

Because the person dependent on barbiturates usually maintains a high blood level of drug throughout his waking hours, it is not of so much significance medically whether he is on short acting, intermediate, or long acting barbiturate. The addict himself, however, typically has very definite preferences, and can get the desired "high" from only one or two of the whole list of barbiturates. Physical dependency can be demonstrated to be developing within two or three days after the abuser begins to take barbiturates; as a rule of thumb, however, addiction is considered to be established in any person whose daily dosage amounts to 800 milligrams or more.

Barbiturate abusers ("pillheads") usually refer to the drugs as "goof-balls"; "goofing" refers to the unsteady gait, slurred speech, and drunken behavior of the chronically intoxicated abuser, who sometimes becomes enraged, abusive, aggressive, and destructive while he is high—again, much like the alcoholic. The names often used for the specific drugs are as fol-lows: blue heavens (amobarbital; Amytal); tooies, or rainbows (a two-colored, two-compound capsule of amobarbital and secobarbital with the trade name of Tuinal); purple hearts (phenobarbital; Luminal); nemmies, or yellow jackets (pentobarbital; Nembutal); red birds or red devils (seco-barbital; Seconal—perhaps the favorite of addicts).

Symptoms of barbiturate intoxication are similar to the effects of exces-sive alcohol ingestion, and when the two are taken together the effects are markedly intensified. At first, the user may feel relaxed, sociable, and free, and the early bienaise produced fills the subject with self-confidence and, often, an overestimation of his capacities. Soon, however, the depressant effect is more obvious. The user becomes sluggish, droopy, fuzzy in his thinking, and his early gaiety passes into gloomy moodiness. Speech is stumbling and slurred, enunciation is painfully exaggerated, and muscular coordination in general is adversely affected. It is difficult for the user to keep his balance—he sways, shuffles, and stumbles, and may have to feel his way along the wall. Finally, he collapses completely into a deep sleep from which he may not wake for many hours, or into a coma from which he may never be roused. During the weeks and months and years he stays on bar-biturates there will be noted a gradual deterioration in social functioning and in general mental and physical status. The irritability that characterizes some barbiturate addicts may develop into paradoxical excitement, despite the huge amount of depressant being ingested, and the likelihood of such a reaction increases with continuing use of drugs.

The marked physiologic dependence and tolerance that develop with barbiturates make sudden, total withdrawal ("cold turkey") very dangerous. For a short time after withdrawal, symptoms of chronic intoxication seem to abate; the user becomes more alert, seems mentally "with it," his speech improves, and he can walk without stumbling or weaving. But soon the alertness becomes apprehension and anxiety, the energy is transformed into tremulousness and agitation. Nausea and vomiting ensue, and the subject becomes panicked and terror-stricken. An electroencephalogram taken at this point shows slowing of the waves with bursts of high voltage activity. Within thirty to forty-eight hours after withdrawal, about 75% of addicts will go into convulsions which may be fatal. And about 60% of patients will go into a delirium (that is, a number of patients will have both types of severe reaction). The delirium too may be fatal; it resembles the alcoholic withdrawal syndrome known as delirium tremens, and in those who recover it begins gradually to abate within about five days.

Because of the dangers inherent in abrupt withdrawal, the advised procedure is to wean the addict gradually, by reducing his maintenance dosage by 100 milligrams per day. With the user who is taking 30 or 40 capsules a day, withdrawal will obviously extend over a long period of time. One practical difficulty encountered with most drug abusers is trying to determine the actual amount of drug taken; since the drug in question is being obtained through illegal channels, there is no guarantee that each capsule sold does in fact contain as much as the pusher claims. Furthermore, the addict himself is notoriously unreliable, both because of drug-induced uncertainty and confusion, and because of a tendency to minimize his dependency, when he says how much he is taking. The usual practice is to administer any drug that must be withdrawn gradually to the point of intoxication; take that point as a base line, and from that base line begin to decrease gradually. Such a method may seem overcautious and wasteful of time; but it is the only certain way to avoid fatal complications in the withdrawal process.

As in the case of heroin addicts, several patterns of barbiturate abuse can be distinguished which rarely overlap: (1) sedation seekers, who use the drugs to alleviate anxiety, sometimes to the point of semipermanent stupors; (2) exhilaration seekers, who have a paradoxical reaction of excitation to barbiturates; (3) "see-saw" abusers, who use barbiturates to counteract the stimulants they also abuse, and (4) multiform abusers, who combine barbiturates with other depressants, especially alcohol and/or opiates. The resultant intoxication is more severe than would be explained by the amount of drug ingested. The chronic alcoholic who has remained dry for a long period of time will frequently be found to have substituted addiction to barbiturates for addiction to alcohol, and the problems in dealing with him once he is withdrawn from barbiturates may be complicated by a tendency to revert to his earlier pattern of addiction.

The following hypnotics and sedatives are available in the U.S. market; some of them will be discussed individually below, but all of them may be abused with similar effects to those described for the barbiturates.

Barbiturates
  Barbital (Veronal)
  Mephobarbital (Mebaral)
  Metharbital (Gemonil)
  Phenobarbital (Luminal)

Drugs With Barbiturate-Like Action
  Chlormezanone (Trancopal)
  Emylcamate (Striatran)
  Meprobamate (Equanil, Miltown)
  Oxanamide (Quiactin)

Barbiturates
  Amobarbital (Amytal)
  Aprobarbital (Alurate)
  Butabarbital (Butisol)
  Diallylbarbituric acid (Dial)
  Probarbital (Ipral)
  Talbutal (Lotusate)
  Vinbarbital (Delvinal)
  Cyclobarbital (Phanodorn)
  Heptabarbital (Medomin)
  Hexethal (Ortal)
  Pentobarbital (Nembutal)
  Secobarbital (Seconal)
  Hexobarbital (Cyclonal, Evipal,
    Sombulex)
  Methitural (Neraval)
  Methohexital (Brevital)
  Thiamylal (Surital)
  Thiopental (Pentothal)
  Allylbarbituric acid (Sandoptal)
  Butethal (Neonal)
  Cyclopentenyl allylbarbituric acid
    (Cyclopal, Cyclopen)
  Butallylonal (Pernocton)

Drugs With Barbiturate-Like Action
  Phenaglycodol (Ultran)
  Mebutamate (Capla)
  Carisoprodol (Soma)
  Hydroxyzine (Atarax, Vistaril)
  Ectylurea (Levanil, Nostyn)
  Ethchlorvynol (Placidyl)
  Methyprylon (Noludar)
  Ethinamate (Valmid)
  Chlordiazepoxide (Librium)
  Hydroxyhenamate (Listica)
  Mephenoxalone (Trepidone)
  Carbromal (Adalin)
  Bromisovalum (Bromural)
  Chloral Betaine (Beta-Chlor)
  Glutethimide (Doriden)
  Chloral Hydrate (Somnos, Noctec,
    Loryl)
  Diazepam (Valium)
  Methylparafynol (Dormison)
  Petrichloral (Periclor)
  Buclizine (Softran)

Non-Barbiturate Hypnotics, Sedatives and Tranquilizers

Ethinamate (Valmid), ethchlorvynol (Placidyl), glutethimide (Doriden), and methyprylon (Noludar) are non-barbiturate hypnotics and sedatives, originally believed to be free of the addicting potential of the barbiturates but now recognized to be just as likely to produce dangerous dependency in susceptible users. Glutethimide, for example, can produce severe dependency in a short period of time, and in many users it has produced an acute cerebral intoxication manifested by mydriasis (excessive dilatation of the pupil), congested and inflamed conjunctivae, depression of the corneal reflexes, ataxia (loss of coordination of movement), dysarthria (loss of ability to articulate properly because of poor coordination of the muscles involved in speech production), facial twitches, reduced activity and thinking, impaired attention and concentration, dejection, and sometimes convulsions. Like the barbiturates, glutethimide is associated with severe deprivation symptoms and must, therefore, be withdrawn gradually to avoid the risk of fatal complications. Other non-barbiturate sedatives and hypnotics with high addiction potential are chloral hydrate and paraldehyde.

The term "tranquilizer" or "tranquilizing drug" is currently used to refer to a group of phrenotropic compounds whose effects are exerted primarily at a subcortical level so that consciousness is not interfered with, in contrast to hypnotic and sedative drugs, which also have a calming effect that is often intimately associated with if not dependent upon a direct interference with consciousness. Two major groups of tranquilizers are recognized: major tranquilizers, or neuroleptica, with principal effect on psychomotor activity, especially when this is increased; and minor tranquilizers or psycholeptica, whose principal effect is on the psyche to reduce anxiety. Included within the major group are such drugs as chlorpromazine (Thorazine), thioridazine (Mellaril), trifluoperazine (Stelazine), fluphenazine (Prolixin; Permitil), and perphenazine (Trilafon). These phenothiazines (a general term for the group) were introduced into this country in 1954 and produced a revolution in treatment for severe psychiatric disorders. There is no doubt about the fact that they have been largely responsible for not only halting but reversing the upward trend in mental hospital populations. Their effectiveness has been maintained now for more than a decade, and it is generally accepted that the phenothiazines are here to stay. It is also generally agreed that these drugs are not generally abused and that they are not associated with the kind of dependency and addiction that are under consideration in this chapter.

The same cannot be said, unfortunately, about the minor tranquilizers. Their effect on severe mental illness may be minor, but their potential for producing hazardous dependency is major. HR-2, the bill passed by Congress in 1966 to control the use of certain sedatives, stimulants, and hallucinogens, specifies certain drugs that have already been demonstrated to have substantial capability of creating hazards to the health of the user or the safety of the community. Within the psycholeptica group the following were listed: chlordiazepoxide (Librium), meprobamate (Miltown; Equanil), and diazepam (Valium). The pattern of abuse with any of them is very similar to that seen with the barbiturates: increasing dosage that finally exceeds the usual range by three, four, or many more times; chronic intoxication manifested in ataxia, dysarthria, decrease in coordination, disturbances in perceptual-motor organization (of great danger for users who drive, or who operate heavy machinery), and disturbances in attention and concentration. Withdrawal also has the same pattern as that seen with the barbiturates and alcohol: for a short time, improvement in the picture of chronic intoxication, then increasing irritability, vasomotor instability, rapid pulse, tremor, fainting episodes, and finally convulsions. In some cases, delirium further complicates the picture, and in a small percentage a chronic schizophrenic-like psychosis develops. It is assumed that such cases were borderline schizophrenics whose underlying disease was triggered into more overt manifestations by the use of the drug.

As with the other drugs discussed, the usual clinical picture as described is complicated by concomitant use of other depressants or stimulants, and especially alcohol which potentiates and exaggerates all the usual effects of the tranquilizers.

Cocaine Dependency

Cocaine is derived from the coca bush, which grows on the mountain slopes in Bolivia and Peru. Cocaine is a direct stimulant to nerve tissue, including brain and autonomic nervous system; in addition, it decreases or removes hunger pangs. The effects are a result of sympathomimetic discharge (such as rise in blood pressure and sweating) and to central nervous system excitation (the user is more active mentally and overestimates his physical and mental capacities). Many have pleasurable illusions and hallucinations. The latter are sometimes of the Lilliputian variety—everything is seen as tiny or shrunken. After these effects wear off, there may be noted motor incoordination, moroseness and suspiciousness, and sometimes, although very rarely, convulsions, or cardiac or respiratory failure. Emotional lability may persist for some time, and suspiciousness may increase to the point of persecutory ideas. Aggressive release may then occur, and the user will turn against his imagined persecutors and may try to kill them. Impotence is usual in cocaine users so that sexual activity is reduced or absent.

Because even long-time users of cocaine develop little tolerance to it, withdrawal usually can be accomplished abruptly with few deprivation symptoms. One typical withdrawal symptom is formication—the "cocaine bug"—a sensation that bugs are crawling under the skin.

Nowadays, pure cocaine addiction is rare. A favorite route of administration is snuffing, through the nose; if continued for long, however, cocaine snuffing can erode the nasal septum, and the nose looks as though it had been chewed by rats. (The fraternity song, "Have a little sniff on me," refers to cocaine snuffing.) Heroin addicts like to combine heroin with cocaine ("speedballs"), because addition of the stimulant to the depressant effects of heroin produces a more pleasurable high. Cocaine is expensive, though, so most addicts settle for the very similar effects that can be obtained with a cheaper speedball whose stimulant component is one of the amphetamines.

Marijuana Dependency

Marijuana is an Indian hemp product of the Cannabis sativa family; although traditionally considered along with narcotic drugs, marijuana (and its cousins hashish, bhang, kief, ma, and charas) is actually a weak hallucinogen and thus more closely related to mescaline and lysergic acid than to any of the opiates. It has been estimated that the popularity of marijuana as an intoxicant is second only to alcohol, and that one in every ten undergraduates in universities on the East and West Coasts is on "pot" (also known as tea, grass, weed, and charge). Marijuana use is also on the increase in Europe, and has recently mounted to almost epidemic proportion among teenage "toughs" in Sweden. Most marijuana used in the United States comes from Mexico—and some believe that the name is derived from two Mexican women of the night named Maria and Juanita who brought a supply with them as they sneaked across the border— although it can be grown easily in the United States.

Most commonly, marijuana is taken in the form of "reefers," shorter and thicker than the usual cigarette and wrapped in brown paper (thus sometimes referred to as "Tootsie Roll"). Smoking two or three reefers gives the desired effect: a dreamy state of partial consciousness in which ideas are disconnected, uncontrollable, and plentiful; at times, euphoria and an excited joyousness, at other times a moody reverie or panic and fear of death; imagination runs riot, and perception is crowded and disturbed; a peculiar distortion of time, such that minutes seem to be hours, and of space, which is broadened so that near objects seem far away; vivid, pleasant hallucinations, often with a sexual coloring; loss of discriminatory ability so that a three-piece honky-tonk band may seem like a symphony orchestra (hence, perhaps, its popularity among some musicians). Under the influence of marijuana behavior is impulsive, mood is elevated, and random ideas are quickly translated into action. The effect of the drug is primarily to release inhibitions, and the majority of smokers remain friendly and sociable during their "tea parties." Prolonged use by those with a psychopathic personality may result in a certain degree of mental deterioration, but no possible causal relationship between violent crime and the use of the drug has ever been demonstrated. Its dangers, none of them very great, are (1) that it will be used by inadequate or antisocial personalities to gain courage to commit aggressive and violent acts; (2) that inadequate, unstable personalities will substitute the pleasurable effects of pot for all efforts to deal with external reality; and (3) that the chronic user will become dissatisfied with the effects of marijuana and will go on to other drugs, including heroin. Physical dependency on marijuana is minimal, so that abrupt withdrawal is generally advisable.

Dependency on Amphetamines and Other Psychostimulants

Like the use of barbiturates, dependency on amphetamines (Benzedrine, Dexedrine, Methedrine, Desoxyn, etc.) is becoming more and more a public health problem. Approximately ten million people each year take amphetamines on their physicians' orders, but at least an equal number take "pep up" pills or capsules that have been obtained illegally. Users refer to them as bennies (Benzedrine), co-pilots (Dexedrine), and footballs (Diphetamine). Not all users become habituated or dependent, to be sure, and many employ them, only occasionally, for example, to stay awake all night to study for an examination.

The chief effect of the amphetamine group is to mask fatigue and to cut down on appetite. For the latter reason, they form the cornerstone of many medically approved regimens for weight reduction. Susceptible persons, however, may quickly become dependent on them because of the energy, alertness, self-confidence, and euphoria that typically accompany their ingestion. They combat the sluggishness and weariness that are part of many heavy drinkers' hangovers, and they afford a quick lift for the person who feels groggy after a night of sleep for which a sleeping pill has been required. The exhilaration, pressured thought, increased phantasy life, rapid speech, and conviction of ability to perceive, think, and perform better, and all the other elements that go into the feeling of "being turned on," are too effective an enticement for many. Despite the fact that amphetamines are not associated with any significant degree of physical dependence, the craving for their psychologic effects is very insistent, and the high degree of tolerance that builds up with continued use is remarkable. It is not unusual for a user to be on 150 pills or capsules a day, and as his dose mounts he becomes increasingly restless, talkative, and irritable, has difficulty sleeping, and may become increasingly apprehensive. Furthermore, his self-confidence is bought at the risk of judgment and impulse control. He is too ready to take on the impossible task, overestimates his ability to stay awake, begins to have visual hallucinations and responds to illusory sensations, and commits gross errors of judgment, for example, in driving a car or truck (amphetamine dependency is known to occur frequently in truck drivers, who get on the habit trying to stay awake and alert through-out drives across the country), in operating a dangerous and/or delicate machine, in judging the distance of speeding traffic when he decides to cross a highway. Some users go on to develop an overt paranoid psychosis—with auditory as well as visual hallucinations, ideas of reference, delusions of persecution, disorientation, and profound interference with all mental and intellectual processes. In all cases of amphetamine dependency, treatment is the same—abrupt withdrawal, followed by attention to the factors that favored establishment of dependency in the first place.

Another stimulant with high potential for dependency is phenmetrazine (Preludin), used medically for its anorexiant properties. Its effects are very similar to those described for the amphetamines. One complication that develops in some chronic users is a characteristic schizophrenic-like psychosis, that begins with feelings of jealousy and self-referential and persecutory ideas. These progress to illusionary misperceptions, hallucinations involving any or all sensory modalities, and often micro-hallucinations (Lilliputian hallucinations). The subject becomes increasingly restless, excited, and delusionally anxious, and often manifests compulsive, ritualistic handwashing. Treatment, as with amphetamines, is abrupt withdrawal; a few of those with complicating psychosis may require electroconvulsive treatment for their delusional state.

HALLUCINOGEN ABUSE

Hallucinogens are agents that can produce hallucinations—sense perceptions to which there is no external stimulus but which arise, instead, from within the subject himself. Any number of drugs can produce hallucinations, but the term is generally confined to those substances which produce psychological changes in a high proportion of subjects exposed to the drug without producing the gross impairment of memory and orientation characteristic of toxic psychoses or drug-induced deliria. The psychological changes produced mimic, to a large extent, the symptoms of the so-called functional psychoses, and particularly the affect disorders (with manic or depressive elements) and the schizophrenias (with interference in thinking, feeling, object-relatedness, relationship to reality, etc.). Thus they are sometimes termed psychotomimetic, or schizometic; others favor the term psychedelic (mind-manifesting) to avoid the perplexing question of how good a facsimile of spontaneously occurring psychosis is the state induced by hallucinogens. Others term them M.A.D. (mind-altering drugs) or consciousness expanding drugs. Even as used in the more strict sense, however, many hallucinogens are known: hashish and marijuana, mescaline (peyote), lysergic acid diethylamide (LSD), adrenochrome, harmine, tetrahydrocannabinol, diisopropyl fluorophosphate (DFP), tetraethylpyrophosphate (TEPP), N-allylnormorphine, bufotenin, psilocybin (from mushrooms), morning glory seeds (ololiuqui), pulp from banana skins, diemethyltryptamine (DMT), and even nutmeg (myristica).

None of the hallucinogens is addictive, at least insofar as physical dependence is concerned, although some tolerance develops to each of them (and in some, cross-tolerance to other members of the group as well; that is, a person who has developed some tolerance to LSD may require a higher initial dose of mescaline than he would have needed to produce the same effect had he had no previous exposure to LSD). Their ability to produce symptoms similar to those of the schizophrenias—which affect approximately 1% of our population and whose sufferers occupy one-half of all hospital beds in this country because of the long-term and often deteriorative nature of the disorders—was the reason for enormous scientific interest in them during the past decade. It was hoped, not unreasonably, that by producing schizophrenic-like symptoms at will, and then studying how each symptom came into being and how each symptom might be controlled by one kind of therapy or another, knowledge would be amassed as to how true schizophrenic symptoms originated and new ways of treating those disorders might be uncovered. These hopes have not yet materialized, although the psychotomimetic drugs have provided heuristically useful models for the study of the biochemical and neurophysiologic substrata of emotions and of emotional disorder. In addition, there is some evidence that LSD may be of some value in treating chronic alcoholism, and, perhaps, other severe disorders as well.

Whatever their ultimate medical use may be, however, few of the hallucinogens are used nowadays for legitimate therapeutic or research purposes; in fact, for every dose used in research or treatment, approximately one-thousand doses are used illegally. The hallucinations, depersonalization, other worldly sensations, torrent of thoughts, intensification of feelings with a simultaneous lessening of "wanting" or "striving," disconnected images including thrusts of awareness of one's own being, and all the other symptoms that may be produced—sometimes pleasurable, sometimes terrible—have made the hallucinogens the new craze among those who would seek out the unusual, the different, the thrilling. It may not be too difficult to understand how this might come about, for the reckless abrogation of control over self and the flirting with danger required of any rider on a roller-coaster may be the fundamental determinants of a search for "thrills" or "kicks" from a cube of sugar moistened with a single drop of LSD.

Unfortunately, however, the track of the hallucinogen "trip" is neither so rigidly nor so carefully laid as the roller-coaster's. Reactions are not totally predictable, even in those who have had previous experience, nor does the trip end at any specified time. Some will be over all effects within six to twelve hours; others will have severe after-effects, which consist of persisting, or in some cases, perhaps, even irreversible mental changes, or delayed reactions that appear unexpectedly when the subject is no longer under supervision or control, or severe reactions of psychotic proportions that require emergency psychiatric treatment. Furthermore, as with amphetamines, interference with judgment is so severe that the person "on the big A" or on the "acid" may endanger his life without realizing it. Suicides, serious suicide attempts, and even homicide have occurred as part of the psychotic state induced by LSD. Many of the serious complications can be controlled or treated with phenothiazine medication; but even this is not fully predictable or certain.

Of all the hallucinogens available, the ones most commonly used in this country at the present writing are marijuana (already discussed in another section because of the separate status traditionally accorded it), mescaline, psilocybin, and lysergic acid diethylamide (LSD-25). Lysergic acid is by far the most powerful, perhaps 5,000 times as potent as mescaline. The users of any of them are seeking particularly the elements of mystical union with the unknown or spiritual ecstasy and rapture, much as many religious groups have for centuries used one or another of the known hallucinogens as an essential part of their rituals and ceremonies. In fact many of today's users talk about LSD as providing them with a "unitive" religious experience, a one-ness with self, with others, with the universe, with God, a feeling that no matter what one's inner thoughts and visions might be, they are experienced by everyone else on the drug: a conviction of communication that often the user has never experienced in real life. For some, LSD (known as "The Chief," "The Cube," "The Hawk"), is a way to stimulate artistic productivity; and even though the more objective self-appraisers admit that most of what they produce under LSD is worthless, they tend to maintain that they would never have produced the one worthwhile picture or chapter without the insight afforded by the drug.

LSD is relatively easy to obtain because its manufacture is not a complicated process, and it has been alleged that chemistry laboratories in many colleges and universities are turning out enormous quantities of it. In New York, it is sold as a colorless, odorless liquid that is usually dropped onto a cube of sugar. A dose costs somewhere between two and five dollars, although as with most such commodities the pushers will set whatever price the traffic will bear. LSD users, though, seem to feel themselves much more ethical, honest, and trustworthy than those who are hooked on H, and they treat the latter with a certain amount of undisguised contempt.

MISCELLANEOUS DRUGS

Among the other drugs that are being abused currently in the United States are the deliriants—a group of substances, many of them volatile solvents, which when inhaled or otherwise ingested produce dizziness, slurring of speech, disturbances in orientation and memory, dream states with visual hallucinations, and, if enough is taken, unconsciousness, coma, and even death. The deliriants are directly toxic, both to brain and to liver, and while they are not associated with a high degree of physical dependency even their erratic and infrequent use is hazardous. Among the deliriants used are model airplane glue, gasoline, lighter fluid, cleaning fluid, and paint thinner (all of which typically are sniffed).

So far, gasoline sniffers have been boys, generally from an unsettled or discordant home where the father is weak, ineffectual, or brutal, and the mother an overindulgent, easily intimidated person, who allowed her child to manipulate her from his earliest years. As a result, the affected child developed little tolerance for frustration, and later in life when his every demand was not instantly met he found in gasoline sniffing a way of re-treating from anxiety into drunken euphoria, often with visual and auditory hallucinations.

Glue sniffing also is largely confined to adolescent and pre-adolescent boys from a background of severe emotional deprivation. They are under-achievers academically, of limited intelligence, are often involved in delinquent activity such as stealing, tend to be impulsively defiant, socially inept, and intolerant of stress. For many, sniffing is used to combat feelings of helplessness and depression and/or as a stimulant to erotic phantasies and behavior. In some, inhalation of fumes can produce a reversible brain disturbance, with disorientation, visual hallucinations, and epileptiform seizures.

Withdrawal from the deliriants should be accomplished abruptly, since no withdrawal or abstinence symptoms occur.

Etiologic Factors in Drug Dependency

The foregoing descriptions of different types of drug abuse have already alluded to some of the behavioral and personality characteristics of drug abusers—they are young, immature, demanding, impulsive, intolerant of control, negative to authority, dissatisfied with ordinary living, constantly on the lookout for new adventures, new thrills, new kicks. We know more about teenage heroin addicts than about other drug users, but the evidence available suggests that even they do not form a homogeneous group, and we anticipate that the difference between users of different drugs will be at least as great as the differences among users of the same drug.

Closest to the stereotype of the addict is the "hustler"—the user whose conventionality is low and whose delinquent tendencies are high. This group is characterized by low tension tolerance, poor impulse control, amorality, emotional instability, stubbornness, and conflict with authority, and it accounts for as many as 80% of heroin addicts. The hustler is often a suspicious loner, whose sensitivity to real or imagined slights alienates him from others. His facade of omniscient bravado covers the insecurity he feels about his sexual identity (many addicts are overt homosexuals), and the anxiety he feels about his poorly controlled aggressivity. Typically unreliable, untrustworthy, and manipulative, he tries to force narcissistic supplies from a reluctant environment, but he does it ineptly and tends to antagonize or otherwise repel those from whom he would seek sustenance. He abrogates responsibility for his actions and his welfare, seeking a magical solution in the strength and control that others will exert over him; but when the magic fails to appear, he retreats from his would-be helpers and sinks into an anxious resentfulness. He convinces himself that it is society that is sick, not he; that society has made him an addict and now would punish him for its own crimes; that the only hope for relief from his pulsations of anxiety and panic, the only possibility of escape from his frightening drives and impulses, lies in drugs. Even though they will not provide the whole answer to underlying problems, drugs will provide a release for tension, an escape from conflict, and a patterned illegal rebellion.

Another type of drug abuser is the uninvolved isolate, whose long-standing and extensive personality problems have interfered with interpersonal relationships and group identification long before he was exposed to drugs. Users in this group are unconventional, unusual, strange, even bizarre; they are passive, dependent, and often immobilized by anxiety. They are not so likely to act out against society as the hustler; rather, they use drugs to safeguard their passivity and dampen their anxieties. At best, their adaptation is an insecure, uncertain one; but perhaps for them, drugs allow more functioning than they could achieve in any other way. It is within this group that most of the overt schizophrenics are found, and because of the nature of the underlying disorder it is difficult to assess the contribution of a drug habit to the personality deterioration that is generally seen over a long period.

In increasing numbers, a third type of drug abuser is seen—a conformist, high in conventionality and low in delinquent tendencies. Many in this group are upper-middle-class adolescents, whose pattern of drug use is a current pattern of rebellion against parents, a rebellion whose main aim is to afford differentiation from the older generation and to establish identification with a peer group. Drug abuse in such youngsters is probably little more harmful than swallowing goldfish was in F. Scott Fitzgerald's time. In schools, drug users form a group united by reason of their shared special experiences. They tend to denigrate those who do not use drugs or, as with LSD users as already mentioned, those who use drugs other than those that are "in" at the moment. Many begin drug use mainly as a means of esthetic enrichment, increased sensitivity, and as part of "getting more experience under my belt." The problems of this group are the problems of adolescents in our culture; the main dangers of conformity to a pattern of drug use are untoward reactions that have not been anticipated or prepared for, and so complete a rebellion against the "Establishment" that school or other authorities feel duty-bound to move against the user.

Perhaps to be included within the third group are those students who use stimulant drugs on special occasions, for very specific purposes, such as to stay awake while cramming for examinations. By far the overwhelming majority of such students move on to ways of life that do not include drug abuse, and only the susceptible minority will make such drugs an end in themselves.

Another type of drug abuser has been labelled the two-worlder, the person who, on the one hand, maintains—at least on the surface—a high degree of conformity with the standards of the community, but, on the other, will flaunt every law or ethic that interferes with his drive for the drug(s) of his choice. Many physician-addicts and nurse-addicts are in this category, and they lend themselves less easily to the usual psychodynamic formulations of drug-dependency than most other drug abusers.

No doubt other forms of drug abuse and drug dependency will be differentiated as our knowledge in this area increases. At the moment, though, we can only say that drug dependence stems from many factors, psychologic, social, economic, cultural, ethnic, and even biologic and physiologic variables, and it seems unlikely that the same formula is applicable to all who are drug dependent. We can confirm in many abusers the usual hypothesis, that they are fixated at a passive, narcissistic level of development, seeking gratification without needing to make any return. For such a user, the drug offers hope of fulfillment of a deep, primitive, oral desire for food and warmth, without having to give and without having to consider reality. Genital sexuality is uninteresting and is bypassed in a regression to the very earliest stage in libidinal development, where libido exists only as amorphous tension energy. Addiction represents an attempt to replace external frustrations with pleasurable phantasies, or to evade internal inhibitions (usually of a depressive nature) by drugging their source, the super-ego.

Yet passive-narcissism and a desire to evade frustration are hardly confined to the drug dependent, and one might wonder if there is anything specific in the metabolic or physiologic constitution of the addict that determines his particular way of achieving such ends. There is much to indicate that the really characteristic trait shared by the drug-dependent and severe, habitual drug abuser is a specific proneness to drugs. Not all who are exposed to drugs become addicts; mere withdrawal of the drug and cure of the associated physical dependence does not remove the psychologic craving for the drug; and most of those who make drug use their way of life have sensed almost from the first dose (or at least long before true physical dependence can develop) that the drug gives them the special kind of relief, that nothing else has ever before provided. Such proneness may well be physiologically determined, and current research is making every effort to define its nature at a cellular level.

Treatment and Rehabilitation

Management of drug dependent people cannot wait until the laboratory provides answers to our many questions about the nature of dependency. Instead, we must face the problem as best we can immediately, for the thousands and thousands of drug abusers endanger their own mental and physical health each time they give themselves another dose. But, what is even worse, they are often committed to the philosophy that their need for drugs justifies any amount of criminal activity that will guarantee them a supply, and, furthermore they threaten society by their tendency to introduce others to their own patterns of drug use.

In general it can be said that the drug abuser cannot cure himself alone; that withdrawal from the compounds on which he is dependent will require strict medical supervision; and that rehabilitation must focus not only on placing him back within his community, but must uncover and control or ameliorate the conditions that contributed to his dependency, at all levels of his functioning and living.

In competent hands, withdrawal of the user from drugs is a relatively simple medical problem, which need not concern us here. But rehabilitation is another matter, for to have any chance of success, any rehabilitation program must be multifaceted and truly comprehensive. It must provide at least the following:

(1) continuity of contact with the rehabilitation team—psychotherapist, vocational counselor, placement worker, physician, nurse, recreation and occupational therapist, social worker, family counselor, etc.— whose exact composition will be dictated by the needs of the specific patient;

(2) experience in healthy group living and interpersonal relationships, such as could be provided in a well supervised neighborhood center;

(3) emergency housing facilities, to help with the severe problems in family adjustment that the drug abuser almost certainly has, and to serve as a refuge from unbearable strain in his own home;

(4) emergency medical facilities to provide quick admission and early

discharge as the patient's fluctuating course and expected frequent relapses will require;

(5) use of those who have kicked the habit for new admissions to the program, as field workers, case finders, and rehabilitation cadre.

Experience gained with many different approaches, used over a period of many years and tried in many different countries, underscores the necessity of developing an individualized approach for each drug dependent person. For most, total abstinence will not be possible, and maintaining that as a goal is unrealistic. Instead, each person must be brought, coaxed, and cajoled into what is optimal functioning for him while treatment for his chronic, and not wholly reversible, disorder continues. Such a program must attend to the patient's physical health, to his relationships to other people in the community (and especially to his family), to his antisocial or criminal activity, and to his drug intake.

Most of the recent advances in management of drug dependent persons have centered about three areas:

(1) Legal measures, including imposition of strict control over any drug with a high potential for abuse, and enactment of laws that will make medical treatment of addiction mandatory;

(2) Group approaches, and particularly the use of residential rehabilitation centers for addicts while they overcome their dependence on drugs; among these programs are Daytop Lodge, Synanon, Teen Challenge, and Encounter;

(3) Pharmacologic agents to antagonize the effects of narcotics. Methadone and Cyclazocine are two such agents that have received much attention recently. Methadone is a long-acting synthetic narcotic that blocks the euphorigenic action of heroin and other opiates thus rendering them ineffective without itself producing narcotic effects. Patients can be stabilized on relatively low daily doses of Methadone, supervised carefully to guard against illicit use of Methadone and to prevent abandonment of Methadone dosage with return to narcotics, and thus freed of their need to spend every waking moment searching for a new supply of illegal drug.

Cyclazocine is another synthetic narcotic antagonist which prevents the action of large doses of narcotics; since it prevents the development of physical tolerance, it controls the factors that ordinarily lead to compulsive build-up in heroin dosage. Published reports to date, though they are few in number, are promising in their results, and Cyclazocine may well take its place alongside Methadone as the pharmacologic mainstay in the fight against addiction.

The pastor's role in meeting the challenge of drug abuse is a complex and important one. It will vary with the specific needs of his congregation, and it will have to be as individualized as the entire rehabilitation program for each abuser. While a judgmental, moralizing approach will usually fail, the pastor cannot let himself become an apologist for delinquency. An understanding of the emotional and psychologic factors that favor abuse of drugs will not by itself resolve dependency on them. Yet armed with such understanding the pastor can become the fulcrum around which rehabilitation efforts turn. His functions include the following:

(1) case finding;
(2) early referral to a physician, drug clinic, or hospital for medical evaluation and detoxification; it must be recognized that preparation of the subject for such referral is often the most important step in his treatment program;
(3) education of the community regarding the nature of the problem and the need for treatment programs;
(4) implementation of rehabilitation plans;
(5) counseling the abuser and his family.

GENERAL REFERENCE

A.M.A. Committee on Alcoholism and Addiction. "Dependence on Barbiturates and Other Sedative Drugs." *J.A.M.A.*, 1965, 193: 673–677.

Bier, W. C., ed. *Problems in Addiction: Alcoholism and Narcotics.* New York: Fordham University Press, 1962.

Connell, P. H. *Amphetamine Psychosis.* Maudsley Monograph no. 5. London: Oxford University Press, 1958.

Dole, V. P. and Nyswander, M. E. "Rehabilitation of Heroin Addicts after Blockade with Methadone." *New York State J. Med.*, 1966, 66: 2011–2017.

Freedman, A. M. "Drug Addiction: An Eclectic View." *J.A.M.A.*, 1966, 197: 878–882.

Hamburger, E. "Barbiturate Use in Narcotic Addicts." *J.A.M.A.*, 1964, 189: 366–368.

Helpern, M. and Rho, Y. "Death from Narcotism in New York City." *New York State J. Med.*, 1966, 66: 2391–2408.

Osnos, R. J. "The Treatment of Narcotics Addiction." *New York State J. Med.*, 1963, 63: 1182–1188.

Solomon, D., ed. *The Marihuana Papers.* New York: Bobbs-Merrill, 1967.

Symposium: *Non-narcotic Addiction. J.A.M.A.*, 1966, 196: 707–723.

Time-Life Special Reports. *The Drug Taker.* New York: Time, Inc., 1965.

Wilner, D. M. and Kassebaum, G. G., eds. *Narcotics.* New York: McGraw-Hill, 1965.

9

COUNSELING THE TEENAGER

Wolfgang W. Riedel, Ph.D.

Introduction

ADOLESCENCE has been defined as a period of transition from child-hood to adulthood which, while not linked to any precise span of years, roughly extends from the onset of puberty to the attainment of sexual maturity, full height and mental potential. Adolescence may be understood as both a developmental and a cultural phenomenon. Most appropriately, it may be defined as a psycho-biological phenomenon, occuring in a social setting. The pubescent individual experiences his biological changes in a cultural frame of reference and reacts to them in line with his social and personal history. Most generally, the hoped-for outcome of this transition period will be the attainment of adult status. L. Cole has described the characteristics of maturity as follows:

> A true adult is, then, a person of adequate physical and mental develop-ment, controlled emotional reactions, and tolerant attitudes; he has the ability to treat others objectively; he is independent of parental control, rea-sonably satisfied with his point of view of life and reasonably happy in his job; he is economically independent; he is not dominated by the opinion of those about him, nor is he in revolt against social conventions; he can get along in ordinary social situations without attracting unfavorable attention; and, above all, he has learned to accept the truth about himself to face reality instead of either running away from it or making believe it is not there. [1]

[1] Cf. L. Cole, and T. Hall, *Psychology of Adolescence*.

For our purposes, we might well add that a true adult is one who has attained a reasonably integrated view of himself as a creature of God, so that he is able to describe and experience his faith as something that is an integral part of him.

The maturational tasks that face the adolescents are indeed formidable; they have been very adequately described by R. J. Havighurst;

1. achieving new and more mature relations with age mates of both sexes
2. achieving a masculine or feminine social role
3. accepting one's physique and using the body effectively
4. achieving emotional independence of parents and other adults
5. achieving assurance of economic independence
6. preparing and selecting an occupation
7. preparing for marriage and family life
8. developing intellectual skills and concepts necessary for civic competence
9. desiring and achieving socially responsible behavior
10. acquiring a set of values in an ethical system as a guide to behavior [2]

None of these tasks can be solved instantaneously, for they involve a fairly prolonged process of trial and error, of the evolving and testing of hypotheses, and of slow and often tortuous growth toward greater integration in any and all of these task areas. Because adolescence, particularly in our culture, extends over a rather long time, many adolescents have little motivation to master these developmental tasks very rapidly. Progress often lags, much to the disappointment of those responsible for the adolescents' welfare. Writers of all persuasions, scientific as well as religious, have pointed to the very real difficulties encountered by most adolescents during this period of transition.

It would seem quite logical that many adolescents would require some assistance beyond that ordinarily provided by the families or even by the school in mastering the complex tasks facing them, and, unfortunately, the Church at the parish level appears to have been less than responsive to their needs. One reason for this may be the lack of training on the part of many clergymen in the area of counseling adolescents. To help eliminate this problem, this chapter intends to provide information on basic counseling procedures with adolescents to aid the prospective pastoral counselor in acquiring the necessary tools to serve effectively the needs of the youths of his parish.

[2] Cf. R. Havighurst, *Human Development and Education*.

Definition of the Counseling Process

While there is no general agreement among professional counselors regarding the exact nature of the counseling process in all of its ramifications, there does seem to exist a consensus as to some of the basic ingredients of the successful counseling process. These have been summarized by Carl Rogers in the form of six basic psychological conditions that are necessary and sufficient to bring about constructive (personality) change: (1) that significant positive personality change does not occur except in a relationship. His first condition then is simply psychological contact; (2) that the client is in a stage of "incongruence" (this term refers to a difference between the actual experience of the individual and his self picture), and when he is even vaguely aware of such incongruence he is anxious; (3) that the necessary condition for a client's constructive personality change is that the therapist be congruent or integrated in the relationship, that is, that he, the therapist, must be freely, deeply, genuinely himself with his actual experience accurately represented by his awareness of himself; (4) that it is necessary also that the therapist experience unconditionally positive regard for his client, or more precisely that he must care for the client as a separate person and permit him to have his own feelings and experiences; (5) that the counselor must experience and try to communicate empathic understanding to the client; (6) finally, that the counselor must be at least minimally effective in communicating both his empathic understanding and unconditional positive regard to the client in a way that the client will definitely perceive that the counselor empathizes and accepts, and not feel that such attitudes do not exist in the relationship as far as he the client, is concerned.[3]

The committee on the definition of the counseling divisions of the American Counseling Association also describes the objectives of counseling by focusing on the contribution of the counselor. They point out: (1) that the client's realistic acceptance of his own capacities, motivation, and self attitudes, (2) that the client's achievement of reasonable harmony with his social, economical and vocational environment, and (3) that society's acceptance of individual differences and the implications for community, employment, and marriage relation are the primary contributions of the counselor.

Having considered these basic ingredients, it seems safe to say that the prospective counselor as a reasonably integrated person, who has unconditional regard for his client, is able to share the client's emotional experi-

[3] C. Rogers, "The Necessary and Sufficient Conditions of Therapeutic Personality Change," *Journal of Counseling Psychology*, 21 (1957), pp. 95–103.

ences at least to some extent, and can communicate his acceptance and his empathy to the client, can be successful. However, he must also remember that the object of the counseling process is not and cannot be the solving of the client's problems by the counselor. Most individuals seek counseling aid because they have not learned to solve their own problems. Therefore, while assistance in the solution of a given problem may afford temporary relief, it does not help the individual to do something about changing the causes of his problems. A counselor should also keep in mind that it is not his task to make the client happy and satisfied. Although it is to be hoped that the conclusion of a successful counseling experience will have brought the client a degree of serenity and relief from previously intolerable anxiety, this is not a goal of the counseling process per se; rather, it is a by-product of the effective counseling process. Other unacceptable counseling goals include efforts to remodel the client to the point where he will be pleasing to a given segment or to all of society, or to persuade him to alter important life decisions in favor of alternate ones preferred by the counselor. Basically, the counselor's chief goal is to maximize the God-given potential of the client to live effectively and happily, without imposing his own views and values on the counselee. This may seem to be an alien goal to the pastoral counselor, and he might well argue that it is the latter's moral responsibility to persuade the client to move toward more ethically acceptable conduct, if he finds the client acting in a morally deviant manner. Nevertheless, experience shows that counseling is most effective where it follows the above suggestions, in other words, where the counselor refrains from attempts to impose his own value system as a model for solutions to problems.

If the counseling relationship prospers, the client will in all likelihood become motivated to model himself after the value system of the counselor, even where the latter has refrained from urging such a change in values. Furthermore, for most Catholic clients seeking pastoral counseling, reemphasis on the moral teachings of the Church should be unnecssary from an information-giving point of view. It is, of course, possible that a prospective client may approach the pastoral counselor for the purpose of obtaining advice. If the request is for information, it may be appropriate to give such information. Where the counselor has reason to suspect that the client (consciously or unconsciously) is seeking to manipulate the priest into solving his life problems for him, it would seem unwise to grant such requests. It would only tend to prolong the exaggerated dependence of that adolescent on others and will do nothing to further the main aim of the counseling process, to allow the client to become more competent in the solving of his own problems.

INDICATIONS AND COUNTER-INDICATIONS FOR COUNSELING

It may be reasonably anticipated that the bulk of prospective clients will be self-referred; we shall therefore focus our attention on this particular group and devote only a few passing remarks to situations where the pastoral counselor may be required to work with clients referred by agencies or institutions. While self-referral is not in itself a predictor of success in the counseling process, it has been the general experience of counselors and psychotherapists alike that self-referred clients tend to profit more from counseling.

While professional counselors ought not restrict their practice to any given group of clients, it would seem wise for the relatively inexperienced counselor to adopt some guidelines to help him decide whether or not he should offer his services to a prospective client. It would seem advisable for the pastoral counselor to restrict his activities to the following types of clients: 1) Those free from severe symptoms of psychopathology; adolescents seeking the priest's help who appear incoherent, are apparently hallucinating and/or delusional, or who show other marked indications of lack of sufficient contact with reality as well as prospective clients with profound anxiety states who appear either deeply depressed or quite agitated would best be referred to other sources. 2) More generally, prospective clients who do not, for any reasons (for example moral deviancy or physical appearance) cause the prospective counselor undue anxiety and make it seem doubtful that he would be able to work with them effectively; those that do cause such anxiety might best be referred elsewhere. 3) Clients who are not expected to have marked "secondary gains" from the counseling relations; clients who are suspect of leaving such gains may also have to be denied counseling. While the present writer does not advise that such cases should automatically be excluded from counseling, the counselor should be thoroughly familiar with the type of gains the client may be expected to have from being engaged in the counseling relationship and attempt to determine how this may interfere with the counseling process. We are here defining "secondary gains" as those conditions which may lead a prospective client to seek counseling not for the intrinsic benefit to be derived from the counseling experience but rather, to escape the consequences of his own behavior in the community or to gain some kind of compensation from entering the counseling process (often of a monetary nature). Typically, in the case of adolescents, we are thinking of such conditions as having a counseling relationship being made a precondition for not being expelled from school or not having to face juvenile court or even court-ordered detention. Similarly, youngsters who may be approaching the counselor in the hope of gaining special consideration in their evaluation in his (the counselor's) school for example, would probably lack the necessary motivation for making the counseling experience a meaningful one. It should be noted that automatic exclusion of any of these cases is not recommended. Rather, each case has to be carefully weighed in terms of the adolescent's past behavior and an appraisal of the circumstances surrounding his request for counseling. 4) Clients who do not primarily need vocational guidance. Those clients whose need for counseling seems to be primarily of a vocational nature should not be accepted for counseling by the pastoral counselor, unless he has been adequately trained in the collection and interpretation of data pertaining to a prospective client's aptitudes and interests. Where such skills are lacking, and request for guidance is forthcoming, it would appear best that the counselor explain to the client his inability to serve him effectively in this area and suggest other resources.[4]

These four counter-indications regarding pastoral counseling are by no means hard and fast rules. They should simply be taken as guidelines for prudent restrictions based on a realistic assessment of the counselor's capabilities and of such factors as may a priori interfere with the counseling relationship. Wherever possible, the refusal of service should be put in such a way that the client does not feel needlessly rejected by the counselor; in each instance, every effort should be made to explain to the rejectee that the counselor is suggesting other referral sources in the best interest of the client and that no personal dislike or negative evaluation is intended by this referral. In the case of those who may possibly be suffering from severe emotional disturbance, the priest might well point out to the youngster that he would be perfectly willing to talk with him but that any such relationship must be supplementary to one involving a mental health specialist (psychiatrist, psychologist or social worker) because he does not feel qualified to cope with the full range of possible problems that the client may be presenting.

Pastoral counseling would, therefore, seem to be intended for and most effective with the great majority of adolescents who are not severely disturbed emotionally, but who find that they are experiencing difficulties in coping with the developmental tasks appropirate for this phase of life as outlined in the initial portion of this chapter. These 10 developmental tasks may be conveniently subsumed under one major heading: the search for attainment of an identity. Erik H. Erikson has addressed himself most elegantly to this problem and has described adolescence in terms of this

[4] C. Wrenn, "Status and Role of the School Counselor," *Personality and Guidance Journal*, 36 (1957), pp. 175-183.

overall goal.[5] Following him, we may define identity as the accrued confidence that one's inner sameness and continuity are matched by sameness and continuity of one's meaning for others. Erikson also stresses that adolescents are trying many identities, and are struggling to integrate many facets of personality. Therefore, a certain degree of instability and changeability of expectations and outlooks are rather normal in this life phase and are not to be confused with the severe disturbance that this lack of an adequate identity may indicate in later phases of life. Sex differences in the adjustment that each adolescent has to make in this period are of particular importance. While the struggle for the choice of an acceptable and satisfying occupation is perhaps first and foremost among the concerns of the male adolescent, this is not a problem of the same magnitude for girls. Elizabeth Douvan and Joseph Adelson have argued persuasively that the completion of the identity formation process in adolescence is only possible for the boy; the average girl's identity depends to a large degree on the status of her eventual husband. If a girl cannot reasonably plan for marriage in the same manner that a boy can plan and strive for an occupational identity, then her identity will not fully develop until after she has married, or, in the case of an apparently increasing minority, after she has made the vocational commitments which were once the sole prerogative of males.[6]

The difficulties that the typical adolescent faces in completing the various developmental tasks appear to have derived mainly from two sources. First, the adolescent is confronted by a revival of the many problems he faced in his development from birth to about the age of six, namely, those of his problem of defining his role acceptably in relation to both father and mother, satisfying his need to control himself instinctually, and alleviating his fears about lack of sufficient dependency (or the converse of it, not being allowed to be independent enough), which, this time, he must work through to a more or less permanent solution. Second, the profound bodily changes that accompany the onset of puberty, and provide most adolescents with some of the physical signs of manhood or womanhood, together with the physiological tensions that accompany the acquisition of greater sexual maturity, both of which motivate the average youngster to seek a redefinition of the "family contract" which hitherto has defined his role, duties, and prerogatives in the family in a way that is now largely outmoded. The notorious inability of most parents to "let go," together with the adolescent's exaggerated drives for independence, usually make this re-negotiation of the contract a mutually painful and vexing one.

David P. Ausubel defined the relationship of the preadolescent child with

[5] E. Erikson, "Identity and the Life Cycle," *Psychological Issues*, 1 (1959).
[6] Cf. E. Douvan, and J. Adelson, *The Adolescent Experience*.

his parents as one of "satellization," [7] and others more sociologically ori-entated speak of "engagement." Therefore, what now must begin is a process of desatellization (in psychological terms), and disengagement (in social terms). These complementary processes are fraught with uncertainty and ambiguity for many adolescents. For, whereas, on the one hand they are bitterly clamoring for release from undue parental bondage, they are at the same time consciously or unconsciously worried about the day when they have to assume complete responsibility for themselves in both an economic and (primarily) personal-social sense. It is only natural, then, that the adolescent will frequently resort to exaggerated claims for independence in the secret hope that it will not be granted, and to reassure himself that he still has a measure of belongingness and safety in the family realm. In a word, then, we can state that the adolescent faces three major problems: 1) he needs to come to terms with his new bodily powers and the instinc-tual pressures that he is now experiencing; 2) he must successfully redefine himself in a dynamic rather than static way opposite the other family members; and 3) he must learn to assume an ever-increasing degree of self responsibility and self determination. Therefore, at this point it might be observed that the vast majority of difficulties that adolescents may seek counseling help for most probably are related to difficulties in one of these three major task areas.

To facilitate the adolescent's transition from childhood to adulthood, he frequently resorts to complex memberships in various peer groups, for to the extent that the adolescent has to reject parental norms and values in order to find and define his own, the peer group provides a ready reservoir of such values and a mirror for the roles and identity rehearsals the ado-lescent undergoes. Contrary to common parental fears, the peer group is usually an extension of the parental value schema. While it may adhere to styles profoundly different from adults and while its members may show rather marked differences in their taste from that of their parents, the basic value scheme of a given peer group usually resembles (and even exaggerates) the normative values embraced by the parents. Profound personal unhappi-ness is very frequently due to the inability of an adolescent to find accep-tance in a desired peer group. Such acceptance is commonly withheld be-cause of the evident inability of the youngster to conform to peer group standards, because of physical or personality difficulties. Thus, very early as well as very late maturing youngsters may find themselves at least tem-porarily excluded from the peer group because of their inability to "fit in" in a physical sense. The emotional suffering, particularly of the late develop-ing boy or girl, is frequently underestimated by the adult. As the late

[7] Cf. D. Ausubel, *Theory and Problems of Adolescent Development*.

developers watch their peers grow into physical adulthood, their own lack of development takes on the character of a major catastrophe and they are often convinced that this condition is irreparable and will, therefore, never change. Adult impatience with this attitude, inspired by hindsight, is highly inappropriate, and contributes to the fact that a goodly number of youngsters seeking counseling aid of the pastor will come from the ranks of "peer-group rejectees."

Space limitations do not allow us to discuss in detail the numerous specific complaints which may be brought to the pastoral counselor. However, some of them, such as problems inherent in pubertal growth, have been discussed in other chapters in this book. We can only reiterate here that the adolescent who is likely to seek help from the pastoral counselor may be expected to have more or less profound difficulties in arriving at an identity which is satisfying to him and acceptable to the society in which he lives.

COUNSELING TECHNIQUES

At this point in our discussion it seems appropriate to introduce the reader to the notion of a "counseling contract," a term which implies that effective counseling depends, to some extent, on the proper understanding of both client and counselor as to what their proper roles are, and what the counselee may reasonably expect in terms of process and outcome. Such an understanding counteracts the development of unwarranted fears which may easily lead to excessive resistance, and even tends to curb to some degree the "transference relationship." By this we simply mean that the client who has undergone appropriate structuring of the counseling process beforehand will be less likely to invest his counselor with attributes and powers which the latter neither possess nor, if he did possess them, would be in a position to use in the manner that the client hopes for. To illustrate, the pastoral counselor is not the client's father and should not be expected to act like one. An emotional attitude on the part of the client which would invest the pastoral counselor with a paternal image could make the counseling process which, by necessity, has to be rather short-term, a rather lengthy, even interminable process.

Structuring, then, simply consists in telling the prospective client what the counselor can and cannot do for him. Usually, the client is told that the counselor will be listening with utmost attention and interest to the client's complaints and feelings and that in this process clarification of his difficulties can be achieved—this in turn, it is hoped will increase the client's ability to deal effectively with life's problems. Rarely is effective structuring achieved at the beginning of counseling. Finally, it should be noted that frequently, the respective roles of client and counselor have to be reclarified throughout the counseling sequence.

What then are the actual techniques that a counselor might be expected to utilize in the counseling process? We shall attempt to list and briefly discuss some devices which have been found useful by counselors of various persuasions. However, it should be noted that the listing is by no means exhaustive and that other techniques are also of considerable value. The ones listed here are recommended because they seem particularly well suited to the counseling of adolescents and also because the counselor who effectively utilizes them is likely to refrain from activities which are beyond his professional skills.

1. First and foremost, the counselor makes a strong and consistent effort to understand the client's content of speech and feelings conveyed by words, gestures, expressions, etc. It would seem particularly important to focus on the feelings expressed by the adolescent client. Very often, some of the thoughts expressed may seem unrealistic, contrary to what common sense dictates, and perhaps even plainly ridiculous. It is here that the counselor must understand that most adolescents are perfectly capable of logical and reality-oriented reasoning processes, and that while their verbalization may not always reflect this, the deviancy expressed in their thoughts is frequently more apparent than real. Adolescents, apparently, are so used to having to attempt to explain their thoughts to adults whom they perceive as uncaring and hostile, that their thinking often appears to have an aggressive overtone or even a paranoid flavor. Many counselors find that after one or two sessions which focus on the expression of feelings rather than the actual words used by the client, they see a remarkable change in the latter's verbalizations.

2. It is also very important for the counselor to convey his understanding to the client by his words as well as by his general attitude. This should not normally take the form of "I know just what you are talking about —I had exactly the same experience several years ago . . ." This writer has frequently found—through bitter personal experience—that one's own youthful exploits have only very limited teaching applications to the problems of today's adolescents, partly because of the changed context of things, and partly because most adults have a vivid memory for the content of their own adolescent experiences, but have conveniently managed to "forget" the affective (emotional) component of these events. Therefore adults are rarely able to really feel the same outrage or shame that their client may be presently talking about.

Rather, this understanding should simply be a sincere effort on the part of the counselor to comprehend what the client is experiencing at this time.

3. The appropriately timed reflection of feelings and thoughts is also important, for this technique not only enables the counselor to convey his understanding to the client, but has the added purpose of helping the client to clarify his thoughts and to give them greater precision.

4. The actual interpretation of the client's thoughts, if attempted at all (and this writer would caution the would-be counselor to be very economical in its use), should be made on a level that the counselor perceives to be within the realm of the client's experience. An interpretation which either states the obvious (by the verbatim repeating of what the client has said, without any additional clarification being achieved) or, which is aimed at the client's "unconscious," will probably not promote profound insights. Rather, it may indeed engender in the client a considerable degree of resistance and feeling of not being understood by the counselor. If the counselor finds it absolutely necessary to give interpretations to the client, they should take the form of questions rather than direct statements. Very often, the device of repeating a critical word in a client's preceding statement in a questioning manner serves the purpose of guiding the client in the desired direction.

5. Occasional remarks about the nature and limits of the therapeutic relationship, the proper expectance in regard to the present situation, and the therapist's confidence in the ability of the client to learn to deal effectively with his problems, will also be necessary.

6. The answering of questions or the giving of information may at times contribute to the client's "working through" of his problems. However, a counselor should studiously refrain from such procedures when he sees that they will increase the client's dependency.

7. As a rule, the counselor refrains from interrupting the client, unless it is obvious that such interruptions are really necessary. Most adolescents (as well as many adults) have had numerous experiences with persons who, with the best of intentions, have plied them with advice, exhortations, and admonitions, but have never paid them the ultimate courtesy of hearing them out.

8. A counselor may also find it very useful to attempt to give the client a synopsis of the discussion of the previous session at the beginning of the next one: Such a procedure frequently saves time as well as provides an over-view of where the client and counselor together have

been. The counselor should also encourage the client to correct, amend or, in any way alter the synopsis and point out that it is being attempted for the explicit benefit of the client.

The Physical Setting for Counseling

Once a potential client has approached the counselor for an appointment, a mutually convenient time should be set for, under most circumstances the counselor cannot interrupt his activity, and counseling in a hallway or while the counselor is engaged in other duties is simply not counseling. The length of the interview (usually 50 minutes) should be discussed with the client beforehand and closely adhered to. It is undesirable for the counselor to arbitrarily shorten the interview time, or to allow the client to extend it beyond the time agreed on. Needless to say, the client may request termination of the interview at any time and this should be granted. If the counselor is forced to cancel an appointment for unavoidable reasons, he should, whenever possible, notify the client beforehand and arrange an alternate time for the interview. If the client has to cancel an appointment, this should be readily accepted unless it occurs too often. Frequent cancellations should be discussed with the client in terms of the meaning for the counseling relationship and may well need to be included in the structuring process. If the client does not meet an appointment without previous notification of the counselor, he should be required to make a new appointment. To enhance the counseling processes, the interview should take place in as much privacy as possible, in an adequate and attractive setting. The counselor should also arrange beforehand that interruptions do not occur (or at least will be minimal), for few things are more distracting to the youngster seeking help than a counselor who is answering the telephone repeatedly while supposedly counseling him, or one who often leaves the room on other business.

These measures are designed to emphasize the reality governing the relationship between client and counselor, and to minimize opportunities for the client to exploit the counselor. They also afford the client some reassurance about the entire counseling process. While informality and a relaxed attitude should characterize the counseling relationship, these should not affect the physical limits governing it.

Special Problems in the Counseling Relationships

The pastoral counselor faces several additional problems in his counseling activities which are either connected with the age of his client, or arise from the fact that he may be playing multiple roles in his relationship to the adolescent seeking his counsel.

Since the adolescent client is legally under age, the question of the pastoral counselor's responsibilities toward the client's parents needs to be explored here. Should the client obtain parental permission to see the counselor before counseling can begin? Should the pastoral counselor ask the prospective client's parents for permission to counsel this child? These are difficult questions to answer, and so most community service agencies and private practitioners serving adolescents will not see an underage client except with the express knowledge and permission of the latter's parents or legal guardians. Occasionally, an agency may permit a few contacts, which are usually defined as being short of a counseling relationship, before parental involvement becomes mandatory. While it may be assumed that the vast majority of parents would be happy to have their youngsters counseled by a cleric, nevertheless, it cannot be concluded that the pastoral counselor does not need to obtain parental advice and consent. It should be remembered that doing so may, of course, jeopardize the counseling relationship and realistically expose the client to parental pressure to discuss with them the nature of his problem, and even put the cleric in the difficult position of having to withhold information regarding his client from the parents, should they request it. Perhaps the most practical solution would be to acquaint the parents of the value of adolescent counseling, and to involve them as much as possible in the discussion of a counseling program for their son or daughter. The cleric might also point out to the parents that in the opinion of moralists almost the same confidentiality that governs the sacrament of confession also applies to the non-sacramental counseling process and that, therefore, for the good of all involved, the adolescent should be allowed to seek help from his pastoral counselor without having to explain or defend this relationship to anyone else, including the family. While it would seem that most mature adults would accept this approach quite readily, it does not follow from this that the clerical counselor would be legally protected in the unlikely case of a lawsuit. If a counseling program is planned in a parish or school, it might be advisable to consult the services of a lawyer to seek greater clarification on this point.

Another possible approach would be to acquaint those concerned with the general purpose of pastoral counseling services, and then to publish in the church bulletin a "negative release slip" to the effect that the parent is presumed to have given his consent to a possible request on the part of his child for counseling by any of the parish priests, unless he returns a (preprinted) slip indicating that he does not wish to have such counseling take place without his specific knowledge.

A second problem area, that of the multiple-role relationships of the clergyman to the prospective adolescent client, does not have legal implications, but nevertheless does include a number of possible difficulties. First and foremost, the pastoral counselor may have a teacher-disciplinarian relationship with the adolescent seeking his counsel, and may feel that it is difficult, if not impossible, to combine two such disparate functions. However, experience shows that this simply is not so, and that the good counselor is usually able to "thin out" his teaching function so that it does not interfere with the counseling experience of his client. In fact, most counselors in public schools have similar dual teaching or disciplinarian roles to play.

A third, and perhaps even more serious problem is that of the conflicting responsibilities of the counselor in terms of safeguarding the interests of his client as well as of the group to which the counselor belongs. Since the counseling relationship is not afforded sacramental protection, the question of confidentiality must be considered, in those instances when the client's actions are obviously damaging to other members of the pastoral counselor's parish or school, or to society at large. Though there is no clear and certain answer to this problem, this writer feels that the primary allegiance of the counselor must be to the individual client, because the client might never have revealed compromising data and thereby endangered himself by discussing his problems with the counselor, had he not been led to believe that any revelation of his would be treated confidentially. However, it should be noted that some counselors and moralists hold that when the common good, the rights of a third party, or the well-being of the individual himself is gravely endangered, the counselor is justified in revealing such compromising data to the proper authorities. If the counselor follows the latter view, and does indeed intend to use the knowledge gained in the counseling process outside the counseling relationship when conscience requires him to do so, the client should be so advised and be given an opportunity to withdraw from the counseling relationship before counseling is initiated. While this may well be more a theoretical problem than a practical one, it nevertheless enters into the definition of the counseling process and therefore cannot be ignored.

Special Procedures in the Counseling of Adolescents

Thus far we have discussed only the one-to-one relationship in treating of the pastoral counseling process with adolescents. However, at least two alternatives are available. First of all, it is theoretically feasible to think about including the parents in one way or another in the counseling process, by offering counseling not only to the individual adolescent, but also to other members of his family or even to an entire family group. Secondly, it is possible to involve adolescents in group counseling. The technique of family counseling is a comparatively new one, and since there are, at present, difficulties, it cannot be discussed in detail in this chapter. Those interested in this technique, will find it adequately treated in a book by Virginia Satir, entitled: *Conjoint Family Therapy*. The pastoral counselor who might find it advantageous to include the other family members in the counseling process should observe the following cautions: 1) the entire family, or at least those members present in counseling are your clients; 2) do not allow yourself to become a referee for family quarrels, for it is almost unavoidable that one or the other members of the family group will attempt to enlist the aid of the pastoral counselor in his struggle against other family members, and to the extent that he is successful, the counseling undertaking is jeopardized. The emphasis in such family counseling, just as in individual counseling, has to be on clarifying the feelings and thoughts expressed by the various family members. Interpretations, advice, and similar guidance techniques are definitely not recommended. The successful family counselor will focus on improving communications among the various family members and on aiding them in the clarification of reality processes. "Depth-oriented therapy" designed to effect a profound personality change is beyond the ability of the average pastoral counselor and should therefore not be attempted.

Group counseling with adolescents may, in contrast to family therapy, be the technique of choice when a number of adolescents are willing to undergo a group experience and when the counselor thinks that greater benefits may accrue to the clients from the group process. This would be especially true for youngsters who feel rejected or isolated from the peer group and who are seen as needing the support and feeling of "being in the same boat" that group membership can offer them.

Effective group counseling demands a thorough understanding of group composition. Unfortunately, research on this point is rather sparse and inconclusive. Nevertheless, while opinions regarding the "proper" compositions of counseling groups differ, it seems entirely appropriate to form counseling groups without any detailed and diagnostic knowledge of the group members' particular personalities or specific problems. To the extent that the counselor has interviewed each prospective group member and excluded those who appear so seriously disturbed that referral to mental health resources seems warranted, he can comfortably expect that there will be similarities among these youngsters sufficient to generate the desirable "being in the same boat" feeling. Even when it appears that an individual is very different from the others, his inclusion need not be an obstacle to a well functioning counseling group. Aside from excluding apparently severely disturbed youngsters, the counselor might well decide to work with groups of one sex only. While there are no theoretical objections to coeducational counseling groups for adolescents, greater freedom of expression may exist in a monosexual group. Traditionally, adolescent counseling groups have been segregated according to sex, because most practitioners have found this to practical advantage.

The counselor may also do well to consider separating groups according to age. It would seem that the difficulties experienced by youngsters in the early stages of adolescence are sufficiently different from the problems that preoccupy the older adolescent, that segregating them into older and younger groups is necessary to further the feeling of belonging and of being understood and accepted.

Let us now consider group counseling procedures. As in individual counseling, a degree of structuring will be necessary to assure adequate functioning of the group. The clients should be informed that the primary purpose of the group is to afford them an opportunity to express themselves freely on any topic that seems to be of importance and interest to them. The counselor might also point out that concentrating on their feelings has often been found to increase the self understanding that is generated by the group process. He should also remind the group that while he is their group leader, he does not intend to assume the role of an advisor or director of activities. Furthermore, the group must understand that it has been established for the benefit of the clients and that no a priori restrictions will be placed on the content or direction of the discussions. The counselor's role should be explained as that of one who is in charge of the physical arrangement of the group including the prompt beginning and ending of the session and the selection of a moderator. As in the individual counseling process, occasional restructuring may be necessary to assure the group that progress toward their goal is possible, and to take care of whatever contingencies that may have arisen in the course of the group's progress. The counselor's role continues to be that of a warm, accepting, and empathetic listener who is able to convey his regard and empathy to the clients and to aid them in the progress of self-exploration through reflection and clarification. Beyond the counselor-client interactions occurring in the individual counseling process, the counselor engaging in group work must pay particular attention to the following problem: the extent to which the group, in contradistinction to the counselor, may be judgmental toward one or more of their members, for it is important that the counselor not allow the group to terminate the session at a point at which a given member has been greatly upset by group comments. When such an event occurs near the closing time of the group, the counselor should prevent the expression of anger or hostility toward a particular member by first indicating that the time is too short to bring this particular line of discussion to a fruitful conclusion, and, then, by reassuring the "target" client that criticism by the group members is not to be taken as a reflection, but rather as a sign of their honest and serious concern for him rather than by forbidding such angry or hostile statements. It should be evident that whenever free self-expression is encouraged or even permitted in a group, the group leader must assume a reasonable degree of control so that each individual will learn that self-revelations need not result in untoward feelings of hurt for him.

Another point that must be considered is group size and frequency of meetings. While some counseling groups have had as many as twelve members, groups seem to function best with from five to seven members, with six generally being considered the ideal number. Research in group dynamics shows that member satisfaction is highest when the group numbers five or six members and decreases sharply when the number is decreased or increased. When there are fewer than five members, the clients tend to feel too much "on the spot" and free expression is hampered. On the other hand, when the group numbers seven or more, some clients feel left out of the process and group cohesion and satisfaction suffer. Group meetings, just as individual counseling sessions, are usually held at least once a week. When the groups meet less often, the group process seems to become diluted and less growth is likely to take place. More frequent meetings are usually impossible because of the schedule commitments of the pastoral counselor.

At this point, it has probably become apparent to the perceptive reader that group counseling demands skills beyond those necessary for counseling individuals. This seems particularly so because of the need for some control over the group process. This writer would therefore strongly recommend that the prospective group counselor gain some theoretical knowledge of small group processes (Cf. Bibliography), and have at least one experience as a member of a therapeutic group before attempting it. Participation in a small group process laboratory (popularly also known "sensitivity group"), would seem to be especially suitable to the prospective group counselor's needs, it will afford the counselor firsthand experience with group process and also give him models of how to guide a group of this type. Engagement in group work without these prerequisites is not recommended, is ill advised and should not be attempted. Such small group laboratories are conducted in many metropolitan areas by various organizations. Information may be obtained by writing to the Case Institute of Technology, at Cleveland, Ohio.

SUMMARY

Techniques of counseling, with special reference to the process of adolescent identity formation, were outlined in the preceeding sections of this chapter. We shall attempt to briefly recapitulate the main points of this process:

1. The adolescent seeking counseling help does not seek "advice" in the common sense of the word. Rather, he is searching for means of improved self definition.
2. This suggests that the counselor's role is not to help the client solve specific problems, but rather to assist him in improving his overall problem solving ability.
3. This can best be achieved through a warm and accepting relationship in which the counselor empathetically attends to the client's thoughts and feelings, and in turn is able to convey his empathy to the client.
4. The counselor refrains from attempts to directly promote insight, but rather, restricts himself to clarification and reflection of the client's feelings and thoughts.
5. The counselor must acquire the ability to listen to the client. (If any single point warrants emphasizing, it is this one. The adolescent who seeks counseling usually has had more than his share of "advice"—if getting advice is as helpful as often assumed, he would not have felt in need of a counseling experience in the first place.)

Having thus summarized the basic points of counseling, we may then conceptualize counseling as a process of disorganization and reorganization of the self at a higher level. Through counseling the client learns to symbolize more accurately a wider range of sensory and visceral experience and to reconceptualize a system of values based on his own feelings and experiences rather than to continue to function with those second-hand values which he has never been able properly to incorporate into an over-all value system.

Though the prospective pastoral counselor, even by close attention to the points discussed above, will not automatically become an effective, skilled counselor, he may well become the kind of person to whom adolescents will come for help by adhering to these principles. In a word, when a pastoral counselor effectively utilizes these principles, he is no longer just one more adult who attempts to remodel adolescents in his image, but rather, a competent counselor who can give ultimate proof of their inherent worth and dignity by allowing them to solve their own problems in their own unique way. This writer can think of no more appropriate goal for those who would aid the adolescent in the arduous and often painful process of "becoming a person."

REFERENCES

On Adolescence:

Ausubel, David P. *Theory and problems of adolescent development.* New York: Grune & Stratton, 1954.

Erikson, Erik H. *Childhood and society.* Second Edition. New York: Norton, 1963.

Douvan, Elizabeth and Adelson, Joseph. *The adolescent experience.* New York: John Wiley, 1966.

Gallagher, J. Roswell, and Harris, Herbert I. *Emotional problems of adolescents.* Revised Edition. New York: Oxford U. Press, 1964.

Hurlock, Elizabeth B. *Adolescent development.* Third Edition. New York: McGraw-Hill, 1967.

Steimel, Raymond J. (Editor) *Adolescence: Special cases and special problems.* Washington, D.C.: Catholic U. Press, 1963.

On Counseling and Therapy with Adolescents:

Arbuckle, Dugald S. *Counseling: An Introduction.* Boston: Allyn & Bacon, 1961.

Balser, Benjamin H. (Editor) *Psychotherapy of the adolescent.* New York: International Universities Press, 1957.

Holmes, Donald J. *The adolescent in psychotherapy.* Boston: Little, Brown & Co., 1964.

Hamrin, Shirley A. and Paulson, Blanche B. *Counseling adolescents.* Chicago: Science Research Associates, 1950.

10

COUNSELING THE RELIGIOUS SISTER

Vincent S. Conigliaro, M.D.

WE SHALL discuss, in this chapter, counseling; counseling of the Religious Sister; and such specific points as: What is counseling; why is it effective; how is it effective; what does it do for both counselor and counselee; what special skills should the counselor have—or what special considerations should he keep in mind—when the counselee is a Religious Sister.

It is essential to understand right from the beginning how little "Counseling of the Religious Sister" can be separated (as a topic) from "Counseling" in general. With Religious Sisters there are, obviously, in-group characteristics, relevant only to Religious Sisters (as there are with any other human groups); consequently, in counseling Religious Sisters, considerations will be appropriate that would be irrelevant to the counseling of other groups. Aside from this, however, counseling of the Religious Sister is, first and foremost, counseling: counseling of human beings in difficulties, individuals that is, with drives, needs, aspirations, conflicts, and fears as any other human beings.

Nor does one find, in counseling Religious Sisters, personalities "*sui generis*" (as contrasted with the personalities found in the laity): just personalities, as unique (and as different from each other) as one finds with any other human beings; and with group determined similarities as secondary (when contrasted to the primary, individually-determined uniqueness) as with groups of soldiers, artists, businessmen or farmers. Counseling of the Religious Sister, therefore, cannot be treated without a thorough understanding of counseling theory and technique in general.

A clear apperception of this point is essential also from a clinical standpoint. In counseling the Religious Sister, one must first see the person, not the habit. The right balance must be struck between awareness of her in-group characteristics (as Religious Sister) and awareness of her uniqueness (as a human being). To approach the treatment of the Religious Sister without appreciation of what it means, experientially, to be a Sister is superficial; it is even more superficial and prejudicial, to approach it only thinking of her as a Sister.

Counseling of the Religious Sister, then, differs from counseling in general only in the obvious fact that the counselee is a Religious Sister. In terms of practical considerations, of course, this means that the counselor must understand Religious life, in its form and in its essence, phenomenologically and psychodynamically. He must understand Religion and religious needs in depth and see them as something other than an "illusion without a future." He must appreciate what the vows of obedience, poverty, and chastity are about; and both the gross appearances and the nuances of community and contemplative life, of cloister and mission, of duties and obligations; understand, in other words, his patient, in this case the Religious Sister, her Religion and her creed, her *Weltanschauung* and her everyday life.

In this chapter, therefore, we shall treat, first and foremost, counseling. Dimensions specifically relevant to Religious Sisters (in the sense described above) will be interpersed throughout the first two parts of the chapter and treated, in greater detail, in its third part. More specifically, our conceptual itinerary will be the following:

Part I is an *INTRODUCTION*. It offers a definition of counseling; it discusses what counseling is and differentiates it from other types of interventions on the psyche.

Part II consists of *GENERAL THEORETICAL AND TECHNICAL CONSIDERATIONS ON COUNSELING*; Section A treats the theoretical aspects of counseling, Section B the technical.

Section A covers the most essential aspects of any discussion on counseling. Counseling technique cannot be learned in a vacuum, divorced from the theory to which they belong. The tendency to learn the "How" instead of the "What" must be firmly resisted in learning about counseling, a highly sophisticated science whose technique cannot be reduced to formulas, blueprints, "Ten-Easy-Steps." This section, with its emphasis on the conceptually sophisticated, psychologically and philosophically complex theory on which counseling techniques are based, should neutralize temptations to use "How-to" approaches.

Part III consists of SPECIAL CONSIDERATIONS IN COUNSEL-ING THE RELIGIOUS SISTER. This part discusses such specific prob-lem areas as neurotic motivations for the religious life, loneliness, boredom, etc.

PART I—INTRODUCTION

In attempting to define counseling before describing and discussing it, one senses that its essence eludes tight, rigid definitions and that (just as with psychotherapy) it suffers when forced into terse, prefatory statements. In reviewing the literature one finds a few excellent definitions of counsel-ing [1*]; yet one is tempted to go along with Egan who, before defining it wrote: "Counseling, as Love, is a many-splendored thing." [2] I propose to dispense (temporarily, at least) with a true definition, and make do with a descriptive statement just giving us an idea of what is it that we are talking about. Let us say, then, that counseling is a special kind of psycho-therapy, aimed at helping human beings suffering from psychological problems; and let us note that counseling is much more closely related to psychotherapy than it is to teaching or guidance. The best way to begin to understand what counseling is (and is not) is through an il-lustration.

Sister Mary rarely asks to confer with Sister Superior; when she does, it is always for everyday matters relating to her teaching second grade in the parish school. Sister is always tidy, composed, and fastidious. She is never late (or early) for anything, her linens are always perfectly in place, her habit always freshly pressed. Today she has asked Sister Superior for an appointment, arrives more than twenty minutes early, is flustered, nervous, and fidgety and whereas she usually looks straight into the eyes of the people she is addressing, today her eyes are consistently low. Without any preamble, she tells Sister Superior that she is having "difficulties" with her children and has been wondering whether it would be against charity and obedience to ask to be relieved from teaching and be transferred to another house where she would only do nursing work. Sister Superior answers. Shortly afterward Sister Mary abruptly looks at her watch, realizes it's almost time for confessions, excuses herself, and leaves. Let us examine this hypothetical, yet typical situation from the viewpoint of the various ways Sister Superior might have handled it.

[1*] In this chapter, authors and works carrying superior numbers will be found in "References," pp. 220–221.

In one case Sister Superior goes over the obligations of charity and obedience with Sister Mary, explaining under what circumstances one would indeed be defaulting on them. This is not counseling; Sister Superior is engaged in religious instruction, spiritual direction.

In a second case Sister Superior asks Sister Mary for details. Predictably Sister gives a long list of intellectual and scholastic problems. Sister Superior, who is the principal of the school and has had years of experience with teaching, indicates to Sister Mary the many different things Sister might do to help herself in her teaching duties. This is not counseling either; Sister Superior is practicing a form of guidance.

In a third case, this is not Sister Superior's day; she woke up early in the morning with a headache and Sister Mary's premature arrival irked and annoyed her. She has no time to answer Sister's questions and dismisses her brusquely by telling her, "Of course, of course, you are supposed to accept difficulties and tribulations. It's part of religious life. Just go back to your classroom and do your best." This, certainly is not counseling either, but unadulterated rejection and oversimplified rationalizing and sermonizing.

In a fourth case, Sister Superior listens to Sister Mary in a relaxed manner and with attention and empathy. She does not close her eyes to Sister Mary's uncustomary behavior: requesting an appointment, arriving earlier, lacking in composure, the fact that she is not looking into her eyes. When Sister Mary poses her opening question, Sister Superior answered it fully and warmly (more or less as in the first case). When Sister Mary describes her difficulties as solely intellectual and academic, Sister Superior listens with attention and possibly follows the approach exemplified in the second case; but does not stop there. She wonders (silently) whether Sister Mary has found it "safer" (emotionally) to perceive her difficulties as purely intellectual (whether, in other words, Sister Mary is lying to herself); then, toward the end of the visit, she says: "Say, let us not make any decisions now. Why don't you come by again to talk of this; or of anything else that may be on your mind." This is not counseling either. In this last case, however, Sister Superior comes closest to it. To begin with, she engages in what I call the "counseling attitude," by which one relates to the "wholeness" (conscious and unconscious) of another person, thus hearing and seeing more than what appears on the surface; and, secondly, takes the indispensable first step preliminary to all counseling—she "structures" the interview.

Let us now see if we are a few steps closer to knowing what counseling is.

1. We see, first of all, that counseling is not "advising" (even though the two words "counseling" and "to counsel"—to advise—are so similar). Advice giving, giving instructions, may be part of what some call "prescrip-

tive counseling"; more regularly, however, they are found in teaching and what is known as "guidance."

2. Nor is counseling simply "tender loving care," "being sympathetic," "listening kindly"—as in the second and fourth cases of our illustration. Physicians, nurses, Religious Sisters have all been kind and loving whenever a patient, a friend, another Sister came to them with a problem weighing on her heart. Being sympathetic is certainly part of true counseling; but with one important difference: in the non-counseling situation usually one openly communicates loving feelings to one's friend in need; in counseling (in which the counselor relates to the counselee's conscious awareness of his difficulties; and the counselee's unconscious facets of personality) kindness and love are expressed more discriminately.

It is important, again, to appreciate the limitations—the "medicinal properties" one might say—of love, if unnecessary frustrations (especially in the frequently "emotionally-tight" quarters of community life) are to be avoided. Love is, to some, very strong medicine; it is to be taken, like sunshine, in very small doses. Also, at unconscious levels of personality, love may have unusual effects on its recipients: it may inhibit, frighten, puzzle, shame, even enrage.

3. Nor is counseling compatible, finally, with authoritarianism, dogmatism, a "Father knows best" attitude, rejection, and impatience a "You just do this and that and you will be okay" attitude.

Let us now summarize all we have been saying so far, explicitly and implicitly with a view to a possible definition of counseling.

Counseling is one of the behavioral sciences, a kind of psychotherapy, a service profession for people suffering with emotional problems. It is something other than teaching and guidance. It is more than indiscriminate lovingness and empathy. It is never authoritarian and rejecting; it thrives on acceptance and relatedness. In counseling, the content of the communication is less intellectual than in guidance and refers to highly unique problems, affecting the counselee as an individual rather than a member of a group or class. The recipients of the service do not lack knowledge, do not want information; they "know the score," so to speak, but can't help themselves: can't do, think, feel what they know they should feel, think and do. Finally, there are, in counseling, such constructs as "counseling attitudes" and "counseling structures" and a counseling theory and technique. Counseling may be defined as a highly specialized approach to the psychologically disturbed individual; a process in which the patient is helped to "take counsel with himself," [3] i.e., to unearth and rediscover his true self from under the rigid armor of repressions and conflicts, thus giving re-birth to his free, non-mechanical, psychologic, and spiritual humaneness.

PART II—GENERAL THEORETICAL AND TECHNICAL
CONSIDERATIONS OF COUNSELING

A. *Theoretical Considerations*

Although all types of counseling (therapeutic, diagnostic, supportive, motivational) are, ultimately, "therapeutic," counseling is first an "approach" to the psychologically disturbed individual; it is, therefore, more than just a method of treatment—somewhat in the same sense that psychoanalysis, a depth-approach to the human mind, is more than just a treatment modality.

Counseling practice is based on a body of scientific knowledge: counseling theory. There is nothing haphazard in the counselor's seemingly casual approach to his patients; behind the "bartender's approach" of the nondirective counselor, a far reaching philosophy of man is to be found.

The theoretical foundations upon which counseling rests basically coincide with the personality theories espoused by the psychoanalysts and the existential psychologists. These are "psychodynamic" theories of personality, the differences between the various theorists and practitioners of counseling being differences as to the emphasis some give to Freudian concepts and others to neo-Freudian or existential concepts.

Of the many aspects of counseling theory only the following will be considered here: 1. the view of man as "man" rather than as a machine or a biological automaton; 2. man as a "wholeness," a "Gestalt," rather than a sum of component-parts; 3. development of personality; 4. dynamic influence of the unconscious; 5. the defensive meaning of symptoms; 6. the power of words.

1. *Man as "man"*

Counseling theory's view of man is refreshingly unlike the many contemporary philosophies viewing man at worst as a machine, predictable as one and just about as interesting, at best as a cybernetic automaton, as Pavlovianly conditionable as his best friend on four legs.

Counseling theory, as indicated above, is refreshingly antimechanical and committed to a unified and humanistic philosophy of man. In counseling, we said, the patient is helped to take counsel with himself; to rediscover, as we can better understand now, his humanity, to re-commit himself (in feelings, in the actual art and practice of living) to a human view of self and others.

From a historic-philosophic perspective, counseling theory as psychoanalysis was a reaction to the mechanistic philosophies. The recoil from over-positivistic and over-rationalistic views of man and the return to the unified, humanistic view of the Judeo-Christian and Greco-Roman tradition started with Freud, the last and great representative of the Rationalism of the Enlightenment era and the first to convincingly show its limitations. Freud was the first to raise the curtain onto the complexity of man's consciousness and unconscious dynamisms and the unknown depths (and heights) of man's mind. Psychosomaticists, neo-Freudian scholars, the existentialists, and then the counseling theorists followed on the trail first opened by Freud, further demonstrating the complex (psychological, biological, and spiritual) nature of man; viewing man as "man" first, "animal" second; essentially unpredictable; existential rather than simply biologic in nature: the only child of nature who "transcends the rest of nature";[6] a life form whose complexity dwarfs that of the most sophisticated computers.

2. Man as a wholeness

This aspect of counseling theory is the psychological corollary to the philosophical conception of "man as man."

a) *The Gestalt concept.* To say that man is a "wholeness" or a "Gestalt," means that man is *not* a "sum" but a wholeness of parts, a wholeness transcending, and different from its constituent parts. Man is not body *plus* mind, but body *and* mind; is not organ A *plus* organ B *plus* organ C, but organ A *and* organ B *and* organ C. Similarly, man's mind is not memory *plus* attention *plus* intellect *plus* emotion, etc., but memory *and* attention *and* intellect *and* emotions.

Before death our body is a product of organs, one influencing the other. After death we become an un-Gestalt, a sum, with each of our organs continuing to live, after the heart has stopped beating, its own individual existence for a few seconds, a few minutes, or a few hours.

This concept has many important implications. If man is a Gestalt, there can be no artificial separation between intellect, emotions, "the spirit," etc. Also, since man is a Gestalt, to affect or diminish a part, will necessarily affect and diminish the whole. Hence a person therefore cannot be "retarded" only in his intellect without being retarded also in his emotions; a person cannot be "physically" sick without also having a "mental" sickness; a Sister cannot have a religious sickness (i.e., inability to pray) without an emotional sickness.

b) *Conscious-unconscious.* Man is a wholeness also in the sense that he is both consciousness and non-consciousness. Patients' problems are partly consciousness. Patients' problems are partly conscious and largely unconscious. Sister Mary went to Sister Superior consciously concerned about her teaching, and simultaneously, with other, unconscious concerns. A Religious Sister may have symptoms of anxiety which she consciously relates to the frustrations of the physical dimensions of her femininity; actually she is anxious for unconscious reasons as well, of which she knows nothing. Another Sister's depression is consciously related, by her, to the fact that she masturbates compulsively; but her depression will be found related to the compulsive masturbation and to many other factors (unconscious) as well.

The conscious-unconscious aspect of man's wholeness has many implications of great import, both clinically and philosophically. Some of its practical implications will be discussed under the section on the "Dynamic Influence of the Unconscious"; one implication that can be briefly discussed now is that things are never *only* what they seem.

Awareness of the conscious-unconscious wholeness results in what can be called the "paranoid commitment of the counselor." Paranoids are suspicious individuals, always discovering connections between unrelated events, always reaching unwarranted conclusions. A good counselor engages in a bit of paranoidism purposefully, to see his patients in their wholeness. He always asks himself: "Why?" and is not satisfied till he can answer his "whys" on several levels, some conscious, some unconscious. In the last case of our illustration, Sister Superior did exactly that. She searched for connections between seemingly unrelated manifestations of Sister Mary's behavior (the early arrival, the unusually ruffled linens and habit, the looking down, etc.), seeking *tentative* but warranted conclusions for the sake of better understanding Sister in as much of her wholeness as possible.

c) *Body-Mind.* Man is a wholeness also in the sense of a complete and never-ceasing integration between body and mind.

Beyond the evidence offered by psychosomatic medicine, the most dramatic illustration of the inseparable unity between body and mind was probably provided in Spitz [7] studies on maternal deprivation. In humans, psychological differentiation occurs within the first week of life. From this time on, psychological needs (for love, emotional security, inter-personal relatedness) will be superimposed upon previously purely biological needs (for food, water, warmth, etc.); from now on, the fulfillment of solely biological needs will be no longer sufficient to preserve life. Foundling infants raised in institutions in which excellent care was provided for their bodies, but whose minds were starving because of the cold emotional climate of the institutions, lost weight (despite forced feeding), became psychomatically depressed, slowly "aged," and eventually died. Post-mortem studies of these infants consistently failed to reveal physical or organic causes for their irreversible wilting. The prophet had a very deep psychological insight who said "Man doth not live of bread alone"; the human animal needs love and a meaningful interrelatedness with other humans as much as he needs food and sunshine.

Another illustration of body-mind integration is offered by the severe psychosomatic conditions (especially skin and intestinal disorders) occuring in infancy-and childhood-schizophrenia. It is as though in the very young mind (that has not yet learned to protect itself through complicated defense mechanisms and sophisticated mental symptoms) rejection of a world experienced as hostile and ungiving is expressed by continuously defecating on it (colitis) or by the development of protective defensive scales over most of one's body (psoriasis).

d) *Body-Mind-Spirit.* Another aspect of man's wholeness is the integration between his biological, psychobiological, and spiritual dimensions. Remaining, because of space limitations, on a superficial level of discussion, one may just reflect that the old statement, *"Mens Sana in Corpore Sano"* should be complemented with *"Religio Sana in Mente Sana."* This concept is of great importance in treating Religious Sisters, whose psychological pathology invariably includes religious and spiritual pathology. Thus one could observe that as man's health ("health" here is meant not only clinically but also ethically) improves or perfects itself, one does find better and better patterns of adaptation first on a strictly psychobiological level, then on an existential level, and finally on a religious-spiritual level. Just as in infancy and childhood psychological as well as physical needs have to be fulfilled if one is to survive psychobiologically, in adulthood and maturity spiritual and religious needs must be fulfilled if one is to survive existentially and spiritually.

3. Development of Personality.

Theories of personality development are a central aspect of all psychological theories and much can be written on the subject. Only those aspects of personality development will be discussed here that are relevant to the treatment of counseling techniques. The concepts discussed here belong to a Freudian, psycholanalytic theory of personality,[8] with modifications that are only minor and supplementations that although original are still within orthodox Freudian context.

In my personal philosophy of life and psychoanalysis, man can be thought of as a life-form capable of functioning at three levels of adapt-ability and response-ability (here one means the ability to respond, not "responsibility" as a moral concept).

The ability to adapt and to respond are two essential characteristics of all life forms, from one-celled Protozoa to man. Even the simplest form of life is capable of adaptation to its environment. If we place an ameba in a medium and drop in some carbonic acid, the ameba will respond by moving away from the acid, thus adapting to the change in its environment. The types of responses of which a life form is capable become progressively more sophisticated as one moves up in the scale of evolution. The responses the ameba is capable of are purely biological and chemical. In man one finds physico-chemical responses (for instance, to the introduction of food in the stomach, the cells lining the inside of the stomach respond by secreting digestive juices), but, also, other responses, extremely more complicated (and less and less "mechanical"): neurological, social, cultural, psychological, and spiritual.

As just mentioned man is a life-form capable of functioning at three levels of adapt-ability: a lowest level, that may be called the "natural-biological level," a middle level, "the natural existential" one, and a highest level, the "spiritual." At the lowest level, man fulfills biological needs, i.e., the need for food, for oxygen, for sex, for the disposal of waste products. At the middle level man fulfills equally important existential needs, i.e., the need for love, for companionship, for security, for prestige. At the highest level man fulfills his spiritual needs, which are understood differently by different psychoanalysts. For Jung [9] spiritual needs are the need for recognition of a "numinous experience" and for a "religious experience" of submission to a deity, for Fromm [10] these needs are the need for co-existence with another human being, co-existence recreating the feeling of at-oneness lost after man's fall (i.e., separation from nature); for a theistically religious psychoanalyst these needs are the need for God and reunion with the Creator.

Personality basically consists of a complex network of responses to stimulations: The reader's personality is right now responding to stimuli, physical stimuli (the temperature of the room in which he is reading; sounds; light; etc.), emotional (feelings about the chapter he is reading); cultural; social; spiritual; etc. In responding to stimuli we adapt to our environment. But why is it that we *have* to respond and adapt? To answer this question we must discuss a third characteristic of life, that is, the "tendency to homeostasis."

"Homeostasis" basically means "equal balance" of tensions, of energy. All life forms are energy systems. Man is a system made of physical energy (enabling him to walk, lift weights, eat and digest food), and psychic energy (enabling him to think, feel, remember, will, etc.). The "tendency to homeostasis" means that all life-forms strive at maintaining a balance, an equilibrium of energy within themselves. Stimuli are energy, too. They disturb the energy equilibrium of the life forms they stimulate, thus causing in them a surplus of energy. This surplus causes a lack of homeostasis, which is experienced subjectively as discomfort, tension, or anxiety. Responses have the function of reestablishing some homeostasis which is experienced, subjectively, as quiescence, comfort, or pleasure.

Responses reestablish homeostasis by getting rid of the stimulus (which had created the energy surplus to begin with). A newborn baby is asleep. As long as his stomach is full, his bladder empty, etc., he is in a state of relatively high homeostasis and remains asleep. Then his bladder may get full; the mass and weight of urine are energy, a stimulus causing a surplus disturbing his homeostasis. The baby will respond by emptying his bladder, thus eliminating the source of the energy surplus (and the attending discomfort) and temporarily reestablishing homeostasis. The same cycle stimulus-homeostatic response is found in coughing or sneezing-out foreign matters, closing one's eyes when lights stimulate the optic nerves, the scratching reflex, etc. In the case of mental stimuli with their more complicated mental responses the cycle also appears. A lecture, interesting or boring, is to each student a stimulus, inevitably creating, with its new, unfamiliar concepts, a surplus of psychic energy in the student's system. This surplus is bound to cause lack of homeostasis and discomfort till such time as the student finds some kind of homeostatic physical, mental, or psychosomatic response: understanding the material, thus making it part of himself, until it is no longer a disturbing foreign body; taking notes, by which the task of having to understand difficult concepts is postponed; intellectual rejection, by which the student "sneezes out" the lecture; daydreaming or falling asleep, etc. Response-ability and adapt-ability, therefore, have the function of protecting homeostasis. We adapt and respond to achieve pleasure and avoid pain; personality is the ways and the means each of us develops in the search of pleasure and in the flight from anxiety.

The stimuli man responds to may be external: lights, sounds, the mental stimulation of parental teaching. The most important stimuli, however, come from within: these are our instinctual needs and wants, our hunger and our thirst, first for food, physical security, biological "pleasure"; later for love, emotional security, existential "pleasure," still later for spiritual security and spiritual "pleasure." Instinctual needs disturb homeostasis too; responses must be found to satisfy these internal stimulations also. When we find the "right" response we achieve some degree of homeostasis; when we do not and instinctual needs remain ungratified, we experience discomfort, tension, or anxiety. In human beings, the apparatus designed to discover, coordinate, and control responses is what we call "mind." Let us see how these concepts may help us in understanding growth and development of personality.

Adapt-ability, response-ability, and the tendency to homeostasis, we said, have the purpose of fulfilling needs. Actually our needs are never totally fulfilled and very often are not even partially fulfilled; as a matter of fact, were our needs always fulfilled, there would be no mental development. Our mind grows from infancy to maturity exactly because our needs are frustrated and new ways (what I call "alternate routes"; what Freud called "displacements" and "sublimations") must be discovered if *some* homeostasis is to be achieved. Life is the endless maneuvering to establish *some* homeostasis. As long as we are alive, we are never completely successful at this; but as long as we are engaging in these maneuvers, we are alive, growing, and developing.

An illustration of this may be found in the human newborn. Before the umbilical cord is cut, oxygen reaches the infant through the cord and the baby is relatively homeostatic. Development occurs as soon as the cord is cut. Now the infant needs oxygen (his first need, his first internal stimulus in his new world) and this need must be satisfied in a new way, through a different response. As long as he does not engage in a new response, the newborn experiences severe lack of homeostasis and the "pain" of asphixia; in engaging in his first response (his first respiratory act, coincidental to his first cry). He has taken his first alternate route, his first detour around that "something" (the cutting of the umbilical cord) interfering with his previous ways of satisfying the need for oxygen. With his first alternate route, the newborn has truly begun to live; had the cord not been cut, had it not been necessary to devise a new way of getting oxygen, there would not have been development nor life. Mental development consists of the development of better and better alternate routes, all in protection against the anxiety caused by the impossibility of satisfying our needs; alternate routes adopted automatically and quite unconsciously.

To better explain the concept of displacement and sublimation in personality development, Freud used the concept of "urging and checking forces." Urging forces are, among other things, our instinctual needs (internal stimulations), urging us to reach those objects through which some homeostasis is possible. Checking forces are all the obstacles coming between urging forces and the needed objects (for instance, the child needs food but mother tells him he should not have any). Checking forces, too, can be external and internal, the latter of much greater importance for personality development; an example of internal checking forces would be prohibitions from one's conscience (or its unconscious equivalent, the "super-ego"). Alternate routes are the displacements taken by our instincts whenever the urging forces need object A, object A is not available or permissible and a similar object, B, is utilized instead of A.

Let us see, as an illustration, how personality develops through the displacements of various instincts.

The oral instinct is the instinct impelling us to "take-things-in" by the mouth. At the beginning of life, this response occurs whenever the stimulus is the need for food. Every time this need is frustrated, the infant experiences anxiety; every time this need is satisfied, he experiences pleasure. Because of the fact that every time milk flowed through the mouth anxiety disappeared and pleasure followed, the infant soon comes to associate pleasure with taking-things-in by the mouth; as a result, all human beings take-things-in by the mouth whenever they are anxious and looking for security (as compulsive eaters and smokers well know). Let us see the steps of displacement of the oral instinct.

From birth to 6–12 months of age the infant satisfies the oral instinct by sucking on the mother's breast. Soon, however, an external checking force will appear: weaning. The oral instinct must find a new object; the normal baby may displace onto his thumb. Now from 6–12 months of age to 2–3 years of age the infant satisfies his oral instinct by sucking his thumb, and as long as his urging forces can focus on the thumb, anxiety is avoided. Note the progress in this first displacement: before, when hungry for food, the baby was totally dependent on mother; now, whenever he is hungry for security, he can depend on himself (the thumb is his own).

Soon, however, another checking force will appear: the child is told he is not supposed to suck his thumb. The oral instinct must find a third object; the normal baby may displace on to sucking lollipops. Now from 2–3 years to 6–7 years of age the child satisfies his oral instinct by sucking on lollipops. Note again the progress in this new displacement: the thumb was a personal object, lollipops are social objects; they can be bought, shared, given as presents to the little boy next door to show our liking for him (one could not very well give him one's thumb to suck on, as a schizophrenic child I once treated used to do). But a checking force will appear again. As the child grows, external and internal checking forces will unmistakably convey to him that it is no longer appropriate for him to go on sucking lollipops. The oral instinct will have to find, again, a new object. The child, adolescent, young man, will displace onto chewing gum, sucking candies, biting his nails, playing an "oral" musical instrument (i.e., the trumpet), playing with his lips, smoking, sucking on a pipe, drinking beer from a bottle, etc. There usually is little resemblance between the last object in the chain of alternate routes and the first one; yet if one follows the chain of displacements link by link, one realizes that object F is indeed similar to object E, and object E to object D, and D to C, etc.

Displacement occurs with all instincts ("partial instincts," biological instincts, psychobiological instincts, social instincts, etc.), because all instincts meet with checking forces. Let us see the development of personality through the displacement of the aggression-instinct.

John is 4 and an only child, until a little brother, Junior, is born. Junior comes between John and his homeostatic objects, his parents; naturally enough John will be angry and jealous. External checking forces will fortunately prevent him from acting out his aggression—his parents, who will physically restrain him whenever he tries to hurt Junior. Internal forces, too, will soon exercise the same checking influence—the realization, on John's part, that, should he continue to act aggressively against Junior, he will lose his parents' love.

Deprived of its primary object, John's aggression must find a new object. He may displace on to animals or toys, become cruel with house pets, very destructive with his toys. As he grows older, however, John will find that, in our culture, cruelty to animals is also frowned upon. Deprived of this outlet too, a new displacement will be necessary: John may develop a sanguine interest in anatomy and biology; now he is "cruel" against frogs and lizards and kills and dissects them for the conscious purpose of studying them. When he reaches an older age, this outlet too may be met with by checking forces of disapproval and aggression will have to be displaced again: John may become interested in hunting; or enter medical school and become a great surgeon. Now he is "destructive" against parts of his patients' bodies for humanitarian reasons, no longer for aggressive ones. There should be little resemblance between the final outlet of displacement (surgery) and the original one, the infantile aggressiveness; but, again, if one follows all the steps of displacement one will find the similarities. When a chain of displacements ends in a final outlet of significant social, cultural, humanitarian, or aesthetic value, the alternate route is called "sublimation."

It is important to understand the difference between a "good" sublimation and a "not-so-good" sublimation. A good sublimation is one in which there has been a large number of substitutive steps between the original and final behavior. This assures that the final behavior (i.e., practicing surgery) is no longer an infantile one, one based on the self-centered characteristics of the natural-biological levels of adaptation. A "good" surgeon, thus, is one whose infantile aggressiveness has been so much modified that he operates only for humanitarian reasons; a "bad" surgeon, one whose infantile aggressiveness has not been sufficiently modified; he enjoys operating too much, is subtly sadistic in his surgery, operates unnecessarily (the knife-happy surgeon).

All adult choices and careers are reached through chains of alternate routes and displacements, with more or less sublimation. A psychiatrist may be a person who experienced, as a child, intense frustration of voyeuristic instincts. Again there should be little resemblance between the final outlet of displacement (psychiatric practice), and the originary one (the curiosity and inquisitiveness by which he tried to avoid anxiety in childhood); but again, if one follows, step by step, the chain of displacements, one will see the similarities. Here too one may see the all-important difference between a good and not-so-good sublimation. A "good" psychiatrist is one whose infantile curiosity has undergone much change, through steps and steps of displacement; as a result he listens and elicits confidences from his patients for his patients' benefits, not to cure his own anxiety. A "bad" psychiatrist is one whose displacement steps have not sufficiently sublimated his infantile curiosity; he asks unnecessary questions of his patients and elicits intimate details from their sexual lives, not for his patients' needs but to fulfill, vicariously, his own needs.

Persons engaged in service-professions (social workers, nurses, the clergy) have usually reached their final professional choice by displacement of dependency instincts. In a healthy (that is well sublimated) displacement of dependency, one takes care of one's own dependency by making oneself dependable to others (which is, of course, the essence of a service profession); someone whose dependency has not been sufficiently sublimated into dependability is a person who "needs" his charges excessively, i.e., the social worker who is accepting of his client as long as the client remains destitute and inadequate and who becomes hostile and vindictive (or tries to retard his client's growth into independence) when his client begins to recover.

4. The Dynamic Influence of the Unconscious

A large portion of man's mentation originates in the unconscious. All psychodynamic schools agree on the existence of the unconscious, divergencies being only on its "quantity" and quality. Only the concept of the "dynamic influence of the unconscious" needs be discussed here, as it is most important in terms of counseling techniques.

By "dynamic influence of the unconscious" Freud meant that unconscious feelings and ideas direct conscious behavior and thinking. The unconscious, is not a foreign body, walled-off from the other components of the mind, but something alive, continuously influencing behavior. Freud likened the unconscious to an iceberg, of which one sees only a small portion, whereas it is the larger, submerged part that makes the iceberg move this way or that, keeps it stable, or causes it to lose its balance. The conscious layers of man's mind are like the top of the iceberg; the unconscious layers like the submerged portion: what we think and feel on the top (consciousness) is largely determined by what we think and feel at the bottom (unconscious). Memories and emotions, therefore, repressed into the unconscious during infancy and childhood, continue to influence conscious behavior and thinking.

> As young Freud was at the station leaving for Paris, his father came to see him off and gave him a watch as a present. Freud opened the package, but, in admiring it, the watch slipped from his hands, fell to the ground and broke in pieces. Freud consciously loved his father and appreciated the gift. As a child, however, he had been quite resentful of his parent. This resentment had been removed from consciousness (where it would have caused much guilt and anxiety) and repressed into the unconscious. The repressed anger caused Freud's hands to slip off the watch, as unconsciously he wanted to reject the gift more than he consciously wanted to accept it.

A gynecological surgeon practicing on the West Coast observed that some of his women patients did not recover uneventfully. Hypnotic regressions to the surgical scene proved that, while under general anesthesia, his patients actually "heard" most of what was being talked about by the doctors; misinterpretations of these data became an unconscious memory which exercised, psychosomatically, a negative dynamic influence on postoperative recovery. (In a case in point, under hypnotic regression a patient "reheard" a voice saying: "This woman will never be the same again." During the operation the surgeon had said those very words, meaning that after surgery she would feel much better. Perception under anesthesia, however, is not very accurate and nuances of feelings and tones are not "heard" accurately. What the patient "heard" was that she would feel miserable and sickly for the rest of her life; which was the way she felt after surgery.)

Doodling, slips of the tongue, accident proneness, seemingly unexplainable moods, irrational "first sight" likes and dislikes, etc., are all illustrations of the dynamic influence of the unconscious.

In infancy and in severe mental sickness the motivation for most mental activities originates largely from the unconscious. In the healthy adult, functioning at the natural existential level of adaptation, the conscious ego possesses enough psychic energy of its own for conscious motivation and some control of unconsciously motivated choices. Here too, one should think in relative terms. The healthier a person is, the less the dynamic influence of the unconscious; in psychoneurotic and psychotic conditions the unconscious exercises a much more pervasive influence over conscious behavior (the obsessive-compulsive, for instance, must engage in many, seemingly meaningless, rituals which he can't explain *consciously* and which he is totally helpless to control by *conscious* will power).

5. The defensive meaning of symptoms

Mental symptoms have a meaning and represent partly successful attempts by the mind to defend itself against pain. Far from being casual and accidental, mental symptoms are always connected with something else (i.e., unconscious). Symptoms are alternate routes gone astray, successful at protecting some homeostasis at one level of personality, but at the cost of anxiety on another level. Painful as they are, however, there would have been an even greater pain (and more acute lack of homeostasis) without them.

A Sister I treated was tortured by obsessive sexual thoughts, occurring at the most inappropriate times and places (i.e., in church, just before receiving Communion). These thoughts disguised unconscious murderous drives which, had they been conscious, would have caused even greater guilt and anxiety.

With another Sister, who extinguished cigarettes by pressing them on her skin, the symptom was a defense against unconscious guilt. She once asked her spiritual director whether she should consider herself "bad" for having impure thoughts. The spiritual director made the mistake of answering her truthfully (he should not have answered her at all); knowing that her thoughts were of an obsessive nature, he told her she was not "bad." She went home and set fire to her habit. Sister needed someone telling her she was "bad." Deprived of external accusations, she had to become self-accusatory and self-punitive (burning).

The defensive meaning of symptoms explains why depressed and anxious patients experience a remission of their symptoms whenever they develop a painful physical illness or, by a "non-accidental accident," break a leg or an arm: the physical pain takes over the punishing previously inflicted by depression and anxiety; already suffering from a tight cast around a leg or an acute peptic ulcer, these patients no longer need to punish themselves by the mental pain of depression and anxiety.

The practical implications of the defensive meaning of symptoms are important and immediate. If symptoms are defenses, removing them prematurely will cause the mind to set up other defenses, other alternate routes, usually more drastic ones, resulting in more severe symptoms, as is dramatically illustrated by the removal of symptoms (that is, defenses) through hypnosis or by the "scrambling" of the personality's defenses by L.S.D.

6. The power of words

This concept is closely related to the one just discussed. Counseling is powerful medicine and words are, to the counselor, what the knife is to the surgeon. Symptoms could be visualized, metaphorically, as props, as defenses against something else; take the props away and the personality can only cave in. Premature tampering with symptoms, therefore (by premature interpretations, rash words, poorly timed advices), may "counsel" some patients into psychosis.

A 28-year-old single, attractive Catholic patient who led a very retiring life consulted her physician because of heart palpitations, stomach pains, tiredness, sleeplessness, and choking sensations. Her doctor correctly diagnosed hysteria and incorrectly concluded that her bodily ailments were the result of her sexual abstinence. (Both sexual abstinence and bodily ailments were symptoms and therefore defenses.) He also felt that she was using shyness and religion as "excuses" for not going out more (which she was); but, again, did not look at the total picture, did not see that her "excuses" were symptoms (i.e., defenses), and "ordered" her to date more and be more flexible with her morals. Eventually, the white-haired, fatherly-looking physician persuaded her and she accepted a date from a man. Shortly afterward she became more depressed and withdrawn: "because of guilt over having allowed her date to kiss her." Her physician took again her "guilt" at its face value, and told her to be more "broad-minded." She did, engaged in heavy petting, and after her date left, overburdened with what she consciously experienced as guilt attempted suicide. Several months after she had started psychotherapy it was found that when she was 5 and 9 years of age, she had been seduced by her psychopathic father. Unconsciously she had come to associate all adult sexuality to the incestuous sexuality experienced in childhood; the guilt and horror attached to the childhood experience had been transferred to all adult sexuality and all sex marital or premarital, "right" sex or "wrong" sex, was "wrong." The fatherly physician forcing her to be more broad-minded represented, to her unconscious, the symbol of the father who had forced her to premature sexuality as a child. Symbolically seduced again, deprived of her defenses of isolation and pseudoreligiosity, she could only experience depression, anxiety and psychotic guilt.[11]

In the above illustration the self-styled counselor gave advices which were wrong both morally and psychologically. Morally sound and psychologically unsound advices are just as unsettling and dangerous.

A young novice told her spiritual directress about her compulsive masturbation. The directress, who only related to the religious aspect of the problem, sternly ordered her to give up the practice at all costs. The novice did, at the cost of severe homosexual panic and intense anxiety.

In "neurotic marriages" husband and wife ("who is afraid of Virginia

Woolf?") need each other in a sickly way. Marital counseling forcefully advising premature separation may result in psychic tragedy. In the "marriage" to Christ and to the religious life of Sisters whose religious vocation has predominantly neurotic, unconscious components, one hears Sisters complaining bitterly of their religious status and saying that once they leave the religious life (i.e., break the "marriage") all their psychic difficulties will disappear. Actually the contrary is often true. To these Sisters, religious life is as much a defense against unconscious drives and conflicts as a neurotic marriage is to some women. Premature or neurotically-motivated exclaustration has made many a Sister (who in the religious life was slightly disturbed and neurotic but at least functioning) into an extremely disturbed, unfunctioning individual once exclaustrated.

While the power of words and the destructive influence of untimely advices must not be underestimated, it must not be overestimated either. Personality defenses have been operating for a lifetime and are often a sturdy and resilient armor which is not easily tampered with. These defenses will collapse only when there is an already advanced ego weakness and a borderline psychopathological condition. It is in these cases that "wild counseling" (just as the "wild psychoanalysis" of which Freud wrote) can precipitate overt psychosis. In counseling, therefore, one must first make an accurate diagnostic evaluation and then strike the right balance between excessive activity and excessive passivity.

B. Technical Considerations

The topic of "techniques" in counseling (as in psychotherapy) should be approached with much caution. While, on one hand, there indeed are "techniques" to counseling, on the other hand, one must not assume that a mechanical understanding or application of such techniques will make anyone a counselor. Hopefully, the previous presentation of counseling theory may have been sufficient to deter anyone from making this assumption.

In counseling and psychotherapy we often work with persons who are looking for easy solutions to life problems. In our culture the idea is still prevalent that man's mind is something of a machine which can be easily readjusted by the right kind of tappings and hammerings. It should be clear from the previous theoretical points that this attitude is fallacious; we are hurt by persons and can only be healed through persons; no mechanistic list of technical points, no mathematical formulas will cure anyone; As C. Wise adeptly phrases it: "Life is a constant process of relationships between ourselves and the world, through which *conditions* are being created . . . that we have learned to call illness or health . . . Any cure or solution can only take place in and through . . . living relationships with (. . . . persons) qualified in heart and mind to give help." [12] Rather than "technical principles," therefore (which might become straitjackets of counseling behavior), let us think of technical guidelines, and let us discuss five of them: listening; non-directiveness; structuring; relationship; attitude.

1. Listening

The "listening" referred to here is a "comprehensive listening," a "listening with a third ear" (T. Reik) and "seeing with a third eye"; a "listening and a seeing in which one is aware of everything the patient 'says'—with his words and with his silence; with his restlessness and his immobility; with the inflection of his voice and with the clothes he is wearing; with the motions of his hands and his feet; with his punctuality or lateness in arriving to the therapists's office." [13]

Sister comes in. The Superior is sitting beside her desk; Sister has the choice of two identical chairs, one on the other side of the Superior (with the desk in between), the other across from the Superior (with no desk in between); she sits across the desk. She is saying something, and if the Superior is willing to listen, she may hear: "I am afraid of this encounter. I need the desk, a barrier, between us." Another Sister comes in 45 minutes earlier; if the counselor is willing to listen, he may hear: "I am anxious. I need you. I wanted to see you sooner."

A patient came for her first session on a relatively cold day; the office, however, was comfortably warm. The first thing she said was: "Is it always this cold here?" She was really saying: "People are always cold with me. Are you going to be cold too?" Another patient opened the session by saying: "As I was coming here I thought: What ideas shall I kick around today? and found I had nothing to talk about." During the session she was silent most of the time; at one point, in adjusting her skirts, she crossed her legs, kicked the ash tray stand, and spilled all the ashes on the rug. She was "talking" all along, even before entering the office, while she was still in the car, and wondering what "ideas" she should kick around during the session; she was saying: "I am angry today. I want to kick you, and this thought makes me feel guilty and uncomfortable. I am afraid I might become conscious of my anger, that's why I am not talking; but I *am* angry, that's why I kicked your ashtray and dirtied your rug." Another patient, right after an interpretation he was unwilling to accept, started scratching his neck and had a violent attack of cough. He was "saying": "You're getting under my skin. That's why I'm scratching my neck; I don't want to swallow your ideas, that's why I am trying to cough them out of me." [14]

In counseling we also listen—to ourselves. Counseling is a "cooperative venture," a meaningful, though temporary, co-existence; the feelings, thoughts, fantasies we experience vis-a-vis our patients are most worth listening to; they may have been engendered by our patients and give us important clues about them.

A beautiful career-woman, charming, flirtatious and engaging, came for her first session of psychoanalysis. As I was listening to her, I was also listening to myself and what I heard was—silence: no response within myself; no feelings of being charmed, no stirrings of engagement. In asking myself why, I first examined the possibility that it was I that was unopen, unwilling to be charmed, unresponsive to being engaged. Since it seemed that I could exclude this explanation, it must have been that she was not sending the messages she seemed to be sending. Actually her charm and flirtatiousness were only a facade behind which hid a frightened, hostile individual. Some time later she told me she had been a lesbian for many years and consciously hated and despised men.[15]

In comprehensive listening, a most essential requirement is to hear what the patient is truly saying, not what one wants to hear; to experience what the counselee causes one to experience, not what one's unconscious or preconscious make one experience.

Sister may have come forty-five minutes earlier not because she is anxious and wants to see the Superior sooner, but because she is hostile and wants to disrupt the Superior's schedule. A supervisee of mine, in discussing a case with me, said: "No doubts about this patient. My third ear tells me he has a severe sexual problem." When he discussed his second, third, and fourth patient in the same terms, and I began to realize that it was the supervisee who had a sexual problem and was hearing, non-verbally, sexual messages coming not from the patient but from himself. A religious Sister I trained had difficulties with patients who had problems with authority figures. She over-identified with her patients and experienced anger at the persons her patients were angry at. After examining her reaction with me she realized that she was transferring some of the anger she felt against her own Superior to those persons her patients felt anger at.

Self-analysis of one's "counter-transference" not only helps the counselor to help his patients better, but also helps the counselor to become more aware of himself vis-a-vis his childhood, adolescence, persons he may have difficulties with in the present; to expand his consciousness; to diminish the power of his unconscious; in one word: to grow. In "good" counseling, then, the patient grows—and the counselor grows.

2. *The non-directive approach.*

All psychodynamically oriented schools of counseling use the "Non-

Directive approach," the differences between various schools being mainly differences of degree of "non-directiveness" and of rationale behind the approach. "Non-directiveness" started with Freud and became popular with Carl Rogers,[16] whose approach, however, has a rationale and a purpose which differ from the non-directiveness of Freudian psychoanalysts.

The non-directive approach has been called many things: "Non-Directive"; "Client-Centered"; "Minimum Activity"; "Active Passivity"; etc., and it may consist of one or more of many approaches. It may be a reflecting, an echoing-back to the patient not so much of his words, but, especially, of his feelings. This is done discriminately and with a great deal of empathy as this is often a crucial starting point in structuring a good relationship.

A Sister came for her first session with a counselor, fearful and unable to utter a word. The counselor said, with a great deal of genuinely experienced feeling: "You must be in a great deal of pain to be unable to talk." This reflecting-back to the patient of the feelings the patient herself was experiencing was a good opening for what was to be a productive session.

Non-directiveness may mean that one's approach is "client-centered": it is what the patient wants to discuss that counts; the patient "sets the line" for the session, and the counselor follows that "line." Non-directiveness may take the form of silence. In psychoanalytic therapy this may have the purpose of frustrating the patient's transference neurosis; in counseling or in supportive psychotherapy this approach is followed in order to interfere minimally with the patient's spontaneity.

The advantages of the non-directive technique are readily apparent. By not intruding into the patient's spontaneity with questions or "instant-opinions" the patient eventually tells us his "story" in its wholeness and not just in its surface dimensions. Feelings are elicited more rapidly and productively. Most significant of all, the patient tells us what is important for him to say, not what is important for us to know.

A counselor who felt he should know more about the patient's family, tried to obtain this information by saying to his patient: "Tell me about your father." In being so "directive," the counselor already structured the relationship in a "vertical," subtly authoritarian form; and deprived himself of the many diagnostic clues that non-directiveness would have afforded him, i.e., how "ready" was his patient to talk about his father; or which parent the patient would have first discussed if left to his own devices. If a question had to be asked at all, it would have been better to ask: "Tell me about your family."

In the non-directive approach the counselor assumes what has been called the "actively-passive position." The counselor listens; waits out pauses of silence; stimulates the patient's continuity of communication by non-verbal (attentiveness, nodding, interest, etc.) or verbal means (saying "Humhum," rephrasing, echoing and reflecting-back words and feelings, etc.). With mild problems this technique may be therapeutic in itself and be both means and ends. The counselor becomes the patient's "oral vehicle," and the patient, by listening to the counselor's clearer re-formulation of his difficulties, may see a road toward a solution. With more severe problems, this approach is mainly a means to an end as it provides the counselor with valuable information with which he can later help the patient help himself.

Having discussed the advantages of the non-directive technique, one should also warn against its abuses. In the first place this is an "ideal technique," toward which one must always strive but from which one must not be shackled into unwavering rigidity. Secondly, poorly trained counselors apply it so strictly that they will ask no questions at all and go through several sessions still knowing little about their patient's chief problems, family constellation, etc. Thirdly, the non-directive technique should be applied with the conscious (and, it is to be hoped, unconscious) rationale of wanting to help the patient, and not to frustrate him unnecessarily, to punish him with silence, or for other counter-transferential motivations.

3. Counseling structure

Flexible as counseling is, it has an inner orderliness, a structure, some of which is communicated to the patient as soon as possible. By structure, one means many things; to mention just a few of its dimensions, one means: roles; formalization of the interview; focusing and goals.

a) *Roles*. The counselor thinks of himself as a professional person engaged in a professional service, and not just as a sympathetic listener, a "good friend," someone that the patient can call on at will. Similarly, the patient is helped to think of herself as someone with emotional problems, seeking a professional healing service. The exact nature of the relationship, of the service, and of the problem must be clearly understood as soon as possible.

A Religious Sister went to a pastoral counselor with what she considered a problem of moral theology for which she wanted spiritual direction. The counselor evaluated the *total* picture and found that she had religious hallucinations as well; he sent the patient to another priest for spiritual direction and took her in for "motivational counseling" for the schizophrenic process.

Patients resist the structuring of roles as a way of resisting change. Since symptoms, painful though they are, are defenses, the patient unconsciously fears the greater pain he would experience if he were changed and deprived of his symptoms. It is a misconception to think that patients want to be "cured" of their illness: they only want to be made comfortable—"Manipulate my symptoms away but do not change me." By confusing roles, by not seeing themselves as patients, they are trying to protect their illness.

b) Formalization of the interview. By this is meant that interviews are by appointment, on the same day of the week and at the same time of the day, last the same length of time, take place in the same place, have complete privacy. This rigid structuring, too, is an ideal requirement and exceptions will be made; but more counseling has been rendered ineffectual by too little rigidity in structure than too much. The counselor, again, keeps in mind that patients resist structuring as a way to manipulate, control, and express various unconscious feelings.

A Sister continuously cancelled her appointments to express hostility against the counselor and to avoid the risk to discuss her unconscious anger, now close to the surface. Another Sister kept on asking a different day for her appointment to test her power to control the counselor. Another consistently came thirty minutes late for her forty-five minute session to test her counselor's "love and acceptance" and see if the counselor would still give her a full-session time regardless of personal inconveniences to himself.

c) Focus and goals. As indicated before, counseling is a professional service and one of the healing sciences. When the patient first comes, the counselor must evaluate his psychological health. He may do so by taking a "history" (age, religious status, presenting problems and their duration, previous emotional difficulties, parents' personalities, siblings, childhood history and personality, etc.), or, preferably, by evaluating nature and quality of the interaction in that first encounter. Whenever possible, the counselor listens to whatever the patient is saying in whatever order the patient prefers; only if necessary does he ask leading or direct questions. He then arrives at a tentative diagnosis. (While the formal diagnosis of any illness is within the province of the psychiatrist, a well trained counselor is certainly qualified to evaluate the severity of a mental disorder and to differentiate it from a solely moral or religious problem.) After this evaluation has been completed, the counselor sets in his mind a tentative "direction" and formulates tentative "goals," i.e., the expectations he can have in helping this particular person. Then, in the course of counseling itself, he will "focus," which means listening to everything the patient says, but responding selectively, that is only to those emotions, and childhood or past experiences which are relevant to the goals previously set.

4. Relationship

By "having a relationship" one means that the patient is "engaged" with the counselor, feels the counselor cares and respects his human dignity, and, especially, accepts him, despite what the patient conceives of as shameful and hideous emotions. When a relationship exists, the patient trusts the counselor and knows that, no matter what he says, the counselor will remain objective and not penalize him for his words or feelings. This patient knows that the counselor is there not to judge but to understand; not to label his emotions as "right" or "wrong" but to help him understand why he feels "wrongly" or "rightly"; not to approve but to accept.

A good relationship is hardly characterized by continuous pronouncements, by the patient, of great admiration, love, and respect for the counselor: such relationship may not be a good relationship at all but a rather tenuous one in which the patient feels so insecure of his standing with the counselor that he has to "buy" the counselor's acceptance by respect and admiration. The hallmark of a good relationship is trust; the patient who trusts his counselor can become angry or express feelings of hatred and contempt. In a good counseling relationship the patient may or may not be conscious of his liking and trust for the counselor; when unconscious, his affection and trust show in deeds rather than in words—in his punctuality, in his cooperativeness, in his willingness to reveal intimate or embarrassing experiences, and, ultimately in his amenability to change. Of a good counseling relationship too, one might say: "By its fruits you shall know it."

5. Counseling attitude

The counseling attitude includes many components some of which have already been discussed. Some of these components are:

a) *Observing all the time,* comprehensively, with the third ear and the third eye.

b) *Asking oneself "why?"* The counselor enters the "paranoid attitude," purposefully, to see his patient's wholeness and to make connections between conscious symptoms and unconscious emotions.

c) *Humility.* This is a special type of humility. It is the humility of appreciating that our patients are complicated "beings," not machines and that therefore it is not easy to see the whole problem and see things as they really are. It is the humility of realizing that complex problems always have multiple causes, so that it is unclever to make quick diagnoses and tell one's patient: "Look, what really bothers you is this and that." It is, again, the humility of being willing to listen and ask oneself "why?" for a long time.

Psychiatrists, psychoanalysts, and pastoral counselors may find it difficult to be "humble" before their patients. We live in a world exalting the healer (especially the medical healer). The M.D. handles miracle drugs; with a masterful stroke of his knife, cuts disease off the body; has, supposedly, the "answers" for health. The psychoanalyst has even more of this magical halo around his head: he talks the strange tongue of symbols, interprets dreams, listens with the third ear and sees with the third eye. Physicians and psychoanalysts are thus particularly exposed to the occupational hazard of developing a "God complex." Pastoral counselors are exposed to the same danger. As men of God, they have knowledge; when parishioners come to them for religious or spiritual matters, they have authority; in taking off the clerical hat and donning the counselor's hat, they may forget that they are no longer God's minister and may be easily tempted to give quick answers and attempt miracles. The same is true of the religious Superior practicing counseling. To make the situation more complicated often patients do not want the healer to be humble, expect him to be God-like, practice miracles, make them well without the patient doing any work at all ("Manipulate my symptoms away").

d) Non-judgmentality. A good counselor's attitude is non-judgmental. This is not the same as having no values (even that is a value); nor is it the same as not committing oneself (even that is a commitment). By non-judgmentality one really means that one is there not to judge on right and wrong but to help a patient understand why he does that which is considered right or wrong.

The patient's own difficulties might make him want us to be judgmental, e.g. the Sister mentioned earlier, who wanted to be told that her masturbatory problem made her "bad." Patients will try to trap counselors into passing judgments in many subtle ways for many subtle reasons. The "judge me" trap may be a red herring having the purpose of diverting our attention from what really matters. A patient once insisted that I tell her whether I thought it was right for her to make love in her roommate's presence. The really important point obviously was not how I *judged* that; but why she should want to make love without privacy in the first place.

e) Understanding. Understanding involves many thngs which have little to do with what we generally mean by this word. Too often we think of an understanding counselor as someone who grins and smiles all the time, is always agreeable, is gentle and unassertive, and goes around dispensing indiscriminate reassurances and approval. This is more the stereotype of a very neurotic counselor than of an understanding one.

A pastoral counselor I once supervised was counseling a hostile and rebellious postulant whose natural mother and whose present Mistress of Postulants were stern and punitive. His patient often acted out her hostility by being late for her sessions or breaking appointments without notification.

The counselor was very "understanding." He remarked to his patient about her lateness only casually, gave her the full session time by cutting into his own rest periods; re-scheduled makeup appointments to his own great inconvenience, and made sure never to appear the least annoyed by his patient's erratic behavior. His conscious rationale for his so-called "understanding" was: "I want her to see that there are understanding people in the world, that not everybody is like her own mother or Mistress of Postulants." Actually, he failed to structure the sessions and appeared "understanding" because of his own neurotic feelings about assertion; he neurotically equated justifiable annoyance (at having his schedule continuously disrupted) with irrational rage and rigidly controlled the annoyance to avoid becoming conscious of the rage. Also, he conveyed to his patient his approval of her often delinquential behavior with the community; his "understanding" disguised his own unconscious rebelliousness and hostility against authority.

Real understanding has mostly to do with the ability to understand human psychology, to feel-with, to have empathy (understanding, standing-under, taking up someone's burden). Real understanding, therefore, includes the components of counseling attitudes already discussed (listening, asking why, etc.) and something else of paramount importance: for understanding to be real, it must be healthy (mature) and loving.

f) Lovingness and maturity. Beneficial understanding is mature and loving. Various forms of understanding may seem identical phenomenologically and yet be motivated by very different unconscious feelings. Just as a parent's concern for a child may be motivated by love or by a wish for control and domination, understanding may be related to loving and mature determinants or just the opposite. Understanding must be loving: or there will not be the concern, the care, the interest motivating one human being to help another one; it must be mature or will be neurotically motivated, with the counselor distorting the patient's needs because of his own unconscious needs. Without lovingness and maturity, the most sophisticated psychological understanding will be a sterile manipulation of mental mechanisms and counseling will be ineffectual.

The mature counselor practices counseling in terms of his patient's needs, not his own. He is actively passive because he believes in the rationale of his technique not because he is disinterested or wishes to work less. When he is active he is so because he believes it is right at the time to be so; not because by being so the patient will love and admire him.

The mature counselor responds to his patients realistically, and not in terms of neurotic reactions set up in him by the patient's symptoms or values. In being loving the mature counselor is also capable of that self-love and self-respect without which there can be no true love and respect for others.

Immaturity in the counselor will result at best in ineffective counseling (the patient comes interminably and nothing beneficial occurs); at worst in psychic catastrophes.

A counselor I once supervised always asked his patients very personal questions of a sexual nature, not to clarify his views on the relevant aspects of his patients' wholeness, but to fulfill, vicariously, neurotic sexual needs of his own (a good example of unsublimated voyeurism). Another counselor's judgmental repression of his patients' anger was less related to the patients' problems than to the counselor's fear of his own hostility. Sometimes immaturity and lovinglessness (as well as lack of training) result in "interminable counseling": the patient keeps on coming for months, sometimes for years and the counselor is unable to end the relationship. One factor frequently responsible for interminable counseling is the counselor's need to be needed, to see himself as indispensable to his patients (an illustration of poorly sublimated dependency).

References

1. Bier, W. C., "Goals in Pastoral Counseling," *Pastoral Psychology*, 1959, 2, 7–13.
2. Cargnelo, D., "Binswanger's Existentialist Anthropology," *Rivista Di Psicologia*, Firenze, Italy, 1967, XLII/3–4, III.
3. Conigliaro, V. S., "Counseling and Psychological Aspects of the Religious Life," *Review for Religious*, 1965, 24/3, May, 337–362.
4. Conigliaro, V. S., "Listening in Counseling and Psychotherapy" (Iona) *Journal of Pastoral Counseling*, 1966, I/I, 53–58.
5. Curran, C. A., "A Catholic Psychologist Looks at Pastoral Counseling," *Pastoral Psychology*, 1959, 2, 21–28.
6. Curran, C. A., "Counseling, Psychotherapy and the Unified Person," *Journal of Religion and Health*, 1963 2/2, Jan., 95–111.
7. Egan, J. M., in *Marriage: A Psychological and Moral Approach*, W. Bier Edit., Fordham Univ. Press, 1965, 212–223.
8. Freud, S., *A General Introduction to Psychoanalysis*. Liveright Publishing Co., New York, 1935.
9. Freud, S., *New Introductory Lectures*. W. W. Norton & Co., Inc., New York, 1938.
10. Freud, S., "An Outline of Psychoanalysis," in: *Int. Journal of Psychoanalysis*, 1940, 21, 83.
11. Freud, S., "Some Elementary Lessons in Psychoanalysis," in *Collected Papers*, Vol. V (Hogarth Press, London) 33, 376–382.
12. Freud, S., *Beyond the Pleasure Principle*. Liveright, New York, New Translation, 1950.
13. Fromm, E., *Man for Himself*. New York, Rinehart & Co., 1947.

COUNSELING THE RELIGIOUS SISTER 221

14. Fromm, E., *Psychoanalysis and Religion*. Yale Univ. Press, New Haven, 1961.
15. Joyce, A. R., "The Priest As Pastoral Counselor," *Marriage: A Psychological and Moral Approach*. Past. Psych. Series No. 4, W. C. Bier, S.J., Editor
16. Jung, C. G., *Psychology and Religion*. Yale Univ. Press, New Haven and London, 1938.
17. Rogers, C. R., *Client Centered Therapy*. Houghton & Mifflin, New York, 1951.
18. Spitz, R., "Infantile Depression and the General Adaptation Syndrome," in: *Depression*, by Hoch, P. and Zubin, J., Grune & Stratton, New York, 1954, 93–109.
19. Wise, C., *Mental Health and the Bible*. Harper & Row, New York, 1956.

11

COUNSELING THE RELIGIOUS SISTER: SPECIAL CONSIDERATIONS

Vincent S. Conigliaro, M.D.

Having discussed counseling in general, we can now consider some specific aspects of counseling the Religious Sister. It may not be superfluous to restate that these considerations cannot be separated from the general considerations on counseling previously discussed; this chapter, therefore, is meaningful only as a continuation of the preceding one.

In a comprehensive treatment of these aspects, one might consider such points as personality types attracted to the Sisterhood; type of emotional difficulties most frequently encountered among Religious Sisters; aspects of the religious life contributing to the development of emotional difficulties among Sisters; psychological mechanisms through which this occurs; special considerations to be kept in mind in counseling Religious Sisters; and many others still. For obvious reasons, only some of these questions will be treated here.

The question of what personality types are attracted to the sisterhood is an important one, since it bears on the question of motivations (conscious and unconscious) for the sisterhood.

In considering this question, one should first dispel the lingering myth according to which Religious Sisters must have personality "problems" to begin with, the myth best expressed by the cliché, "One must be neurotic to want to become a nun." The irony about this myth is that it could apply, with the same quality of only superficial validity, to many other all-involving, deeply self-committing service professions (Albert Schweitzer type of missionary medicine, some types of nursing, some kinds of social work, etc.). That this is a myth is clearly indicated by the many Sisters, who, despite the psychological and social hardships of their life, remain sane, vibrant individuals, psychically and existentially alive and creative. To say that these Sisters had "problems" to begin with, or that these problems did not materialize because of divine grace or natural accident, is to misunderstand both psychology of nature and theology of grace.

In thinking about this question, rather than approaching it—as the above myth does—from the viewpoint of "normal vs. abnormal," "problems vs. no problems," one should consider the following points:

1. Since Freud, personality characteristics are viewed as being arranged on a continuum, "normal" and "abnormal" being concepts of which we all partake to various degrees.

2. What we like—what we do—the career we choose, is related to unconscious as well as conscious factors. Unconscious "character layers" related to such early alternate routes as early incorporations and identifications, are most important in shaping one's external character and personality type.

3. Each unconscious character layer, before taking its final form, has been molded, worked upon, changed, and rechanged by the work of the alternate routes. For instance fixated infantile dependency on one's mother may appear in later life as simply displaced, equally helpless and clinging, dependency on mother superior; or as sublimated, quite helpful and reliable dependability to other Sisters.

4. Unconscious character layers do not, by themselves, make a person normal or abnormal; what matters in this respect, is these layers' psychodynamic state; i.e. the kind of changes each character layer has undergone before a stabilized personality structure has been attained.

People attracted to the "service professions" (nursing, social work, psychiatry, the clergy, the sisterhood) do indeed have unconscious character layers and personality characteristics different from those of persons attracted to other works or professions. Note that there are *characteristics*, not "problems," and that they are *different*, not "healthier" or "unhealthier." In the unconscious character layers of those attracted to the sisterhood, one invariably finds residues of infantile dependency, more or less displaced and/or sublimated into dependability. The quality of sublimation, again, will make the whole difference between an emotionally mature Sister and an emotionally immature one. These residues can be thought of as the central core of a cluster of other, more superficial, less and less unconscious, character layers. Each of these characteristics will be in varying psycho-dynamic states (as described in (3) and(4) above), and it is this state that will determine whether Religious life is entered for healthier or less healthy reasons. It is not a question, then, of whether only "normal" or "abnormal" personalities are attracted to the sisterhood; but that the sisterhood attracts individuals with *similar* unconscious character layers in *varying* psychody-namic states; individuals with healthier motivations and individuals with less healthy ones.

What has been said above clearly indicates our belief that the calling to the sisterhood can indeed by approached on a natural (psychological, existential) level. The supernatural dimensions of the profession, of the calling, the workings of divine grace in religious vocation, are beyond our scope and competence (whatever they are, however, grace presumes on nature; it is the nature of the calling that concerns us here).

Religious life, then, as any other profession, is entered with a combina-tion of healthy and unhealthy, conscious and unconscious motivations. To the healthier Sister, it offers opportunities for existential richness and the fullest expression of her personality; to the less healthy, opportunities for an impoverished, restricted existence and the fullest expression of her neurotic potentials. When chosen mainly on the basis of healthier motivations, the "calling" was exercised, mainly, by the essence of religious life and its psychological opportunities for the reinforcement of sublimative adapta-tions; when chosen mainly on the basis of conflictual unconscious drives, the calling was exercised, mainly, by the accidental properties of religious life and its psychological opportunities for the reinforcement of repressive and reactive adaptations (i.e., the expression, under disguise, of disturbing unconscious drives).

The vow of Chastity may have appealed as an opportunity to express emotional frigidity, heterosexual fears, homosexual tendencies; the uni-sexual, all-female environment may have been chosen for the same uncon-scious reasons. The habit, the uniform, may have appealed to unconscious conflicts on exhibitionism. Cloistered, strictly silent orders may have been chosen less to enhance one's meditative faculties than because of schizoid tendencies; and contemplative orders selected less in relation to the psycho-logical values of asceticism than because of unconscious conflicts about "doing."

The vow of obedience may have appealed to a Sister mature enough to *wish* to be obedient and dependent on others' wills; this Sister can relate to the will of God beyond her Superior's will and knows that obedience neither infantilizes her nor diminishes her dignity as a self-determining individual (she *chooses*, actively and autonomously, to be passive and dependent, a *sui generis* expression of the power of feminine surrender). On the other hand, the vow may have exercised an unconscious appeal because of fear of authority, pathologic passivity and dependency, conflicts about self-determination and the like.

In the treatment of the Religious Sister, therefore, her religious status on one hand is not to be overlooked, on the other hand it must be considered from the view point of a two-fold (conscious and unconscious, spiritual and emotional) significance. Emotional difficulties found among Sisters may be non-specific (similar to those found in the lay population) or specific (related to, or expressed through, the religious status); the fact not to be overlooked in either case is that they affect a Religious Sister: specific or not, they will have to be considered within the context of the two-fold significance religion and religiosity have for each Sister and in terms of how they relate to (1) the accidental properties of religious life (i.e., that which is "external" to the Sister) and, (2) the unconscious personality traits of each Sister (i.e. that which is "internal" to the Sister). Let's examine some more of these problems in terms of this two-fold context.

We might begin with loneliness problems. Religious life, especially community life, is rarely a life of loneness and needs not be one of loneliness. Yet many Sisters bitterly complain of loneliness and feel threatened by it in their psychic stability.

Whereas loneness results from the absence of any kind of communication with other human beings, loneliness corresponds to the absence of meaningful, gratifying communication. One may be lonely and not alone (at a cocktail party one is not enjoying); and alone and not lonely (for a while, at least; by communicating, through memories, daydreams, and fantasies, with one's significant friends).

The need to communicate, to be "at-one" (rather than "al-one," all by oneself) is a powerful human need, the frustration of which inevitably creates tension, anxiety, or depression. In loneliness, however, rather than absence of other humans to be at-one with (i.e., an "external" factor), one finds unconsciously-determined inability to communicate within the lonely person (i.e., an "internal" factor).

In older days, such external factors of religious life as stricter silence rules, more rigid interpretations of the Book of Customs, stronger taboos on particular friendships, etc., did narrow realistic possibilities for meaningful communication. Even then, however, loneliness was not univalently related to external factors alone and was also explainable in terms of individual Sisters' unconscious reactions to such factors. Today, with greater recognition of the human needs of the religious and greater appreciation of the

"Religio sana in mente sana" philosophy, accidental features of religious life interfere less with opportunities for meaningful communication and the loneliness phenomenon is more and more related to internal factors, i.e. individual Sisters' personality problems.

In the lonely Sister one usually finds unconscious conflicts about relating, with fear, inability, or unwillingness to communicate. The defense mechanism of repression is widely employed, by which mechanism a Sister may repress the awareness of her own worth as a communicant ("who would want to talk to me? I have nothing to give"); the awareness of other Sisters' worth as communicants ("how can I enjoy talking to them? They are all old gals, with nothing in common with me"); or the awareness of the possibilities for communication existing in her community (as with a Sister who interpreted the community's customs on outside contacts to suit her unconscious needs). On a deeper level of personality, this repression is usually related to other, equally unconscious, conflicts and drives.

At the inception of treatment Sister N's major complaints revolved around loneliness. Over the previous ten years she had been transferred from one house to another (at her request) at least four times. In each house she had found herself lonely and, to use her own words, "incommunicado." She explained away her loneliness by the usual rationalizations: the other Sisters were too old, too young, too intellectual, not intellectual enough; the rule frowned, anyway, on particular friendships and "wants us to be all alone with Christ." Actually her teaching and missionary order offered its members many opportunities for meaningful communication; social and recreational life, although narrow from a secular point of view, was remarkably free. Because of her loneliness in the religious life, Sister had been obsessively ruminating for the previous two and one half years whether she should seek exclaustration or dispensation.

Sister used repression as outlined above. In her case, repression was more specifically related to the need to repress deeper threatening emotions, i.e., rage, possessiveness, and dependency. To be close to others, to relate, to communicate meant, to Sister N, to run the risk of expressing rage; to become contemptuous and be found contemptible; to become possessive and overdependent and then be controlled and possessed. Throughout her childhood her own mother's love had always had "strings attached"; to love and to be loved meant also to be infantilized and possessed.

In treating the lonely Sister, therefore, the experience of loneliness must be disassociated from the external factors it is often related to. The patient must be helped to recognize that her loneliness says something *about herself, not about the religious life*; and that it is a symptom of a more pervasive malady, a symptom that cannot be treated in a vacuum or magically cast off by one more transfer (or by leaving the religious life altogether).

Sisters who can't make up their minds whether to leave the community often have a semiconscious inner certitude that "it won't make any difference anyway." Sister N knew that she would carry her fear of relating wherever she went and to whatever she might be.

It is again only when the patient is helped to take counsel with herself, and her wholeness as a human being is restored, that the symptom of loneliness will disappear, to be replaced by the vibrant need and desire to be with others.

Problems of boredom are very similar to the problem of loneliness, the psychodynamics of boredom being closely related to those of loneliness. Except in extreme cases (massive sensorial deprivation of prisoners in solitary confinement or astronauts in space capsule training) boredom is related to repression: of stimulations coming from without and of stimulations (feelings, especially) coming from within (in response to the "boring" situation, a situation which far from being objectively boring is subjectively exciting and threatening). Both in loneliness and boredom there is a defensive turning-into-oneself, a "playing-with-oneself" (which is an attempt at distracting oneself from the threatening stimulation): daydreaming (playing with one's memories); fingering one's habit, pencils, crucifix; playing with one's body (rubbing one's eyes, scratching, pulling one's nose); or becoming introspective and masturbating.

Sister E, member of an active teaching order and of a young, stimulating, 12-Sister house, was perpetually bored, especially while in the company of the other Sisters or of some of the adolescent girls she taught. Her "ennui" severely interfered with her teaching and praying and eventually depression and masturbation developed too. Her boredom was related to repression of strong homosexual feelings she experienced whenever other women were in the same room with her.

Compulsive masturbation is frequently encountered in treating the religious (although not much more frequently than in treating lay women of comparable age, nubile status, and socioreligious culture). In some cases the problem is associated with moral scrupulosity and intense neurotic guilt (super ego anxiety): a guilt which Sister (aided, in this, by the external factor of her religious status and by literal interpretations of the vow of chastity), will obsessively rationalize in terms of the moral-spiritual aspects of masturbation. In other cases the obsessive-compulsive structure of personality will appear in ritualizations of behavior, rigid overscheduling of time, stubbornness, fastidiousness; or in the form of "compulsive non-compulsivity" and compulsive defying of all rules, customs, and authorities.

The neurotic guilt may undergo repression and manifest itself through somatic symptoms (fatigue, dizziness, tachicardia) unconsciously symbolizing punishment and atonement.

Compulsive masturbation is, essentially, a symptom of an obsessive-compulsive psychoneurosis or character neurosis; therefore it is invariably associated with conscious and/or unconscious anger and rage. In compulsive masturbation (just as in compulsive smoking or eating) an originally pleasurable activity has been turned into a self-punitive, minimally pleasurable one.

In counseling Sisters with compulsive masturbation one again sidesteps the symptom and relates to the whole person. Because of the fact that Religious Sisters (just as "devout" lay Catholics) might make utmost use of the moral aspects of masturbation, counseling must be structured without delay and the patient helped early to recognize the psychological dimensions of the problem. When this is resisted, reflective-interpretative means may be used to help the patient to realize that she "moralizes" in all aspects of her life, i.e. thinking in terms of right-wrong rather than "why?"; labeling, rather than understanding, her behavior, her thoughts, her feelings. This analysis usually leads the patient away from the symptom and on to the relevant aspects of her illness (having experienced moralizing, puritanic, censoring parents, childhood problems with authority, etc.).

The principles of counseling theory previously discussed are relevant here too and will again direct the technique of treatment: Sister is a "whole" person; her masturbation is only one facet of a complex, pervasively affected Gestalt; the roots of her illness are deep in her unconscious, not on the surface of her symptoms; only by listening, nonjudgmentally, to her "whole" story, thus offering her a human corrective relationship, can she be again at ease with her whole self rather than diseased.

In homosexuality, too, "Things are not always what they seem"; and the true nature of the *illness* cannot be apprehended by considering only the external symptoms of the *disease*.

True homosexuality, a condition related to early oral-stage pathology and resulting in faulty identifications with the parent of the opposite sex, is a severe mental condition, whose pathology transcends the solely "sexual" deviation. It is infrequently encountered among the religious; the nature of the illness is such that the unconscious character layers producing it are not consistent with character layers producing motivation (healthy or unhealthy) for the religious life; and its severity is such that religious affected with it are usually diagnosed and screened out early in their postulancy or novitiate years. More often one encounters in the religious life situational homosexuality or the less severe forms of homosexuality. These are conditions related to anal- or phallic-stage pathology, in which rather than sexual deviation or a deviant sexual identity there are, mainly, heterosexual conflicts or conflicts of other instincts. In these cases the unisexual environment of the religious life encourages the expression of these conflicts through homosexual channels.

Sister B, an attractive and feminine person, referred to this writer because of overt homosexuality, also suffered with depression, compulsions, and neurotic guilt. Over the past eight years she had been involved homosexually with three older Sisters. A previous therapist, mainly impressed by Sister's depression, had subjected her to electric shock treatment with no beneficial results.

In relating to Sister's "wholeness" one was mainly impressed by her conflictual, ambivalent attitude over dependency. (When she first came into my office, while her voice was saying, "I am a mess, Doctor, I need you," her self-possessed and composed demeanor and bravely smiling face were saying: "I am O.K. I don't need anyone.")

Throughout her life Sister had developed a philosophy of utmost independence and self-reliance with perfectionistic standards on work and obligations supporting and actuating it. One must work very hard, she felt, and never give in to minor ailments. One must always help others but must never let others help oneself. One must always be cheerful in the company of people because one is not to burden others with one's troubles. With this philosophy of life, Sister was very much appreciated in her house and a true pillar of her community; even when sick she continued to be a hard worker, an excellent teacher, and everybody's (but her own) friend and support.

Sister's rigid, robot-like self reliance was a defense against very strong dependency drives which simply terrorized her and had, therefore, to be repressed (their partial sublimation into dependability had contributed to motivating her to enter the religious life). Originally she had come to fear dependency because her very undependable alcoholic parents had made her fear that dependency on them was quite unsafe; throughout childhood and adolescence, therefore, instead of being mothered and dependent, Sister had to mother and be dependable (once, at 10 years of age, Sister developed acute appendicitis. Before mother could panic, Sister calmly reassured her that everything was O.K., coolheadedly instructed her to get a taxi and imperturbably directed the astonished driver and the by-now hysterical mother to the hospital). She carried over this attitude and her fear of dependency and helplessness into the religious life and adulthood.

Sister's homosexual behavior was her only outlet for the symbolic expression of her frustrated needs to depend and be mothered (as well as other unconscious drives and conflicts: symptoms are always "over-determined," i.e. energized by various unconscious mechanisms simultaneously). In homoerotic behavior Sister was overdependent, clinging, filial, selfish, demanding: all things she should have been, and could not be, as a child and an infant. In her homosexual relationships she was not only exacting nurture from a symbolic mother but also taking symbolic revenge on her by showing complete lack of interest and affection for her partners once she was sure they were "in love" with her.

In counseling the homosexual Sister, therefore, one must, again, "see" the whole person, and not just the symptoms; and understand the illness (rather than just the disease) in its unconscious determinants. Counseling will be of little help in true homosexuality. In less severe cases, counseling must first guide the Sister to recognize what inner drives and needs are hiding behind her homosexual behavior. In so doing one is already relating to the whole person, rather than just the homosexual symptoms, and the experience will be corrective to some degree. These drives and needs must then be liberated from their conflictual relationship to other needs and components of personality; only thus can they be channelled (or, possibly, sublimated) into socially, existentially, and spiritually acceptable directions.

Sisters are often referred for counseling with the general diagnosis of "immaturity." Psychiatrically this term is meaningless, for it covers a multitude of conditions; to understand, and treat, the "immature" Sister, then, one must try to understand her immaturity more specifically and in its causes and unconscious determinants.

Immaturity has to do with inability to be (vis-a-vis other human beings as well as oneself) what one could and should be, considering age, talent, abilities, circumstances, etc. The immature Sister is a Sister who has not grown as much as her age, status, obligations, etc., demand and warrant.

The immature Sister cannot do things others can. She cannot be depended on and cannot depend on herself. Her emotions are juvenile in quality and fluctuate like a child's from elation to depression, from submission to primadonnaish assertion, from meekness to temper tantrums. She talks too much or too little, is overly shy or inappropriately bold. With her "friends" she is over-possessive, clinging, and jealous; with her "enemies" petty, catty, and spiteful: It is obvious that inherent to immaturity is a chronic state of tensions and frustrations: for the immature Sister, unable to perform as she could and should; and for those around her, who must put up with her, support her, and carry her weight.

Immaturity is a symptom, a "language in code," having its specific "defensive meaning." It is actuated by such basic defenses as fixations and regressions, defenses through which gratifications are sought and partly achieved that had been feasible, but had been frustrated, years before. The immature Sister, thus, derives certain gratifications, symbolically and unconsciously, by being immature; the key to understand her *in the present* is in understanding what *past* gratifications she is now seeking a duplication of.

Development from immaturity to maturity consists of a gradual relinquishing of earlier, simpler modes of gratification in favor of more and more civilized modes (acceptable to the biological components of personality and also to the psychological, social, existential, and spiritual components). In our previous discussion on personality development (page 201) we showed how growth rests on urging forces (promoting gratifications), checking forces (causing frustrations), and alternate routes (upon which growth and development ultimately depend). We grow (relinquish earlier gratifications, i.e., sucking our thumb, in favor of sucking a lollipop) because of (*a*) our parents, who by being exceedingly strict about it make it impossible for us to go on sucking our thumb; and (*b*) we ourselves do not want to go on sucking it because our parents do not and we want to be like them; besides, there are more advantages to sucking on lollipops than to sucking on thumbs. The more our parents help us to grow by (*b*), the easier our process of relinquishing primitive modes of gratification; the more our parents made us grow by (*a*), the harder to give up these modes and the harder not to return to them later in life.

Fixation, then, is the condition in which a quota of our urging forces remains over-attached to a primitive mode of gratification. It is related to the pain and anxiety caused by checking forces applied too soon (infants weaned too early) or too stringently and harshly, thus interfering with a gradual (at the child's own pace) relinquishing of earlier modes of gratifications. It is as though the fixated personality were saying: "I haven't had enough of this particular pleasure; it is taken away from me too soon; I won't, therefore, relinquish it in favor of a more mature pleasure." Once the fixation has developed, it will be subjected to alternate routes as previously discussed (page —); fixated thumb sucking may be displaced onto overeating, oversmoking, or gullibility (being a "sucker"); fixated infantile biting may be displaced onto biting sarcasm, vitriolic talking, "chewing people up with words;" etc. Fixations, also, will be returned-to (regressions) in later life whenever painful anxiety and frustrations are re-experienced: which is exactly what the immature person does (every time her mother harshly restrained her from masturbating, M.H. retaliated against mother, and protected herself from the anxiety of giving up masturbation by giving herself to the gratification of an anal drive—uncontrollable diarrhea, as incontinent as before toilet training. As a young religious today, Sister M.H.

develops functional colitis whenever the Superior rightly or wrongly "crosses" her).

The above discussion on fixation and regression should clearly show that:

1) Every human being has fixations, because each of us, having been brought up by human, thus fallible, parents, has experienced frustrations in childhood. That this is so is clearly demonstrated by the fact that every adult has occasional regressions to previous fixations. In the face of the inevitable difficulties of life, whenever realistically anxious or sad we over-smoke and overeat (regressions to oral-stage fixations); have bouts of constipation or diarrhea or periods of stubbornness and overscheduling of life (regressions to anal-stage fixations); masturbate or engage in compulsive sexuality of one type or another (regressions to phallic-stage fixations); find it impossible to wake up on time in the morning or are irresistibly attracted to afternoon naps (infancy and childhood fixations); etc. Thus the difference between the immature and the mature person is only a difference of degree: the different degree, duration, and intensity of fixations and regressions.

2) The fact that the immature person derives gratification from his immaturity does not make him a malingerer or a person deliberately (or consciously) trying to draw attention to himself. The immature does crave for attention—only because he didn't have enough of it when, in childhood, he was entitled to it; his symptoms are unconsciously-operating attention-getting devices; there is, however, no conscious pleasure in the gratification of his unconscious drives; and because of the conflictual psychodynamic state in which these drives are, a very high price in anxiety, guilt, and shame is being paid even as these drives are being gratified.

Counseling the immature Sister, therefore, is counseling of a person entangled in a web of fixations and regressions, a web compelling her to do, time after time, that which only in childhood could and should have given her pleasure; and which, now, can only attract upon her shame, ridicule, and more rejection—which in turn only frustrates her more and keeps her immature longer.

Superiors of immature Sisters are often caught in a dilemma. Giving in to the patient's immature demands will cause resentment and anger in other Sisters, with the attending problem of morale; not giving in frustrates and depresses the Sister even more and will at times make the Superior feel guilty. What is she then to do? She (the Superior) will have to be herself, and demand of the immature Sister as much (or as little) as her heart and her mind dictate; but, simultaneously, she *must* address herself to the Sister's whole person (i.e., the hunger for relationships underlying the external anger and cattiness), address herself to the inner person hiding behind the immature person, and refer Sister for counseling or psycho-therapy.

Her treatment, therefore, is directed at understanding the specific factors that had interfered with her growth; at discovering why drives and needs that could have been harmoniously integrated into an adult personality (and unconflictually fulfilled through it) were not and had to undergo fixations. In so doing one is already relating to the whole person, her present and her past, her conscious and her unconscious. And this relating, as we can better understand now, is already therapeutic because it will gratify some of the repressed and fixated drives.

A Sister once said: "No one had ever listened to me with so much atten-tion and respect before. It makes me feel, for the first time in my life, that some of these long-buried things I am talking about are worthwhile, are not odious; it makes me feel that I may be worthwhile and not odious, in spite of being such a little child in so many areas of my life."

Simultaneously to this, a corrective experience (through the intermedia-tion of transference) is being offered. The therapist becomes a parent and counseling becomes home; the earlier, more primitive modes of gratifica-tions are consciously re-experienced (in words, fantasies, dreams); in the benevolent, permissive, care-full atmosphere of therapy, previously experi-enced checking forces are re-experienced and better understood; till the immature modes of gratifications can be freely given up because new ones are now available.

Sister E's immaturity took the form of being and thinking of herself as "a little girl." She always felt as if she were the youngest and the least knowledgeable and experienced of the entire community. She clung over-dependently to some of the older Sisters in the house, exhibited what some have called "whole," rather than "holy," obedience, and maintained a very naive, over-idealized, almost ethereal image of herself, the world, and espe-cially "the facts of life." (She related to sex the same way pre-puberty Vic-torian children were supposed to. As an intriguing psychosomatic corollary, she stopped menstruating the day she entered religious life, at 18, and was still un-ovulating and amenorrhoic at the time she initiated treatment). Her "little-girl-ness" was not noticed (and had, probably, been further fostered) during the years of her religious formation and did not become a severe prob-lem (and the source of intense frustration) till after profession.

Among other factors, Sister's fixation to dependency was related to over-whelming unconscious fears of giving in to intense, primitive sexual desires. Her mother, evidently, had the same problem: an extremely repressed woman, she showed a consuming preoccupation to repress her own sexuality by con-tinuously talking against (rather than about) sex to Sister E; and by plaguing her, inappropriately and prematurely, with sexual prohibitions and taboos (Sister was only 7 when mother took one of her dolls, sewed up its bottom and told her "I'll do this to your bottom if you don't watch out with boys when you grow up"). Sister, thus, came to equate growing-up with dangers, specifically sexual dangers. Therapy, among other things, made her aware of her sexual fears and desires and helped her to see that defenseless as she might have been as a child, in the face of strong instincts, she was no longer helpless now and could indeed channel her sexuality in directions appropriate to her age, religion, and status. Through the corrective intermediation of transference, the therapist became a mother, who accepted Sister E's right to sexual feelings and to discover by herself the best way to control them; and a father (one of the "boys" mother had forever warned her against) who did not take advantage of her as she consciously feared and unconsciously hoped. Therapy was, therefore, a corrective experience, through which Sister could re-experience her whole self (including her arrested, repressed sexuality) without "sewing herself up" (incidentally, also Sister's menstrual cycle returned to normal).

With Sister L, immaturity took the external form of difficulty (try hard as she might) to fulfill her religious obligations (especially morning prayers and Mass) and underachievement at school (a very bright, perceptive person, she rarely obtained grades higher than C in college). With Sister L, immaturity was tied to the unconscious conviction that female authorities would disapprove of her if she were mature, authoritative, self-reliant, and independent. This idea, in turn, was related to Sister's unconsciously equating being authoritative with being authoritarian, being mature and independent with being tyrannical and autocratic. More specifically, Sister L had had, in her childhood, a very competitive relationship with her mother, a confused, insecure person who on one hand wanted Sister L to achieve, on the other squelched her and made her feel guilty every time she achieved. For Sister L to become mature, to achieve, meant to displace her mother (later her Superior) from the "throne" of the house (later of the Convent), which she longed for, and simultaneously felt much guilt and anxiety about (who would or could love her if she were "on the throne"? whom could she depend on if she "were on top"?). Counseling, among other things, made Sister L aware of her competitiveness, desire to succeed, ambivalence about it, and of the various ways and means by which she sabotaged her efforts toward mature achievements thus assuring the appearances of immaturity and underachievement. She became able to dis-associate her Superiors from her mother and no longer to equate self-control and self-reliance with controlling and dominating others. What, essentially, was curative was, again, the corrective experience of transference, through which the counselor became a non-competitive, accepting parental figure who recognized her right to achieve and who would not withhold his affection and care because of her achievements.

Immature Sisters may come for counseling consciously convinced that their immaturity affects only one aspect of their personality as if it were possible to be immature only sexually, or only religiously, or only as far as assertiveness is concerned, and be mature in all other areas. This attitude must be understood for what it is—a symptom, a first line of defense, an attempt to avoid change by fragmenting (in one's mind) one's wholeness and pushing to the fore just one particular aspect of one's general dysfunction. In counseling Sisters with "compartmentalized immaturity," one, again, must sidestep the localized symptom and relate to the whole person.

Superiors, directresses of training, at times make the mistake of viewing a Sister's spiritual immaturity as if it were in a vacuum, i.e., unrelated to Sister's immaturity in charity, aggressiveness, sexuality, working habits, etc.

Immature Sisters will occasionally protect their illness by convincing themselves that nothing is the matter with them that a better Superior, a better Community, more perceptive and giving friends, etc., would not remedy. These are often pathetic cases; for, with no insight (on Sister's part, and, frequently, everybody's around her) on the internal nature and origin of the problem, no therapy is sought, Superior and other Sisters feel responsible and guilty ("maybe it is our fault that she is so unhappy"), the wrong moves are decided upon (a transfer, for instance) . . . and Sister remains as unhappy, after each of these steps, as she was before.

In counseling these Sisters, early focusing and structuring are essential. As soon as possible, Sister will have to see that the other Sisters' lack of warmth and perceptivity is "their problem"; and that what one is concerned with, in the counseling situation, is Sister's reaction to the other Sisters' personalities. In most cases it will again be through the counseling relationship itself that Sister will realize (if she can realize it at all) that the problem is internal, part of herself, rather than external.

Externalization of internal problems may occur in the direction of religious life as a whole: "If I only were not a religious, I would be O.K." In these cases Sisters leave the religious life, only to feel as anxious or depressed "outside" as they were "inside." This may result in a complete emotional and spiritual deterioration, particularly regretful in the case of former Sisters whose vocation and spirituality could have been saved had therapy been instituted before dispensation. In other cases exclaustration, obtained while Sister is undergoing therapy, is indirectly therapeutic through the mobilization of internal problems it may provoke.

> Sister J, another "little-girl" case, had been debating for years as to whether she should leave religious life. All her problems, she felt, were caused by it: Superiors were cold, Sisters clannish, community spirit not what it was supposed to be. Sister longed to return to her parents, whom she visited as often as permissible and whom she experienced as warm and loving. (Interestingly enough, her parents, just as unhappy as Sister J, also externalized the sources of their problems and were convinced that, if only Sister came back home, they would be all right). With their encouragement (and despite warnings to the contrary from her therapist) Sister finally applied for exclaustration. After a few weeks at home, the "honeymoon" was over, serious problems between Sister and her parents appeared, and Sister became acutely

anxious and depressed. From a concrete and immediate point of view this exclaustration—one would say—had been disastrous. From a long-range, psychotherapeutic perspective, however, it had actually happened to be the right move: it showed Sister J that her problems were more internal than external; and to the extent that they were external, her relationship with her own mother was much more relevant to her difficulties than her relationship with her Mother Superior. (Sister J incidentally, returned to the religious life 15 months later.)

In counseling, on the other hand, Sister V, a repressed and depressed young Sister, exclaustration would have been more damaging than therapeutic. Sister V also externalized her problems and projected her fear of loving and of being loved on everyone around her. The type of community she lived in, however (relaxed, easy-going, fun-loving), and the Sisters and Superior she lived with (warm, interested, dynamic), gave her the unique opportunity to work out her problems right in the house.

A major generalization one can make, then, about this matter is the following: Except in extreme cases, in which life in the convent (or life outside the convent) would be extremely painful because of specific, realistic, external factors, the question of whether the Sister is or is not exclaustrated is secondary to the question of whether Sister is or is not able to rightly perceive the true source of her difficulty; and whether she is or is not receiving counseling and psychotherapy.

To conclude, a few words ought to be said on the counseling of Sisters with difficulties in interpersonal relationships, i.e. Sisters who "can't get along" (with other Sisters; with their Superior; or, in the case of Superiors, with their subordinates). This type of problem too (like "immaturity") is a "catch-all" problem, embracing a number of psychiatric difficulties and expressing a variety of unconscious dynamisms.

After all, the way one gets along with people, the quality, the "style" of one's interpersonal relationships, is the point of convergence of one's entire personality, the apical point onto which and through which are channeled all of one's alternate routes, displaced and sublimated instincts, unconscious character layers in their various psychodynamic state, etc. Personality is the "mask" (cfr, latin, *Persona*, the mask donned by the actors to impersonate various *characters*), the public (conscious, external) version of our private (unconscious, internal) character; the way this "mask" relates to others is a function of the internal character. It has been said: The way one relates is the language of the inner person. It could be said: Tell me how you get along with others and I'll tell you who you are.

"Transference," in our opinion, is the most important and the most frequently operating unconscious dynamism underlying difficulties in interpersonal relationships. "Transference" is responsible not only for difficulties between Superiors and Sisters but also for difficulties between older Sisters and younger Sisters; "old-breed" (regardless of chronological age) and "new-breed" (again, regardless of age) Sisters; peer Sisters; and is certainly operating to various degrees in the reactions of many Sisters to some of the changes recently initiated by the II Vatican Council.

Sister F has an unconsciously-determined need to "play games" with her Superior; regardless of the Superior's responses to her "games," the Superior is always wrong and Sister F always dissatisfied, the result being a very disturbed (and disturbing) interpersonal relationship between the two. For instance: At breakfast time Sister F stage-whispers something, in the Superior's presence, about the coldness of community spirit in the house: "One might feel miserable," she says, "yet one has to get up and have breakfast with everybody else." In the evening, she does not appear at the community meal. The Superior, motivated (at least consciously) by love, concern, and humility brings a tray of food up to Sister F's room. Sister F accepts it grudgingly, then bursts into tears and says: "Stop treating me like a child! What is the matter with you, anyway?"

For Sister A (Superior in the house) Sister L, is never right: if Sister L is deferential, Sister A experiences her as fawning and false; if assertive, Sister A finds her disrespectful and disobedient. No matter how much Sister L tries to stay out of the Superior's way, Sister A is always around, finding faults with her; the two are getting along with each other so poorly that a transfer soon becomes necessary. When Sister L, however, has been transferred, Sister A finds herself becoming equally impatient and fault-finding with Sister P. Both Sister L and Sister P, Sister Superior reveals months later, reminded her exactly of her younger sister, 10 years her junior, who had also been in the religious life and had left before taking final vows.

Sister H can't get along with Father L who hears confessions at her convent and teaches religion at the convent's school. However, because of administrative and academic matters, she has to see him continuously. She dreads the thought of her daily conferences with him and not much is accomplished at the meetings because of her dislike and contempt for him. Her major complaint is that he is too soft and tender hearted with the children; he lets them "get away with murder"; she is coming to hate the children too for the love and respect they have for him. Much later in therapy, Sister H discovers that Father L related to the school children somewhat as her own father related to Sister H's 9 younger brothers and sisters.

What is "transference"? Transference is a *sui generis* emotional posture, particularly recognizable in psychoanalytic psychotherapy but actually occurring, to varying degrees of recognizability, in other intimate relationships (husband and wife; soldier and N.C.O. on the battle front; pastor and curate; superior and sister; etc.). In transference one experiences toward present persons and situations feelings which are minimally related to what these persons and situations realistically are; inappropriate feelings, therefore, bearing little relationship to the feelings these persons and situations should realistically engender. In transference, rather, one experiences a duplication of the conscious and unconscious feelings one had about significant persons (parental figures) and situations (childhood events) from one's past. These feelings are now *unconsciously* ("transferred") onto the present persons and situations, who have come to *unconsciously* represent, symbolically the past persons and situations. Transferentially, then, a Sister experiences her Superior not as the Superior objectively is but as Sister consciously (and, especialy, unconsciously) experienced her own parents when she was a child. Her feelings toward the Superior are less related to what the Superior actually is, does, and stands for than to the feelings Sister had about what her parents were, did, and stood for.

Transference motivates behavior as well as feelings. In transferential behavior, a Sister will act toward her Superior not realistically but as she acted (or wanted to) with her own parents in childhood (transference being a "remembering and repeating through actions and feelings").

From what has been said so far, it should be apparent that: (1) the influence transference exercises upon conscious behavior is only one aspect of what has been previously described (page 206) as "the dynamic influence of the unconscious"; (2) since conscious behavior is always influenced, to some degree, by the unconscious, it is also always influenced, to some degree, by the unconscious dimensions of transference; (3) transferentially-influenced behavior is unrealistic, subjective, and neurotic: to a degree directly proportional to the degree to which transference participates to its determination. Behavior is never totally realistic, fully objective: normal (more objective) and abnormal (more subjective) behavior differ only in the different degrees to which transference influences it. Especially considering this last point, it should be already understandable why transference should be an important factor in the psychogenesis of interpersonal difficulties (in or out of the Religious life).

Sister F was re-living, with Sister Superior, the manipulative and exploitative climate she had experienced, in childhood, with a very disturbed mother, with whom neurotic "games" had to be played if one were to survive physically as well as psychically; and experiencing her Superior as infantilizing and destructive as her own mother had actually been. Sister A was transferentially re-living, through her feelings toward Sister P and Sister L her sibling rivalry against her younger sister; Sister H re-living her feelings about her own father's partiality to the younger siblings.

Interpersonal relationships between Sisters, then (why Sister A does not get along with Sister B, why Sister C does get along with Sister D), can be truly understood only if their transferential dimensions are also considered. Sisters will get along poorly or richly with other Sisters (or with aspects of spiritual and community life invested with personal, symbolic value) less because of what these Sisters and these aspects are, than because of how they are subjectively experienced through the distorting glasses of transference.

We can realize, then, that it is naive to try to explain the transferential reactions affecting religious Sisters (and the disturbed interpersonal relations thus engendered) by considering only the external factors of religious life. In determining quality and intensity of transferential reactions, the characteristics of the person toward whom the transference develops (i.e., what Mother Superior is like) or of the environment within which the transference grows (i.e., the convent's atmosphere) are important but secondary. A Junior Executive in I.B.M. is more likely to develop intense transferential reactions toward the older Vice President with whom he relates frequently than to another Junior Executive from a different department with whom he is not competing for promotion and who is more or less his age. Sisters are more likely to develop transferential reactions toward their Superior than to other Sisters in the house. In general, the more "parental" a figure is (attitudinally or symbolically, through the power or authority invested in that figure), the more likely it will be that persons subordinately relating to it will develop transferential reactions. That these external characteristics, however, are far from primary in transference-determining value is clearly indicated by the many instances in which a person's behavior toward a "superior" figure is only minimally transferential in nature; or the instances in which transferential reactions are experienced toward younger or "inferior" persons. What is primary, then, in determining a person's transferential reactions, is that person's own psychodynamic structure of personality.

Accidental features of religious life will promote transferentially-based relationships, less because of what these factors are than because of the psychodynamic structure of the persons exposed to these features. The fact that Sisters may be referred to as "Daughters" and Superiors as "Mothers"; the potential and latent implications of the very word "Superior"; the reality of the Superior's authority over the Sisters in the community; the vows of obedience and chastity—are all accidental features of religious life which may indeed infantilize Sisters and "motherize" Superiors; but those Sisters will be infantilized (and Superiors motherized) who from the depth of their unconscious had already looked upon these features as opportunities for the release of their transferential needs. The fact, again, that one can observe so many obedient and deferential Sisters who can, at the same time, relate joyfully, vibrantly, and maturely to their Superior demonstrates the naivete of believing that religious life is bound to promote transferential relationships in everybody.

Much is written today on the so-called "unrest" among the religious, and its connections with the recent changes catalyzed by the II Vatican Council. This unrest, is frequently a "ferment" rather than an unrest, a very promising and fertile ferment, harbinger of still more changes in the accidental aspects of religious life; changes rendering this life more self-fulfilling and, simultaneously, saintly and spiritual in the broader, more "worldly" context of an apostolate relevant to today's social, psychological, and political ills. When it is a true unrest its neurotic manifestations (psychoneurotic anxiety, anger or depression about the "new Church" or the "old Church"; character-neurotic passivity about—or resistance against—the changes) are often related to transference; or, more precisely, to the frustration of unconscious, transference-based, neurotic expectations from religious life.

We are not suggesting that attitudes about changes in religious life, (pro—or against) are, necessarily, neurotic or transferentially-determined. As indicated earlier, phenomenologically identical manifestations of religiosity may be unconsciously and genetically quite different in nature, so that in one case one finds a largely neurotic religiosity and in another a largely authentic one. The same can be said of attitudes about changes; it is when these attitudes have largely neurotic, transferentially-determined origins that they are accompanied by a neurotic, highly personalized "unrest." Sisters, we said elsewhere in this chapter, may have entered the religious life because of neurotic motivations; because of a sick religiosity; hoping to find, in the structure of religious life, a new protection and a new armature for their collapsing defenses. They may have entered unconsciously seeking opportunities for a transference to a grim, wrathful, and vengeful God (father figure?) or a rigid, strict, and ungiving Superior (mother figure?); or looking forward to an authoritarian system of life, in which they would be over-deferential and over-submissive to their elders, when younger sisters; and selfishly authoritarian and tyrannically domineering toward younger sisters when older themselves. They may have entered with the unconscious anticipation of a life of silence (whole rather than holy) and isolation (permanent and uncommitted). Upon discovering that the Superior is a "person" indeed, warm, feminine, and fun-loving; or that the God her elders talk about is a loving, forgiving Father first when the fresh winds of change force upon her a different relationship to the lay community, to non-Catholics, to men; or expose her to a flock of young, pop-music-loving (but no less good and holy), free and easy (but no less respectful in the true sense of the word "respect") postulants; and cause her to relate to novices who don't go along with her grim determination to be somber and austere at all costs—when all this happens, she can only feel alienated and bitter, unable to get along with everybody, young and old, and resistive to all changes, good or bad.

12

MARITAL PROBLEMS—PSYCHOSOCIAL AND PASTORAL CONSIDERATIONS

A. C. Zarkadas, A.C.S.W.

But God did not create man as a solitary. For from the beginning 'male and female He created them' (Gen 1:27). Their companionship produces the primary form of interpersonal communion [1]—Vatican II

The ideal of interpersonal communion expressed in the quotation above is realized when husband and wife actualize their capacities to relate so as to become one—a family. That is, they relate in such a way that, while each one loses himself in the other and is thereby enriched, neither loses his unique individuality nor deprives the children of theirs. This unremitting capacity and longing to relate to others, to care and to be cared for, to love and to be loved—to give himself to the other and to receive the other unto himself is innate to man, for it is his nature to be a social being. People who, unfortunately, cannot find opportunities to gratify this basic demand, seem to shrivel up and die, and if they are married, their marriage dies too. This tragedy, with its attendant despair, not only affects the couple involved, but so often profoundly affects their children.

When efforts are made to "heal" dying marriages, the complex nature of marital problems quickly becomes apparent, and the counselor soon realizes that the two troubled people are seeking to gratify a multiplicity of needs

---

[1] W. Abbott, S.J., *The Documents of Vatican II*, 211.

and wishes. Because these needs and wishes are often contradictory they result in greater confusion and further alienation. Consequently, the coun- selor's efforts, no matter how logical, and appropriate, meet with intense and confounding resistance, and often only add to the confusion. There are many explanations for this development. Some of them, of course, have to do with the troubled individuals themselves. But others result from the counselor's defective approach. This chapter—a sociological, psychological, and pastoral consideration of this many-faceted marriage problem—it is hoped will contribute to a deeper understanding of the interplay of forces that lead to disrupting marital situations, stimulate the development of a creative approach to counseling these troubled people, and reflect on the preventive possibilities that such understanding suggests.

SOCIOLOGICAL PERSPECTIVES ON THE AMERICAN FAMILY

Traditionally, all cultures have provided stabilizing forces and supports for the family, for "when we survey all known human societies, we find everywhere some form of the family, some set of permanent arrangements by which males assist females in caring for children while they are young." [2] The need for a permanent familial arrangement has a biological foundation for not only is it utterly impossible for a human infant to survive without mothering, but the nurturing relationship between a human infant and its mother must last for a significantly longer period of time than for any other known living creatures. Furthermore, the need for a permanent union also has a psychological basis, for the nurturing relationship contributes directly to the emotional development of the child.

Essential, if the family is to provide for the socialization of its young by conveying to them a cultural and social inheritance, is a set of moral values, customs, traditions, and skills, and a meaningful identity with their society.

Since these biological, psychological, and social needs are essential for the continuation of human society, it is understandable that society places a high premium on family stability, and erects barriers to prevent family breakdown. However, despite the acknowledged interdependence between the family and society to the extent that neither can thrive without the other, there has been, in recent years, a significant increase in the number of family breakdowns. A few sociologists, notably Sorokin and Zimmerman, have expressed the concern that the family (and, by implication, civilized society) is in danger of disappearing from the American scene. On this point, Professor Sorokin writes:

[2] M. Mead, *Male and Female*, 188.

The family as a sacred union of husband and wife, of parents and children, will continue to disintegrate. Divorces and separations will increase until any profound difference between socially sanctioned marriages and illicit sex-relationships disappears. Children will be separated earlier and earlier from their parents. The main socio-cultural functions of the family will further decrease until the family becomes a mere overnight parking place mainly for sex-relationships.[3]

Zimmerman has expressed similar conclusions, warning that, "There is little left now within the family or the moral code to hold (the) family together." [4] However, while it is obvious that the increase in family breakdown is real and significant,[5] others are not so pessimistic, but feel that there is really little question but that the truth about the future of the American family lies somewhere short of these extreme views. Nevertheless, their suggestion that we should return to the type of family life that existed a hundred years ago,[6] seems to beg the question, for there is little historical evidence to show that we could reverse either the current changes in family structure or the direction our society has taken.

What are these irreversible changes in family life and new movements in society? Well, from a time nearly one hundred years ago, when divorce was practically unknown in this country, the American family, as a social unit, has undergone some significant changes that are directly related to other social, economic, and cultural phenomena. Briefly, the American family is evolving a new structure and function in response to our evolution from a primarily rural society to an increasingly urban and industrial one. It is also being affected by the greater emphasis our culture places on individualism, competition, and the application of democratic principles to social life. Burgess observes that, taken together, these influences amount to a social revolution.[7]

As a consequence of this revolution, the family of a hundred years ago, which might be called the extended kinship family, has become the companionship, or isolated conjugal unit of today. This transition has been described quite well by sociologists who note that the two families differ in several aspects. They point out that the extended kinship family was essentially paternalistic with authority residing in the husband and father; that the division of labor between males and females was fairly clear and

---

[3] P. Sorokin, *Social and Cultural Dynamics* 4. 776.

[4] C. Zimmerman, *The Family and Civilization*, 796.

[5] P. Jacobson—P. Jacobson, *American Marriage and Divorce*, 96.

[6] C. Zimmerman—M. Frampton, *Family and Society*, 129–130. P. Sorokin, *The Crisis of Our Age*, 203.

[7] E. Burgess, "Economic, Cultural and Social Factors in Family Breakdown," *American Journal of Orthopsychiatry* 24 (1954) 465.

distinct, and that inasmuch as Industry was primarily contained within the family, roles were dictated by the family's needs, which invariably eclipsed the needs of its individual members. At its best, the extended kinship family was a benevolent authoritarian institution. As such, it contained all the questionable assets and the real liabilities of authoritarianism. It was, however, admirably suited to a rural society where progress, and sometimes survival itself, depended on maintaining close family ties with a role and function for each member.

The emphasis on the priority of family objectives over those of its individual members, and related emphasis on conformity, public opinion, convention, and the secondary role assigned to women resulted in an *externally* stable family life. Examination of the steadily increasing rate of family breakdown in the past one hundred years clearly shows this to be true. According to conditions existing in 1955, Jacobson estimated that one of every four marriages contracted that year would end in divorce.[8] Thus, considered from a structural point of view alone, there is little question but that the extended kinship form of family life resulted in greater stability.

Just as the earlier family evolved in response to the prevailing rural situation, the family of today is adapting to the present urban situation. Burgess and Locke describe this evolving family as follows:

> The form of the family that appears to be emerging in modern society may be called the companionship family because of its emphasis upon intimate interpersonal association as its primary function. Other characteristics of the companionship family are: the giving and receiving of affection; the assumption of equality of husband and wife; democracy in family decisions, with a voice and a vote by the children; the personality development of its members as a family objective; freedom of self-expression which is consistent with family unity; and the expectation that the greatest happiness is to be found in the family.[9]

One of the paradoxical aspects of the dynamic adaptation of today's family is that its struggles to embrace the very cultural values that have made our country great result in its appearing to be a less stable family system. It would appear that much of the urgency to reinstitute the earlier family system arises from this paradox. As has been stated earlier, the majority of sociologists clearly see that this is impossible. They suggest instead that society provide supports to buttress the promise that today's family holds, thus making the fulfillment of that promise a reality. This new type of family emphasizes the dignity of all its members, and can actualize the development of each member's personality and potential to

[8] P. Jacobson—P. Jacobson, *op. cit.*, 148.

[9] E. Burgess—H. Locke, *The Family, From Institution to Companionship*, 2nd ed., 651.

participate and to contribute in our modern world. To achieve this potential fully, today's family desperately needs the support of an informed society—a society which not only is motivated by its immediate self-interest (the reduction of breakdown), but which recognizes as well the vastly superior possibilities that are potentially available to its future generations.

Since we are at present in a state of transition, our efforts on the family's behalf are sometimes tinged with ambivalence. Much depends upon how this ambivalence will be resolved. A striking example of this is the great resistance that attends society's efforts to relieve the economic difficulties of many of our families. It is common knowledge that for those at the lower rungs of our economic ladder it is often tempting for the husband to "leave" his family to make it eligible for economic aid. We condemn him and establish elaborate welfare programs to provide for the now fatherless family. All this in the face of irrefutable evidence that a broken home is a statistically significant factor in the histories of both juvenile and adult delinquents.[10] This is an area in which our society could support these families *as whole families*, and without ambiguity or ambivalence. Fortunately, the current trend seems to be in that direction.

In other areas, we have more successfully initiated efforts in the family's behalf. These efforts, though less dramatic than a guaranteed income to all families, nonetheless hold much promise for the future. Among these are the introduction of courses in family living and marriage at various levels of our educational system. Many communities have instituted "cooling off" programs in their courts of domestic relations, and frequently these programs provide a kind of "first aid" counseling during the mandatory cooling off period to couples seeking separation and divorce. The professional preparation of physicians, attorneys, and clergymen is increasingly emphasizing the importance of happy family life, making them more attuned to the presence of marital conflict. Adult education programs frequently provide general courses in psychology which emphasize the dynamics of interpersonal relations in marriage, family living, and parent-child relations.

An outstanding development has been the increase in public and private agencies and clinics devoted exclusively to supporting family life with a host of services. Not surprisingly these services in many respects parallel the supports that flowed from an extended kinship way of living. In addition to professional counseling, they offer such auxiliary services as: substitute homemakers, camping programs, temporary foster care of children, legal services, budget counseling and others. The Family Service Association of America, a national pace setting affiliation of family counseling services,

[10] *The Challenge of Crime in a Free Society*—A report by the President's Commission on law enforcement and administration, 44.

describes the purpose of its member agencies as contributing to harmonious family relationships, strengthening the positive values in family life, and promoting healthy personality development and satisfactory social functioning of various family members.[11]

In the main, these are preventive services designed to reinforce the family's natural tendency to maintain its integrity and to remain intact. Often they are so much a part of the very fabric of society that we overlook the important contribution they make. The pre-Cana and Cana conferences and the Christian Family Movement are explicit supports under Catholic auspices which hold great potential. However, despite society's efforts to buttress families' attempts to adapt to our times, there are families for which these are of little avail. These are the families for whom the threat of family breakdown is neither a statistic nor a regrettable social phenomenon, but rather an excruciatingly painful and uniquely individual reality. These are the people who, becoming aware of the need for some kind of help, seek out marital counseling. They approach the experience with preconceived ideas that reflect their own internal needs and the usual popular misconceptions.

PSYCHOLOGICAL PERSPECTIVES OF MARITAL CONFLICT

What people actually experience in the course of working on their problems depends upon whom they turn to for help. There is great variation in the activities, vis-a-vis the client, that are referred to as marital counseling. It is somewhat ironic that so distinctive a name has gained such common usage, connoting as it does a misleading sense of homogeneity of practices that in reality does not exist. Despite the existence of a relatively small group that view marriage counseling as a distinct profession (in 1962, the Directory of the American Association of Marriage Counselors contained fewer than 450 names, including non-clinical members),[12] most of the work in this area is done by members of the major therapeutic professions: psychiatry, social work, and psychology. When these practitioners speak of marital counseling, it is not in terms of a distinct professional discipline, but as a conflictual area of life to which they apply their varied professional skills.

The actual experience of help is further complicated by the many interpretations practitioners place on the significance of the marital difficulty. There has been a tendency on the part of some to emphasize the inter-

[11] Family Service Association of America, *Scope and Methods of the Family Service Agency* (infra).

[12] E. Nash—L. Jessner—D. Abse, *Marriage Counseling in Medical Practice*, 302.

actional factors to the exclusion of other aspects. When this happens, the marital complaint is often viewed in an isolated way, unrelated to the individual's unconscious intrapsychic contributions to the relationship. Not infrequently, some one aspect of the interaction itself is isolated and receives disproportionate attention. Examples of this kind of development are the emphasis on "togetherness" of a few years ago, and the more recent concern with "communication." The latter is also an example of how a single aspect, the breakdown in communication, is made the focal point of efforts to intervene in the disturbed marital relationship. The thinking here goes something like this: people in the midst of marital conflict invariably exhibit some degree of lack, or distortion, in communication; since this is the case, they must be helped (encouraged) to communicate, and all efforts are concentrated in this direction. There is unquestionable appeal to this conceptualization. It is straight-forward and logical. The therapist feels in control of the situation since he has arrived at a direct, and causal-like relationship between the disturbance in communication and the conflict in the marriage. What is left unanswered is *why* the disturbance in communication. The answer to that question is of the utmost importance if the therapy is to be more than a form of advice giving. Yet, marital counseling too often means exactly this for many who seek it, and, unfortunately for many who presume to undertake its practice. As a result, definitions of marital counseling are noteworthy for their vagueness and their disproportionate emphasis on treating the "marriage" or the "interpersonal relationship" toward the goal of an undefined "better adjustment."

It is our position that most marital problems are expressions of intrapsychic conflicts of one or both spouses. As such, they are susceptible to understanding and diagnosis.[13] They signal the individuals' continuing efforts to deal with their unresolved conflicts. It is helpful, therefore, to conceptualize the marital problem (whatever its specifics) as a "symptom" that makes its appearance in the marital area, and represents one or both spouses' efforts to maintain their psychological integrity. The presence of actual neurotic symptoms indicates that the ego's defensive efforts have miscarried, and that the ego has suffered a defeat.[14] The symptoms represent a compromise between instinctual demands and external realities; they allow partial gratification of the instinctual demand and pay a price for this partial gratification through the pain which symptoms always produce. It is helpful to assume a parallel view of marital conflicts.

In some instances, it is true that one or both partners exhibit signs of the

[13] R. Blanck, "Marriage as a Phase of Personality Development," *Social Casework* Volume 48 (1967) 154.
[14] A. Freud, *The Ego and the Mechanisms of Defense*, 193.

classical neuroses or psychoses. Experience suggests, however, that when this is the case (particularly when only one partner is ill), therapy is more frequently sought in terms of the specific neurotic or psychotic symptomatology, and seldom in terms of a marital problem. The majority of individuals who do seek therapy in terms of unhappy marital relationships do not exhibit frank psychological symptoms. The marital relationship itself is the vehicle, so to speak, for their internal difficulties. This is a less costly—in intrapsychic terms—expression of their difficulties and many times serves as an entry into therapy that would otherwise be unacceptable to the person. This also helps to explain the high incidence of serious emotional problems in persons whose presenting complaints revolve around the marriage and, from a practical point of view, emphasizes the futility of concentrating therapy in the interactional aspects of the marriage to the exclusion of other factors. Few people initiate therapy with the statement, "I have a problem and it's making my marriage unbearable." More frequently it is, "my marriage (or spouse) is impossible and this makes me miserable."

Although it is beyond our scope to examine this complicated phenomenon in minute detail, it will be helpful to look at some of the implications of the latter presenting complaint. It immediately gives rise to three formidable technical tasks: 1) moving the focus from the marriage back to the individual; 2) understanding the individual's intrapsychic contributions to the marital relationship; and 3) engaging this individual in a therapeutic relationship on the therapist's terms. The third task is particularly difficult for reasons that are obvious when the marital problem is viewed as a reflection or extension of intrapsychic conflicts. Such individuals have a vested interest in maintaining the focus upon the marriage and avoiding, at all costs, the more painful analysis of themselves. The tenacity with which they "hold on" is in direct proportion to the internal risk they sense. As a maneuver, it is similar (but not identical) in purpose to the significance of the ego's mechanisms of defense. An example of this is projection, the ego defense that permits an intolerable affect or motive expression only in terms of another—"I'm not angry at her, she's angry with me." This leaves the ego free, in a sense, yet enslaves it from ever coming to terms with the affect or motive it has disowned.

Ego defenses are employed to protect the ego and restrict the development of anxiety.[15] Nullifying the defenses precipitously may overwhelm the ego with anxiety and result in withdrawal from therapy, or worse. Prudent therapists respect the ego's defenses, accepting them as necessary to its integrity. This general psychotherapeutic maxim has equal applica-

[15] *Ibid.*, 193.

bility to individuals whose presenting complaints are in terms of their marital relationships. Thus, the therapist's view of the marital conflict, i.e., what it signifies, is no mere intellectual exercise. To view such concerns only as problems in interpersonal relations that have no meaningful history prior to the marriage, no relatedness to the intrapsychic make-up of the marital partners, and treatable as "here and now" phenomena, is to fail to utilize what we know about human psychology.

It is also erroneous to conceive of the forces at work in the lives of individuals as consciously directed maneuvers and, hence, as responsive to logical discussion, reprimand, exhortation or mediation. Painstaking work is required to understand their nature and the reasons for a person's resorting to such patently unproductive means. During training seminars, one often hears young therapists, correctly perceiving that a man is doing precisely those things that alienate his wife, exclaiming, "That's crazy, if he wants her to love him, why doesn't he. . . ." They are completely missing the point of the man's difficulty: he can't seek love because he has never felt loved. An emotional cripple, he is doomed to compulsive repetition of unsuccessful maneuvers to maintain the illusion that he is lovable without really testing it, and to keep at bay the terrible emptiness, the frightening rage, and desolate depression that haunts his every waking moment. These are the men and the women who fail in marriage. To intervene in such emptiness is the work of the therapist.

In the spectrum of therapeutic activities, therapy with partners or individuals whose presenting complaints are focused on the marital relationship is one of the most difficult. Almost invariably these are people whose psychosexual development and ego-adaptive capacity has been stunted, and who are unequal to the multiplicity of demands that marriage makes. The object of therapy is to promote maturity by releasing the inherent growth potential of the individual, which is a long and slow procedure.[16] The nature of its demands tries both therapist and client, often to the limits of their endurance. The client struggles to maintain the maneuvers he has utilized within the very process that is designed to ultimately mitigate their influence. The therapist strives to understand that struggle for what it is, and to remain free enough to avoid responding to the client's maneuvers. Unquestionably, the inclusion of both spouses in therapy further complicates the process. Despite such complications, however, most therapists recognize the advantages inherent in working with both partners. At present, a variety of approaches to the therapy of marital conflict reflects this view. As has been indicated earlier, these are colored by the practitioner's school of thought and psychological orientation (e.g. analytic versus non-

[16] R. Blanck, *op. cit.*, 154.

analytic). Ultimately the choice of approach will depend on the therapist's formative professional experiences and incline toward procedures with which he has achieved some measure of competence. Greene has suggested the following quite comprehensive classifications of the dynamic therapies: [17]

I. *Supportive therapy*
    A. Counseling—an orientation stressing socio-cultural forces and explicitly acknowledging the implications of the "here and now" situation.
II. *Intensive therapy*
    A. Classical psychoanalysis—an individually oriented approach.
    B. Collaborative—the marital partners are treated by different therapists, who communicate for the purpose of maintaining the marriage.
    C. Concurrent—both spouses are treated individually but synchronously by the same therapist.
    D. Conjoint—both partners are seen together in the same session by the same therapist.
    E. Combined—a combination of
        1. individual, concurrent and conjoint sessions in various purposeful combinations;
        2. analytic family therapy; and
        3. group psychotherapy.

Although individual professionals tend to become identified with particular therapeutic methods, it is a fact that, but for one exception (psychoanalysis), Greene's approaches to the therapy of marital conflict can be, and often are, utilized by members of all the major therapeutic professions (psychiatry, social work, psychology). Common to all, as a basic point of departure, is the *dynamic* relationship between objective reality and the subjective inner world. What this signifies for the understanding of marital conflicts is that the conflict (objective reality) is related inextricably to the subjective inner world of the spouses. Such dynamic relationships cannot be understood by the methods of the physical sciences, but rather by the empathic capacities of the therapist. This intensified capacity for empathic understanding is another characteristic of the dynamic therapies. Their successful practice requires considerable formal training followed by extensive supervised experience and, for most, a personal experience with psychoanalysis or psychotherapy.

Supportive efforts of fairly short duration are usually the treatment of choice in reactive situations, where there is little or no history of prior marital conflict and no significant pathological processes are evidenced. The object of such an effort would be to re-establish a prior level of conflict-

[17] B. Greene, *The Psychotherapies of Marital Disharmony*, 3.

free functioning. Implicit is the expectation that, once this is achieved, the spouses' internal resources and their motivation to maintain the marriage will take over. A supportive approach is equally applicable in situations that contain gross pathology, and the spouses' egos appear unequal to the added stresses that more intensive, uncovering efforts would introduce. In these instances, therapy is of prolonged duration, and rarely less than several years. Not infrequently this supportive therapeutic experience makes it possible to move into more intensive activities as the ego becomes stronger. The intensive therapies are specialized approaches. However, all are generally directed at enhancing the ego's capacity to deal with reality in more mature and less costly ways by utilizing its (relatively) greater strength to observe, understand, and struggle with its self-defeating tendencies. In brief, the supportive approach tends to hold the person together; the intensive approaches tend to encourage the person to take himself apart so as to better reorient himself.

The treatment of people whose presenting complaint is marital conflict should encompass more than an understanding of the institution of marriage and the acquisition of psychological gimmickry. It must preclude simply telling people what is wrong and what to do about it, and must have no place for a manipulative, or coercive, attitude. Most important, its psychology must be consonant with an I-Thou philosophy. Too often, even people who should know better adopt a simplistic, almost mechanistic, psychological orientation whose end result is to reduce humans to objects—a chilling prospect.

Pastoral Considerations

The road to therapy is a circuitous one. For most people seeking help with a marital problem it is frequently preceded by appeals to more natural resources. Together with other reasons which will be referred to later, it goes far in explaining the regularity with which physicians, attorneys, and clergymen are approached about such problems. To begin with, the members of these professions are each community's natural guardians of secrets; for most people this is an important social, as well as psychological consideration. Invariably the approach is in terms of a legal, medical, or spiritual problem, and is seldom expressed directly in terms of help with a marital conflict. In other words, the person uses the language of the intermediary person being approached. With the attorney, it can be a request to institute proceedings for separation, divorce, annulment or separate support. The request might take the form of "get me out of this marriage." Superficially, it seems an appropriate request to make of an attorney. Frequently, however, examination of the situation in detail reveals that grounds for the action requested are insufficient, or even entirely missing. Now it must be asked, why does a person seek such legal action? Requests of this kind are in the nature of a demand, more than a seeking of the attorney's advice. In itself, this is remarkable—the expert is being told what the solution must be. It is not his expertise in the law that is being sought, but the "power" he represents. Like the therapist, the attorney is faced with the problem of shifting from the presenting request to what the problem may really be.

The approach to a physician follows similar lines. Now the language is somatic, and medical or surgical treatment is requested. It is a somewhat more subtle approach in that the patient can really be experiencing physical discomfort, and who is more appropriate to turn to than the physician? Here the insistence on a medical or surgical procedure is the counterpart of the demand to the attorney. Many times the patient does not verbalize his insistence, but his physical discomfort does this for him. The perceptive physician, having ruled out organic origin of the discomfort, begins to think in terms of functional origins. Like the attorney, he is faced with the task of enabling the patient to relinquish his presenting complaints, and to consider with the physician other contributory factors.

The clergyman is available for the most complicated modes of approach. In part, this is due to his traditional role as shepherd, mediator of right and wrong, and man of God. He stands explicitly for the permanence of marriage, and he gives evidence implicitly through his own life, of his commitment to the Christian moral code. Catholics call him "Father," and address him as "Reverend" (revered one). In his person abides the real, lifelong commitment to be a pastor to all. Saint Gregory's, "The Pastoral Rule," expresses beautifully the pastor's relationship to his flock:

> The ruler should be a near neighbor to everyone in sympathy, and exalted above all in contemplation, so that through the bowels of loving-kindness he may transfer the infirmities of others to himself . . . Those who are over others should show (sic) themselves to be such that their subjects may not blush to disclose even their secrets to them; that the little ones, vexed with the waves of temptation, may have recourse to their pastor's heart as to a mother's breast, and wash away the defilement they foresee to themselves in the solace of his exhortation and in the tears of prayer.[18]

In each of his roles, he becomes the subject of all the attitudes, feelings, expectations, confusions and other displacements that his flock attaches to

[18] P. Baute, "The Work of the Pastoral Counselor," *Insight* 2 (1963) 3–4.

his office and to him. Each encounter, thus, is colored by the tendency to see in the priest the fulfillment of every exaggeration or abbreviation in "character" that is consonant with the imperatives of the person's particular psychological makeup. This confusing phenomenon is best understood in terms of the Freudian concept of *transference*. Of this, Karl Stern says:

> Not long after the psychoanalytic method proper had been inaugurated, Freud was struck by a peculiar fact. During treatment the physician became an object of love and hatred. The patient's attitude toward the doctor went through phases of an intense emotional coloring. These phases were mysterious. They could not, like ordinary love and hatred, be explained by the actual situation. The mystery was solved when it was found that in such a setting the physician was not a neutral figure but represented, under disguise, a powerful figure from the patient's infantile background. Usually he was a parental figure, a father or a mother, or a sibling figure, a brother or sister. The love or hatred experienced during the treatment were not directed toward the analyst, but toward someone else in whose place he stood. The patient was not aware of this. But when it was interpreted to him at the proper moment he learned to realize something which is so highly important to us if we want to understand ourselves; namely, that all our emotional relationships are tainted by a carryover. That which determines our earliest relationships—the original "plot" which is played between ourselves and those huge over-lifesize *dramatis personae* of the family—has an impact on all the later dramas of life. We paraphrase it, we vary it a bit, but what we really want to do is to play it over and over again. And the reason why so many things go mysteriously wrong between ourselves and people around us, at school, at work, in marriage, is that we repeat performance of a play which was actually, in every single case, unique.[19]

Colorations like these play a part in all relationships, but particularly in those that, by their very nature, recreate parent child-like configurations. Though usually less intense than in the therapeutic relationships, the attorney-client, physician-patient and pastor-son relationships are also examples of such configurations. Each contains the elements of authority (parent) and petitioner (child); each of these professionals is the repository of real power and knowledge; and each is in the position of granting or withholding. These are the factors that together with the individual's predisposing life experiences result in the "as if" qualities that are seen in such relationships.

To repeat, the priest is a particularly vulnerable object of such colorations—to be more accurate, he is a particularly vulnerable target for distortions. As the mediator between man and God, the distortions often contain elements having to do with God as well as with the man of God; for, in the main, people's relationships to God are themselves colored by

[19] K. Stern, *The Third Revolution*, 111.

their primary relationships to their parents. Thus, the individual's relationship to the priest he is turning to is multiply-determined. Primarily it reflects elements of his earlier parental relationships but is influenced, as well, by his relationship to God and the nature of his presenting problems. It may also be influenced by earlier "formative" contacts with other priests. Whatever its antecedents, it is a unique relationship and, tempting though it may appear to catalogue its many variations, efforts in this direction will ultimately detract from its uniqueness. Each person must be met

> . . . as if there was no one else in the world, as if there existed no recognized method of treatment in "such cases," as if there had never been any similar situation in the history of man, as if textbooks, formulae, and even previous experience were as remote as the Himalayas.[20]

The purpose of the pastoral relationship is to bring man to God. This end is facilitated, at the natural level, by the priest's welcome, acceptance, direction, and mediation as a man relating to other men.[21] Each encounter between priest and men is a potential opportunity to further this purpose. Men, however, approach the encounter in many ways and under various guises; as has been suggested, they introduce distortions that are reflective of their habitual manner of relating. For example, a man who turns to his priest for help with, "My wife refuses to sleep with me. Tell her that she must," may be conveying many things in addition to revealing that he and his wife are having problems. In the dialogue that follows, if the priest doesn't agree to the man's request immediately, he may sense a subtle threat—that he is less than he purports to be. The threat, of course, is directed to the priest's identity as a man of God, for if he fails to uphold the man's marital rights, it is interpreted as equivocation; implicitly, and sometimes explicitly, the priest is made to appear less priestly. Should he in fact feel threatened and respond, possibly with sharp questions as to the man's obligations to his wife, an interesting development has taken place. Two threatened men are playing the same game.

The point of this vignette is that the priest, like all men, carries within him the propensity to infect his relationships unrealistically. To the extent that this happens, his welcome and acceptance are circumscribed. To be truly effective, the priest must extend his welcome and acceptance to all men. To achieve this he must also be open to the stirrings of his own emotions; extending to this part of himself an equal welcome and acceptance. The degree to which he (or anyone) succeeds in this makes him that much more available to others, for, in the final analysis, they are men like

[20] H. VanZeller, We Die Standing Up, 112.
[21] A. Godin, The Pastor as Counselor, 26-64.

himself. Accepting himself is the necessary prelude to accepting the other and permits meaningful discussion of the other's situation.

This discussion should be in the nature of a sympathetic exploration to determine the boundaries of the problem, what precipitated the present plea for help, the duration of the problem and its progression, earlier efforts at relief and their result, and the presence of bizarre qualities that may indicate serious pathology. In addition to assessing the nature of the problem, the exploratory process is the vehicle for furthering the relationship, getting to know the people involved, and determining whether the situation is one the priest will work with exclusively, or will refer to another professional person for additional specialized help. The very nature of some situations, as is the case when little or no empathy is felt, call for early referral. These are situations that frequently feel "alien" and are suggestive of a psychosis or a borderline state. In the remaining far more numerous instances, this decision rests entirely with the pastor; he must be guided by his experience, his realistic assessment of his competence, and the needs of the situation as revealed by his exploratory activities.

When referral is indicated it is often felt as a rejection by the person being referred; frequently the one making the referral may unwittingly contribute to this by his own attitudes. This would be the case if the referring person views it as a loss, or conversely views it with relief. People are acutely sensitive to both verbal and non-verbal nuances of this kind, and often respond in ways that jeopardize the referral. Ideally, referrals should reflect what is necessary for the person with the problem, and should be unencumbered by other reasons. The pastor can facilitate this process and minimize feelings of rejection in several ways: 1) by being comfortable with his decision to refer, 2) by knowing the helping people, agencies, hospitals, clinics, etc. in his community so that his confidence in their professional competence carries over to the one being referred and 3) by demonstrating his continuing concern through the ongoing pastoral relationship. Too often a referral is viewed as a surrender, or abdication—a literal turning over, or away from; and too often insecure professionals reinforce this view. A continuing relationship motivated by pastoral concern is not "interfering"; on the contrary, most therapists welcome the encouragement it provides to the person to work on his problem, though the opportunity to express this seldom occurs. In the two illustrations of a pastor's activities that follow, therapists and pastor have never met to discuss the individuals concerned.

A couple in their mid-forties came to the rectory because of the husband's heavy drinking. The wife threatened to leave if the husband didn't stop drinking. In the course of two meetings with the couple it became clear that the man was confused and disoriented; the drinking seemed to be a secondary problem. After several months of effort by the priest, the wife and the family physician, the man accepted hospitalization for his emotional illness. Shortly after this, the wife spoke to the priest of her own serious drinking problem and many difficulties with her adolescent children. She accepted referral to the local family counseling agency and the priest continued to see her weekly, supporting her efforts there and demonstrating his concern for the family. After a year of hospitalization and therapy at the agency, all of the family "spontaneously" returned to the practice of their faith.

A couple, parents of three children, came to the rectory to ask whether the priest thought the husband needed psychiatric help. The husband had been afflicted with scruples since adolescence. He had had a number of confessors over the years. One way his problem manifested itself is in his feeling that he does not "hear" Mass validly if his attention wanders; he often went to two or three Masses on a Sunday to fulfill his Sunday obligation. His wife, realizing the pain her husband suffered, went with him. This Sunday, the husband wanted to bring his six-year-old son to a second Mass because the son fell asleep during the first Mass. At this point, the wife insisted that they do something lest he foist his scruples on their children. The pastor called a psychiatrist who indicated he would see the husband. The pastor arranged to see the couple after the husband had been seen by the psychiatrist. During the past two years, the husband has been seeing the psychiatrist weekly and the pastor twice a month. The focus of the pastor's meetings has been on understanding God, prayer and participation in the Sacramental life of the Church. The wife is seen by the pastor on an irregular basis, as she feels the need. Their meetings seek a deeper understanding of scripture and support her encouraging her husband to continue with the doctor. The great emotional stress of the husband has been an opportunity for this family to grow in the Christian life.

In large measure, the benefits to these two families flowed from the pastor's continued involvement with them and from the competence of the professional resources they turned to for specialized help—resources he introduced and encouraged them to use. These actual situations clearly illustrate the pastor's potential as a force for the *prevention* of marital and family breakdown, a consequence so readily perceivable in these situations that little more need be said about it.

There are many other aspects of the illustrations that merit attention. Foremost of these is the complete absence of censure denoting true pastoral concern for *persons* rather than for their acts. It can also be said with a fair degree of certitude that the outcome would have been different had the first man's drinking been seen as the real problem, and the obsessive nature of the second man's difficulty been underestimated. Complications arising from the pastor's "coloring" his participation in favor of either of the spouses were avoided; he gave himself to each according to their needs, and to each he remained a man of God. It is of interest that with one family his mediation was (and continues to be) explicit; with the other it was less so, yet his pastoral concern, no less for one than for the other, "influenced" both families in the same direction. His simple, straightforward activities personify the great strength of the truly pastoral relationship, beside which the current claims for *pastoral counseling* as a quasi-therapeutic approach pale. This is not to say that priests (or religious) should not pursue advanced studies in social work, psychiatry, or psychology. On the contrary, there is great value in the mastery of such specialized knowledge and skills. Such training can have an immeasurable impact on their personal fulfillment and on the fulfillment of others, but more important, it may ultimately enrich the life of the Church in countless ways.

The priest, or religious, who desires to acquire such knowledge and skill must be prepared to submit to the same training that is required of others. To imagine that preparation for Holy Orders, or for the religious life, offers a unique advantage to the pursuit of such studies is deceptive. There are ample indications that, for many, such earlier preparation is actually no small obstacle. Interestingly enough, the chief spokesmen for this view are those very priests and religious who have successfully worked through the complications and achieved a comfortable resolution of earlier ambivalences —ambivalences that resolved, primarily, around the acquiring of an additional role: the role of the therapist. The decision to pursue such a goal must, in the final analysis, remain an individual matter between the aspirant and his, or her, superiors. However, because motivation usually involves a multiplicity of factors with affective components that are often not readily apparent, such aspirations should be examined openly and preferably with the counsel of others who have undergone similar training, whenever possible.

Fortunately the utilization of knowledge from the behavioral sciences is not limited only to those who wish to acquire specialized training. It is available to all who are interested in enriching their understanding of themselves and of others. Nor need the implications of this knowledge be reserved for a select few. Ideally, all priests and religious should be introduced to its potential and the possibilities for its creative application to their everyday pastoral activities.

A group of activities referred to earlier as explicit supports for today's family, namely, the pre-Cana and Cana conferences and the Christian Family Movement, is an area that could be further enriched from creative applications of knowledge from the behavioral sciences. Though these activities depart in form from the one-to-one model of the pastoral relationship, they remain opportunities for each participant to experience the pastor's welcome, acceptance, direction, and mediation. Knowledge of

small-group dynamics suggests that the preventive possibilities of these experiences will be enhanced by: 1) keeping the activities parish-based, 2)
limiting the participants to a reasonable number—four to six couples, and
3) providing for permanence in each group member's relationship with
the pastor. To enhance these group activities in these ways extends to them
the many benefits of the individual pastoral relationship, provides a climate
in which to learn from each other through the exchange of ideas and questions, and serves as a source of strength in meeting the trials that come to
all men.

Though serious marital conflict is not the destiny of all marriages, each
marriage does have its conflicts. In their efforts to resolve or adapt to these
problems people will continue to turn to their priests. Though they approach him in various ways, under many guises, each encounter will have
its explicit, or implicit spiritual dimensions. Some will speak directly of this
as they seek to learn more of God, of God's way with men and to enrich
their own relationship to God. Others, less aware of these same yearnings,
or overwhelmed by the circumstances of life, will approach the encounter
with the pastor in terms of human concerns and pain. However he is approached, regardless of his specific response, as "a near neighbor to everyone
in sympathy"; his life bears witness and his pastoral concern reveals *to all
men* the God who is Father, Redeeming Brother, and Sanctifier.

BIBLIOGRAPHY

Baute, P., O.S.B., "The Work of the Pastoral Counselor," *Insight* 2 (1963)
    3–7.
Bier, W., S.J., Ed., *Marriage: A Psychological and Moral Approach*, New York
    1965.
Blanck, R., "Marriage as a Phase of Personality Development," *Social Case-
    work* 48 (1967) 154–160.
Freud, A., *The Ego and The Mechanisms of Defense*, tr. C. Baines, New York
    1946.
Freud, S., M.D., *A General Introduction to Psycho-analysis*, tr. J. Riviere,
    New York 1935.
Godin, A., S.J., *The Pastor as Counselor*, tr. B. Phillip, New York 1965.
Greene, B., M.D., Ed., *The Psychotherapies of Marital Disharmony*, New York
    1965.
Johnson, D., *Marriage Counseling Theory and Practice*, New Jersey 1961.
Nash, E.—Jessner, L., M.D.—Abse, D., M.D., Editors, *Marriage Counseling in
    Medical Practice*, New York 1964.

13

GERIATRIC COUNSELING

Jeanne G. Gilbert, Ph.D.

FREUD, the pioneer in psychoanalysis, rejected older persons for psycho-analytic treatment. He stated, "If the patient's age is near or above the fifties the conditions for psycho-analysis become unfavorable. The mass of psychical material can then no longer be thoroughly inspected; the time required for recovery is too long; and the ability to undo psychic processes begins to grow weaker." [1] Later psychotherapists, whether Freudian, neo-Freudian, or non-Freudian, tended to follow the lead of the master and to reject the possibility of benefit coming out of work with the aged. Without any scientific or empirical evidence, they assumed that an older person could not learn, would be resistive to all change, and could derive no benefit from any therapeutic effort other than institutionalization in a home for the aged. Fortunately, in time a few brave souls questioned this stereotype and succeeded in breaking the pattern when they learned that older people can and do respond to therapy of all types. They discovered that some aged individuals, even with well developed psychoneuroses or psychoses, derive considerable benefit both from psychotherapy and from ameliorative physical measures.[2]

With the constantly advancing life span we are finding increasing numbers of people in the older age bracket. This means that we can normally expect also to find increasing numbers of emotionally disturbed and men-

---

[1] S. Freud, *Collected Papers*, 1, p. 271.
[2] Cf. J. Gilbert, *Understanding Old Age*.

tally ill persons at this period of life. In addition to this normal expectancy, the number is swollen by those individuals who in later life experience a reactivation of earlier emotional disturbances and are affected by the special stresses to which the older person is subject in present day society. Thus, the urgent need of counseling or psychotherapy with middle aged and geriatric patients can be appreciated. However, this is something which requires not only an interest in and a liking for older people, but also definite training in counseling in general and in geriatric counseling in particular.

STRESSES TO WHICH OLDER PEOPLE ARE SUBJECT

In order to treat geriatric patients effectively, it is important to understand some of the stresses to which they are subject and some of the ways in which they meet these stresses. Stresses may arise from within the individual himself because of changes in the aging organism or from a rejecting or unaccepting environment.[3]

The normal aging process consists of a certain amount of decline in the physical, mental, and emotional functioning of the individual. These declines in efficiency do not occur at the same time in all individuals or at the same time in all areas in a particular individual. Thus, we may find a person of only 35 or 40 years of age who is "old" in the sense that he seems no longer able or inclined to engage in any physical activity, seldom has a new idea or learns anything new, and is so rigid and self-absorbed that he resists all change and cannot give anything of himself to other people. On the other hand, we may find a person of 70 or more who is "young" in the sense that he is still physically active, full of new ideas and interested in learning new things, and is flexible, ready for change, and willing to extend himself for other people. Nevertheless, physical, mental, and emotional changes will occur at some time in all individuals who live long enough.

When a disturbed person needs help or advice one of the first persons he usually consults is his priest, minister, or rabbi. It is therefore most desirable that the clergyman not only have some knowledge of counseling but also that he be aware of the usual problems confronting the older person and alert to the special needs of the person consulting him. There are many problems which he himself can handle by sympathetic, understanding listening, emotional support, and some practical, common sense advice. Other members of the family too may be more willing to listen to the advice

[3] Cf. J. Gilbert, "Stresses That Attack Older Persons," *New York State Legislative Committee on Problems of Aging.*

and suggestions of a clergyman than to those of a stranger. In other instances, the clergyman will recognize that certain problems are beyond his competence and if he has made himself cognizant of community facilities, he will refer his counselee to the proper resources for the help he needs.

When aging occurs in one part of an individual faster than in another there is an alteration in the smooth running of the organism, and this may occasion stress to the person involved. For example, changes in general appearance, such as increased bulk, balding or graying hair, and wrinkled skin, or in physical strength, speed, and endurance may be quite disturbing to an older person, and if he can not accept them, he may react by denying and trying to disguise them or by overemphasizing them in order to gain some special end he has in mind. Slower recovery, while normal with advancing age, may presage early physical disintegration and death to some older persons.

The decline of the efficient functioning of the sensory organs is distressing to many people. It is most frustrating not to be able to see or to hear as well as one used to, and some aging persons tend to become suspicious when they find they cannot understand what is being said by those around them.

Dental conditions, which may be associated with digestive difficulties, may cause trouble not only because of the associated eating and digestive problem but also because of the embarrassment occasioned by the inability to find comfortably fitting dentures. The resultant cosmetic picture is often a blow to the ego.

The climateric, although a normal part of the aging process, causes distress to some women. "The waning or loss of sexual power is a blow to the ego which arouses intense anxiety and compensatory desires in many individuals. It may arouse feelings of uselessness that one is no longer ABLE to reproduce and serve the race, and general feelings of inadequacy. Of course, many individuals are able to withstand these stresses because they have developed other areas of satisfaction in life, but those who have always considered the physical areas, and particularly the sexual aspects, all-important find these normal physiological changes difficult to accept." [4] In addition to these psychological effects there are the very real physical and emotional reactions resulting from *estrogen deficiency* associated with the menopause in women.[5]

The normal aging process of the human body is often accelerated by the

[4] Gilbert, *op. cit.,* p. 48.

[5] R. Wilson, and T. Wilson, "The Fate of the Non-treated Post-menopausal Woman: a Plan for the Maintenance of Adequate Estrogen from Puberty to the Grave," *Journal of the American Geriatric Society,* 11 (1963), pp. 347–362.

abuses it suffers throughout the years of living, so that we find far too large an incidence of chronic disabling physical conditions and decreased efficient functioning of organs and systems which should have remained healthy. No doubt, the majority of emotionally healthy people in later maturity accept with a certain amount of equanimity both the normal and the abnormal physiological changes that occur with advancing age and deal with them as effectively as they have dealt with other stresses they have experienced throughout life. It is those who cannot accept these changes and who deal with them either by trying to deny them with physical over-indulgences or by using them to gain attention or to control their environment who will need the help of the counselor or therapist.

The same holds true of changes in *intellectual functioning*. Assuming that he has normal intelligence to begin with, a person does not grow stupid as he grows older but the character of his thinking and reacting may change. Although his years of living may tend to make his thinking more mature and seasoned, his thinking, acting, and learning of new things tend to slow up with the years. He remembers the old things and the bygone days well but finds it increasingly difficult to absorb new ideas and to learn new material; this often results in an increasing disinclination to try the new. Because he is generally less flexible and adaptable, his thinking may become more rigid. The healthy older person accepts these losses in a matter-of-fact way and tries to compensate for them by keeping alive the learning habit and by devising ways of helping himself to recall those things which are important to remember. The unhealthy individual may either be unable to admit any losses and try to cover up memory lapses by fabrication, distortion, or projection, or may use his declining memory as a defense against doing what he does not want to do, or forgetting what he does not want to remember.

Decrease in the elasticity of the personality as one grows older makes it more difficult to deal with physical, intellectual, or emotional problems which may arise, makes it more difficult to cope with new situations, and makes it more difficult to respond to therapy or counseling. However, the life pattern of emotional response will determine to a large extent how the individual will respond to physical, intellectual, or emotional stresses attendant upon the normal aging process.

Stresses emanating from the environment may become increasingly difficult to cope with when inner resources are also failing, and certainly in present day society there are more things to cause emotional stress to older persons than there were a few generations ago. To begin with, the modern cultural accent is on youth, and to be old is to be discarded. The modern home is small and there is no place for the aging relative. In this day of desegregation only the old people are segregated—in old folks' homes, old age centers, and retirement villages.

The modern business wants youth, refuses new jobs to older persons, and encourages or forces retirement of those older persons still employed. *Early retirement* with limited funds on which to live taps not only the basic problem of existence, but also wreaks havoc on the self-concept. True, there are some compensations: Medicare, old age pensions and assistance, social security, low cost housing, low cost travel, etc. Nevertheless, these are often insufficient to satisfy the healthy mind of an older person even though he may have an aging body. He may still feel the need to be a part of the world around him, and it may be a strong blow indeed to his ego to feel that after having given many years of service to his family and his job, he is now discarded, neglected, rejected, and no longer of any use to anyone. If he has held a position of importance or authority or if he (or she) has been the head of a household and the pivot around which the activity of its members has revolved, it may be doubly difficult to step down and to accept rejection without feeling disturbed about it. The healthier ones accept these losses as an inevitable aspect of the normal aging process and find their own new niche by contented disengagement or by developing new interests or other interests which have long attracted them but which the pressures of work and daily living have never before permitted them to pursue. The unhealthy ones react with all kinds of emotional problems for which they may need counseling or psychotherapy.

Recurring deaths among one's contemporaries and friends may bring added stress to the older person for they tend to intensify already existing feelings of rejection, insecurity, and loneliness. There is not only the sense of personal loss but also the feeling that one's own end may not be in the too far distant future. When one is young death is seldom thought of in terms of oneself; if feared, it is usually in terms of possible loss of a loved parent or grandparent. But when one is old and sees his contemporaries dying, the realization that he may be next is inescapable.

Types of Therapy

With older as with younger patients any type of therapy can be successful, success depending, of course, upon the problem, the skill of the therapist, and the particular patient being treated. Problems may run the gamut from mild upset over a situational difficulty to psychosis and deterioration, although apathy, depression, and anxiety are probably found more often than others. Assuming a skilled therapist, the type of therapy to be used with a patient will depend on the problem and on the financial assets, the inner resources, and the motivation of the patient. Some problems are obviously the result of certain circumstances in the environment which the patient very much wants and needs help in clearing up. These may require only a few counseling interviews and can often be handled quite well by an understanding clergyman. Other problems may be of more serious nature and the result of factors lying deep within the personality of the patient; thus, they will require a longer period of therapy by a trained therapist, and the therapy will be quite different from the relatively superficial counseling interviews used in treating problems emanating from mild environmental stress.

Psychoanalysis, the traditional form of psychotherapy, is a lengthy and an expensive procedure. Daily treatment for a period of several years or more is expensive both in time and money, and few older people can afford either. However, with certain types of problems, which require an entire personality reconstruction, and with a wealthy older patient with a flexible personality, traditional psychoanalysis can be a most effective form of psychotherapy.

Short term therapies are probably more practical to use with most older patients since they require less time and are less expensive. Short term therapy may be directive, non-directive, or psychoanalytic in nature and the success of any of these methods will depend on the patient and the particular problem involved as well as on the skill of the therapist. With some patients a certain amount of direction is necessary in order to stimulate them to do something constructive about their problems.

Group therapy is a method which lends itself particularly to the needs of older patients. The comradeship and rapport built up with other group members as well as the therapist, the realization that others are experiencing similar problems, and the opportunities for reality testing in small groups are especially beneficial.

Individual Counseling of the Older Patient

When an older person seeks help with his problems it is usually with considerable reluctance and fear. Often he will first consult his pastor, and if the clergyman is able to handle the problem, he should do so at once. If, however, he recognizes that the disturbance is beyond his depth, he should take the time to prepare the patient for referral to the proper source for help.

Because of the prevalence of guidance counselors in schools and colleges, school and job screening tests and interviews, and psychological and psychiatric examinations for the armed services, younger people are more likely to accept a visit to a psychologist's or a psychiatrist's office in a matter-of-fact way than older people who have had no experiences of this sort. For this reason, it is especially important that the *setting* in which the older person is seen be as attractive and homelike as possible. Coldness and too much formality may intensify already existing feelings of fear and of not belonging and thus inhibit verbalization of problems. However, when the surroundings are pleasant and the therapist shows warmth, acceptance, and interest in him and in his problems and accords him the respect and dignity his years merit, most older people verbalize quite freely. In fact, the problem then often becomes not one of getting them to verbalize but of trying to stem the flow of words before the next patient arrives. Thus, it is most important that there be, in the very first interview, a clear understanding of the time limits for each subsequent interview. Time limits and fees are business matters which should be established during the first interview.

The History

When the patient is comfortably settled (and usually a comfortable chair is more effective than a couch), he should be permitted to present his problem and to tell his story in his own way with a minimum of interruptions and questions from the counselor. Of course, it may be desirable at times for the therapist to interject a question, to make a comment, or to repeat a phrase for the purpose of clarifying a point, emphasizing some aspect of the problem, or promoting insight, but these occasions should be rare. There is also certain information the therapist or counselor will want to know about the patient, and it may be necessary for him to guide, question, or direct the conversation in such a way as to elicit this information.

In addition to the presenting problem or problems, the therapist will want a complete history of the patient so that he can understand his life style—his pattern of reacting not only to what he sees as his present stress but also to previous stressful situations throughout his life. He will want to know something about his early development and his life and relationships with his parents, siblings, and friends; he will want to know details of his education and his work history; he will want to know about his marriage and his relationships with his wife and children; and he will want information concerning his community, personal and social relationships during his middle and later years. Last, but by no means least, he will want a complete health history with details of illnesses, accidents, and injuries, particularly in the past ten years of his life.

The Physical Condition

If the older patient has had a recent physical examination, the results should be learned by consultation with his physican; if he has not had a recent examination, he should be referred for one before getting too deeply involved in therapy. As many emotional problems may mask as physical complaints so also may many physical problems be responsible for the manifestation of emotional difficulties, and this is especially true with older patients. Although some emotionally unstable patients may use physical complaints as threats to "ungrateful" offspring in order to keep control, to punish, or to gain attention and sympathy, some patients may become extremely cantankerous and difficult to live with because of an underlying and unrecognized physical condition. An example of this can be seen in the following report of a middle aged couple referred for marriage counseling:

Mr. and Mrs. A were both in their early fifties and had experienced a fairly satisfactory married life for about 25 years but were now on the verge of separation because of constant bickering, quarreling, misunderstandings, and suspicions. Mr. A was a good-looking, successful business man who seemed affable but frustrated and bewildered about the whole situation. He said, "I can't understand it. We had a good life and we always got along well. We worked haid but we pulled together. Now all the kids are married but two, and they're almost through school and ready to take off. Things should be easier; we have enough money so we don't have to worry any more, but all we do is fight. Maybe it's my fault, I don't know, but it seems that everything I do and everything I say, she takes my head off. I just can't please her. She used to be so sweet but now . . . , she's AWFUL! I can't stand it any longer; I just got to get away. The doctor says it's the change of life, but how long can that last? You can't take it forever. Even my daughters can't wait to get back to college. She nags them to death too."

Mrs. A had been a pretty woman but her prettiness was marred by a distraught, harassed look with little frown and anger wrinkles around the eyes and mouth. She said, "Our marriage has gone sour. I know it and it's all my fault. I can't eat or sleep right and I get so depressed and irritable that I'm always jumping on someone. I don't want to, but I just can't help it; everything annoys me. You can't imagine what it's like—the way I feel all the time—it's awful."

Further conversation with this couple revealed that Mrs. A was nearing completion of the menopause. She had been experiencing menopausal symptoms—headache, backache, hot flashes, night sweats, and extreme irritability and fatigue—for about ten years. For the first few years she had been able to endure these symptoms in silence and hide her irritability from her family because she felt certain that her condition was a normal change of life which would soon pass, but as the condition worsened with the years, she became increasingly unable to cope with it.

The first step in the treatment of this couple was to refer Mrs. A for a complete physical examination. A severe estrogen deficiency was found, and

she was placed immediately on suitable dosages of estrogen and proges-
terone. In the meantime, both Mr. and Mrs. A came for counseling interviews. They were seen both individually and together. As her physical
condition improved and she began to feel better, Mrs. A began to
understand herself and to cope more adequately with her problems. Mr. A
gained an understanding of his wife's condition, became more sympathetic,
and gave her the attention she often needed. Six months later everything
seemed to be working out well for this couple: there had been no separation, and there seemed to be greater sympathetic understanding and rapport
than there had been for years. Counseling in this case was quite direct and
carried on at the same time as medical treatment. Without the medical
treatment it is doubtful if the situation could have improved, and without
psychotherapy it is doubtful if the medical treatment alone would have
sufficed to re-establish this marriage which was on the point of dissolution.
The importance of the physical examination in geriatric counseling cannot
be over-stressed.

Environmental Conditions

In counseling the older person it is also extremely important to understand his environmental situation, and in order to do this it may be necessary to interview other members of his family as well as the patient himself.
Most patients tend to project the blame for their misfortunes or miseries on
to family members or those with whom they live. Without a true understanding of the actual home situation and of the people closest to the
patient, little constructive help can be given to him. In some instances the
disturbance lies entirely within the patient himself so that the main focus
of counseling must be on trying to effect changes within him. In other
instances, the patient's disturbances may be directly attributable to difficult environmental circumstances, in which case the main focus may be on
environmental manipulation. Sometimes, of course, both the individual
himself and others in his environment must be treated. Examples of environmental situations which required altering can be seen in the following
two cases:

Mr. B, aged 75, was brought to the office by his daughter, Mrs. C, a
pleasant, middle aged woman who treated him like a small child, taking off
his coat and hat, straightening his tie and hair, and leading him to a chair
to sit down. Mrs. C, who was interviewed first, stated that she was very
worried about her father and did not know what to do. He had come to live
with the family several years previously, following the death of his wife to
whom he had been very devoted. He was welcomed in the home, but conditions were crowded so that he had to share a room with one of the young

sons of the family. The young son did not mind at first because, although infrequently seen, Grandpa had always been a favorite with the family. Now, however, things were different: Grandpa wandered aimlessly around the house all day long, cried constantly, and showed no interest in anything. Mrs. C spent considerable time with him, trying to cheer him up and get him interested in things. After awhile the crying stopped, but he continued to withdraw from everyone although he was in no way difficult to handle. In the last six months, however, the situation had worsened seriously: he seemed confused and if not watched, would wander outside and get lost in the neighborhood looking for his wife. At home he seemed unable to find the bathroom and consequently was often incontinent. He toyed with his young grandson's model airplanes and in his efforts to "fix" them, usually destroyed them. He had to be reminded to bathe and helped to dress. A short time previously he had got up in the middle of the night and gone to the kitchen to "cook breakfast" and turned on the gas stove without lighting it. Fortunately, his grandson heard him get up and followed him, thus avoiding a possible catastrophe. The whole family was upset by the situation.

When interviewed, Mr. B proved to be a deteriorated old man who was apparently suffering from a senile psychosis. His presence in his daughter's home was destructive to family unity, detrimental to the normal development of the children, and possibly dangerous to the safety of the household. Outpatient therapy for this man was not indicated since it was felt that he was in need of the kind of treatment which could best be carried out in a psychiatric hospital. Some time was spent in helping the daughter, who was quite devoted to her father, to accept this placement, and the case was not pursued further.

The second case concerns Mrs. D who was referred by the Pastor of her Church because of unhappiness and dissatisfaction with her life. Mrs. D proved to be a healthy, well preserved woman in her early sixties. She was well dressed and could easily have passed for ten years younger than her actual age. She lived with her son and his wife and child and she spoke in glowing terms of her son and grandchild but said that she could not get along with her daughter-in-law. She said her husband had died early in their marriage but had left enough money so that she was able to bring up her only son without too much financial strain. She said, "We had such happy times together, he and I. I kept the house and his clothes just the way he liked them, and I cooked all the things he loved, and I let him have his friends and they all liked me too. Everything was just lovely until SHE came along. Of course, I wanted him to get married, but I knew this was not the girl for him. It was the only time he ever went against my wishes. Now she won't talk to me and she doesn't want me to cook or mend for my son. I don't have much income; I spent it all on him and now I have nothing; I feel miserable."

Later interview with the younger Mrs. D confirmed much of what her mother-in-law had said but with a somewhat different interpretation. She said, "I don't really *HATE* her, I guess, but I just can't *stand* her. She is a good woman, I suppose, but she treats my husband like a little baby, and he practically stands on his head if she has a headache or a sore toe. It's *my* home and *my* child, but you'd never know it. He doesn't want a wife; he just wants his Mommy; he should have married HER!"

Obviously, all members of this family need help, and particularly the senior Mrs. D and her son. If possible to effect the separation, Mrs. D should be encouraged to move into quarters of her own, seek at least part time employment to supplement her income, and develop friends and outside interests of her own. She will also need therapy so that she can learn to understand herself and her reactions and gain an appreciation of the detrimental effect she has had on her son's psychosexual development and marital adjustment. She is intelligent and well educated so that it can be hoped that these things, along with her genuine affection for her son and grandchild, will enable her to effect some much needed changes. Needless to say, her son and his wife will also need therapy if they want to make anything worthwhile of their marriage.

The Goals of Therapy

On the basis of the evaluation, it must then be decided whether this problem which is presented is one which can be helped and, if so, to what extent. This means that goals should be set up before therapy actually begins. These will be both immediate and long term goals, the immediate ones being those which we might reasonably expect to achieve within a relatively short time and the long term ones being those which we might hope to achieve at some more distant time in the future. The immediate goals will usually concern the more practical and urgent aspects of everyday living such as, for example, needed medical care or change of living arrangements. The long term goals are more likely to involve changes in personality or in long established habits of reacting. Since the choice of goals must depend upon the physical, intellectual, emotional, and social assets and liabilities of the patient, it is important that the counselor or therapist be aware of these assets and liabilities. Although assets should be stressed and built up, ignorance or disregard of limitations or weaknesses might well lead to unrealistic goals for the patient and consequent failure of counseling.

The therapist must be aware of and realistic about how much his patient can stand physically, whether he is keen enough to gain insight into himself and his problems and can learn to modify his patterns, and how much his personality and emotions can withstand. He must ask himself whether his patient at this time is physically well enough to live on his own in the community or requires care in a hospital or home for the aged. If the answer is doubtful, he must then consider how much and what kind of physical rehabilitation will be necessary to enable him to function adequately in the community.

The therapist must appraise his patient's natural *intellectual assets* and determine to what extent he has deteriorated and how motivated and able he is to learn and to change. No matter how skilled the counselor may be, he will have little success if his patient is very dull or so deteriorated that he is unable to learn or to change his patterns of reacting, or if he has absolutely no motivation to change or to have anything different than it is. In cases of this sort it is obvious that goals must be short term and very practical.

Goals of therapy must also be considered within the *social framework*. For example, goals will be quite different for an individual living in an institutional setting from one living in the community. In an institutional setting, whether it be a hospital or a home for the aged, the impact of the individual on the group must be appraised, as well as the influence of the group on his adjustment difficulties, and therapy geared according to these considerations and the attitudes of the personnel of the institution. If he is living in the community, his *living arrangements* can be either beneficial or detrimental. If he is living with intelligent and understanding relatives or other persons, it may even be possible to make use of these others as adjunct therapists, whereas if he is living with rejecting, disparaging persons, it may be possible to accomplish little unless these persons also be treated or he be removed from the environment.

Financial assets are an important and practical aspect of the social framework. Obviously, the community-living older person with unlimited income can afford long term therapy which would be impossible for the person who must live on Social Security benefits. The financial situation would also have considerable influence on the *recreational outlets* and the *friendships* formed by the older person. Since loneliness is one of the most prevalent and painful ailments of the older years, counseling goals for these individuals must proceed within the framework of present and potential friendships and recreational outlets.

Another important thing to be considered in setting the goals for therapy is the *life style* of the individual to be counseled. From the preliminary material already secured, the therapist should have gained insight into the way this particular person has customarily reacted to stressful situations he has encountered throughout his lifetime. When an individual has reached the upper years of life he may be helped to change his pattern of reacting and behaving to a certain degree, but it is highly unlikely that he will drastically alter his basic life style, so the counselor must set his goals within this framework.

The final important thing to consider in setting the goals of therapy is the *personal desire of the patient*. This means that the therapist must not use his own personal bias to set the goals but rather that he should accede to the wishes of the person with whom he is working, even though these may run counter to his firmly established convictions regarding the best way to grow old and to resolve problems. For example, the counselor may feel certain that the only way to keep happy and to stave off the encroachment of age is to keep busy and to engage actively in the life around one, but a particular patient may prefer retirement to a rocking chair with gradual disengagement from the world around him. Any attempt to draw this individual into active, useful, or recreational pursuits would probably be doomed to failure so that counseling would be a waste of time. The case would be the same if the situation were reversed, and the counselor could think only of the merits of disengagement whereas the patient himself wanted only to work and to keep as actively a part of the life around him as possible. The therapist must always be aware of and respect the personal wishes of his patient and work within this framework, remembering that it is not necessary to try to develop an entirely new personality but rather, to help this particular person to live more happily and effectively in the world. Self-determination and self-direction are important for every adult human being and should be fostered, not destroyed.

The counselor who works in the geriatric field must genuinely like older people and always remember to treat them with respect and dignity. This is a field which requires endless patience and often is very discouraging. Older patients are often slow moving, slow to get new ideas, and resistive to change. They may have destructive habits of thinking, feeling, and reacting which are so firmly established that it is extremely difficult, if not impossible, to effect any change. The counselor who is unprepared for this and lacks optimism may develop the feeling that he is working on a dead-end street and that all his efforts will prove fruitless. This may result in negative transference toward the geriatric patient with hostility which quickly transmits itself to the patient and bolsters his stubbornness and resistance.

Before attempting to work with the aged, the therapist should be aware of his own feelings toward aging in general and toward older people in particular. He must have worked through his feelings toward his own parents and resolved his conflicts with them. Only if he has achieved full emancipation from his parents so that he can meet them on a warm yet mature basis will he be able to meet with his geriatric patients on a mature, adult basis. The counselor plays many roles for the older person, these roles alternating from time to time and from situation to situation. Probably initially the counselor is viewed as a son or daughter and treated accordingly. If the patient feels anger and hostility toward his offspring or views him as rejecting, he will probably respond at first to the therapist with hostility and resistance. Later, when he finds the therapist kind, accepting, and helpful, he may view him as the "good" son or daughter he always wanted but never had. At other times the patient will put the counselor in the role of parent or sibling and reactivate with him his earlier feelings toward these family members.

Finally, the counselor must be fully cognizant of the community facilities, both in-patient and out-patient, available for help of the aged.

PLACEMENT OF GERIATRIC PATIENTS

Although it is desirable to aim for independent living for the older person, there are times when this is impossible because he is incapable of assuming full care of himself and requires some outside help. The amount of help and care he will need in his every day life will determine to a large extent the living arrangements necessary for him. Townsend has devised a rating scale for self-help and self-care which might well be used as a guide when trying to decide what type of placement is best suited to a particular individual.[6] Those who rate highest on this scale are deemed fully capable of looking after themselves whereas those who obtain the worst scores (highest numerically) are able to do little or nothing for themselves. When removal from their home is considered desirable for those who obtain the best scores (lowest numerically) on this scale, residence in an apartment of their own might be arranged or placement in a boarding or foster home for older people, depending upon the wishes of the individual patient.

When an individual requires help in his daily living, institutionalization may be necessary if his relatives will agree to this placement. Again, it will be helpful to resort to Townsend's rating scale as a guide to the correct placement. There are many reasons for institutionalization, and these reasons will also play a part in the selection of the most suitable institution for a particular patient.[7]

When an individual has a *chronic disabling physical condition* which so incapacitates him that he is no longer able to look after himself and needs

---

[6] P. Townsend, "Measuring Incapacity of Self-Care," in R. Williams, C. Tibbitts, and W. Donahue, *Processes of Aging*, 2, pp. 269–288.

[7] Cf. E. Wasser, "Creative Approaches in Case Work with the Aging," *New York Family Service Association of America.*

constant nursing care, he probably requires placement in a hospital for chronic diseases. If both patient and relatives object to hospitalization and if the presence of the disabled person does not affect the normal growth and development of children in the home, family relations are excellent, and there are sufficient funds for constant nursing care, it might be possible to care for the patient at home, but this is seldom the case. Usually, even though he may not realize it, a patient cannot only receive better care in a hospital than he can at home but he can also maintain better family relationships when he is not the constant burden he usually proves to be when he is cared for at home. Sometimes, however, even though the burden at home is almost intolerable, it will be necessary for the counselor to work both with the patient and with his family in order to effect placement.

At times adult offspring are unable to consider placement for an ill and aged parent because of their great love for him and fear of making him feel hurt and rejected. In other instances, inability to place the ill parent stems not from a strong attachment to the parent but from strong guilt feelings which may be the result of a deep underlying resentment masking as affectionate concern and inability to separate. These underlying motives must be understood by the counselor before he can hope to guide the patient and his relatives toward placement. Often the clergyman who has had contact with the family over a period of years can be especially helpful in this respect because he may have a greater awareness of family relationships than can be secured, even by a trained counselor, in one interview.

However, before any older person is placed outside his home setting, he should receive ample preparation for the change. Whether his condition be psychological, psychosomatic, or physiological, an elderly person generally feels more comfortable and secure in familiar surroundings and if he can receive the attention and care he requires, his recovery might be facilitated by remaining in these surroundings. But if placement is necessary, the need should be presented tactfully and with much reassurance on the part of the physician, the counselor, and the family since the immediate reaction to uprooting from familiar surroundings is often one of intense anxiety which may develop into pathological agitation.[8] At this time, the clergyman can often supply this much needed reassurance and support to the patient and to his family.

The transition phase will also be smoother if the patient has frequent contact with familiar people in the early days of his hospitalization or institutionalization. As the older person often turns to religion as his days grow shorter, even though he may have neglected this aspect of life in his earlier years, his clergyman can be especially helpful at this time, not only

[8] Cf. N. Cameron, *The Psychology of Behavior Disorders.*

in his role of clergyman but also as counselor and friend. However, whether at home or in an institution, the patient should be encouraged to become as independent and self-sufficient as his condition warrants and not permitted to use his illness to gain attention, to control his environment, or to satisfy his dependency needs.

The situation with a *senile psychosis* is much the same as that with a chronic disabling physical condition. The patient may feel more comfortable in familiar surroundings but unless family relationships are excellent and funds plentiful, he can usually receive more adequate care in a mental hospital and be less disruptive to the normal development of children in the home. Despite earlier opinions to the contrary, the prognosis for recovery from a senile psychosis is by no means hopeless and various therapeutic approaches are proving helpful.[9] However, most of these approaches, such as drugs, electroshock, hydrotherapy, occupational therapy, and group therapy (especially if these therapies are used in combination) can best be carried on in a hospital setting. The main task of the counselor is to help the patient and his family to accept this placement. However, if the theory postulated that senility may be precipitated by the threat of death because this is the senescent defense against this threat [10] has any validity, possibly the counselor may also be able to avert the development of some senile psychoses by working to remove or reduce the terror of the death threat.

Ongoing counseling and support by the clergyman can be invaluable in this area. Perhaps more than any other person, the clergyman can help individuals to develop a philosophy of life and death and to accept the fact of inevitable death and the probability of life in the hereafter. Even when it is too late to develop a real philosophy of life and death, the clergyman by his very presence with his staunch beliefs and his willingness to listen with empathy, may help to allay fears and provide much needed strength to the older person who is disturbed about the possibility of his impending death.

Placement may also be necessary when an older person, although not chronically disabled or psychotic, *cannot look after himself independently and has no funds or family to provide this care in the community.* Placement in these instances will probably be in a residence for older people. Adequate preparation for this placement is obviously necessary for some older persons may interpret placement as a complete rejection by society or as somewhere to go and wait for death. In preparing him, the counselor

[9] D. Rothschild, "Senile Psychoses and Psychoses with Cerebral Arteriosclerosis," *Mental Disorders in Later Life* (ed. O. Kaplan), 2nd ed. pp. 289–291.
[10] Morgan, R. F., in *Psychological Reports*, 1965, pp. 305–306.

must consider not only the impact of the placement itself but also the impact of the personnel and the residents on this particular individual. He should be allowed ample time to ventilate his feelings regarding placement and to discuss the pros and cons of this type of living. In addition, the counselor must consider the impact of this individual's personality on the other residents of the home to which he is going. If he is normally adjusted and reasonably easy to live with, he will probably make a normal adjustment to the institution and to the people in it and they, in turn, will accept him. However, if he is selfish, cantankerous, demanding, and fault finding, adjustment will be more difficult both for him and for the other members of the home. In cases of this sort a period of counseling prior to entering a residence for older people is important. This counseling is not only for the purpose of helping him to accept placement but also for the purpose of helping him to understand how his behavior influences his acceptance or rejection by other people and to want to modify unpleasant characteristics of reacting which have brought him rejection in the past. An individual may fear rejection and both want and need acceptance and yet, his very fear of rejection sometimes causes him to react in ways destined to bring nothing but rejection. If his whole pattern of living has been one of selfishness and disregard of others, it may not be possible to effect any drastic change in his basic selfishness, but it may be possible to teach him that selfish behavior gains him nothing—neither attention nor power. Persons of this sort will probably need counseling not only before entering a residence for older people but also while they are in the home. Many of these individuals, after a period of individual counseling, respond well to group therapy.

The clergyman is in a unique position in so far as counseling is concerned because his role is confusing. Traditionally, he plays an authoritarian, judgmental role, whereas the role of the counselor is the reverse. The clergyman's parishioners come to him for advice and counsel when they are in trouble or are confused about questions of right or wrong. They are looking for direct answers to their problems and if they do not get them, are quite likely to reject both the clergyman and their church. In addition to other considerations, this would be most unfortunate because it would take away from older persons one of their greatest sources of comfort. On the other hand, since they are looking for direct answers, they may be more ready to accept the advice of their clergyman than of anyone else. His very position carries an aura of authority, whether or not he himself is an authoritarian person. Thus, a certain degree of authoritarianism may be desirable as well as inevitable for the clergyman-counselor if this authoritarian approach can be combined with empathy and a lack of condemnation and emphasis on sin. Sin must be dealt with in the confessional not in the counseling situation.

In older as well as in younger age groups, many people tend to *somatize their difficulties* and after physical disability has been ruled out, these problems must be dealt with in the usual way and the patient helped to understand that his physical stress, although real, stems not from organic illness but from the emotional stresses and pressures to which he has been subject. However, among older people the practice of using illness or the threat of illness to control the environment and gain much desired attention is quite popular too. The illness may be non-existent or it may be of mild, moderate, or severe degree, but the important point is that the patient, either consciously or unconsciously, is using his illness to control his environment, build up his own importance, or maintain his self-esteem. While any physical condition must be ameliorated to the extent that this is possible, the patient must gain insight into his own behavior and the reasons for it, so that he will be motivated to make constructive use of the strengths he has within him. Removal of secondary gains from his illness will help in this respect, and this holds true whether he resides in the community or in an institution. Independent thinking, decision making, and living, within constitutional limits, should be a goal for all patients.

Many older persons in the community who seek help do so because they are *despondent, discouraged, depressed,* and *anxious.* If the individual's physical condition is satisfactory, these feelings, as well as other maladjustive reactions, are usually in response to social pressures, to pressures arising from within the self, or to pressures from both sides.

Social pressures may be the result of bored inactivity and loneliness following enforced retirement, insufficient income, lack of friends, or unhappy living conditions. If the counselor is aware of existing community facilities, many of these pressures can be alleviated and the patient's outlook improved with only a brief period of therapy or counseling. Many older persons do not know about all the clinics, hospitals, institutions, Social Security, Medicare, and other benefits available to the aging; nor are they aware of ways of supplementing inadequate incomes, and the counselor must be sufficiently conversant with these to provide his client with all the necessary information and, if need be, help him by making some direct contacts for him. Many lonely older persons are also unaware of adult education courses and senior citizen recreational centers which they might utilize. Here again, the counselor can be of great practical help and often, when these pressures are relieved, the patient's depression lifts and he is once more able to function in his usual way. Likewise, when home conditions are unhappy but the older person does not want to enter an institution for the aged, he should be made aware of other community facilities for living arrangements for older people, such as low cost apartments or boarding homes, and helped to find one he likes. Thus, the geriatric counselor, and most particularly, the geriatric clergyman-counselor, must often play a more active role in the life management of his patient than a counselor who works with other age groups might play with his patients.

Sometimes, despondency and depression are grief reactions at the loss of a loved one. In these cases, a false cheerfulness on the part of the counselor is generally ineffective. It is better and of more comfort to the patient to share his grief with him, and help him to find new patterns of rewarding interaction through the release of his feelings.

At other times, the despondent and depressive feelings may be a *reactivation of earlier attacks of depression*. In fact, it has been said that psychoneuroses and psychoses seldom occur for the first time in later life in well integrated persons except when brain damage is present. Usually they are either exacerbations of long existing personality traits or a reactivation of earlier psychoneuroses or psychoses. In these cases, if the condition is not severe enough for hospitalization, a combination of medication and psychotherapy prove most effective, always guarding against the possibility of suicide. The clergyman has a definite role here and can sometimes prove invaluable in cases of potential suicide since religion is often the greatest safeguard against self-destruction. Therefore, if he will keep himself constantly available during severe depressive periods, the clergyman may sometimes avert disaster.

In some instances, despondency, depression, and pessimism are the life style of the patient. The depression is usually not as great as may appear on the surface and anxiety may be absent, but the lifelong pattern of thinking and reacting is one of pessimism. The individual always takes a dim view of everything and seems to derive a certain amount of satisfaction out of being miserable. If a picnic is planned, he is sure it will rain or the food will be inedible or the insects will spoil the day; he worries that he will never have enough money to last the rest of his life; he is certain the counselor will lose interest in him; he knows the clouds in the sky portend a hurricane or a blizzard; and the cold he has is certain to cause his death from pneumonia. Nothing is ever quite right for him, and the future is all black. He knows no other way of thinking and would feel bewildered if deprived of his pessimism as a way of enhancing his self-importance. The counselor could probably never make a cheerful personality out of such a gloomy character, but he might be able to help him to understand how his relationships with others might improve if he would keep his dire predictions to himself. If possible to stimulate, the development of constructive, rewarding interests and activities will help to take the patient's attention away from some of his unhappy thoughts and conversation. Group therapy is also helpful in some instances.

Aside from the psychotic and the organic areas, the geriatric patient with depressive trends, psychosomatic complaints, and/or anxiety can usually be helped by medication prescribed by a physician, psychotherapy, and assistance in managing difficult social areas, but the *apathetic, withdrawn patient* often proves most resistive to change. The task seems to be to induce him to take an interest again in the life he has given up, and this may require great ingenuity on the part of the therapist. Too much time on one's hands with nothing to do but think about oneself is likely to result in maladjustments and emotional disturbances of many types and in varying degrees, and the outlook often seems so impossible to the individual that he can see no point in making an effort to change things. Enforced retirement when one is not ready to leave the labor market, has insufficient income to last the rest of his life, and has few inner resources to keep alive his interests and zest for living often results in feelings of this sort. Fortunately, despite enforced retirement at earlier ages in some quarters, there is a movement in the opposite direction and successful efforts have been made to rehabilitate even those older workers who are disabled.[11] More people are beginning to recognize and point out the fact that the older person does not necessarily present a picture of deterioration, that many are flexible, vigorous, and alert, and that the condition of many could be improved by interesting, creative, remunerative work.[12] The counselor should remember that even in working with apathetic geriatric patients, interesting, useful activities and remunerative work often exercise the greatest pull toward normality if the patient can be induced to attempt these. An example of this can be seen in the following case:

Mrs. X was a 64 year old woman who had become increasingly withdrawn and apathetic since the death of her husband the previous year. Her only son had been killed in the service of the U.S. Army some months before the death of her husband. Although well educated and a teacher prior to her marriage, Mrs. X had devoted her entire married life to the care of her home

[11] Cf. H. Rusalem, R. Baxt, and L. Barshop, "The Vocational Rehabilitation of Older Handicapped Workers: Demonstration of Feasibility of Vocational Rehabilitation for Vocationally Handicapped Persons 60 Years of Age and Over," *Federation of Employment and Guidance Service*, 16 (1963).

[12] J. Wallin, "The Psychological, Educational, and Social Problems of the Aging as Viewed by a Mid-Octogenarian," *Journal of Genetic Psychology*, 100 (1962), pp. 41–46; A. Repond, "L'hygiène Mentale de la Sénescence et de la Vieillesse," *Vita hum*, 5 (3) (1962), 142–160; Cf. J. Birren, R. Butler, S. Greenhouse, Sokoloffil, and Yarrow, R. Marion, "Human Aging: a Biological and Behavioral Study," *Public Health Service*, U. S. Dept. Health, Education, and Welfare, Publ. No. 986.

and family, enjoying all her recreation and entertainment in their company. When both her son and her husband had gone she felt she had nothing left to live for; she had no friends or interests, and no one had any need of her. A friend and former employee of her husband became concerned about the situation when he visited her and brought her in for help. She proved to be an attractive, intelligent woman but she was apathetic and indifferent to everything. After trying in vain for several weeks to get her interested in one of the senior citizens' recreational centers, the counselor finally asked her if she would help an underprivileged, foreign born youngster who was having difficulty with his school work because of his lack of knowledge of the English language, saying that she had failed to secure the help the child needed through any of the usual channels. The child's plight seemed to strike a spark of interest in this woman, and she agreed, albeit somewhat reluctantly, to undertake the job. Within a short time a remarkable change took place in this woman: she looked alive again and actually seemed enthusiastic about the work she was doing. Someone needed her, and she was once more of some use in the world!

Contrary to popular opinion, marital problems occur all too frequently in later life. Surprising numbers of older couples are finding their later years unhappy because of increasing bickering and incompatibility. This may be due to mental or physical illness of one partner, unaccepted decline of sexual vigor with nothing sound or constructive to take its place, enforced retirement with decreased income and no satisfying interests, emotional immaturity, or failure of one or both partners to grow intellectually. Thus, after the children have grown up and left the home, nothing remains to hold the two together.[13] If psychosis is not involved nor hospitalization required, the counselor can often be effective by working with each partner alone and then seeing the two together. Each partner must learn not only to understand himself and the part he is playing in the failure of his marriage but also to understand his partner's viewpoint. Assuming these partners are not really enjoying a life of bickering, as some few actually do, each must be helped to see what a lonely, empty life he would lead if a separation were to occur, and then encouraged to find mutual interests and develop spiritual values which might draw them closer together and solidify their crumbling marriage. Working out his own problems individually with the therapist offers a sound beginning and then being forced to really listen to the partner's viewpoint helps the readjustment process to proceed more rapidly. Usually, when strong feelings are involved, and two people try to discuss their problems alone, neither one really *hears* what the other has to say so that the end result is another quarrel. In the therapeutic situation, on the contrary, each one is required to sit quietly and listen while the partner discusses his problems and the marital relationship as he sees it

[13] Cf. J. Gilbert, "The Elderly Couple in Marriage," *Marriage* (ed. W. Bier, S.J.).

with the result that greater rapport and mutual understanding are generally developed. The clergyman has a special role here because often he is the first one consulted when things are not going right in a marriage, so that he has a better opportunity to work with the situation before it reaches the point of imminent dissolution.

GROUP THERAPY

The aim of all psychotherapy or counseling, whether individual or group, is to improve the patient, that is, to help him to adjust as comfortably and effectively as possible to himself and to the environment in which he lives. In the process of accomplishing this, certain things take place: identification and transference, catharsis, insight, reality testing, and sublimation.

Whereas in individual therapy the patient has the therapist with whom he can form a relationship, in group therapy he has other group members as well as the therapist with whom he can relate; instead of one therapist he has many adjunct therapists. By its very nature the group must stress social factors and the relationships between people, since people, when together, react to each other. This interaction between people promotes the processes of therapy and frequently stimulates the resolution of problems. Thus, it can readily be seen how particularly applicable group therapy might be in the treatment of geriatric patients. These people are often lonely, hurt by feelings of rejection, despondent, and irritable. Consequently, the feelings of acceptance, support, friendliness, and communal problems which develop in a group are especially beneficial to them.

The setting for group sessions with geriatric patients should be as comfortable and informal as possible. Comfortable chairs placed informally with ashtrays at hand are desirable, and soon it will be found that each will choose his own spot which he will take every session save occasionally, when a leader with whom he identifies is absent and he appropriates his chair. Coffee or tea with crackers or cookies placed in a readily accessible spot where the members can serve themselves helps to create an informal atmosphere which is conducive to conversation.

The counselor in geriatric group therapy is essentially a passive, nondirective therapist. He introduces the members to each other, explains the purposes of group therapy, and points out to the members that the group is essentially *their* group and consequently the conversation will center around *their* problems, what *they* want to talk about, remembering always that what is said in the group is confidential and not to be discussed with anyone else outside the group. He then lets the members proceed in their own fashion. Sometimes, if the group is slow to get started or there seems to be a long lag in conversation, the therapist may interject a question or comment to get things started. Also, he may occasionally try to draw out a particularly reticent patient, offer support to a patient who is especially distressed, or ask a question to stress a particular point or elicit a much needed interpretation but, in the main, his role is basically passive and accepting. If specific information is requested as, for example, about community resources, he will supply this if he can, but most questions about feelings, reactions, and behavior he will reflect back to the group.

Individuals in the group will form *identifications and transferences* with other group members as well as with the therapist, reacting to them as they have to other significant persons in their past lives. For example, a person may react to different ones in the group as to a father or mother, husband or wife, sibling, son, or daughter, behaving toward them as he once did or as he now feels toward these individuals in his life. Thus, attachments and hostilities are formed which must be worked through. After awhile, other members are quick to see these identifications and bring them to the attention of the group, and this helps in the readjustment process. Occasionally, a member identifies so strongly with the therapist that he unconsciously assumes his mannerisms and tries to fit the role in which he sees him.

Catharsis, while sometimes easier to initiate in individual than in group sessions, often continues more readily in a group because the knowledge that others have experienced similar reactions and feelings tends to reduce anxiety and guilt. Sometimes, in geriatric groups, the very support and encouragement of other group members tend to prolong the purging of innermost thoughts and feelings beyond the point where it is good for the group and the individual at that time. In these instances, it is usually another group member who steps in and shuts off the flow in a direct way that the counselor in his role could never do. Also, even though a person might not make use of catharsis himself, he often will derive considerable benefit from just listening to others.

Listening to others as they attempt to achieve insight also promotes *insight* into one's own problems. In addition, many bright older people, even though they may know little about themselves, have learned much about other people during their years of living and thus are able to help them to achieve insights into their problems in a quite direct way.

The older person might find the group an especially safe place in which to *test reality*. In this small sample of society he can try out his new ways of feeling and reacting and his changed viewpoints and see how they are received without the fear of rejection. If he is in error or should modify his behavior still further, other group members will be sure to point this out to him.

Group members will also help an individual to find ways of *sublimating* his unattainable and unacceptable wishes and behavior and deriving satisfaction through other mediums. Companionship, friendship, and sharing of creative activities and recreational outlets may often mean more to an older person than to one who is younger and has more energy and initiative to seek something on his own.

An interesting example of successful group therapy can be seen in the case of a 63 year old woman who was very despondent and depressed and felt lonely, rejected, and alone. She lived with her married daughter and her family, but she and her daughter quarreled constantly and she frequently went to her room in a huff. She was quiet for her first few sessions in the group but then one day suddenly poured forth all her feelings of loneliness, frustration and unhappiness. Her daughter was ungrateful and unloving, never listened to what she had to say, and seemed to want to get rid of her, etc. etc. A lively discussion followed, and some of the comments and questions brought out by the other members were both interesting and enlightening. "Why should she be grateful to you—just because you bore her? That wasn't her fault; it was yours. She gives you a home; maybe you should be grateful to her." "Why should she listen to you? She's grown up and married; she's got a mind of her own; leave her alone." "She probably does want to get rid of you. Why should she want you around when you're quarreling and finding fault and trying to run things?" "It's *her* home and she's entitled to things the way *she* wants them. I had the same trouble until I moved out, and now we're the best of friends." The reactions of the other group members were upsetting at first but when she showed her distress they offered her support which gave her some reassurance. Gradually, she began to understand herself better, decided to move to an apartment house set up for older people, and became quite busy in both volunteer service and recreational activities. At the age of 68 she remarried and when last heard from, was living contentedly with her husband in Florida.

SUMMARY

The increasing number of older people in our population necessarily results in increasing numbers of mentally ill and maladjusted persons in this age bracket. However, contrary to earlier opinions, many of these older disturbed persons can and do respond both to medical therapy and to psychological counseling.

In order to treat geriatric patients effectively, it is important to understand the special stresses to which the older person is subject, these stresses emanating from within the self and from the present day cultural environment which tends to discard and segregate the old. Stresses arising from within the self include both the normal and abnormal decline of efficient physical, mental, and emotional functioning of the individual. Reactivation of earlier emotional problems and mental disturbances also impose special stress.

The understanding and trained clergyman can often be most helpful in dealing with minor problems but should be sufficiently aware of severe emotional problems to know when to refer an individual for intensive psychotherapy.

Any type of therapy can be successful with geriatric patients, depending upon the problem, the patient, and the therapist, but, generally speaking, short term therapies and group therapy seem to be somewhat more effective and practical than traditional psychoanalysis.

In counseling the geriatric patient it is most important that a complete history of the patient be secured and a report of a thorough physical examination. It is important also to understand the environmental conditions under which the patient lives, and to gain this understanding it is often necessary to interview other family members as well as the patient.

Therapeutic goals, both immediate and long term, should be set up with the patient within the social framework and the framework of his personal assets and liabilities. Living arrangements, financial resources, the life style and the personal desires of the individual must be considered.

The geriatric counselor must be one who genuinely likes older people, has resolved his conflicts with his own parents, and is fully cognizant of community facilities available for help of the older person.

Hospitalization may be necessary for a chronically disabled or a mentally ill old person when he can secure better care in the hospital or his presence in the home constitutes a menace to the well being of other members of the family. Placement may also be necessary for an older person who cannot look after himself independently and has no funds or family to provide this care in the community. Whenever placement is necessary, the patient should receive careful preparation for the change; if relatives are in the picture these too should be prepared to take the step toward placing the older person. The trained clergyman-counselor can be particularly helpful in this situation. He also has a special role to play in helping to allay fears of death and in the development of a philosophy of life and death.

Many older persons either somatize their difficulties or use illness, either consciously or unconsciously, to gain attention or to control their environment. Others may show depression, anxiety, or apathy and withdrawal tendencies. Treatment of these problems will be handled in much the same way as similar problems in other age groups, and identification, transference, catharsis, insight, reality testing, and sublimation will take place.

The establishment of companionships, recreational outlets, and creative and useful activities is especially important for patients in the upper age brackets.

Group therapy, because of its stress on social factors and interpersonal relationship, is an especially good therapeutic approach with geriatric patients.

BIBLIOGRAPHY

Birren, J. E., *Handbook of Aging and the Individual*, Chicago: University of Chicago Press, 1959.

Birren, J. E., Butler, R. N., Greenhouse, S. W., Sokoloffil, and Yarrow, Marion R., "Human Aging: a Biological and Behavioral Study," *Public Health Service*, U.S. Dept. Health, Education, and Welfare, Publ. No. 986, 328p.

Bromley, D. B., *The Psychology of Human Aging*, Baltimore, Md.: Penguin Books, Inc., 1966.

Donahue, Wilma and Tibbitts, C., *The New Frontiers of Aging*, Ann Arbor: University of Michigan Press, 1949.

Foulkes, S. H. and Anthony, E. J., *Group Psychotherapy*, Baltimore, Md.: Penguin Books, 1965.

Freud, S., *Collected Papers* (Vol. 1), New York: Basic Books, 1959, p. 271.

Gilbert, Jeanne G., *Understanding Old Age*, New York: Ronald Press Co., 1952.

Gilbert, Jeanne G., "Stresses That Attack Older Persons," New York City Legislative Committee on Problems of Aging, 1954.

Gilbert, Jeanne G., The Elderly Couple in Marriage, in Bier, William C., S.J., *Marriage*, New York: Fordham University Press, 1965.

Havighurst, R. J., Factors Which Control the Experience of Aging, Gawein, 13 (4), (1965) pp. 242–248.

Kaplan, O. J., *Mental Disorders in Later Life*, 2nd ed., Stanford: Stanford University Press, 1956.

Morgan, R. F., "Note on the Psychopathology of Senility: Senescent Defense Against the Threat of Death," *Psychological Reports*, 16 (1), 1965, 305–306.

Repond, A., "L'hygiène Mentale de la Sénescence et de la Vieillesse," *Vita hum*, 5 (3), 1962, 142–160.

Rockwell, F. V., Psychotherapy in the Older Individual, in Kaplan, O. J., *Mental Disorders in Later Life*, 2nd ed., Stanford: Stanford University Press, Chapter 16, 423–445, 1956.

Rothschild, David, Senile Psychoses and Psychoses with Cerebral Arteriosclerosis, in Kaplan, O. J., *Mental Disorders in Later Life*, 2nd ed., Stanford: Stanford University Press, Chapter 11, 289–331, 1956.

Rusalem, H., Baxt, R. and Barshop, I., "The Vocational Rehabilitation of Older Handicapped Workers: Demonstration of Feasibility of Vocational Rehabilitation for Vocationally Handicapped Persons 60 years of Age and Over," *Federation of Employment and Guidance Service*, 16, (1963) 49p.

THE CONTRIBUTORS

REVEREND EUGENE J. WEITZEL, C.S.V., M.A., S.T.D. is a member of the Chicago Province of the Clerics of St. Viator. He was born in Chicago, Illinois, but his family soon returned to Springfield, Illinois, where he received his elementary and secondary education and attended Springfield Junior College (now Springfield College) in Illinois, graduating in 1947. He completed his undergraduate studies at St. Joseph's College, Collegeville, Indiana and was graduated with a Bachelor of Arts degree in Philosophy in 1949. Shortly after graduation, he entered the novitiate of the Viatorian Fathers and pronounced his first vows in February of 1951. After accepting teaching assignments at St. Philip High School in Chicago, Spalding Institute in Peoria, Illinois, and Cathedral Boys' High School in Springfield, he completed his studies for the priesthood and was ordained in 1959. At this time he also received the Licentiate in Sacred Theology from The Catholic University of America. While teaching at St. Philip High School in the early 50's he attended De Paul University and was graduated with the degree of Master of Arts in Education in 1952. After ordination, Father Weitzel was assigned to Griffin High School (formerly Cathedral Boys' High School) where he taught English, U.S. History and Religion for the next five years. In 1964, he returned to C.U.A. to begin his studies for the doctorate in Sacred Theology and was graduated two years later. During the two years of his graduate studies, he taught both Pastoral Theology and Catechetics at the Viatorian Seminary in Washington, D.C. After Graduation, Father Weitzel was again assigned to Griffin High School as an Assistant Principal in Charge of Extra-Curricular Activities, and Chairman of the Department of Religion.

Father Weitzel has edited five books including this one. They are: *Father Connell Answers Moral Questions* (CUA Press); *More Answers to Contemporary Moral Problems* (CUA Press); *Follow the Rubrics* (CUA Press); *Contemporary Pastoral Theology* (Bruce). He has also contributed to professional journals, taught in adult education programs, given retreats and days of recollection to teenagers and religious women, and lectured to numerous civic and religious groups.

REVEREND JOHN W. STAFFORD, C.S.V., Ph.D. Provincial of the Chicago Province of the Clerics of St. Viator, was graduated from St. Viator's College, Bourbonnais, Illinois in 1930. After completing his theological studies at The Catholic University of America in 1934, he was ordained to the priesthood in 1934 and he received his doctorate in psychology from Louvain Uni-

286

versity in 1939. A year later he joined the Faculty of The Catholic University of America where he taught in the Department of Psychology and Psychiatry. In 1947 he was named Department Head and retained that post until he became Provincial in 1959. Presently he is Chairman of the Advisory Board of the Chief of Chaplains of the Veterans Administration, and Chairman of the Sensory Studies Section of the Department of Health, Education and Welfare. He is a frequent contributor to professional journals, and has lectured extensively.

MAGDA B. ARNOLD, who was a Dunlap Scholar in 1940 and 1941 and received her doctorate in Psychology a year later, has taught both in Canada and in the United States. As a college professor, she has taught at some of the best known colleges for women in the U.S., including Wellesley College, Bryn Mawr College, and Barat College. She was also a Putnam Advanced Research Fellow at Radcliffe College in the early 50's and is presently on the faculty of Loyola University. A member of the American Psychological Association, her fields are emotion, personality, and neuropsychology. Her works include: *Excitatory Theory of Emotion, Human Person* (co-author), and *Emotion and Personality*.

ALEXANDER A. SCHNEIDERS, Ph.D., who was born in Sioux City, Iowa, on February 2, 1909, began his brilliant career as a college professor more than 30 years ago at Loyola University. A well-known lecturer and writer in the fields of mental hygiene, adolescence, and personality dynamics, Dr. Schneiders received the Family Action Award in 1951. He is a member of both the American Psychological Association and the American Catholic Psychological Association. His works include: *Introductory Psychology, Psychology of Adolescence,* and *Personal Adjustment and Mental Health*.

REVEREND GEORGE A. KANOTI, who is assistant to the Dean of the School of Sacred Theology and Director of Moral Studies at The Catholic University of America, was born in Lorain, Ohio on April 15, 1934. He received his Bachelor's degree and Master's from St. Louis University in 1958 and 1961 respectively, and his doctorate from The Catholic University of America in 1966. Along with his teaching duties in the School of Sacred Theology, he has contributed to a number of professional journals, including the *Journal of Pastoral Counseling*.

REVEREND JOHN F. HARVEY, O.S.F.S. has written and lectured extensively on the subject of homosexuality and was a contributor to Father Joseph F. X. Cevetello's book, *All Things to All Men*. He has also contributed articles on inversion to such well-known publications as *Homiletic and Pastoral Review, Theological Studies,* and the *Bulletin* of the Guild of Catholic Psychiatrists. Father Harvey, who is presently an instructor of Theology at De Sales

Hall in Hyattsville, Maryland, received both his Master of Arts degree and his doctorate in Sacred Theology from The Catholic University of America in 1946 and 1951 respectively. He is also Head of the Department of Theology at Dumbarton College of the Holy Cross in Washington, D.C.

NORMAN J. ROSE, M.D., who is presently Chief of the Bureau of Epidemiology of the Department of Health of the State of Illinois, received his Bachelor's degree and his doctorate in medicine from North Western University in Evanston, Illinois. He also received a Master's degree in Public Health from the University of Minnesota. After completing his internship at West Surburban Hospital in Oak Park, Illinois, in 1934 he entered private practice. Seven years later, he joined the Illinois Department of Public Health as Assistant Chief of the Bureau of Tuberculosis Control, and a year later was named District Health Supervisor of 25 Illinois counties. He held this post until 1949. During these early years of public health service, Dr. Rose was also Chief of the Bureau of Epidemiology, a division of the State Bureau of Communicable Disease Control. For some time, beginning in 1954, Dr. Rose was also Chief of the Division of Maternal and Child Health. In the course of his long public service career, Dr. Rose has become a recognized lecturer in the area of public health.

ROBERT J. CAMPBELL, III, M.D. was born in 1926. He received his M.D. degree in 1948 from Columbia University College of Physicians and Surgeons in New York City. A member of the American Psychiatric Association, he is Chief of the Outpatient and Psychiatric Service of St. Vincent's Hospital in New York City. He was certified by the National Board of Medical Examiners in 1949 and received his license to practice medicine that same year.

WOLFGANG RIEDEL, Ph.D. is presently the Director of Training at the Counseling Center of The Catholic University of America, and a member of the faculty of the Department of Psychology and Psychiatry. Born in Marienbad, Czechoslovakia on April 5, 1930, he received his Bachelor's and Master's degrees from the University of Delaware and his Ph.D. from Temple University. He is a clinical consultant at the National Institute of Mental Health, and a consultant to the Jewish Social Service Agency in Washington, D.C. He has contributed a number of articles including "Anxiety Level and the 'Doubtful' Judgment," "Psycho-physical Experiment," and "Diagnostic Assembly of M.M.P.I. Items Based on Comery's Factor Analysis," to a number of professional journals.

VINCENT CONIGLIARO, M.D. was born in 1928. He was graduated from the Facoltà di Medicina e Chirurgia dell'Università di Palermo in Palermo, Italy in 1952. He became a licensed psychiatrist in 1959 and is presently engaged in private practice. He is an active member of both the American Psychiatric Association and the American Geriatrics Association, Inc.

A. C. ZARKADAS was born on December 13, 1921. He received his A.B. from St. Anselm's College in 1949 and his M.A. from Boston College's School of Social Work in 1952. Presently he is engaged in private practice in psychotherapy and is on the staff of the Family Counseling and Guidance Center, Inc., in Boston, Massachusetts. He is also an instructor in Psychology at St. John's Seminary and a Consultant to a Canadian religious community.

JEANNE GILBERT, Ph.D. received her Master's degree from the University of Pennsylvania, and her doctorate from Columbia University in 1935. She began her career as a teacher in the public schools of New Jersey but later joined the staff of St. Charles Guild Clinic and became a member of the faculty of the Department of Psychology at Fordham University. As a psychologist, she specialized in Child Psychology and Mental Deficiency. She is a member of the American Psychological Association and the American Association for the Advancement of Science.

INDEX